Supporting Reading in Grades 6–12

Supporting Reading in Grades 6–12

A Guide

Sybil M. Farwell and Nancy L. Teger

 LIBRARIES UNLIMITED

AN IMPRINT OF ABC-CLIO, LLC
Santa Barbara, California • Denver, Colorado • Oxford, England

Library of Congress Cataloging-in-Publication Data

Farwell, Sybil M.
   Supporting reading in grades 6–12 : a guide / Sybil M. Farwell and Nancy L. Teger.
     p. cm.
   Includes index.
   ISBN 978-1-59884-803-8 (pbk.) — ISBN 978-1-59884-804-5 (ebook)
1. Reading (Secondary) 2. Children—Books and reading. 3. School librarian participation in curriculum planning. 4. Motivation in education. I. Teger, Nancy L. II. Title.
   LB1632.F37 2012
   428.4071'2—dc23   2012010826

ISBN: 978-1-59884-803-8
EISBN: 978-1-59884-804-5

16   15   14   13   12   1   2   3   4   5

This book is also available on the World Wide Web as an eBook.
Visit www.abc-clio.com for details.

Libraries Unlimited
An Imprint of ABC-CLIO, LLC

ABC-CLIO, LLC
130 Cremona Drive, P.O. Box 1911
Santa Barbara, California 93116-1911

This book is printed on acid-free paper ∞

Manufactured in the United States of America

To my family for their support of my professional work (and hobby) of school librarianship, especially to my husband who graciously took over the kitchen duties. SMF

To my parents, William and Lucy E. Thomas, who instilled in me an unquenchable desire to learn, as well as a strong work ethic. NLT

Contents

Acknowledgments xiii

PART 1: OVERVIEW

1   Introducing the Read, Explore, Analyze, Develop, Score (READS) Concept 3

    AASL Resources 4

    Evolution of READS Guidelines. 4

    Structure of READS 5

    Use of READS 6

2   Implementing READS 8

    Developing a Literate Community 11

    The Plan for This Book. 12

PART 2: READ AS A PERSONAL ACTIVITY

3   Guiding Readers' Choices 19

    Library Environment 19

    Individual Reading Guidance. 19

        Time for Checking Out. 22

        Reading Interests. 23

        Reading Surveys 23

    Reading Guidance Techniques for Groups. 24

        Displays 24

        Reading Lists and Bookmarks. 26

        Reading Programs and Celebrations 26

        Booktalking 27

        Online Selection Tools. 27

        Quick Strategy Ideas. 29

       Reading Aloud 30

       Friendly Staff 33

4   Connecting Learners to Resources 39

   Audiobooks and Other Digital Media 39

       Educational Benefits of Audiobooks 42

       Advantages for Struggling and Special Needs Readers 43

       Audiobook Formats 45

       Audiobook Activities 45

   Library Orientation 46

       Challenges to Delivering Ideal Orientations 48

       Planning Orientation Activities 49

       Formal Assessment Options 51

   Public Libraries 52

       Opening Basic Communication Lines 53

       Sharing Resources 55

       Public Librarians in Schools 55

       Students in Public Libraries 56

       Co-Production by School and Public Librarians 57

   Academic Libraries 58

       Visits to Academic Libraries 59

       Academic Librarians in K-12 Schools 60

       Academic Librarians' Involvement in Reading Promotion 61

   Museums and Other Community Resources 63

PART 3: EXPLORE CREATIVE WORKS

5   Identifying Literary Genres and Themes 77

   Working with Genres 77

       Activities Introducing Various Genres 81

       Student Genre Activities 86

       Which Literary Selections? 87

       Fiction: Realistic Fiction 89

       Fiction: Historical Fiction 92

       Fiction: Fantasy 93

Fiction: Short Stories 95

Poetry 96

Nonfiction 97

Nonfiction: Biography 102

Drama 104

Picture Books 105

Magazines and Newspapers 107

Graphic Literature 109

Multiplatform Works 110

Working with Themes 111

6   Exploring Social, Cultural, and Historical Contexts 129

Personal Identity 129

Social Issues 134

Appreciation of Cultural and Ethnic Diversity 136

Historically and Culturally Significant Works 141

7   Appreciating Literary and Artistic Excellence 151

Awards for Literary Quality 153

American Library Association and Divisions 153

Other Professional Organizations and Groups 154

Lists of Resources 155

Popularity Awards 157

Intellectual Freedom 157

Practices within the Library 160

Direct Instruction and Collaboration 161

Teacher Support and Training on Intellectual Freedom Issues 164

Community Advocacy for Intellectual Freedom 164

PART 4: ANALYZE CREATIVE WORKS

8   Identifying and Analyzing Details of a Work .173

Importance of Background Knowledge 173

Background Knowledge Strategies 175

Vocabulary Development Strategies 176

Inferences and Predictions 179

Central Ideas and Supporting Details 181

Summarizing and Paraphrasing. 183

    Summarizing—Lesson Ideas. 183

    Paraphrasing—Lesson Ideas 184

9 Understanding the Literary Techniques and Complexities of a Work 189

Author Studies 189

    Working with Authors 191

    Word Choice and Figurative Language 192

Illustrator Studies 193

Literary Elements 195

    Plot. 195

    Characters. 197

    Setting 200

    Point of View 201

PART 5: DEVELOP A LITERARY-BASED PRODUCT

10 Creating and Producing a Product. 211

Choosing a Presentation Method 212

    Assessing Resources 212

    Project Suggestions 214

Generating and Organizing Ideas 217

    Organizing Ideas. 217

    Designing the Product 219

Creating the Product 223

    Importance of Writing 223

    Working Individually or in a Group 223

    Encouraging Good Work Habits. 225

Respecting Copyright Laws and Intellectual Property Rights. 227

Communicate and Evaluate Work 228

PART 6: SCORE READING PROGRESS

11 Participating in and Reflecting on the Reading Experience 237

Literacy Committee 237

Schoolwide Reading Celebrations 239

    One Book/One School 239

    Battle of the Books. 240

    National Reading Promotion Programs. 241

    Family Literacy Events. 241

    Specialized Programs and Groups 242

    Sustained Silent Reading (SSR) 244

    Summer Reading Programs. 247

    Mentoring. 253

    Book Clubs 257

    State Readers' Choice Programs 264

    Reading Motivation Programs 265

Lifelong Learning 277

    Habits for Lifelong Learning and Lifetime Reading .279

    Reflection 280

    Essential Questions. 281

    Lesson Approaches. 282

    Reflection on Reading and Learning 293

    Structuring Essential Questions 296

    Mini-Lesson Ideas for Lifetime Reading and Lifelong Learning. 297

Coda: Open Questions and Final Thoughts 298

PART 7: APPENDICES

Appendix A: READS Annual Calendar—Ninth and Tenth Grades. 313

Appendix B: READS Grade Summaries 315

Appendix C: READS K-12 Chart—Read as a Personal Activity 330

Appendix D: READS Overview 347

Index 353

Acknowledgments

We are grateful to the multitude of librarians, teachers, administrators, and other colleagues who have informed our professional journey. We are also deeply appreciative of the contribution of Carol Bernstein, former library media supervisor for Miami-Dade County schools, Florida, who initiated our collaborative partnership on library curriculum projects.

Part 1

Overview

1

Introducing the Read, Explore, Analyze, Develop, Score (READS) Concept

The basic goals of school library programs have endured for many years: to provide resources and services, to promote reading, and to teach information literacy skills. Historically, the reasons for adding libraries to schools more than a century ago were to provide subject area resources beyond the textbook and to promote reading.

Though we continue to observe outstanding examples of students' involvement in reading activities in our libraries today, the general consensus is that reading scores are still lagging. Various causes for the lack of improvement in reading skills have been explored in the professional literature, ranging from disengaged students, increasing populations of second language learners, to the digital generation theory.

Consequently, it is clear that the traditional work of school librarians concerning reading promotion is more important than ever. The Nation's Report Card: Reading 2009 issued by the National Center for Education Statistics presents results of the 2009 National Assessment of Educational Progress (NAEP) in reading. The report shows that reading scores for 75 percent of the nation's eighth graders were reading below grade level and only 3 percent scored at an advanced level. Furthermore, as part of the 2009 implementation of NAEP, 4th, 8th, and 12th grade students were asked, "How often do you read for fun on your own time?" Percentages of students responding "almost every day" were 44 percent in 4th grade, 21 percent in 8th grade, and 18 percent in 12th grade.

However, the challenge is to balance the time spent on reading-related instruction and promotion with the need for teaching the research process and information literacy skills. Obviously, the two instructional imperatives frequently overlap, but significant time must be devoted to the essential tasks of connecting students with literature and teaming with teachers to ensure that students develop critical reading comprehension skills. To facilitate these goals, READS provides a continuum of reading skills for each grade level to enhance the delivery of a quality reading promotion program. Additionally, through a collaborative agenda with classroom teachers, READS provides a structure for developing a literature-based instructional program that incorporates an inquiry-based approach. Consequently, this scope and sequence becomes a companion document to the information literacy instructional program.

AASL RESOURCES

In recognition of the current national concern about reading skills, the American Association of School Librarians (AASL) issued a position statement, *The School Librarian's Role in Reading*. This statement evolved from the *Standards for the 21st-Century Learner*, published by AASL in 2007, which outlines the skills students need for reading, as well as the skills needed to conduct research using multiple literacies and resources. A wealth of reading resources have been developed by a national AASL committee and posted on the AASL site, and linked to the reading role position statement. For example, the *School Librarian's Role in Reading* toolkit includes four PowerPoint presentations, multiple handouts on reading strategies, scenarios for reading involvement in various types of library programs, a bibliography, self-assessment guidelines for school librarians, and Web 2.0 resources.

The national school library standards, *Empowering Learners: Guidelines for School Library Programs*, are based on nine common beliefs of the profession and encompass the two core approaches to school library instruction: reading and inquiry.

First, reading is a window to the world. Reading is a foundational skill for learning, personal growth, and enjoyment. The degree to which students can read and understand information in all formats and all contexts is a key indicator of success in school and in life. As a lifelong learning skill, reading goes beyond decoding and comprehension to interpretation and development of new understandings.

Second, inquiry provides a framework for learning. To become independent learners, students must gain not only the skills but also the dispositions to use those skills, along with an understanding of their own responsibilities and self-assessment strategies. Combined together, these two elements build a learner who can thrive in a complex information environment.

EVOLUTION OF READS GUIDELINES

Tracing the evolution of READS, we can look back to 1984. In that year, the School Library Media Services section of the Florida Department of Education published *Information Skills for Florida Schools K-12*. This instructional scope and sequence covered the entire range of content to be taught in a school library program: orientation, organization, selection and utilization, comprehension and application, presentation of information, and appreciation. The use of resources, literature appreciation, and reading guidance were merged in this model.

In the 1990s, several districts in Florida developed their own documents to provide structure for the instructional activities of school librarians. These documents also merged information literacy skills with reading promotion and literature appreciation activities. In 2005, FINDS (Focus, Investigate, Note and Evaluate, Develop, Score), a research process model, was first posted on the SUNLINK site and the Florida Department of Education (DOE) website. This publication focused on information literacy skills, but did not include literature appreciation and reading promotion.

As a result of the No Child Left Behind legislation, an increased emphasis on standardized tests, and a growing concern over low student reading performance, all educators were strongly encouraged to become actively engaged in contributing to student reading achievement. Within this context, work began on a school library grade-by-grade document that would provide an infrastructure for the traditional library literature appreciation and reading promotion activities.

Additionally, several national documents influenced the development of READS. When AASL's *Standards for the 21st-Century Learner* were published, both information literacy and literature appreciation were combined together. Those standards also integrate multiple literacies (e.g., digital, visual, textual, and media), as well as stressing the need for students to learn how to work in groups; these concepts have all been incorporated into READS. The workforce requirements first described in the Secretary's Commission on Achieving Necessary Skills (SCANS) report and refined in the *Framework for 21st Century Learning* from the Partnership for 21st Century Skills are also imbedded in READS. The National Education Technology Standards and Performance Indicators for Students from the International Society for Technology in Education are integrated to ensure that the document would reflect the constant changes in information technologies.

To further add depth and relevancy of coverage, several publications and position statements from the National Council of Teachers of English (NCTE) and the International Reading Association (IRA) are referenced, including the *NCTE/IRA Standards for the English Language Arts* and the *Standards for the Assessment of Reading and Writing*. NCTE's *Adolescent Literacy: A Policy Research Brief* also provides insights into the literacy challenges of secondary students.

Finally, the national Common Core State Standards for English Language Arts are integrated into the READS document. This initiative is a state-led effort coordinated by the National Governors Association Center for Best Practices and the Council of Chief State School Officers and, to date, almost all of the states have formally approved the Common Core Standards for implementation in their schools. Of particular note are the areas of coverage included in the document: Reading: Literature; Reading: Informational Text; Reading Foundational Skills; Writing; Speaking & Listening; and Language. The companion document for grades 6–12, *English Language Arts Standards: History/Social Studies*, provides additional specificity concerning the literacy skills needed for career and college readiness.

STRUCTURE OF READS

READS—Literature and Reading Promotion Guidelines is available online at the Florida DOE and at http://readsresources.wikispaces.com in two formats: grade summaries and K-12 charts. The five components of the document are *Read* as a personal activity; *Explore* characteristics, history, and awards of creative works; *Analyze* structure and aesthetic features of creative works; *Develop* a literary-based product; and *Score* reading progress. Each skill has been correlated to the AASL Standards and the Common Core documents. Each component of READS begins with "the student will," identifying the skills that each student should master.

READS formalizes, qualifies, and quantifies the valuable contributions of school librarians to the education of students. The selection of the five components is grounded in both the traditional work and current best practices of the school library profession, which includes, but is not limited to, these activities:

- sharing stories with students to acquaint them with quality and developmentally appropriate literature;
- introducing award-winning books and media;
- discussing genres and history of literature and media;
- using multicultural literature to address the self-esteem needs of adolescents and to introduce all to world cultures;

- focusing attention on the various formats of fiction and informational texts with emphasis on the reading and comprehension skills needed for both print and digital formats;
- exploring the school's curriculum and students' interests to give direction to collection development;
- providing individual reading guidance;
- analyzing literature and media to develop understanding and new knowledge;
- providing opportunities for students to react to literature and media as well as to express their creativity;
- introducing valuable learning resources in the community (e.g., public libraries, museums, parks);
- creating teachable opportunities focused on responsible use of ideas or information (e.g., intellectual property rights and legal use of information); and
- coordinating assessment strategies with READS and Common Core Standards.

USE OF READS

First, the skills in READS are ideal for use in school librarians' lesson plans. The skills are written from a student's point of view and are straightforward, providing a clear understanding to anyone reading the plans. Though not all school librarians are required to submit lesson plans to administrators, these documents are highly valuable as communication devices for sharing best practices in in-services, mentoring situations with new school librarians, conference sessions, and professional portfolios. The very act of transferring ideas for teaching a lesson to paper helps to clarify and improve teaching; the process necessarily includes reflecting on which procedures work best for student learning. Examples of READS lesson ideas are featured throughout this book. In addition, multiple links to web-based lesson plans are available for each component of the curriculum.

The second use of the READS skills can provide an express lane to developing credibility with administrators and staff members. The skills are phrased in familiar language and help to demystify the work of the school librarian. A paramount goal of school librarians is to collaborate with colleagues, so that instruction in the school library is integrated into classroom units of study. A prerequisite for successful collaboration is demonstrating knowledge of the curriculum, needs of learners, and instructional competence to teachers and administrators; therefore, the use of READS, awareness of current trends in professional journals, and understanding of district requirements in the various curricular areas will go a long way in developing the respect school librarians yearn for and deserve. In a sense, the use of defined curriculum documents validates the claims of school librarians that their efforts make significant contributions to the academic preparation of students.

A third advantage of using the READS guidelines is that they provide a common language for the ultimate goal of school librarians: embedding library goals and activities into the culture of the school and the School Improvement Plan. This accomplishment often brings increased funding and staffing for libraries; it has been known to improve working conditions for school librarians, which, for elementary personnel, could mean flexible scheduling or at least a combination of flexible and fixed schedules.

Because the use of READS by school library personnel in a school district brings a common understanding of the potential benefits of school library activities, vertical articulation between grades and school levels in a feeder pattern is facilitated. For example, in the past, a school librarian at the middle school or high school level might find great differences among the reading skill sets of incoming students from various schools. When school librarians at all middle schools feeding into a particular high school provide similar yet individualized programs, students will come to high school with a common base of skill levels.

Finally, the use of the READS continuum of skills can also bring balance to the school library program planned and implemented in a school. By observing which skills are covered in a specific period of time, school librarians may decide to include activities from other components of the curriculum to broaden the range of experiences that students receive. Students benefit from a mix of fiction and nonfiction, vocabulary work and discussion of story elements, award-winning books and current online sources, production activities, and reflection on reading progress. In addition, by understanding the skills recommended for each grade, school librarians can discern which prerequisite experiences prepare students for the next grade's work (e.g., if students in fifth grade are required to create bibliographies, students in third and fourth grades need to know the location of the essential bibliographic elements and how to record them in list format). Through involvement in the blend and balance of activities described for each grade level in the READS document, students progress developmentally in the use of school library resources, acquisition of reading skills, and appreciation of literature and creative works.

WORKS CITED

American Association of School Librarians. (2007). *Standards for the 21st-century learner*. Chicago, IL: American Library Association.

American Association of School Librarians. (2009). *AASL position statement on the school librarian's role in reading*. Retrieved from http://www.ala.org/ala/mgrps/divs/aasl/aaslissues/positionstatements/roleinreading.cfm

American Association of School Librarians. (2009). *Empowering learners: Guidelines for school library media programs*. Chicago, IL: American Library Association.

Florida Department of Education. (1984). *Information skills for Florida schools K-12*. Tallahassee, FL: State of Florida.

National Center of Education Statistics. (2009). *The nation's report card: Reading 2009*. Washington, DC: U.S. Department of Education.

National Council of Teachers of English. (2007). *Adolescent literacy: A policy research brief*. Retrieved from http://www.ncte.org/library/NCTEFiles/Resources/PolicyResearch/AdolLitResearchBrief.pdf

National Council of Teachers of English/International Reading Association. (1996). *Standards for the English language arts*. Retrieved from http://www.ncte.org/standards

National Council of Teachers of English/International Reading Association. (2009). *Standards for the assessment of reading and writing*. Retrieved from http://www.ncte.org/standards/assessmentstandards

National Governors Association Center for Best Practices/Council of Chief State School Officers. (2010). *Common Core State Standards Initiative*. Retrieved from http://www.corestandards.org/

2

Implementing READS

In today's educational setting, demands on the school librarian's time are increasing while budgets and staff are decreasing. This situation results in the school librarian having to make difficult, but necessary, choices concerning program delivery. These facts also emphasize the need for a targeted, focused approach to library programming to ensure that the library resources and instructional programs address the learning and teaching challenges of the school community. The ultimate goals, of course, are to improve student achievement and to develop successful lifelong learners.

To meet these goals, school library programs base their objectives and activities on several foundational principles. In the following chart, library principles are correlated to the READS framework and the Common Core English Language Arts Standards to illustrate how these agendas support each other and work together.

The Common Core Standards (CCS) are the work of the National Governors Association and the Council of Chief State School Officers. Conley (2011) asserts that "the stated goal of the standards is to specify key knowledge and skills in a format that makes it clear what teachers and assessments need to focus on" (p. 17). He further explains that "the standards' developers also hope that creating national consistency in expectations will lead to better uses of student learning data, higher-quality curriculum materials, teacher-preparation programs aligned with key content standards, and research results that identify what works" (p. 17).

In 2010, AASL published a *Position Statement on the Common Core College- and Career-Readiness Standards* to establish the importance of library programs in implementing the Common Core Standards. The document declares that, "As students strive to meet the rigor of the standards, certified school librarians will play an essential part in ensuring that 21st-century information literacy skills, dispositions, responsibilities and assessments are integrated throughout all curriculum areas." As we know, school librarians are in a unique position to impact the quality of a student's educational experience and to be collaborative partners in the implementation of curriculum standards across content areas.

According to Loertscher and Marcoux (2010), "The nature of education is changing and so is the work of the teacher-librarian" (p. 8). Loertscher and Marcoux further explain, "Being conversant on the CCS and other sets of standards is a central role teacher-librarians can have." To facilitate this agenda, school librarians provide equitable access for all school stakeholders to literature and information resources in various formats and can make collaborative connections for teachers and students to those resources and national standards. To highlight the correlation between the READS framework and the national standards, a

School Library Foundational Principles	READS Examples					Common Core State Standards—English Language Arts—Examples*
	Read	Explore	Analyze	Develop	Score	
The school librarian:	The school librarian will:					The student will carry out:
Knows collection and resources both in and outside of the school	• Read—Connects students and teachers with specific books, digital materials, and community resources (e.g., museums, public, and academic libraries) • Explore—Facilitates students connecting with historically and culturally significant works • Analyze—Provides context to make authors/illustrators intellectually accessible to students • Develop—Connects students/teachers with online production tools • Score—Introduces students to resources that support lifelong learning					• Reading: Informational Text—10 Read and comprehend literary nonfiction in the grade text complexity band . . . • Reading: Literature—10 Read and comprehend literature in the grade text complexity band . . . • Writing—6 Use technology, including the Internet, to produce, publish, and update individual or shared writing products . . .
Knows the students and school community demographics and can make connections to resources for individual stakeholders	• Read—Provides resources that reflect ethnic and cultural backgrounds of students • Explore—Introduces students to cultural diversity through literary resources • Analyze—Connects literary elements (e.g., characters, setting) to students' backgrounds and interests • Develop—Pairs students' strengths with production methods (e.g., artist with visual medium, writer with text-based product) • Score—Engages students in statewide and/or national reading promotion activities					• Reading: Literature—3 Analyze the impact of the author's choices . . . • Speaking and Listening—5 Make strategic use of digital media in presentations . . . • Speaking and Listening—1d Initiate and participate effectively in a range of collaborative discussions: Respond thoughtfully to diverse perspectives . . .
Knows school/district curriculum and has a holistic perspective on instructional needs and makes connections for reading across the content areas	• Read—Provides subject content informational texts that reinforce and expand on instructional program concepts • Explore—Integrates genre literature into content areas (e.g., science or historical fiction) • Analyze—Integrates reading skills (e.g., identifying purpose or point of view) into content area readings and projects • Develop—Encourages teachers and students to develop literary-based projects throughout the curriculum • Score—Connects subject area content to real world situations					• Reading: Informational Text—6 Determine an author's point of view or purpose . . . • Writing—9 Draw evidence from literary or informational texts to support analysis . . . • Writing—2a Write informative/explanatory texts: Introduce a topic; organize complex ideas, concepts, and information . . .

(Continued)

School Library Foundational Principles	READS Examples					Common Core State Standards—English Language Arts—Examples*
	Read	Explore	Analyze	Develop	Score	
Understands the national educational agendas, including professional organizations (e.g., ALA/AASL, NCTE, IRA, ISTE) and the Common Core Initiative	• Read—Teaches students to critically view or listen to literary works • Explore—Explores with students the concept of intellectual freedom and First Amendment rights • Analyze—Promotes critical evaluation of literary works • Develop – Teaches students digital citizenship responsibilities • Score—Emphasizes to students school-to-world connections					• Writing—8 Gather relevant information from multiple authoritative print and digital sources . . . avoiding plagiarism and overreliance on any one source and following a standard format for citation. • Speaking and Listening—1d Initiate and participate effectively in a range of collaborative discussions: Respond thoughtfully to diverse perspectives . . .
Understands reading theory and is familiar with leaders in the field and the professional literature	• Read—Promotes reading fluency by providing a broad range of reading materials • Explore—Reinforces students' understanding of text requirements of various genres • Analyze—Promotes reading comprehension through building vocabulary knowledge • Develop—Assists students with encoding new understandings into visual products • Score—Promotes reading fluency by motivating students to read in independent reading programs					• Writing—3c Write narratives to develop real or imagined experiences or events: Use a variety of techniques to sequence events . . . • Writing—2d Write informative/explanatory texts: Use precise language, domain-specific vocabulary, and techniques . . .
Understands language arts theory/strategies and are familiar with leaders in the field and the professional literature	• Read—Encourages students to read, view, and listen for pleasure and personal growth • Explore—Provides multiple opportunities for students to interpret meanings in stories, poems, or plays • Analyze—Reinforces students identifying main and supportive details of a work • Develop—Reinforces writing skills needed to create a product • Score—Motivates students to read by providing literary celebrations (e.g., Banned Books Week, Teens Read Week)					• Writing—6 Use technology, including the Internet, to produce, publish, and update individual or shared writing products . . . • Reading: Literature—7 Analyze multiple interpretations of a story, drama, or poem . . .
Embraces digital literacy and consistently integrates technology applications into the library and school-wide instructional programs	• Read—Understands differences in printed text and online reading • Explore—Integrates media genres into the instructional program (e.g., documentaries) • Analyze—Integrates visual and digital literacies into subject area content • Develop—Uses Web 2.0 tools to produce student projects • Score—Integrates digital tools (e.g., blogs) into independent reading programs					• Speaking and Listening—5 Make strategic use of digital media in presentations . . . • Writing—8 Gather relevant information from multiple authoritative print and digital sources, using advanced searches effectively . . .

School Library Foundational Principles	READS Examples					Common Core State Standards—English Language Arts—Examples*
	Read	Explore	Analyze	Develop	Score	
Understands school-wide role of the school librarian and how the library program relates to the school's mission, goals, and curriculum, supporting and enhancing the learning environment	• Read—Refers to students' reading scores and matches resources to their individual and curricular needs • Explore—Promotes an appreciation for creative works by introducing students to award-winning materials • Analyze—Supports students' reading comprehension skills by reinforcing basic concepts (e.g., identifying main idea) • Develop—Integrates digital tools throughout the curriculum • Score—Encourages students to monitor their own reading progress					• Reading: Informational Text—7 Integrate and evaluate multiple sources of information presented in different media or formats . . . • Writing—9 Draw evidence from literary or informational texts to support analysis . . .
Recognizes that the overall goal is to create and nurture the continued development of a literate community	• Read—Consistently promotes reading to the broader school community • Explore—Connects students to social and political resources • Analyze—Promotes students' in-depth understanding of literary works • Develop—Engages students in publishing their creative products to share with the broader community • Score—Facilitates students' connections to lifelong learning					• Reading: Literature—9 Demonstrate knowledge of foundational works of American literature . . . • Writing—6 Use technology, including the Internet, to produce, publish, and update individual or shared writing products . . .

*Excerpted from *Common Core State Standards for English Language Arts*. National Governors Association Center for Best Practices and Council of Chief State School Officers Commercial License. Copyright © 2010. Used with permission of NGA Center/CCSSO.

correlation chart at the beginning of each chapter shows the match between the READS framework and the Common Core English Language Arts Standards.

DEVELOPING A LITERATE COMMUNITY

Library principles and curriculum initiatives provide the underpinnings for supporting the creation and ongoing development of a literate community, a linchpin goal of school library programs. However, achieving this goal requires a systematic and planned approach that makes the best use of all available resources and technologies. For many school librarians, this requires rethinking programming and instructional activities to more closely align with those of our colleagues in other content areas and with the evolving nature of literacy.

In 2001, Prensky identifies two kinds of content that have a direct impact on the literacy skills that students need in order to function successfully in the 21st century. He identified "'Legacy' content (to borrow the computer term for old systems) and 'Future' content" (p. 4). Prensky defines legacy content as including "reading, writing, arithmetic, logical thinking, understanding the writings and ideas of the past, etc.—all of our 'traditional' curriculum. It is of course still important, but it is from a different era." He defines future content as "digital and technological," including software and hardware, and so on. But he goes on to explain that future content also includes *the ethics, politics, sociology, languages and other things that go with them*" (p. 4).

Today, library, language arts, and reading professionals have embraced the changing nature of literacy. Definitions of literacy are evolving as professional organizations and authors consider the impact of new communication modes. According to Kinzer (2010), current definitions recognize literacy practices both in and out of the academic setting. He observes:

> While someone decades ago was literate if he or she could decode written text, comprehend it, and write an alphabetic message within the constraints of grammar and other conventions defined within the audience that would take up the given text, now a literate individual must be able to communicate and interact with a wide variety of digital media that incorporate but move beyond alphabetic text. (p. 53)

Ohler (2009) observes that, "Just being able to read is not sufficient" (p. 9). He emphasizes that, "Being able to read and write multiple forms of media and integrate them into a meaningful whole is the new hallmark of literacy" (p. 9). Consequently, digital, visual, and text-based literacies are interwoven into the READS scope and sequence, reflecting the expanding role of technologies, but also including traditional reading and writing literacies. An additional by-product of the enhanced role of technologies is that it has resulted in a more connected society. Within this socially connected environment, it is important to recognize that today's young adults are socially, technologically connected and that sharing reading experiences and information is an important part of their lives. Preddy (2010) affirms this observation by stating that, "Students' minds are attracted to entertainment and all things social" (p. ix). She further adds that, "This generation needs, and even thrives on, social interaction; reading must become social too" (p. ix). Therefore, in an effort to meet the needs of our students, implementation ideas using a variety of formats and learning configurations are included in each section of READS.

THE PLAN FOR THIS BOOK

The READS framework is not a step-by-step process similar to a research process. It is, however, an interwoven set of competencies and skills that are linked to curriculum standards and that support the AASL *Standards for the 21st-Century Learner*. It is important for the school librarian to have a firm grasp of the sections in READS to understand how they support one another and the national curriculum standards.

However, this book is not necessarily meant to be read from cover to cover, but rather to be referenced for ideas on how to implement the READS framework to effectively support the school's literacy initiatives. The chapters in this book are based on the sections of READS and may be used independently or sequentially, depending on the needs of the learning community. Background information and implementation activity suggestions are provided for many topics throughout the chapters. School librarians can pick and choose what is important to the school's curriculum and community, making informed choices in programming that are based on a continuum of student-based literature and literacy skills activities.

A cohesive plan can be formulated at the beginning of the year and implemented and/or modified as the year progresses. At the end of the year, an Annual Correlation Chart can be presented to the administration that will indicate the involvement of the library program in the ongoing effort to improve students' literacy achievements. (See Appendix A.) This chart can be an ongoing reminder throughout the year when posted in the library, tracking library literacy-based instructional and promotional activities. For added impact, the chart can be produced as a poster for display in the library and for presenting to the administration.

To facilitate implementation, lesson plans and additional online resources are listed within each chapter, as well as a works cited list and further readings. The lessons are intended for use by librarians and classroom teachers, depending on the local instructional patterns and expectations. The authors recognize that many of our colleagues across the country are in the position of teaching regularly scheduled classes in the library. It will be beneficial for the school librarian to become familiar with district curricula, resources, and requirements for various departments in the school as preparation for instructional planning. The READS curriculum provides a flexible framework for reading instruction centered in the library and coordinated with language arts and other content area curricula.

A wide range and selection of lessons have been gathered so that librarians will be well prepared for collaborative planning sessions with teachers and/or departments. Some lessons may be used by the librarian and others recommended for use by teachers. A librarian and a teacher can collaboratively implement various roles in a particular lesson, depending on the topic and complexity of the instructional plan. In other situations, lessons may be designated for particular grades, depending on the local curriculum (e.g., certain literary genres might be covered in particular grades). Some comprehensive lessons or units, ideal for collaboration, may begin with introducing fiction or nonfiction genres to students in Explore, extend to comprehension activities including specific skills or reader response in Analyze, and culminate with a product created by an individual or group in Develop.

Lesson plans have been linked from multiple online sources, with some lessons included from print journals. Many lessons correlated to the READS components are included from the ReadWriteThink web site, which is a project of the National Council of Teachers of English and the International Reading Association. Certain lessons from this source could be embedded into a district language arts curriculum, so time invested in learning about local teaching resources and requirements will be helpful in determining how to use these materials. Some materials from ReadWriteThink were collaboratively developed by a staff member from that organization and AASL and are particularly suited for use by school librarians (e.g., "Exploring Plagiarism, Copyright, and Paraphrasing" and "Students as Creators: Exploring Multimedia"). The ReadWriteThink site provides many interactive graphic organizers for use with their lessons. However, these versatile tools can be used with lessons developed at the local level and, therefore, are included separately in our READS Lessons and Activities lists as resources.

Many lessons and activities from The Learning Network of *The New York Times* are included in the resource lists. These lessons support many curricular areas (e.g., science, language arts, social studies, fine arts, technology, and math) and often feature breaking news stories. A variety of instructional materials are offered including word of the day (terrific for morning announcement programs), independent comprehension activities for

---

READS LESSONS & ACTIVITIES

Explore: Identifying Literary Genres and Themes

Nonfiction

Identifying nonfiction text structure. By Michael Stencil Sr. *School Library Monthly*, 27 (6), 13–15. (Gr. 6–8).

K/W/L chart. (Resource) Tool for analyzing topic or news article. The Learning Network: The New York Times. (Gr. 6–12) http://graphics8.nytimes.com/images/blogs/learning/pdf/activities/KWL_NYTLN.pdf

Magazine redux: An exercise in critical literacy. By Valerie A. Stokes. Includes Online Magazine list. ReadWriteThink. (Gr. 9–12) http://www.readwritethink.org/classroom-resources/lesson-plans/magazine-redux-exercise-critical-214.html

Podcast: New and noteworthy nonfiction. (Resource) ReadWriteThink. (Gr. 6–12) http://www.readwritethink.org/parent-afterschool-resources/podcast-episodes/noteworthy-nonfiction-30755.html

---

current news articles, and lesson plans, which may include a current news topic or link to a virtual museum source.

Lessons written by librarians from around the country are gathered into an online publication, *From the Creative Minds of 21st Century Librarians*, and hosted by the Center for Digital Literacy at Syracuse University. This publication is edited by Marilyn P. Arnone, Ruth V. Small, and Barbara K. Stripling and is available online at http://digital-literacy.syr.edu/projects/view/83. While the major focus of this e-book is inquiry skills, several links to lessons addressing reading topics are integrated into our READS Lessons and Activities lists.

In this excerpt from the READS Lessons and Activities for Chapter 5, Explore: Identifying Literary Genres and Themes, entries of instructional material links include a lesson from a periodical, an online resource from The Learning Network, a lesson from Read-WriteThink, and another resource from ReadWriteThink that could be used with students or as a staff inservice on new informational books. Please note that quotation marks are used for the titles of lessons or resources referred to in the chapters to differentiate them from the titles of books or periodicals.

In addition, a READS Internet Resources list is provided for each section of the curriculum. These Internet sites may contain background information useful in implementing a lesson (e.g., The Biography Maker, Jamie McKenzie) or a source for poetry (e.g., Academy of American Poets). Other examples of Internet sites are The Pulitzer Prizes and Defining Internet Freedom from the U.S. Department of State. Various websites are intended for student use or for use by educators; some sites may also be appropriate for inclusion in a school library web page.

Other features created for this book to assist in implementing READS are a Literary Genre Framework in Chapter 5, a Web 2.0 Tools chart in Chapter 10, and a comprehensive chart of state readers' choice programs in Chapter 11.

WORKS CITED

American Association of School Librarians. (2007). *Standards for the 21st-century learner*. Chicago, IL: American Library Association.

American Association of School Librarians. (2010). *Position statement on the Common Core College- and Career-Readiness Standards*. Retrieved from http://www.ala.org/ala/mgrps/divs/aasl/aaslissues/positionstatements/collegecareerstandards.cfm

Center for Digital Literacy, Syracuse University. (2010). *From the creative minds of 21st century librarians*. E-book. Retrieved from http://digital-literacy.syr.edu/projects/view/83

Conley, D. T. (2011). Building on the Common Core. *Educational Leadership, 68* (6), 16–20.

Kinzer, C. K. (2010). Considering literacy and policy in the context of digital environments. *Language Arts, 88* (1), 51–61.

Loertscher, D. V., & Marcoux, E. (2010). The Common Core Standards: Opportunities for teacher-librarians to move to the center of teaching and learning. *Teacher Librarian, 38* (2), 8–14.

National Governors Association Center for Best Practices/Council of Chief State School Officers. (2010). *Common Core State Standards Initiative*. Retrieved from http://www.corestandards.org/

Ohler, J. (2009). Orchestrating the media collage. *Educational Leadership, 66* (6), 8–13.

Preddy, L. B. (2010). *Social readers: Promoting reading in the 21st century*. Santa Barbara, CA: Libraries Unlimited.

Prensky, M. (2001). Digital natives, digital immigrants. *On the Horizon, 9* (5), 1–6.

Part 2

Read as a Personal Activity

3

Guiding Readers' Choices

The best strategy for filling our secondary school libraries with young people enthusiastically searching for reading materials is to offer a wide array of books, magazines, and online resources on a broad range of topics and reading levels, displayed both on orderly shelves and in eye-appealing displays. These resources must be promoted by knowledgeable, friendly staff members who understand the adolescent psyche, are tuned in to student interests, and have the time and patience to work endlessly to match fiction and nonfiction titles and sources with each student.

LIBRARY ENVIRONMENT

Whether housed in a traditional library setting or a spacious learning commons, the environment must be welcoming, hopefully with spaces for those patrons who seek a quiet reading spot, as well as areas for typical adolescent social interactions and group activities. Controlling such environments, particularly during lunch times in large high schools, can be somewhat like trying to herd cats, but the old adage that an empty and quiet library serves no one should strike a note for all librarians in this age of accountability and recognition of the need to reconstruct secondary education. The key to this issue of library environment is balance, calling for respectful consideration of others by all patrons.

In this chapter, strategies for getting books into students' hands will be explored, including reading for personal, recreational, and academic reasons. The concept of balance is also paramount in considering which reading promotion activities to embrace, as students have a variety of attitudes toward reading when they enter secondary schools; by employing a range of approaches, the chances of reaching all students increase. In addition, the role of the school librarian in influencing students to read will be described in terms of personal activities, collaborative efforts, including supporting teachers and other educators, and ongoing collection development.

INDIVIDUAL READING GUIDANCE

Many come into this profession because they love to read and want to be involved with spreading the joy of reading to young people. They envision one-on-one sessions with students, discussing a wonderful book, then recommending the next terrific title. This form of personal reading guidance is still appropriate but less common as some of our secondary schools now have a large number of students. One of the authors' former

READS Component	READS Indicator	AASL *Standards for the 21st-Century Learner**	Common Core State Standards—English Language Arts**
Read as a personal activity			
The student will:			
1.1 Select and read literary and informational resources at an appropriate reading level.	1.1.1 Choose age and ability appropriate literature to read based on interest or curriculum need.	• 1.1.2 Use prior and back-ground knowledge as context for new learning. • 4.1.1 Read, view, and listen for pleasure and personal growth. • 4.1.2 Read widely and flu-ently to make connections with self, the world, and pre-vious reading. • 4.1.7 Use social networks and information tools to gather and share information. • 4.2.4 Show an appreciation for literature . . . • 4.4.1 Identify own areas of interest. • 4.4.2 Recognize the limits of own personal knowledge.	• Reading: Informational Text—10 Read and com-prehend literary nonfic-tion in the grade text complexity band . . . • Reading: Literature—10 Read and comprehend literature in the grade text complexity band . . .
	1.1.2 Choose age and ability appropriate informational texts to read based on in-terest or cur-riculum need.	• 1.1.2 Use prior and back-ground knowledge as context for new learning. • 4.1.1 Read, view, and listen for pleasure a nd personal growth. • 4.1.2 Read widely and flu-ently to make connections with self, the world, and pre-vious reading. • 4.1.4 Seek information for personal learning in a variety of formats and genres. • 4.1.7 Use social networks and information tools to gather and share information. • 4.2.4 Show an appreciation for literature . . .	• Reading: Informational Text—10 Read and com-prehend literary nonfic-tion in the grade text complexity band . . .

READS Component	READS Indicator	AASL *Standards for the 21st-Century Learner**	Common Core State Standards—English Language Arts**
		• 4.4.1 Identify own areas of interest. • 4.4.2 Recognize the limits of own personal knowledge.	• Reading: Literature—10 Read and comprehend literature in the grade text complexity band . . .
*Excerpted from *Standards for the 21st-Century Learner* by the American Association of School Librarians, a division of the American Library Association, copyright © 2007 American Library Association. Available for download at www.ala.org/aasl/standards. Used with permission. **Excerpted from *Common Core State Standards for English Language Arts*. National Governors Association Center for Best Practices and Council of Chief State School Officers Commercial License. Copyright © 2010. Used with permission of NGA Center/CCSSO.			

high schools once had more than 5,000 students and 4 school librarians, but recently was cut back to 1 school librarian for the current population of over 4,000. Each student still has the same needs for reading encouragement and promotion, even as staff ratios have been cut, and the best solution is to combine individual and group reading guidance techniques.

School librarians have the opportunity to provide individual reading guidance when students come into the library looking for books independently, whether by their own choice or to meet a classroom requirement. Sometimes, students present a friendly face, requesting a good book, and these situations are pleasant encounters. The basic reader's advisory principles are put into action. Focus on the reader, asking: (1) What was the last book you read and consider great? (2) Who is your favorite author? (3) What is your favorite genre? (4) What is your favorite nonfiction topic? Working in a library environment enriched with displays and stacks of bookmarks and brochures featuring lists of titles on popular themes and topics makes the task of finding the right book for each reader much easier. If, for example, the school librarian can bring the student to a display of books on the state reading promotion program for that particular year, several appropriate choices can be described (on various reading levels) and the student left to check cover illustrations and details. A valuable technique for working with adolescents is to provide choices, so that the student has control of the situation and remembers the pleasant experience in the library.

In another scenario, a teacher brings a class into the library for checkout, with some students rushing to the shelves in search of books by their favorite author or topic. Alas, not all students will be so eager to select a book. The demeanors of some students reflect resentment of the assignment. This is the time when we must call on both our repertoire of reader advisory strategies and a reservoir of patience. Take a deep breath, remember that pleasant experiences in libraries contribute to the development of lifelong readers, and then vow to never embarrass students about their reading level!

Here are some typical questions or statements from students:

• Student 1: "How can I find a book to read? There are so many books in this library!"

   Comment: This question could be a pleasant conversation opener, a reflection of an unmotivated reader (Beers, 2003), or could indicate a lack of knowledge of the layout of the library and of the function of the library catalog. A first-line approach would be to query

1. Reading is rewarding.
2. Reading builds a mature vocabulary.
3. Reading makes you a better writer.
4. Reading is hard, and "hard" is necessary.
5. Reading makes you smarter.
6. Reading prepares you for the world of work.
7. Reading well is financially rewarding.
8. Reading opens the door to college and beyond.
9. Reading arms you against oppression.
10. Reading develops your moral compass.

From: Gallagher, Kelly (2003). *Reading Reasons.*

the student on favorite reading genres and to demonstrate the use of the catalog and online sources to find similar books. Provide paper and pencil for the student to record the call number and accompany the student to the shelves to find the book. Another option could be to direct the student to a display of titles on the favored genre, thus narrowing the range of choices for students who may be overwhelmed by larger secondary libraries.

- Student 2: "There are no good books in this library!"

Comment: This negative approach could indicate lack of reading skills and/or resentment toward reading in general, the classroom teacher, the particular library, or even the school librarian. Proceed cautiously! Try asking about favorite movies, games, or hobbies to connect to reading recommendations. Refer to displays of favorite books for each grade, selected by students.

- Student 3: "I don't like to read!"

Comment: This statement may be a cover for low reading ability, inadequate self-esteem, a poor attitude toward schooling in general, or a preference for other activities. In some cases with a scheduled class, this statement was followed by an emphatic "I am not going to check out a book!" At this point, a referral to the classroom teacher, hopefully in the room, is the best approach. It can be counterproductive for a school librarian to insist that a student check out a book. When dealing with students in a negative frame of mind, it can be helpful to keep the 10 reading reasons offered by Kelly Gallagher (2003) firmly in mind and to pass on one or two of them in a light-hearted manner, accompanied by a smile. If it is obvious that the student is not in the mood for a reasoned discussion, consider offering an invitation to the student to return to the library another day for a conversation about finding a good book to read.

- Student 4: "I don't have time to read!"

Comment: This may be an excuse, but does not necessarily reflect a dislike of reading. This statement is typical of aliterate students (Beers, 2003), who have the ability to read but fall into a pattern of not reading beyond classroom assignments. Recommend a great book of short stories, which can be read between other activities, or perhaps a graphic novel.

To be most effective in matching students with books, a school librarian must know books, must be familiar with characteristics of adolescents, must be current with reading research, and must exhibit almost magical intuitive powers in dealing with secondary students. Sometimes, enthusiastic first-person recommendations of books work well; other times, less is more. For example, when talking with boys about books, a low-key approach may be best, such as suggesting a book and making a comment that another guy read this book recently and liked it.

Time for Checking Out

In many secondary schools, students primarily check out books during independent time before or after school, or during lunch. Teachers may occasionally schedule classes in the library for circulation of books, often on specific content area topics. However, in some middle schools, a regular circulation period, often biweekly, is arranged for all language arts or English classes. This practice at least ensures that all students have the opportunity to select books within the school day.

Circulation patterns in high schools are typically lower than in middle schools. Administrators and staff may be concerned that students with a documented need to improve their reading skills are not reading self-selected titles on a regular basis. A solution in some school libraries is to schedule remedial reading classes to come for book check out. In many districts and states, students who have not achieved a certain score on the state reading examination are assigned a reading class in addition to the usual language arts or English class or students are assigned to a language arts class by reading scores. In this case, it can be helpful to request in advance from the teacher a roster for the class with reading levels for each student.

Reading Interests

Fortunately, all schools have many students who love to read and are vocal about it! Providing the books that appeal to these students is the most pleasant part of the school librarian's job. The publishing phenomenon of the Harry Potter and Twilight series has impacted library circulations and bookstore sales, creating great press for reading and reflecting the choices of many teens.

The responsibility of the library professional is to include but move beyond the blockbusters to gather titles reflecting a wide range of reading interests. Teri Lesesne (2003) observes, "There is no one template for a reader. . . . There is no typical librarian, no typical teen, no typical YA book." She observed that adolescents like humor, nonfiction (boys especially), mysteries, and so on, but this list is certainly not complete.

Much has been written, from a variety of perspectives, about encouraging reluctant readers. The common theme emerging is the importance of providing materials the students like to read. Jones, Hartman, and Taylor (2006) report that boys are more inclined to read informational text, including hobbies, sports, and things they want to do; magazines and newspapers; comic books and graphic novels; escapism and humor; with some groups reading science fiction and humor.

Kylene Beers (2003), reflecting on her effort to determine what her reluctant students wanted to read, ultimately determined that students usually would not like the same books she chose. After listening to reluctant readers, she concluded, "They want books that give them information that fits into their world. They want it to help them with the issues they face right now."

Boltz (2008) studied reading preferences of both boys and girls in fifth grade and found that "boys want action and adventure, even in their nonfiction selections. Girls prefer story and narrative." Boltz encourages other librarians to conduct interviews with students in their schools: "The first step is to make a determined effort to find out what is of interest, and then for teachers, [librarians], and parents to commit to finding and making available materials that match these interests."

Reading Surveys

A traditional reading advisory strategy that targets individual reading preferences but may be implemented primarily in groups is the reading survey or inventory. These instruments are intended to provide information about individual students that will facilitate the process of making appropriate recommendations of reading materials by school librarians and/or teachers. The student choices of literature genres may also be useful to librarians for collection development purposes.

The role of the librarian in providing and using reading interest surveys will vary from school to school. Providing examples of surveys to teachers may be the extent of involvement. Generally, in secondary schools the ratio of students to librarian is very large, likely prohibiting widespread implementation of surveys with individual follow through on the data provided. However, a librarian, in collaboration with teachers and reading coaches or leaders, may decide to use this strategy with groups of reluctant readers or intensive reading classes. To make the task of answering questions more appealing to students, consider the use of online resources such as Survey Monkey.

Reading surveys are available online and in various professional books. One survey by Denice Hildebrant is posted on the Young Adult Library Services Association (YALSA) site. Other surveys are available from ReadWriteThink. For links to surveys and lessons on book selection and other reading strategies, see the READS Lessons and Activities list in this chapter. Surveys are also included in Wood and Harmon's *Strategies for Integrating Reading & Writing in Middle and High School Classrooms* (2001); Jones, Hartman, and Taylor's *Connecting with Reluctant Teen Readers* (2006); and Atwell's *The Reading Zone* (2007).

A reading survey proved to be a useful technique for one of the book's authors when assigned by school administrators to mentor high school students who had failed the state standardized reading test. Each professional in the building was assigned to four or five failing students and personally evaluated on the increase in reading achievement by each student. Little direction by administration was provided for this task, except to act as a mentor, encouraging the student, listening to concerns, and serving as an advocate when appropriate. The largest issue for all faculty members was *when* to find time to meet with students individually. During the second year of receiving this assignment, a process for assessing the student's reading patterns was developed, including the use of a survey. A profile was created for each assigned student using several years of reading grades on the state test, a Lexile Reading Level (provided by the reading coach), and library circulation records from the Destiny library catalog. During the second or third meeting with each student, the short reading survey was implemented. Based on that data and the reading profile, subsequent meetings involved one-on-one reading guidance sessions. While results were not spectacular (one student passed a retake of the test within weeks and exited the mentoring program; another student transferred; an ELL student improved significantly, etc.), at least a process using the training and skills of a school librarian was developed and implemented. An additional plus was data to be used in the required reporting of the mentoring experience; in this case, the administrator in charge was the school principal!

In the reading survey used in the mentoring project, in addition to questions on favorite genres, students were asked about books in the home, use of the school and public library, hobbies, and after-school activities. These answers provided openers for discussion during mentoring sessions on how to use the library catalog, use of time, and so forth.

READING GUIDANCE TECHNIQUES FOR GROUPS

A variety of techniques may be employed to meet the reading needs of groups of students. An advantage of these group strategies is that many teenagers do not like to be singled out in front of their peers, but respond favorably to a broader approach to promoting reading. In addition, in a single space of time, a school librarian can reach many more students using group techniques than with individual encounters.

Displays

Displays can serve both practical and aesthetic functions, creating centers of books on certain themes, genres, or reading programs and offering colorful and creative decorative elements for the library. Displays can be built around current events in the school or world, type of literature, holidays, or a myriad of other topics. A very useful ongoing tabletop display in a high school may be centered on a particular series of books, such as the Bluford series by Townsend Press. This series of books on inner city teens of primarily minority groups have great appeal for students looking for easy reading fiction titles on current realistic themes. A bright poster on the series drew attention to the multiple copies of the books filling a tiered plexiglass rack on a table with a colorful plastic covering. Since the books in the series are written by various authors, they would not stand together in the fiction stacks; therefore, this display made it easier for students to quickly find the books they wanted. This idea was introduced at a state library conference and was easily duplicated in the library with great success. One sheepish teen male was accompanied to the circulation desk by his girlfriend who declared, "I told him he *has* to read this book!" This area was a favorite of students in a hurry to check out a book before the bell rang and some would apologetically explain, "I've got to have a book for silent reading next period!" Townsend Press provides the posters free with any order and sells the books directly to libraries for $1.00 each!

The creation of displays is an easy way to connect with schoolwide events and observances. When the school was preparing for a visit by an International Baccalaureate (IB) team to assess the school's curriculum and promotion of internationalism, a display board was developed with a collage of scenes from other countries found in travel brochures, magazine ads, and photos with the caption "Fiction from Around the World." All the titles featured settings in other countries. This display was reused several times over the years when parent events for IB were scheduled. The group of books used expanded as new titles were purchased and was easy to retrieve as a Destiny library catalog category was created, providing easy access to the titles.

An entire display can center around one book title. A contemporary novel featuring the King Arthur legend, *Avalon High* by Meg Cabot, inspired a display of books on the King Arthur legend itself and other fiction titles with references to the traditional British legend. The free-standing display board included a poster of King Arthur, the cover of Avalon High, a toy spinner, and the caption "Avalon High: A Spin-Off from the King Arthur Legend." A poster of King Arthur was easy to locate on the Internet and inexpensive. The display included the works of Mary Stewart, T. H. White, Howard Pyle, T. A. Barron, and others.

Rotating groups of books are the stars in this activity for a class or group in the library to select books. Librarian Cathy Belben (2007) describes this practice as rotating stations. Set up groups of six to eight books on each of seven to eight tables, depending on the size of the class; the books may be on a single genre or mix of genres, including as many new books as available. After the teacher assigns all to small groups, students will spend five minutes at each table looking at books and choosing one that is most appealing before moving on to the next table. Students use browsing skills (e.g., looking at covers and descriptions, flipping though the book), and after visiting all displays, each group will select one most appealing book and describe it to the other students in the class. An extension of this activity would be providing colored card stock cut to bookmark size for student use to record the call number and title of book they would like to check out and read later.

Other Ideas for Displays

- Olympics, Super Bowl, World's Series, or other sporting events
- New books: a perennial favorite

- Genres of literature
- Read-alikes (e.g., titles like *Twilight* or *A Child Called It*)
- Book or movie tie-ins
- "Have you heard a good book lately?"
- Pop culture
- Current events (e.g., elections, awards)
- College (e.g., admission, choices, preparation)
- Quick bio reads (easy-to-read biographies including graphic novel versions)
- Earth Day
- Multicultural themes (e.g., African American history, Hispanic heritage)
- Women's history
- Historical events
- Curriculum themes (e.g., photography, careers, artists, the Elizabethan era)

Reading Lists and Bookmarks

Printed materials sometimes accompany displays but more often are placed on or near circulation desks. Commercial bookmarks are offered by many sources and are popular with students, especially girls. Local production of customized bookmarks has been facilitated by user-friendly software and is sometimes a project for library aides, media production students, or volunteers. In addition, numerous websites now offer printable bookmarks on many topics.

The creation of reading lists of books in your library on various themes is a great way to promote books to adolescents. As noted in this chapter, some teens prefer to avoid a face-to-face discussion about books, but might pick up a bibliography of titles on a favorite theme.

A quick way to display reading recommendations while saving paper is to post choices on a school or library website. This option will be discussed further in the section on online selection tools.

Reading Programs and Celebrations

Most states have reading programs targeted to specific age groups, typically sponsored by state professional organizations or state school library personnel. Florida offers the Sunshine State Young Readers' Award for the sixth to eighth grades. For high school students, the program is Florida Teens Read, featuring both fiction and nonfiction titles. The programs are similar in that students read from the annual lists of books and then vote for their favorites statewide in the spring. The authors of the books selected by students statewide are honored at the state professional school library conference. This topic will be discussed further in the Score component of READS.

Other reading celebrations are sponsored by national professional organizations. Teen Read Week is scheduled in the fall of the year by YALSA and offers new themes each year to promote reading. The American Library Association designates April for National Library Week and offers a variety of reading promotion products for sale, including posters, bookmarks, pamphlets, and more. An adaptable product is the READS poster software, which allows the creation of reading posters featuring local people. These literary programs offer many opportunities to celebrate reading and to connect students with books.

Booktalking

This group strategy encompasses a range of possibilities, beginning with school librarian presentations, live and online, and extending to talks by students. Basically, booktalking is simply discussing books to entice readers; books may be grouped by themes, genre, favorite titles, or other ways. Booktalks have been described as commercials for a book, as teasers, as a verbal blurb similar to the ones on the book cover, and, more recently, as a book trailer, evolving from movie trailers. Many school librarians write their own, sometimes including brief passages from the book. The flexible rules for writing them are simple: Never talk about a book you haven't read or don't like; give the author and title; show the cover; keep it short; never tell the ending; and maintain eye contact with the audience.

Sometimes PowerPoint presentations are created to accompany booktalks, including covers, in case a student checks out the book just before the class files into the library; of course, having visuals available as you talk helps to maintain the attention of students. An additional advantage of the PowerPoint format is the ability to add a slide listing read-alikes or books similar to the featured title. Heather Gruenthal provides a pertinent example in an article in *CSLA Journal* in 2008: "I have chosen *A Child Called It* by Dave Pelzer and connected this book to other problem novels on a slide entitled, *Life Is Rough*! By linking popular books to others with similar themes, you broaden students' ranges of choice so that they realize that there are a number of desirable books in their favorite genre."

Booktalks are now readily available from other sources. Several youth librarians have published collections of booktalks, including Joni Bodart, whose work is often used in children's and young adult's literature classes. Ruth E. Cox Clark has conducted booktalking sessions at conferences and published several books on the topic. She emphasizes the entertainment aspect of booktalking and describes three styles of talks she employs, "excerpt (read a portion of the book aloud), discussion (talk about a character or an incident from the book), and first person (become a character in the book)," in an article in *Library Media Connection* in 2007. She reports, based on her experiences in public and private schools, the first person style booktalk was the favorite of students.

For all of the advantages of booktalking to encourage reading, there is a downside for librarians. After preparing a booktalk of 8 to 12 or more titles, one class can check out all the copies available. Certainly, the booktalk can be repeated later to another group, but not within a time frame of several weeks. Joyce Valenza discussed her issues with booktalking in her blog, *Neverendingsearch*, in August of 2007:

> True confession: I was never a good booktalker. I did it at every level. I spent a week quickly reading or re-reading about 10 or so books around a theme, around a genre, the new titles. . . . When the grabbing was over, the waiting lists began. Then the next class arrived. . . . I simply couldn't read or re-read fast enough. . . . I needed booktalk support. Booktalk rehab. I craved intervention. Web 2.0 rescued me.

Online Selection Tools

Catering to many students' preferences for Internet-based activities, online book selection tools can provide an alternative to personal reading guidance. Web 2.0 features allow preservation and reuse of a school librarian's own booktalks, as well as taking advantage of the many book promotions posted by school and public librarians, book publishers, and students. Many booktalks are now available on the Internet, including those by veteran Nancy Keane, http://nancykeane.com/booktalks. She provides booktalks online in both print and podcasts. In addition to the hundreds of podcasts, Nancy Keane's site provides a listing of the reading promotion programs from various states with titles, with booktalks for many of the books. Another veteran booktalker, Joni Bodart, also has a website, thebooktalker.com, which offers a concise description of the technique in a section titled "What Is a Booktalk?" She also includes an archive of her talks and a list of her 10 favorites, as well as new talks (Reynolds, 2005). In some cases, multiple booktalks are available for books, a particularly useful consolidation of resources. Just as you should like a book to booktalk it, you must feel comfortable with the written booktalk to use it. Having multiple approaches available allows the combination of features you wish to share about a title, saving time but allowing convenient personalizing of the presentation.

Another online option is using book review websites. See our READS Internet Resources for these sites; some feature reviews written by students (Flamingnet) while others offer reviews developed by librarians. Cathy Belben (2007) reports on a student activity using these sites that she calls "Internet Book Quest." The assignment requires students to visit a specified number of preselected websites, select one title from each, and write about why the book appeals to them. The next step is to check the local online catalog to determine if the library owns the book and check out the book. If the library doesn't own the book, the title information and rationale for purchasing the book could be submitted to the school librarian.

> **Free Online Book Review Sites**
>
> Flamingnet (YALSA): http://www.flamingnet.com/
> Teen Reads: http://www.teenreads.com/
> Teenspoint: http://www.teenspoint.org/readingmatters/index.asp

Another potential source for online readers' advisory is the Books & Authors subscription database from Gale. This product replaces Gale's What Do I Read Next database and offers an interactive approach with a teen-friendly look. In a review in *School Library Journal* in 2009, Shonda Brisco writes, "Users today, especially teens, approach digital content with a range of build-in expectations, from the ability to customize to creating new content to the opportunity to interact with others." This subscription service allows searches by title, author, keyword, series, genre, subgenre, award winners, expert picks, and more. A feature called the Reading Room allows a user to collect book titles, book reviews, or other information to save and to share with others through the web. Teens can add their own reviews or provide ratings for books they have read.

EBSCO offers Novelist and Novelist Plus as an embeddable readers' advisory subscription service. When added to a school or public library's online catalog, this product allows students and staff to search for books in a variety of ways, including author, title, genre, keyword, series, and more. In addition, it features professional resources for educators, including book discussion guides, booktalks, and curricular connections (Brisco, 2009).

In many schools, the advanced features of the online library catalog itself can be a convenient selection tool. For example, the Destiny library catalog can display the top 10 circulating titles in the school, which holds appeal for many of today's students. This catalog recently added a new display option, Destiny Quest, which displays the top 10 circulating titles, resource lists prepared by the librarian, and a new arrival section. Also, a drag-and-drop feature allows students to search the catalog and create a customized book list that will remain available until the user deletes it. This list of items, called "my info," could be created by conducting a search on the student's own reading range, using Lexile or Accelerated Reader levels, which could also be combined with desired subject headings.

The latest twist to booktalking is the book trailer. These visual and audio book promotions are now available on various Internet sites and provide a creative opportunity for student production projects, which will be addressed in Chapter 10. Currently, digital cameras are being used for easy production and uploading of book trailers. Many book trailers are posted on Facebook or YouTube, but not all schools are allowed access to these sites by district filters. One alternative to use in schools is to post the digital product on a library's website. At this point, you can envision a hybrid mix of booktalking strategies, combining live school librarian talks with book trailers or other formats.

Quick Strategy Ideas

- Create a booktalking kiosk in the library, featuring talks by the school librarian or students, with appropriate signage.
- Provide a printed list or bookmark with the booktalking titles, so that students have a handy reference.
- Collaborate with teachers on the theme of the talk, to maximize student appeal and curricular usefulness.
- Consider using a reverse strategy as recommended by Jeanne Ziemba that includes a book curse in a talk; describe how you don't like a particular book because science fiction is not your favorite genre or it is too gross for your taste. Likely students will respond warmly to such a ploy! (personal communication, October 6, 2009)
- Include a mix of nonfiction and fiction titles in a talk. You may even use magazine articles, websites, or database selections on a topic, to promote various formats of information.
- Some prefer to connect one book to the next in some way in a booktalk (e.g., another mystery, same author, wicked stepmothers, another sport).
- Provide a context for the booktalk, to meet a classroom requirement, enhance a certain reading skill, and so on.
- Use props to focus attention on a book and make it memorable.
- When planning the sequence of a booktalk, save a particular juicy one to insert where needed, perhaps when the class is becoming restless! A contributor to LM_NET called this a silencer!
- Occasionally, include a book you haven't read if it fits the theme, but admit you haven't read it yet.
- Use booktalks, particularly with a visual element, as part of a morning news show.
- Include a few very short books in a talk to a class with reluctant readers.
- Display all the books prepared for a talk and select students from the audience to pick the one to hear next.
- Incorporate music into a booktalking session when appropriate: think suspenseful music for a theme of mysteries or jazz for Harlem Renaissance titles.
- For movie and fiction tie-ins, use a brief snippet of the movie as an introduction to the talk.
- Peruse the audiofiles of KUOW Public Radio for public librarian Nancy Pearl's booktalks and discussions. She occasionally includes YA book reviews and many of her adult titles appeal to older students.
- After collaborating with the teacher, use booktalks to help students select a book for their reading circles project.

Reading Aloud

Reading aloud is a time-honored strategy for creating interest in books. In the past, reading aloud to students was associated with public and elementary school libraries. Today, reading aloud is also recommended for middle and high school students, which will be a shift in the day-to-day practices of most secondary school librarians. When one of the authors moved to secondary schools from elementary about five years ago, one of her regrets was the impression, "I can't read aloud any more!" Jim Trelease (2006) echoed that impression in *The Read-Aloud Handbook*, "By middle school, almost no one is reading aloud to students." The prevailing thought was that research skills were the focus of secondary school librarians and that the pleasure of sharing stories must be left behind in elementary school.

Trelease (2006) and Beers (2003) point to *Becoming a Nation of Readers* (Anderson, Heibert, Scott, & Wilkinson, 1985) as establishing the need to read aloud to students in all grades. This landmark study referred to reading aloud as "the single most important activity for building the knowledge required for eventual success in reading." This directive was from the report of the Commission on Reading, established in 1983 by the National Academy of Education and the National Institute of Education, funded by the U.S. Department of Education.

The latest guidelines from the American Association of School Librarians (2009) outline appropriate actions for school librarians in the area of reading, including motivating "learners to read fiction and nonfiction through reading aloud, booktalking, displays, exposure to authors and other means."

Keith McPherson, writing in *Teacher Librarian* in 2008, provides a compelling rationale for reading aloud to secondary students:

> Read-alouds are not just time fillers. Repeated read-alouds are one of the greatest teaching venues we have for modeling powerful and meaningful reading strategies. They are, by far, one of the greatest literacy links between the classroom and the school library. They are also one of the greatest learning gifts we as teacher-librarians can give to our students, their families, our own families, and our community. (p. 14)

The development of background knowledge and vocabulary is one of the most convincing reasons to read aloud to students. The disparity of educational achievement among students with home backgrounds devoid of books and the modeling of reading by parents is a great concern and should be a prime motivator for school librarians to address this equity issue in a multitude of ways. In *Horn Book Magazine* in January, 2010, Christine McDonnell, a librarian in Massachusetts, commented on the benefit of reading aloud to secondary students:

> As the world spins faster and communication shrinks to the size of Twitter, we need to make room for the sound of a voice reading a story: details creating another place; the well-paced unfolding of plot; the blossoming of character; the luxury of language. Thus is culture passed on, through story shared, language spoken and heard. (p. 73)

Middle school librarian Alison G. Follos regularly reads aloud to students in sessions she calls Reader's Workshop. In an article titled "Change the Literacy Depression in Your School: Read Teens a Story" (2007), she writes, "It is a comfortable combination of literature appreciation, book club, and literary circle format. It is time to expose the top titles and engage students who too often walk past, not into, the library." She combines strategies during 40-minute sessions, including not only read-alouds, but also booktalking, reader response including journaling and literary conversations, and talk about authors.

Considering all of the reasons and possibilities for reading aloud to secondary students, how is a school librarian to make the decision to devote time to this technique? The answer to that loaded question will depend on the individual, the school setting, the needs of the student population, and the requirements of school administrators. While all students potentially will gain from reading-aloud experiences, groups that would benefit most from this technique will be English Language Learners (ELL), Exceptional Student Education (ESE) students, and low-functioning readers. Another major consideration is allocating time for implementing inquiry/information literacy activities that have been based on content objectives and collaboratively planned with teachers. The unfortunate reality is that librarians must make difficult decisions about how to divide their time among the many activities with potential benefits to the students and staff in their schools.

Once a decision to schedule a read-aloud session is made, the next issue is what to read, which is dependent on the characteristics of the target group. Among general criteria for book selection are student interests, age of the students, and reasons for the reading session (Follos, 2007). Other qualities to consider include rich language, engaging plots, and titles unlikely to be read independently by most students in the group (McDonnell, 2010). Including a variety of authors adds the benefit of steering students to other books for independent reading. It is strongly recommended that each book is first read in its entirety before sharing with a group to avoid potentially awkward situations with language or appropriateness. Teri S. Lesesne (2003) reinforces the need to read a book in advance and extends it with what she calls the 3 Ps of reading aloud: "preview, practice, and personalize." She refers to reading aloud as a performance, which is enhanced by practice. She recommends that all who read aloud personalize the experience, adding their emotions and emphases to the text.

When planning a read-aloud experience with a group, after deciding what to read, a decision must be made on how to conduct the session. Emphasizing vocabulary from the work is one of many options. Depending on the language level of the students in the targeted group, one choice is to introduce a few key words before beginning the selection. This brief discussion could be conducted orally or through a display of the words, using a variation of a word wall on a bulletin board, poster, or through computer projection, which would add a second method of processing the terms. Another possibility is to pause to clarify the meaning of a word while reading, taking care not to disrupt the flow of the text too much.

To extend the value of time spent reading, Lapp and Fisher (2009) recommend pairing read-alouds with think-alouds. This technique, used by a librarian or content area teacher, scaffolds the reading comprehension and writing strategies taught by reading and language arts teachers. In this read-aloud example from Lapp and Fisher on the topic of racial profiling, the listening audience was a junior class mix of cultures and languages, but all reading significantly below grade level. After reading a section of the book, the educator reader said:

> *I think it's interesting here, what the author does. I notice the opening sentence and how it makes me want to read more. I want to know more about the application of racial profiling, as the author says. But then I notice that the author used some signal words to help me organize my thinking about the text. The author says "One explanation" and then shares the information but then says "An alternative explanation" and then presents the other side. I like the way the author framed*

this and presented both sides of the issue. I'm going to add that structure to my notes because I might want to use it in my own writing. For now, I know it's helping me remember that there are at least two sides of this issue. I'll read on and see what the author says (p. 588).

From reflection on this think-aloud example emerged a useful application for school librarians. Before beginning a fiction or nonfiction selection, one could think aloud about the selection of a particular book, reviewing and extending guidelines for book choice, including reading the blurb in the book, checking the author's credentials or other works, noting the level of the text and number of pages, reviewing the book's description in the library catalog, considering prior reading on the topic, and so on. Another application of this strategy is to locate several appropriate books or periodical articles on a topic, think aloud about the selection criterion, and then allow students in the group to choose which one to be read aloud. This procedure will increase student engagement in the activity, adding to the benefits of a read-aloud.

The possibilities for planning read-aloud encounters are many, ranging from regularly scheduled sessions for a year, semester, or six-week period to a single event. A read-aloud could even be video-recorded and replayed for other groups in a department. The occasion could also be a school-wide or community literacy celebration. Another choice is the setting for the read-aloud, which doesn't always have to be the library. Sometimes, it is preferable for the librarian to read in the classroom, providing a less disruptive environment than a library filled with other classes involved in research projects.

In addition to reading aloud personally, other important roles for librarians are to recommend titles to be used by teachers or other educators in the building and to ensure that the library collection offers appropriate titles for use as read-aloud selections. Addressing the situation of aliterate students, who can read but choose not to, Dr. G. Kylene Beers (1996) analyzed activities that students liked and loathed. She found that uncommitted and unmotivated students are not likely to voluntarily go to a library or buy books at a book fair; however, these same students will listen to a teacher read an entire book aloud.

Many secondary science teachers are matching fiction and nonfiction books with science concepts and reading aloud to their students to assist students in connecting science to their own lives and to increase understanding of the subject matter (Delo, 2008). This teacher suggests that because students have higher listening levels than reading levels, it is practical to incorporate reading aloud of relevant fiction and nonfiction books with independent reading of textbooks. Her article in *Science Teacher* includes lists of read-aloud titles matched with science concepts in addition to a discussion of tips for merging science and literacy activities. Bircher (2009) is another high school science teacher who regularly reads aloud to her students; she urges her colleagues to consult with their school and public librarians when searching for appropriate titles. Bircher writes, "Using . . . literature in the classroom has allowed my students to become interested in difficult concepts from the first day of study and has provided greater incentive to engage in scientific inquiry."

Reading lists and suggestions from these two articles written by science teachers provides an excellent bank of information to be used by librarians in in-service training sessions for their own science departments. Spreading the word about the advantages of reading aloud to students in content areas, a proven reading strategy for promoting student achievement (Carbo, 2008), can facilitate the creation of more engaging learning opportunities in a school. By displaying appropriate books, citing research findings, offering booklists and web links, and summarizing implementation tips of these two authors, a school librarian can link resources and teachers in an exchange that becomes mutually beneficial. Delo (2008) offers another perspective on reading aloud, which may be popular with teachers. She considers reading aloud to be a flexible "reserve" activity; if her class had to relocate to another space because of air-conditioning problems or other reasons, she takes along her reading selection and makes good use of the time.

Excellent resources for creating read-aloud lists in science include the annual Outstanding Science Trade Books for Students K-12, published by the National Science Teachers' Association in cooperation with the Children's Book Council. These lists appear in professional journals, *Science Teacher* and *Science for Children*, and are also available online at nsta.org/publications/ostb. The State of California Department of Education provides listings of science topics with corresponding fiction and nonfiction titles, complete with recommended age groups at www.cde.ca.gov/ci/sc/ll/index.asp. A third recommended online source is the book search from the University of North Carolina-Wilmington at http://appserv02.uncw.edu/booksearch/BookSearchResultsAll.asp.

Friendly Staff

In addition to maintaining a positive attitude in all interactions with students and staff personally, a school librarian is responsible for ensuring that all library staff members encourage students to read, sharing titles they have read themselves, working flexibly with students with a focus on the ultimate purpose of libraries, to provide opportunities and resources to encourage reading for pleasure and learning. When interviewing personnel for a clerical position, ask if the individual likes to read and to recall the book completed most recently. One librarian was surprised when interviewing candidates for the library clerk position with an assistant principal to hear only one of six candidates respond that she read regularly and named titles read. That person received the librarian's vote for the position and, fortunately, was ultimately hired.

Library student aides, whether volunteers from another class in the school or enrolled in classes taught by the school librarian, must also present a friendly and helpful face to patrons. Evaluation forms used for students can include criteria for patron service (e.g., interacting pleasantly with patrons, providing prompt assistance).

Establishing procedures and policies that invite student and staff use of the collection and services are crucial. Particularly in high schools, the school or district office may require strict accounting of fees owed to the school, limiting student participation in pep rallies, field trips, proms, and even graduation ceremonies. While necessarily complying with school rules, the library staff can discuss such issues with students in a pleasant manner, perhaps offering to hold a book for check out until the overdue item is returned. Some school libraries even arrange for students to work off fees owed in the library, as parents and guardians may not be able to pay for lost items.

READS LESSONS AND ACTIVITIES

Read as a Personal Activity

Select and Read Literary and Informational Resources at an Appropriate Reading Level

Adopt a book project. By Lindsay Cesari. *From the creative minds of 21st century librarians*: E-book 249–251. (Gr. 7–9) http://digital-literacy.syr.edu/page/view/221

Authentic persuasive writing to promote summer reading. By Traci Gardner. ReadWriteThink. (Gr. 9–12) http://www.readwritethink.org/classroom-resources/lesson-plans/authentic-persuasive-writing-promote-312.html

BOOKMATCH: Scaffolding independent book selection. By Linda Wedwick and Jessica Ann Wutz. Includes Teacher Scripts for BOOKMATCH Lesson. ReadWriteThink. (Gr. 6–8 up) http://www.readwritethink.org/classroom-resources/lesson-plans/bookmatch-scaffolding-independent-book-1172.html

Developing a definition of reading through investigation in middle school. By Amy Mozombite. Includes Reading Survey and Interactive Profile Publisher. ReadWriteThink. (Gr. 6–8) http://www.readwritethink.org/classroom-resources/lesson-plans/developing-definition-reading-through-11.html

Developing reading plans to support independent reading. By Traci Gardner. Includes Interactive Graphic Map ReadWriteThink. (Gr. 6–8) http://www.readwritethink.org/classroom-resources/lesson-plans/developing-reading-plans-support-836.html

Girls read: Online literature circles. By Helen Hoffner. ReadWriteThink. (Gr. 6–8) http://www.readwritethink.org/classroom-resources/lesson-plans/girls-read-online-literature-970.html

Great "read alouds" from The New York Times. (Resource) By Katherine Schulten and Amanda Christy Brown. The Learning Network: *The New York Times.* (Gr. 9–12) http://learning.blogs.nytimes.com/2010/02/25/great-read-alouds-from-the-new-york-times/

I remember that book: Rereading as a critical investigation. By Tom Lynch. Includes Sample Rereading Essay Rubric. ReadWriteThink. (Gr. 9–12) http://www.readwritethink.org/classroom-resources/lesson-plans/remember-that-book-rereading-1150.html

My history as a reader. (Resource) The Learning Network: *The New York Times.* (Gr. 9–12) http://graphics8.nytimes.com/images/blogs/learning/pdf/2010/20100304readinghistory.pdf

Podcast: Reading text sets. (Resource) 11/12/2010. ReadWriteThink. (Gr. 6–12) http://www.readwritethink.org/parent-afterschool-resources/podcast-episodes/reading-text-sets-30672.html

Reading attitude survey. (Resource) ReadWriteThink. (Gr. 6–8) http://www.readwritethink.org/files/resources/lesson_images/lesson110/attitude.pdf

Reading interest inventories. (Resource) Cedar Rapids Community Schools. (Gr. 6–12) http://www.st.cr.k12.ia.us/reading/readinginterestinventoriesChoicePage.htm

Reading interest survey. (Resource) By Denice Hildebrand. (Gr. 6–12) http://www.ala.org/ala//mgrps/divs/yalsa/teenreading/tipsenc/reading_interest_survey.pdf *Reading sampler (a.k.a. speed dating for books).* By Donna Smith. *From the creative minds of 21st century librarians*: E-book 265–267. (Gr. 9–12) Accessed October 2010: http://digital-literacy.syr.edu/page/view/221

Reading survey. (Resource) ReadWriteThink. (Gr. 6–8) http://www.readwritethink.org/files/resources/lesson_images/lesson11/ReadingSurveyHandout.pdf

READS INTERNET RESOURCES

Select and Read Literary and Informational Resources at an Appropriate Reading Level

A book and a hug. By Barb Landridge. http://www.abookandahug.com/
Book Leads Wiki. http://bookleads.wikispaces.com/
Book pass: The power of choice: Reading activity. Murray Hill Middle School. http://murrayhill.wikispaces.com/Book_Pass
Book tasting in the library. By Buffy Hamilton. The Unquiet Librarian. http://theunquietlibrarian.wordpress.com/2011/09/29/book-tasting-in-the-library/
Books for boys. The Web Home of Michael Sullivan. http://www.talestoldtall.com/B4B.html

Books for middle and high school age. Cooperative Children's Book Center: University of Education: University of Wisconsin-Madison. http://www.education.wisc.edu/ccbc/books/detailLists. asp?idBookListCat=4

The center for the book in the library of congress: Teens. http://www.read.gov/teens/

eBook search: A guide to free e-books. By Joyce Valenza. Springfield Township Virtual Library. http://springfieldebooks.wikispaces.com/

Flamingnet. Book reviews. http://flamingnet.com/

The Florida book review. http://www.floridabookreview.com/

Free e-books by Project Gutenberg. http://www.gutenberg.org/wiki/Main_Page

Guys read. Edited by Jon Scieszka. http://www.guysread.com/

The Horn Book. Publications about books for children and young adults. http://www.hbook.com/Default.asp

International children's digital library (ICDL). http://www.icdlbooks.org/

Internet archive. (E-books) http://www.archive.org/

Jacketflap. Book searches and information. http://www.jacketflap.com/

James Patterson's READKIDDOREAD.com. http://www.readkiddoread.com/home

KidsRead.com. http://www.kidsreads.com/authors/au-curtis-christopher-paul.asp

Me read? No way! A practical guide to improving boys' literacy skills. Ontario, Canada. http://www.edu.gov.on.ca/eng/document/brochure/meread/meread.pdf

Nancy Keane's children's literature website. http://nancykeane.com/

The Reader's Bill of Rights. http://www.ftrf.org/ala/divs/yalsa/teensreading/tipsenc/tipsencourage.cfm

Reading interest inventories. Cedar Rapids Community Schools. http://www.st.cr.k12.ia.us/reading/readinginterestinventoriesChoicePage.htm

Reading interest survey. By Denice Hildebrand. http://www.ala.org/ala//mgrps/divs/yalsa/teenreading/tipsenc/reading_interest_survey.pdf

Reading planet. Reading is fundamental (RIF). Ages 6–15. http://www.rif.org/kids/readingplanet.htm

Reading promotion. By Nancy Keane and Nancy White. AASL Smackdown. http://aaslsmackdown.wikispaces.com/Reading+Promotion

Teens.librarypoint. Central Rappahannock Public Library. http://teens.librarypoint.org/

Ultimate teen reading list. http://www.teenreads.com/features/ultimate-reading-list.asp

YALSA: The hub: Your connection to teen reads. http://www.yalsa.ala.org/thehub/

Displays

Bulletin board ideas. Kathy Schrock's Guide for Educators. http://school.discoveryeducation.com/schrockguide/bulletin/index.html

Creative library displays. http://www.creativelibrarydisplays.com/articles-directory/

Skerricks: Ideas and inspiration for your school library. http://www.creativelibrarydisplays.com/articles-directory/

Your search for bulletin board ideas is over. Education World. http://www.educationworld.com/a_curr/curr273.shtml

WORKS CITED

American Association of School Librarians. (2009). *Empowering learners: Guidelines for school library media programs.* Chicago, IL: American Library Association.

Anderson, R., Heibert, E., Scott, J., & Wilkinson, I. (1985). *Becoming a nation of readers: The report of the Commission on Reading.* Champaign-Urbana, IL: Center for the Study of Reading.

Atwell, N. (2007). *The reading zone: How to help kids become skilled, passionate, habitual, critical readers.* New York: Scholastic.

Beers, K. (2003). *When kids can't read, what teachers can do: A guide for teachers 6–12.* Portsmouth, NH: Heinemann.

Belben, C. (2007). There are no booktalking police: Alternatives to stand-and-deliver presentations. *Library Media Connection, 26* (2), 28–29.

Boltz, R. H. (2008). What we want: Boys and girls talk about reading. *School Library Media Research,* 10. Retrieved from http://www.ala.org/ala/mgrps/divs/aasl/aaslpubsandjournals/slmrb/slmrcontents/volume10/what_we_want.cfm

Brisco, S. (2009). Readers' advisory goes 2.0: Books & Authors lets readers do more than just read. *School Library Journal, 55* (1), 67–68.

Clark, R.E.C. (2007). Become the character! First-person booktalks with teens. *Library Media Connection, 26* (2), 24–26.

Delo, L. (2008). Reading aloud: Integrating science and literature for all students. *The Science Teacher, 75* (5), 33–37.

Follos, A.M.G. (2007). Change the literacy depression in your school: Read teens a story! *Library Media Connection, 25* (7), 20–22.

Gallagher, K. (2003). *Reading reasons.* Portland, ME: Stenhouse.

Gruenthal, H. (2008). 21st century booktalks! *CSLA Journal, 31* (2), 23–24.

Jones, P., Hartman, M. L., & Taylor, P. (2006). *Connecting with reluctant teen readers.* New York: Neal-Schuman.

Lapp, D., & Fisher, D. (2009). It's all about the book: Motivating teens to read. *Journal of Adolescent & Adult Literacy, 52* (70), 556–561.

Lesesne, T. S. (2003). *Making the match: The right book for the right reader at the right time, Grades 4–12.* Portland, ME: Stenhouse.

McDonnell, C. (2010). What makes a good read-aloud for middle graders? *The Horn Book Magazine, 67,* 66–73.

McPherson, K. (2008). Reading: Lifelong literacy links into the school library. *Teacher Librarian, 36* (1), 72–74.

Reynolds, T. K. (2005). *Teen reading connections.* New York: Neal-Schuman.

Trelease, J. (2006). *The read-aloud handbook.* Retrieved from http://www.trelease-on-reading.com/rah-ch1.html

Valenza, J. (2007). *Booktalking 2.0.* Message. Retrieved from http://blog.schoollibraryjournal.com/neverendingsearch/2007/08/01/booktalking-2-0/

Wood, K. D., & J. M. Harmon (2001). *Strategies for integrating reading & writing in middle and high school classrooms.* Westerville, OH: National Middle School Association.

FURTHER READING

Albright, L. K. (2002). Bringing the Ice Maiden to life: Engaging adolescents in learning through picture book read-alouds in content areas. *Journal of Adolescent & Adult Literacy, 45* (5), 418–428.

Allen, J. (2007). *Inside words: Tools for teaching academic vocabulary grades 4—12.* Portland, ME: Stenhouse.

Beck, I. L., McKeown, M. G., & Kucan, L. (2008). *Creating robust vocabulary: Frequently asked questions & extended examples.* New York: Guilford.

Beers, G. K. (1996). No time, no interest, no way! The 3 voices of aliteracy: Part 2. *School Library Journal, 42* (3), 110–113.

Bircher, L. S. (2009). Reading aloud: A springboard to inquiry. *The Science Teacher, 76* (5), 29–33.

Bodart, J. (2009). *Radical reads 2: Work with the newest edgy titles for teens.* Lanham, MD: Scarecrow.

Booth, H. (2005). RA for YA: Tailoring the reader's advisory interview to the needs of young adult patrons. *Public Libraries, 44* (1), 33–36.

Braunger, J., & Lewis, J. P. (2006). *Building a knowledge base in reading* (2nd ed.). Urbana, IL: National Council of Teachers of English.

Carbo, M. (2008). *Educating everybody's children: Diverse teaching strategies for diverse learners* (rev. ed.). Alexandria, VA: Association for Supervision and Curriculum Development.

Chance, R. (2008). *Young adult literature in action: A librarian's guide.* Westport, CT: Libraries Unlimited.

Clark, R. C. (2009). Listening to teens talk back: Teen responses to booktalking styles. *Voice of Youth Advocates, 31,* 501–504.

Cox, R. E. (2002). *Tantalizing tidbits for teens: Quick booktalks for the busy high school high library media specialist.* Worthington, OH: Linworth.

Cox, R. E. (2005). *Tantalizing tidbits for middle schoolers: Quick booktalks for the busy middle school and jr. high library media specialist.* Worthington, OH: Linworth.

Cox, R. E. (2007). *Tantalizing tidbits for teens: More quick booktalks for the busy high school library media specialist, Vol. 2.* Worthington, OH: Linworth.

Drogowski, P. P. (2009).Time well-spent: The intermediate read-aloud. *School Library Media Activities Monthly, 25* (6), 19–20.

Easley, D. (2004). Sharing the gift of literacy: How to get your students hooked on books. *Techniques, 79,* 36–40.

Fleharty, C., & Smith, S. (2007). User-friendly libraries. *Library Media Connection, 26* (1), 22–23.

Follos, A.M.G. (2006). *Reviving reading: School library programming, author visits and books that rock!* Westport, CT: Libraries Unlimited.

Franklin, P., & Stephens, C. G. (2008). Get students to read through booktalking! *School Library Media Activities Monthly, XXIV* (7), 38–39.

Gallagher, K. (2009). *Readicide: How schools are killing reading and what you can do about it.* Portland, ME: Stenhouse.

Grimes, S. (2006). *Reading is our business: How libraries can foster reading comprehension.* Chicago, IL: American Library Association.

Hall, L. (2006). Why read aloud? *Southwest Review, 91,* 386–397.

Jones, J. B., & Zambone, A. M. (2008). *The power of the media specialist to improve academic achievement and strengthen at-risk students.* Columbus, OH: Linworth.

Keane, N. J. (2009). *The tech-savvy booktalker: A guide for 21st century educators.* Santa Barbara, CA: Libraries Unlimited.

Kindle, K. J. (2009). Vocabulary development during read-alouds: Primary practices. *The Reading Teacher, 63* (3), 202–211.

Knowles, E., & Smith, M. (2003). *Talk about books! A guide for book clubs, literature circles, and discussion groups, grades 4–8.* Westport, CT: Libraries Unlimited.

Mahood, K. (2006). *A passion for print: Promoting reading and books to teens.* Westport, CT: Libraries Unlimited.

McQuillan, K. (2009). Teachers reading aloud. *Principal Leadership, 9* (9), 30–31.

National Reading Panel. (2001). *Report to the nation: Teaching children to read.* Retrieved from http:// www.nichd.nih.gov/publications/nrp/upload/smallbook_pdf.pdf

Reading4Life @ your library: Position statement on the library media specialist's role in reading. (2009). AASL. Retrieved from http://www.ala.org/ala/mgrps/divs/aasl/aaslissues/positionstatements/roleinreading.cfm

Scanlan, P. (2010). If books could talk. *Library Media Connection, 29* (3), 28.

Schall, L. (2007). *Booktalks and beyond: Promoting great genre reads to teens.* Westport, CT: Libraries Unlimited.

School library media specialist's role in reading toolkit. (2009). Retrieved from www.ala.org/ala/mgrps/divs/aasl/aaslissues/toolkits/slmsroleinreading.cfm

Thomas, C., & Littlejohn, C. (2003). *Still talking that book! Booktalks to promote reading grades 3—12, Volume IV*. Worthington, OH: Linworth.

Varela, A. (2008). Reading aloud in a high school ESL setting (English as a second language). *ESL Magazine, 61,* 21–26.

Young, T. E., Jr. (2010). Marketing your school library media center: What we can learn from national bookstores. *Library Media Connection, 28* (6), 18–20.

Zehr, M. A. (2010). Reading aloud to teens gains favor. *Education Week, 29* (16), 1, 12–13.

4

Connecting Learners to Resources

In today's libraries, bookstores, and virtual spaces, young people have choices among formats for accessing text. Even at the turn of the 21st century, the vast majority of people read printed books for pleasure and information. A decade later, a shift occurred, with many readers using e-books, online newspapers and magazines, and audiobooks, among other options. In this chapter, we will look at the range of resources for gaining meaning from text. In addition, the focus will expand from the school to public and academic libraries, museums, and the electronic and virtual worlds of mp3 players, cell phones, iPads, and websites. Now, the school librarian will team with others to encourage students to expand their reading horizons into the community and virtual worlds.

Online resources are the clear choice of most young people for listening and viewing. Though Google and other search engines are frequently used, students have favorite sites for particular needs. When asked about her purposes for Internet use during the summer months, a sixth grader responded that she uses it to locate new movie reviews and to follow all the links to her favorite books and movies, particularly the *Twilight* series. Today's teens and tweens go automatically to the Internet to locate information on their interests and hobbies. For example, those who want sports news scroll through their Internet favorites to Sports Illustrated/CNN or ESPN's Sportscenter.

AUDIOBOOKS AND OTHER DIGITAL MEDIA

The New York Times, the bastion of the printed word, as proclaimed in each issue, "All the News That's Fit to Print," is now making podcasts available for some of its stories. In August, 2010, the lead article in *The New York Times Book Review* was Sam Sifton's review of *Four Fish: The Future of the Last Wild Food* by Paul Greenberg. A note inside the publication refers readers to the weekly podcast features, which included an interview with Sam Sifton on *Four Fish* (http://graphics8.nytimes.com/podcasts/2010/07/30/30bookreview.mp3). Many secondary students are interested in the topic of the environment and its impact on people. If both the podcast and printed newspaper were called to their attention by a librarian, one would think more students would become aware of this important nonfiction book.

In *Redefining Literacy 2.0*, David Warlick (2009) describes the dramatic change in information-seeking patterns: "It was only a decade ago that we were largely limited to the information printed in books and stored in our libraries and classrooms, from which we taught our children about the world around them. Today, we take for granted the fact

READS Component	READS Indicator	AASL *Standards for the 21st-Century Learner**	Common Core State Standards—English Language Arts**
1. Read as a personal activity			
The student will:			
1.2 Select listening and viewing resources for enjoyment and information.	1.2.1 Choose age and ability appropriate resources for listening and viewing activities (e.g., audiobooks, podcasts).	• 1.1.2 Use prior and background knowledge as context for new learning. • 4.1.1 Read, view, and listen for pleasure and personal growth. • 4.1.3 Respond to literature and creative expressions of ideas in various formats and genres. • 4.1.7 Use social networks and information tools to gather and share information. • 4.4.1 Identify own areas of interest. • 4.4.2 Recognize the limits of own personal knowledge.	• Reading: Informational Text—10 Read and comprehend literary nonfiction in the grade text complexity band . . . • Reading: Literature—10 Read and comprehend literature in the grade text complexity band . . .

* Excerpted from *Standards for the 21st-Century Learner* by the American Association of School Librarians, a division of the American Library Association, copyright © 2007 American Library Association. Available for download at www.ala.org/aasl/standards. Used with permission.

** Excerpted from *Common Core State Standards for English Language Arts.* National Governors Association Center for Best Practices and Council of Chief State School Officers Commercial License. Copyright © 2010. Used with permission of NGA Center/CCSSO.

that we can casually use the World Wide Web to look up spur-of-the moment interests, the answers to nagging questions, seek reliable references and casual comments, or research major topics that influence us all" (p. x).

Clearly, advantages abound for the instant information status of the Internet. Remember how sometimes you would turn on the car radio to catch only the end of an interesting broadcast and couldn't rewind it to get the full presentation? Recently, part of a National Public Radio (NPR) interview with the folksinger Jewel included selections from her new album that were played, one with full band, and the other with only acoustical guitar. Because many students are now taking guitar lessons, looking up the NPR website and locating and listening again to the interview and songs reassured that the web link could be posted for interested students.

NPR is only one of thousands of news media outlets, museums, government offices, educational institutions, and others providing their content on the Internet through podcasts. A recent format emerging in the last decade for online media delivery, an estimated 10,000 podcasts on a variety of topics existed in 2005 (Hew, 2009). As evidence of the attention accorded to this new information delivery system, in 2005, the *New Oxford American Dictionary* chose podcasting as the word of the year (Eash, 2006). The term podcast is derived from iPod and broadcasting and refers to the process of capturing an audio or video presentation and making it available on the Internet. Users may directly access and play the media file on a computer, download a podcast to a computer or MP3 player to play later, or subscribe to a feed of continuing episodes of a series. The ease of obtaining podcasts to be played on commonly used equipment is a distinct advantage. Add portability to the list of advantages when storing podcasts on smartphones, MP3 players, or tablets (e.g., the iPad).

The capacity to store information until needed in your own digital device provides both convenience and improved learning potential. Individuals can access files at their convenience and listen to them as many times as needed. Hew (2009) refers to this advantage of a podcast as "the time-shifting ability that it affords." These features are especially valuable for auditory learners, second language learners, struggling readers, and others with special learning needs.

To find relevant podcasts on a particular topic, check one of the major directories:

- iTunes Store, http://www.apple.com/itunes/podcasts/
- Podcast Alley, http://podcastalley.com
- Podcast Directory, http://podcastdirectory.com
- The Education Podcast Network, http://epnweb.org

Other traditional research sources have recently made their information available in both auditory and print formats. Whenever a Gale database is accessed, the user first encounters the printed page with the options of "Download MP3" or "ReadSpeaker Help" for all print selections. If accessing multimedia materials in Gale databases, information first presented in audio format on NPR Radio is displayed in print format, with a link to the podcast.

When a student is searching for information on a topic of personal interest, school librarians must seize the moment to not only show the location of print, visual, and digital materials in the library but also to guide the student through locating resources in the databases. This one-on-one time is the most productive way to convince the student of the value of articles, photos, and podcasts from the databases.

A common scene today is a young person sitting or moving with an earpiece in place. It could be music streaming from the headset or perhaps the words of a book. We could be witnessing the integration of technology and literacy, as teens and tweens are increasingly listening to books for class assignments or personal reading pleasure. Librarians can expedite the acquisition of literacy skills by providing a selection of audiobooks to accommodate the preferences and needs of young listeners.

In elementary schools, audiobooks with accompanying paperbacks are staples of library collections, used extensively by classroom teachers and sometimes librarians for independent learning centers. However, when a certain librarian first moved to a secondary school in 2004, there were no audiobooks in sight, except for a few foreign language titles. Moreover, the school had many struggling readers and English language learners. When moving from middle to high school two years later, the situation for audiobooks was similar. When the availability of grants from the local public education fund was announced, she approached a friendly intensive reading teacher and discussed the possibility of adding audiobooks to the collection. The result was a joint application for a grant to add multiple audiobooks to the library collection.

The teacher and librarian wrote the grant together, including specific procedures for measuring student reading improvement from the use of the audiobooks. Fortunately, the grant was funded and orders were placed for the audiobooks, including recommendations of titles from the teacher. A mix of Playaways and CDs were chosen, with mostly fiction and some nonfiction titles. Most titles chosen had low Lexile levels, to meet the needs of students and the district reading initiative; however, titles without Lexile levels were also included, especially when requested by the teacher. Several titles were chosen because they were required reading by the language arts department. Funds for a rack to display the audiobook cases in the library were also part of the grant request, so that students would have immediate access to the sound recordings.

Two years later, when the librarian issued an invitation to the staff to apply for the grant, the same intensive reading teacher stepped forward to collaborate again. However, this time, the teacher requested the purchase of extra copies of books to use with the audiobooks. After determining that the same grant request would be funded a second time, the librarian and the teacher began to generate a list of titles for purchase. The teacher's list began with the two *Twilight* series books with audiobooks available at that time. To address the teacher's concern about multiple copies of a book to use with the audiobooks, the librarian looked at existing titles with multiple copies already in the collection. After looking at titles used in the state high school reading program for the current and previous years, sufficient titles with audiobooks available were selected. Because language arts department funds and other library funds were available for print materials, the decision was made to use all of the grant funds for audiobooks.

Educational Benefits of Audiobooks

The educational reasons for providing audiobooks for students to use in classrooms and for personal reading pleasure are many. Prominently, the advantages of reading aloud to students, discussed in depth in Chapter 3, extend to using audiotapes. As students listen to books, they are immersed in the reading comprehension process, developing fluency, gaining vocabulary, acquiring language, and moving toward improved achievement (Grover & Hannegan, 2005; Wolfson, 2008). Also, because the various audiobook formats are the same or similar to the technologies typically chosen by young people today for listening to music, this method of experiencing novels and nonfiction may be more readily accepted.

"Listening to audiobooks mimics the benefits of reading aloud that children should experience early in their lives, but listening to audiobooks has the advantage of literally placing control of the medium into the hands of young adults. They can stop the recording when they want to and listen again to the sections they didn't understand or want to hear again for the pleasure of it," writes Rosemary Chance (2008).

Top 10 Educational Benefits of Teen Audiobook Listening

10. Removes any stigma of lower reading levels or "uncool" genres.
9. Increases vocabulary skills.
8. Improves speaking and writing skills.
7. Introduces storytelling, an important tradition in human history.
6. Engages imagination by allowing teen to create mental images of the story.
5. Improves listening skills—essential in this multimedia world.
4. Makes mundane yet necessary tasks more tolerable.
3. Keeps teens informed of popular books or latest releases from favorite authors.
2. Improves ability to multitask and complete assignments simultaneously.
1. Listening is an important step for becoming a lifelong reader.

From: "Tune into Teen Listening" posted on *Books on Tape* site: http://library.booksontape.com/2009-pdf/literacy/teenlistening.pdf

School and public librarians who make audiobooks available to students may increase the amount of time that young people experience literature (Cardillo, Coville, Ditlow, Myrick, & Lesesne, 2007; Lesesne, 2007). Secondary students spend considerable time commuting from school to work to sports practices, and so on, and may enjoy listening to stories during these minutes and hours. Long family car trips may be more tolerable to the sounds of an audiobook appealing to all or individual stories through headsets. Also, students engaged in repetitive, perhaps tedious tasks including mowing lawns, cleaning house, or training for fitness or sports can listen while busy with other activities.

Today's audiobooks are narrated by authors or professional readers, with excellent sound values. In some recordings, all voices are portrayed by one reader, such as Jim Dale with the Harry Potter series. Dale created more than 250 characters in this series, which was his first audiobook (Cardillo et al., 2007). Author Bruce Coville started his own audio production company, Full Cast Audio, and typically uses multiple readers for each book. He employs a director to ensure the literary and technical quality of the recording and gives special attention to the selection of readers whose voices will work well together.

Expert readers can accentuate linguistic and cultural aspects of a book. Books including characters with distinctive dialects and accents can be difficult reading for those not familiar with the culture. Hearing such texts read aloud can contribute to comprehension of the work. Also, hearing Dickens or Austen read with a British accent can intensify the cultural experience of the novel.

Mary Burkey, middle school media specialist and reviewer of audiobooks for *Booklist* and *Book Links*, suggests that the use of audiobooks can contribute to the development of reading stamina. "One often-overlooked literacy skill is that of stamina, the ability to stick with a story until the reader or listener falls into the tale. Audiobooks offer an ambience that allows listeners to become immersed in long-form literature," she explained in a *Book Links* column in 2009.

Pam Spencer Holley (2009), past Young Adult Library Services Association (YALSA) president and audiobook columnist for Voice of Youth Advocates (*VOYA*), contributes information about using audiobooks in schools and libraries on the Books on Tape website. She compiled this list of benefits received by listening to audiobooks.

Advantages for Struggling and Special Needs Readers

Wolfson (2008) considers listening to audiotapes to be powerful oral language experience. He writes, "Since the reading process develops through our experiences with oral language, audiobooks simply provide another opportunity to increase the understanding and appreciation of the written word (p. 105)." He also points out that some audiobooks, such as Playaways, offer variable speeds, which can be useful for special needs readers who may need a slower pace to follow the words in the text.

Kylene Beers (1998) expresses concern that the level of reading aloud by teachers and librarians diminishes as students reach middle school and high school, reducing the benefits of hearing books read. "The use of audiobooks with struggling, reluctant, or second-language learners is powerful since they act as a scaffold that allows students to read above their actual reading level. This is critical with older students who may still read at a beginner level. While these students must have time to practice reading at their level, they must also have the opportunity to experience the plot structures, themes, and vocabulary of more difficult books" (p. 4), Beers writes. Focusing on listening to stories while following text on a page, she includes in her article in *School Library Journal* (April, 1998) a quote from a ninth grade student she had interviewed: "I hate those baby books. That's why I like listening to books and following along. Then I can be in the same discussion as everyone else in my class. Just 'cause I got problems with my skills doesn't mean I don't have opinions about stuff" (p. 4).

Reading experts consider discussion of literature as an essential part of the reading experience (Lesesne, 2009; Wilhelm, 2007), validating the importance of using this story form with struggling readers and ELL students. Beers (1998) described the specific benefits of this process: "Through discussions, ideas are formed, tried out, discarded, adapted, and negotiated. Meaning is explored and refined. Critical thinking leads the way as students debate similarities, offer differences, and discuss the issues the author presents" (p. 5).

Because the use of audiobooks with students with special needs can contribute significantly to improving their performance in classrooms, school librarians have an opportunity to contribute to creating an equitable learning environment by providing collections of audiobooks for titles required in the curriculum, in addition to a broad selection on topics of interest to students. By offering these resources for use in classrooms, the school librarian supports the efforts of teachers to enable students to participate fully in high-quality learning activities.

In a 2004 American Library Association (ALA) conference session titled "Reading or Cheating? Using Research to Support Audiobooks in the Literacy Landscape," presenter Ronda B. Baker, a language arts teacher, dramatized the impact of using audiobooks with struggling readers by presenting case studies of a student with a low IQ, another from a limited English home, and a third who was a high-functioning autistic male. She summarized the benefits to these students, which were increased reading ability, increased standardized test scores, and a jump in the books each read for pleasure. She also stressed the value of making available a range of audiobooks, creating the opportunity for struggling readers to participate in classroom discussions, emphasizing not only the literary advantages of such participation but also the boost to the student's self-esteem and increased confidence in his or her own ability. Attendance at this professional conference session made a significant impact on the school librarian, leading to the involvement in the grant writing projects described earlier in this chapter. Handouts from the session summarized the research behind the use of audiobooks and were vital in meeting the requirements of the grant.

Audiobooks appeared in the educational market in the 1930s to meet the needs of blind and physically or visually impaired individuals, as an alternative to books in Braille, according to information posted on the American Foundation for the Blindwebsite. These audiobooks require a special player, which is provided by the American Foundation for the Blind (2005). Today, this organization continues to meet the needs of many people in the United States through the Talking Book Program, which is administered by the Library of Congress. If students in your school are eligible for these services, visit the website at www.loc.gov/nls/.

The traditional selection process for audiobooks for school libraries begins with curriculum needs, an assessment of student characteristics (especially large numbers of ELL, struggling, or limited vision learners), and teacher or student requests. You will also want to select popular titles to entice reluctant and avid readers to listen to a story, both for pleasure and to complete assignments. Several professional organizations include audiobooks in their annual lists of recommended resources. ALA's Notable Children's Recordings, sponsored by the Association for Library Service to Children (ALSC), features audiobooks for preschoolers through ninth graders. The annual list of the YALSA is Amazing Audiobooks for Young Adults. These lists are published in *Booklist*, *Books & Children*, *School Library Journal*, *Young Adult Library Services*, and online.

Fortunately, the identification of quality audiotapes has become even easier with the establishment of the Odyssey Award in 2008. With the full title of Odyssey Award for Excellence in Audiobook Production, this prize is sponsored by ALSC and YALSA to identify the best audiobook produced for children and/or young adults. The chairperson of the first Odyssey Award committee, Mary Burkey, developed a glossary of terms used to describe the features of this medium, *Talking the Talk: An Audiobook Lexicon*, which is available online at http://www.audiofilemagazine.com/features/fea1007.html.

Other excellent sources of information on the titles available and ways to use them in schools and libraries include columns in *Booklist* and *VOYA*. Mary Burkey writes a column "Voices in My Head" for *Book Links* and blogs as Audiobooker. Respected educator Teri Lesesne produces a column for *VOYA*, Audio Talk. Other journals with occasional features on audiobooks include *School Library Journal*, *The Horn Book*, and *Library Media Connection*. H. W. Wilson includes audiobooks in the subscription-based online product, *Nonbook Materials Core Collection*.

Audiobook Formats

Audiobook collections in secondary schools typically involve several forms and devices including CDs, cassettes, Playaways, and various download formats. The Playaway is the leading preloaded digital audio player and comes with a battery, lanyard, and earbuds. Some school libraries provide the battery and replacement earbuds while others assume that students have their own earphones and batteries. Teacher requests for audiobooks depend on the hardware available in their rooms and the purpose for using the product. Some teachers use audiobooks as a listening activity with the printed books for individuals or small groups. Today's students are most comfortable with a downloaded format, though issues arise for management in school libraries. Many students have their own listening devices, but not all. According to the Audio Publishers Association (2010), CDs represented 65 percent of all audiobook sales in 2009, followed by downloads with 29 percent, preloaded products (e.g., Playaways, etc.) 4 percent, and 1 percent each for cassettes and MP3 CDs. At the present time, audiobooks are expected to continue to be available in multiple formats.

Audiobook Activities

To motivate teens to consider adding audiobooks to their listening repertoire, suggest titles featuring musical connections. The plot in *Fairest*, by Gail Carson Levine, is told through story and song; this recording is published by Full Cast Audio, with original music and performances by professional musicians (Myrick, 2008). Another recently published book with an innate connection to music is *Good Masters! Sweet Ladies! Voices from a Medieval Village*, by Laura Amy Schlitz. The Recorded Books staff quickly recognized the potential of this story and procured the audio rights before the book won the 2008 Newbery Medal (Myrick, 2008). Shannon Hale's *Book of a Thousand Days* is a favorite historical fiction read in which the main character sings healing songs in the tradition of her native Mongolia; the audiobook version has received great reviews, praising the original music created by Full Cast Audio (Burkey, 2008b).

Slogans for Audiobook Displays

Tune in to Literature
Energize Your Exercise Routine with an Audio-
book
Dream Away with a Romantic Audiobook
Spice Up Your Listening with a Good Book
Expand Your Listening Options
Hear the Stories of Their Lives (Biographies)
Travel the World through Your Earphones
Turn Up Your Learning with an Audiobook (Non-
fiction)
Plan Your Holiday/Summer Listening Experience

The strong bond between music and words is evident in Walter Dean Myer's *Jazz*. This is a prime example of a picture book with appeal to secondary students and multiple uses in the curriculum including music genres, the Harlem Renaissance, the 1920s, and more.

These and many other fine audiobooks featuring music utilize the theory of multimodal learning championed by Howard Gardiner in *Multiple Intelligences* (1983). Author Bruce Coville, president and founder of Full Cast Audio, explains the impact of combining music and story, "Music opens you emotionally so that the words can come in with more strength and power, hit your brain and your heart at the same time" (quoted by Burkey, 2008b, in Audiobooks Alive with the Sound of Music).

Although most school librarians enjoy reading aloud, some are less comfortable reading poetry to secondary students than sharing other genres. Audiobooks to the rescue! From individual selections to novels in verse (e.g., Karen Hesse's *Out of the Dust* and *Locomotion* by Jacqueline Woodson), quality productions are available. If promoting poetry as a genre, it is totally appropriate to leave the read-alouds to the professionals on audiobooks (Burkey, 2008a).

Recognizing that many teens prefer to find their reading and listening materials on their own, create displays of audiobooks in a prominent place in the library. Promote the use of audiobooks for a variety of purposes with one of the captions listed in the informational box. For mixed displays of books and audiobooks, try one of these slogans: Pick your Favorite Format or Learn It Your Way (nonfiction).

Promote your audiobook collection to the faculty, as teachers with students with special needs can be your best ally in encouraging students to listen to books. Many teachers appreciate and use audiobooks themselves, especially those who participate in exercise regularly. A teacher in one high school library brought in two boxes of audiobooks she had purchased for her sessions on a treadmill. Those titles appropriate for students were added to the library's collection and the others were made available to staff.

LIBRARY ORIENTATION

A pleasant and informative introduction to the library program and facility in a new school can set the stage for continued use of resources and services throughout the years. Students moving one school level to another have many questions and concerns about how to adjust to the new environment. A library orientation can offer the first opportunity to check out books, learn the procedures used in the school, and hear about the reading and learning experiences planned for the year. Our professional standards emphasize the use of activities which enable students to become independent users of information and ideas and which offer "equitable access to books and reading, to information, and to information technology" (*Empowering Learners: Guidelines for School Library Media Programs*, 2009).

Library orientations in elementary schools often feature literature activities, saving the lessons on the arrangement of the library, use of the catalog, and variety of reference

READS Component	READS Indicator	AASL *Standards for the 21st-Century Learner**	Common Core State Standards—English Language Arts**
1. Read as a personal activity			
The student will:			
1.3 Use community resources for recreational and informational needs.	1.3.2 Visit museums, galleries, science centers, and parks virtually or in person (e.g., Smithsonian museums, Museum of Science and Industry).	• 1.2.2 Use prior and background knowledge as context for new learning. • 4.1.1 Read, view, and listen for pleasure and personal growth. • 4.1.2 Respond to literature and creative expressions of ideas in various formats and genres. • 4.1.4 Seek information for personal learning in a variety of formats and genres. • 4.2.1 Display curiosity by pursuing interests through multiple resources. • 4.2.2 Demonstrate motivation by seeking information to answer personal questions and interests . . . • 4.3.3 Seek opportunities for pursuing personal and aesthetic growth. • 4.4.1 Identify own areas of interest. • 4.4.2 Recognize the limits of own personal knowledge.	• Reading: Informational Text—10 Read and comprehend literary nonfiction in the grade text complexity band . . . • Reading: Literature—10 Read and comprehend literature in the grade text complexity band . . .

*Excerpted from *Standards for the 21st-Century Learner* by the American Association of School Librarians, a division of the American Library Association, copyright © 2007 American Library Association. Available for download at www.ala.org/aasl/standards. Used with permission.

**Excerpted from *Common Core State Standards for English Language Arts*. National Governors Association Center for Best Practices and Council of Chief State School Officers Commercial License. Copyright © 2010. Used with permission of NGA Center/CCSSO.

materials until later in the school year. However, in secondary schools, the instructional pace is faster and librarians tend to make the most of the first visit by incoming groups of students, usually through language arts classes.

School librarians use a variety of formats, groupings, technologies, and strategies for orientations. We can identify multiple characteristics of an engaging and purposeful orientation:

- creates a warm, welcoming environment for all;
- introduces the library staff to students and invites follow-up encounters;

- communicates the circulation procedures and library guidelines for behavior;
- meets the needs of every student, regardless of prior experiences in libraries;
- enables each student to use the library catalog to find resources;
- proves the relevance of library resources and services to academic success;
- introduces reading activities available throughout the year;
- inspires courteous treatment of fellow students and ethical use of information;
- motivates each student to become a lifetime library user;
- connects library instruction to an authentic curricular assignment;
- incorporates some form of assessment;
- engages every student in the orientation activities;
- recognizes the social nature of teens and incorporates peer interaction;
- demonstrates school procedures for accessing the Internet and saving data files;
- ensures that each student leaves with books in hand.

This list may be extended by local reading initiatives. For example, if students are required or encouraged to read books on Lexile or Accelerated Reader levels, then they need to know how to locate books in the catalog on their level. If a Sustained Silent Reading program is in place in the school, all students need books the first week of school.

Challenges to Delivering Ideal Orientations

The first challenge to delivering ideal orientations is the sheer number of students needing an introduction to the library. In the past, a middle school or high school would typically have two to four librarians, depending on the size of the school and the district. With recent staff reductions, a high school of 3,000 students or more may be served by a single librarian.

The second challenge is arranging equitable access for all students. In many schools, the goal is to provide orientation for the incoming class of students to the school. However, what about new students to the campus in other grades and students enrolled in virtual classes? How can these students receive information about the library?

Another issue is the wide gap in library skill levels of students. Some really do know their way around the library and just need to learn about checkout procedures and passwords for online resources. Others cannot locate the call number of a book on a certain topic in the catalog and retrieve the book from the shelf! The reality is that students have attended various schools within a secondary school feeder pattern with differing levels of instruction in the use of library resources. The focus must be to provide support for students in learning to use library systems to find reading, listening, and viewing materials for personal and classroom purposes.

Secondary school librarians usually view library orientation from one of two perspectives. One school of thought is that any orientation to the use of the library should be linked to a classroom assignment, so that students understand the relevance of the instruction. The learning experience should be collaboratively planned by the school librarian and the teacher, merging instructional objectives and goals with students researching a content area topic. Typically, such an instructional sequence would take about a week in the library. Students could rotate through stations using various research sources to answer questions devised by the librarian and the teacher in an authentic, hands-on experience. In an excellent example of such an approach, students sampled the flavors of reference sources and then made ice cream themselves in a culminating activity. In effect, an instructional unit such as this serves as an orientation to the library program and to the inquiry process.

Another view is that all students in the targeted grade should be involved with basic orientation as early in the year as possible, so they can check out books and will be prepared for content area assignments. An overview of the library program will typically be provided, covering introductions to the staff, location, and arrangement of resources within the library, a review of types of resources, circulation policies and procedures, a brief preview of reading activities and research assignments, and introduction to other district requirements.

Planning Orientation Activities

Early in the planning process, objectives for the orientation will provide direction for the activities to be included. The planning for the orientation may involve the library staff only but may include the department chair and/or teachers from the department through which classes will be scheduled for the sessions. Some practitioners suggest that students should be involved in the planning process to bring the perspective and interests of the targeted audience to the table. This is the time for attention to the comprehensive list of characteristics of an ideal orientation. It is unfortunately difficult to address all the desirable characteristics in one presentation, so priorities must be established, depending on the intentions of the librarian, the realities of the school setting, and resources available, among others.

As part of the planning process, the librarian can take a fresh look around the library facility. Is attractive, directional signage in place? Does the arrangement of the room send the signal that students are welcome? Do book and media displays invite students to pick up titles for reading pleasure? How many computers are available for student use during orientations?

After determining the purpose and objectives of the session, the next orientation decision to be made is the format of the presentation. The explosion of technological presentation methods in the last decade has expanded the options for communicating with students. Considering all of the desirable characteristics and the need to provide ongoing instruction for students absent during the scheduled session as well as those students new to the school in other grades, the best decision may be to offer multiple delivery methods for learning about the library program.

Class sessions will be appropriate for most, so will be explored first. Within a single session, the librarian may work with the full group, small groups, and individual assignments. The preparation of a video or DVD requires upfront time but can be effective in showing closeups of areas of the library or scenes from around the school or community. New students will enjoy seeing upper class members reading and using online resources. PowerPoint presentations are commonly used and offer the additional benefit of easy differentiation for various groups. These multimedia presentations may focus on typical scenes of the library or may include various themes.

Some school librarians prefer adoption of a theme for the year, including props, decorations, and dressing up, especially for middle school groups. Terri Vrabel (2008) writes about a successful orientation with a pirate theme, complete with "valuable treasures" as giveaways for students. In *Using Pop Culture to Teach Information Literacy, Methods to Engage a New Generation,* Linda Behen (2006) describes sessions built around Survivor or The Amazing Race themes.

More traditional game formats are sometimes used, including bingo, Jeopardy, or scavenger hunts (Steward, 2008). Check the archives of LM_NET for details on various approaches. Some of these activities stress vocabulary associated with the library, reading, and information literacy skills, which provides added value, particularly for ELL and special education populations. Try out an orientation word wall (or series of posters) to introduce procedures and vocabulary simultaneously. If one of your objectives is to introduce procedures for saving files on the server and accessing the Internet in the school, include appropriate technology terms in displays.

A strategy that would surely appeal to a middle school audience would be the use of a reader's theater segment live or on video or DVD to demonstrate the correct way, or better yet, wrong way, to check out books. A common practice is the requirement of an identification card to check out materials; needless to say, tweens and teens forget or lose cards and borrow one from someone else. Chris Gustafson wrote a reader's theatre script about a borrowed ID card and shared it in an article in *Book Report* in 2002. For a high school audience, try a script about the dreaded obligation list used in many schools. If a student owes the school money for anything, including library books, supposedly they cannot attend pep rallies, proms, or receive a diploma. Imagine the humorous yet dramatic possibilities!

Another approach that can help promote understanding of procedures and allow immediate use of resources is to combine direct instruction with an exploratory activity. The intention may be to have students find records for books in the catalog and then retrieve the book from the shelves using call numbers, to locate certain types of information in reference books and in online databases, or to practice locating details required to create bibliographic citations for research projects. The goal may be to ensure that each student show competence at these tasks, or working in pairs or groups may be an option. An activity that could work in pairs or with groups is to assign students to create text sets on a particular topic (e.g., a sport, type of music, hobby, fiction genre, science or history subject, etc.). Students would have to use the catalog to locate call numbers and retrieve books from the shelves.

Even when orientation sessions with each class are implemented, it is advantageous to also use a handout or brochure with basic facts about the services of the library. In an effort to provide some student involvement in the process, headings for facts such as the library hours and database passwords were included on the brochure, but not the specific details. Students were directed to fill in the facts when the details were provided on a screen, so the attention of at least some daydreamers could be redirected to the orientation. Extra copies of these documents (with details written in) can be provided to teachers for students who were absent. Keep a stack available at the circulation desk for students who enter the school at a later time. It is also helpful to distribute completed brochures to the mailboxes of all staff members, including administrators, to keep them informed of library services.

Some librarians have explored other ways to inform students about literacy services. Another option is an individualized system, with students working from a printed or online assignment, combining instructions with activities carried out independently. The instruction could be provided on video and posted on a website. Two library educators, Annette Lamb and Larry Johnson, suggest that orientation could be transformed into a required web-based project to save time and increase appeal to students. In *Teacher Librarian* in 2008, they wrote:

> Create a series of short instructional videos along with practical ideas and strategies that can be placed on your web site. . . . You will still want to provide a short, motivating introduction to the

library, but by using web-based materials you will be encouraging young people to use the virtual resources as well as the physical library materials. (p. 69)

A school library website from Jefferson Davis Middle School in Virginia features videos of a welcome to the library, a sequence on library procedures for signing in, and a tour of the library. A text section provides details on what is expected of students in the library. This site, http://dav.sbo.hampton.k12.va.us/pages.library.html, created by librarian Nancy Terrell is a wonderful example of how essentials of orientations can be posted online and made available to students who transfer to the school during the year.

Another benefit of this web-based approach is the potential for using it with the increasing number of students assigned to a high school but taking some or all classes virtually. To ease the task of preparing an online presentation, perhaps an overview program could be prepared by a group working at a district level, to be expanded with modifications for local library policies.

A variation on the individualized approach to library orientation is the use of iPods within the library. A state conference presenter described her experience in a middle school with recording video segments including directions to walk to a certain area of the library (e.g., fiction or biography) and listen to instructions on the types of materials and organization. The use of the online library catalog was part of the exercise. Small groups of students would come to the library, pick up their iPod, and work at their own pace through the directions and assignments.

In a high school in Texas, librarian Carolyn Foote uses an iPad to provide orientation to parents and students. She writes about the advantages of using this versatile tool in *Multimedia & Internet@Schools* in 2010:

During our annual Back to School Night, I was able to roam the library using the iPad to demonstrate our databases, show off our website, and call up photos of the library construction, all while moving about and greeting parents. The portability and table-style design makes it a handy on-the-go tool for librarians. (p. 18)

Imagine having sets of iPads available for delivering the most engaging orientation sessions ever! Students can access video clips of reading activities, view instantaneous catalog and database demonstrations, and immediately conduct personal searches, and explore the library's website, all made possible using an iPad.

Formal Assessment Options

If a decision is made to include formal assessment as part of a student orientation session, additional issues must be considered. If a pretest and post-test model is selected, items must be written or located and administered prior to the orientation. In two years in a middle school, one librarian implemented this model. In the first year in this school, a set of 25 questions were developed by the two school librarians and implemented with all sixth grade students prior to the orientation. A class set of questions was prepared and scantron forms provided for students to use during the administration in language arts classrooms. The adoption of this procedure was motivated by an administrative requirement to document improvement in student achievement as a result of teaching by all staff members, including school librarians. A spreadsheet was set up for each sixth grade class and individual scores entered on the pretest for each student. Later in the year, after orientation and subsequent information literacy skills lessons, students were post-tested and the improvement or lack of it calculated for the media specialists' annual performance reviews.

The next year, as other teachers in the school heard about the project and how well it was viewed by administrators, the school librarians were asked by teachers in the social studies department if they could be part of the action project. During the previous year, these teachers had collaborated with school librarians on a research unit on ancient civilizations and had a vested interest in ensuring that their students became proficient in reading nonfiction materials and developing other information literacy skills. As a result, the social studies teachers joined the school librarians in using students' improvement on the information literacy skills assessment for their professional development project, and orientations were scheduled through social studies classes, which all sixth grade students were required to take. The teaming with the social studies department proved to be mutually beneficial in several ways, resulting in positive results for staff and students. The annual orientation to the library was integrated into the school program and through increased collaboration between the school librarians and the teachers, instructional activities were expanded and improved.

After moving to a high school, one librarian learned from the professional literature about the Tools for Real-Time Assessment of Information Literacy Skills (TRAILS) program. This free online assessment project for information literacy skills was developed at Kent State University as part of the Institute for Library and Information Education (ILILE) initiative and is funded by the U.S. government (Schloman & Gedeon, 2007). It is the result of collaborative discussions by high school and academic librarians who were concerned about students' high school-to-college transition. The original test for ninth graders was based on competencies in information literacy from the Ohio Academic Content Standards and is consistent with learning requirements in AASL's *Standards for the 21st Century Learner* (2007). Items were developed to measure students' skills in five areas of information literacy: develop topic; identify potential source; develop, use, and revise search strategies; evaluate sources and information; and recognize how to use information responsibly, ethically, and legally. One of the excellent features of this product is that students may take online quizzes on all or one of the skill areas. Most importantly, after students complete a pretest and post-test implementation, the program calculates improvement in performance for both individuals and classes. Since the assessment first became available in 2006 targeting ninth graders, tests have been developed for sixth graders and third graders (Owen, 2010).

The TRAILS program is most effective for an instructional program that begins with an orientation and continues with instruction linked to specific research assignments from teachers. However, to be truly indicative of a student's learning, it needs to be administered before orientation, as many topics usually covered in those initial sessions are included in the test. An orientation that is combined with a research unit would work well, with the librarian and teacher able to choose one of the five areas for assessment or the total package.

PUBLIC LIBRARIES

To foster a love of reading as a personal activity, school librarians can share their knowledge of literature, their passion for stories in all formats, and a commitment to the power of libraries to serve as equalizing forces to provide vast opportunities for all who want to learn; these are the traits and beliefs shared by all librarians. School and public librarians working together form a natural coalition with tremendous potential for increasing access to books and motivation of young people to read now and throughout their lives. Through efforts now to encourage students to use public libraries, school librarians can ease the transition of young people into the adult world of public libraries. More immediately, we can encourage the use of library services during evenings, weekends, and summers, after our school library doors are closed.

Though school and public librarians attend some of the same courses in the basic studies and philosophy of librarianship, courses in school librarianship have rarely placed emphasis on working with public libraries. Tasha Squires (2009), a public librarian, reports a similar experience:

> In library school, this topic rarely comes up during public library classes. Most students on the public library track take coursework on serving youth or adults, including children's literature, reference, and readers' advisory classes. School library media classes, when they do address collaboration, tend to focus solely on collaboration between school librarians and teachers.

However, in the harsh light of recent reductions in staffing for school and public libraries, the time has come to reach out to community partners. Speaking from the school library position, the first thing heard when suggesting outreach from colleagues is a loud chorus, "We don't have TIME!" The response is to remember why school librarians signed up to serve as librarians: to encourage students to read personally and by every other reasonable means, in classrooms, at home, and, yes, in public libraries. It is reasonable, logical, beneficial, and a means of extending our influence into the future to join public librarians in creating opportunities for students to read and learn throughout the year.

Fortunately, many articles and two recent books, *Library Partnerships: Making Connections between School and Public Libraries* (Squires, 2009) and *Librarians as Community Partners: An Outreach Handbook* (2010), provide how-tos and great examples of activities. See the bibliography at the end of this chapter for details on these sources. From professional organizations, the AASL/ALSC/YALSA Interdivisional Committee on School/Public Library Cooperation has collected descriptions of partnerships from libraries around the country and displayed them online. A program at the ALA Annual Conference in 2010, Growing Learners Together, featured highlights of the cooperative programs. To find summaries of these activities, go to the wiki at http://wikis.ala.org/readwriteconnect/index.php/AASL/ALSC/YALSA_School/Public_Library_Cooperation.

Opening Basic Communication Lines

The first level of a school and public library partnership is sharing information about resources, needs, and user groups. This step allows school librarians to identify specific current learning needs of students and long-range needs including access to public library resources after the school doors close. At this initial level, communication can take the form of mailing, telephone calls, e-mails, or personal discussions. Fortunately, both groups of librarians establish outreach to other libraries as a priority for their members. The school library literature encourages members to contact public libraries in their communities (Bush, 2006; *Empowering Learners: Guidelines for School Library Media Programs*, 2009; Squires, 2009).

From the public library perspective, calls have also been issued to initiate contact with the schools in their community areas (Brehm-Heeger, 2008; Rutherford & Shanks, 2004; Squires, 2009). Contact lists of public libraries have sometimes been created by school districts, but if this resource is not available in your district, it would be a worthwhile project for a school librarian group. It could be that the public library system in your county has already organized a list of schools and staff members. Rutherford and Shanks (2004) report that the Chicago Public Library created a questionnaire for their youth librarians to use to conduct an inventory of the needs of the public schools in their areas, facilitating the development of relationships.

As soon as the information is available, school librarians should inform their public librarians about annual reading lists (e.g., state literature programs and school summer required reading lists). Generally, these lists are published in the spring before summer vacation and should be promptly communicated to public library contacts. Some school librarians distribute bookmarks of state reading program titles to students and teachers before school ends and students may head to the public library immediately to look for the books. Libby Gorman (2010) conducted a study on summer reading lists in schools in North Carolina. She interviewed local educators about the purposes of the lists, who created the lists, and how the lists were communicated to students and parents. She concluded:

> Educators should consider collaborating more purposefully with the public library, particularly in terms of assuring book availability. Since summer reading occurs during a time when educators cannot be present to help students, it makes sense that they use this opportunity to expose students to public library service. (p. 55)

In general, schools handle their required reading lists in a variety of ways, with some featuring classic titles and others using current books; some schools have certain required titles for specific grades, and additional reading required from a list of available titles. In a merging of state literature programs and required reading lists, one high school specified a certain title for each grade and required an additional two books from the state reading list for the year.

Major school research assignments with deadlines are another topic of great interest to public librarians, who have adopted a phrase for this, "assignment alerts." The AASL/ALSC/YALSA Interdivisional Committee on School/Public Library Cooperation has included Assignment Alert Programs as one of the content areas on their very useful wiki. Some public library systems offer an online assignment form (e.g., Multnomah County School Corps—http://www.multcolib.org/schoolcorps/assign.html), making the process even easier. For those working with public library systems without an online assignment service, Joyce Valenza provides a form, Mass-Assignment Alert, for school librarians to complete and forward to public libraries with details of a project in her book, *Power Tools Recharged* (2004). Just as in school libraries, public librarians may want to place some books on reserve, in order to accommodate large numbers of requests for materials on narrow topics. Science fair topics and deadlines are examples of assignments with large numbers of students involved. The national History Fair organization (http://www.nhd.org/) announces a general theme each year in advance, which should be shared with public librarians. If local school district curriculum departments have set deadlines and guidelines for the program, these should also be provided to public library partners.

Other types of information that school librarians may want to share with public librarians are student groups requiring special services (e.g., blind or hearing impaired students) and foreign language material needed, among others. Other types to share include specific research models, research paper requirements, or bibliographic style requirements; reading promotion programs used (e.g., Accelerated Reader or Reading Counts); any major literacy themes selected for students; or curriculum requirements in various grades.

From the public library perspective, campaigns to register students for public library cards are a major initiative and the success of this effort is clearly in the best interests of both library groups. Since public and private school librarians have access to most students in a community, distributing printed and media-based promotional materials through schools is a productive approach. Also, activities scheduled for tweens and teens in community public libraries can be posted and distributed to students through schools. Summer reading programs fill a real need to keep students involved in literacy activities during the months out of school and is a research-based approach (Allington & McGill-Franzen, 2008; Gallagher, 2009) promoting academic success and lifelong reading goals. In addition, a newsletter or directory listing public library services available to schools could open doors to further communications.

School librarians can share public library news, services, hours, location, and other pertinent information in newsletters, brochures, or fliers distributed to students, parents, or other community agencies, school announcement programs, presentations to parent groups, and should be a standard part of a school library website. If your library does not currently have these connections, you might consider making them to promote professional partnerships and to improve lifelong learning opportunities for students in your school.

Sharing Resources

A common service of public libraries is the issuance of special educator library cards, enabling the check out of more resources than typical patrons. This is a helpful service to teachers and librarians who need multiple materials for class activities. In an unusual scenario, one school librarian in a new facility needed books with older copyright dates for an activity requiring students to evaluate and select the best books on a particular topic. One of the evaluative criteria for the assignment was currency, and the new library collection did not have a wide selection of books with older copyright dates. Boxes of books from the public library provided the volume of materials needed for this project. Another situation that places a strain on school library collections is the decision by some grade level teams for all teachers in the group to cover a topic (e.g., dinosaurs or the Holocaust) at the same time; public library collections can be the solution again.

Some public librarians have created book collections or kits that offer materials on frequently requested topics. "Buckets of Books" is the title of the program at the Multnomah County Library in Oregon. You may want to view their list of topics available at www. multcolib.org/schoolcorps/bucket.html. Some public libraries offer a delivery service for materials selected by school staff through online catalogs or materials that are part of a public library's special collections. In some cases, a school district's courier system is used to provide delivery of materials. This delivery service can increase the chances that a busy school librarian and teachers can take advantage of the public library traveling collections.

Public Librarians in Schools

Booktalks by public librarians in school libraries and classrooms are a reality in many places across the country. What a wonderful bonus for overworked school librarians! Rutherford and Shanks (2004) point out that this is a great way to make contact with teens who may come into the public library to locate the titles included in the booktalk. In some situations, public librarians may bring books with them that teens can check out on the spot after the booktalk (Van Linden Tol, Vasquez, & Westover, 2005). The success of booktalks can be ensured by prior communication between school and public librarians about the characteristics of students in selected classes and how circulation of public library books will be handled, if it is planned. Tasha Squires (2009) has other recommendations for advance preparation for school presentations: public librarians need a school map and bell schedule in advance; the teacher should stay with the class; avoid overscheduling; and, if time allows, plan a shared lunch by the school librarian and public librarian in the staff lounge to foster relationships with teachers.

A range of other literacy activities conducted by public librarians have been documented in schools around the country. Some public librarians offer storytelling services that are especially appreciated in middle schools. Sullivan (2003) suggests connecting storytelling with geography units on various countries or Greek or Native American mythology and other folklore. Joint book clubs are offered during lunchtime or after school (Boddy, 2006; Wepking, 2009). This arrangement offers a school librarian who has not yet worked with reading clubs an opportunity to work with an experienced colleague in this valuable activity. Several book discussion groups in schools are included in the School/Public Library Cooperative Programs wiki.

Some public librarians welcome the opportunity to come into schools and teach research skills. Certainly, a reinforcing voice or new perspective for search skills and focus on quality resources will be welcomed by school librarians. Linda Homa, reference librarian at the Public Library of Union County, visits ninth grade classrooms to demonstrate online reference tools and other public library services. In what must be a high interest session, she also shows students how to download audiobooks from the public library collection to MP3 players or iPods using the Overdrive Audio program. Read about Linda's projects on the wiki of the AASL/ALSC/YALSA Interdivisional Committee on School/Public Library Cooperation, under the heading Public Library Visits to Schools.

Public librarians are ideal guest speakers or performers for parent events in schools. Whether the occasion is a routine parent teacher meeting or a major literacy extravaganza, parents will benefit by learning about public library services and will enjoy reading or storytelling activities. Additional details on planning school-wide literacy events will be included in Chapter 11.

A final area in which school and public librarians work together to serve their patrons and support literacy skills is through sharing digital materials from public library collections. Mary Burkey (2008) suggests that students in school libraries can benefit from public library resources using downloading options. She shares some of her resolutions on maximizing learning with digital materials:

> I will install the download software (available for free on the public library web site) on school computers, so teachers and students may use their library cards to download materials not available in our school.
>
> I will offer ongoing educational workshops for students, teachers, and parents on what's available through their public library's 24/7 web site.
>
> I will share with the musicians and authors in my school the possibility of adding local content to the public library's downloadable materials.
>
> Most important, I will partner with my public librarian to establish virtual branches in the school library, the classroom, and student's homes. (p. 52)

Students in Public Libraries

Beyond the usual reading promotion, check out of materials, interlibrary loan services, and space for homework, public librarians are offering programs that can impact various areas of students' lives and promote lifelong learning. For many, the public library is the only place that provides computers and the Internet for their use once the school doors are closed. Technology training programs and reference services are also vital services. Homework help programs, both live and in virtual settings, and after-school activities support many students. A wide range of literacy services, starting with readers' advisory services and including book clubs, author events, poetry slams, contests of many types, tutoring, creation of books reviews, book trailers, and so on, are designed to meet the needs of young people and to encourage lifelong reading habits. College and career planning, music and other hobbies, self-help topics, film screenings, video game tournaments, and e-mail discussion groups are among the myriad of other activities available in various public libraries.

In addition, public libraries in some communities invite students to become part of advisory councils to share their ideas on useful programs and purchases. This opportunity to participate in councils with public librarians offers students opportunities to develop and practice leadership and public speaking skills.

The summer is an active period for public libraries, when most offer special programming to attract young people of all ages and their parents to their facilities. In light of recent research and publicity on summer reading loss for students, the value of encouraging reading during school vacations is paramount (Gorman, 2010; Wepking, 2009). For secondary students, providing support for assigned reading from schools is a major focus. Some public libraries offer discussion sessions on assigned books, often with support materials (Rutherford & Shanks, 2004). Activities offered to teens in the summer include not only reading clubs but also writing contests (Mahood, 2006). Themes for reading programs vary from the latest trend in books to around the world reading trips or to reading around a state.

Co-Production by School and Public Librarians

To this point, our discussion of school and public library interactions has focused on programs that were primarily planned by one group or the other, with cooperation in implementation by the supporting partner. In a more comprehensive approach, school and public librarians are joining hands and efforts in planning programs and events together. Some of the types of activities already discussed including books club and summer reading programs could be organized jointly, combining resources of both organizations (Rutherford & Shanks, 2004). You will be inspired by some of the accounts of joint programs described on the wiki of the AASL/ALSC/YALSA Interdivisional Committee on School/Public Library Cooperation, including Performer's Showcase, One Book Two Villages, Partners in Education, and Professional Development Partnership. A stand-out joint program showcased on the wiki is Middle School Survival Program from Las Vegas, Nevada, which features school staff members as presenters and provides several informational handouts for parents and students on study skill tips, adolescent development, and booklists. The novel aspect of this program is an opportunity for students to practice with combination locks.

School and public librarians have also joined forces in planning and implementing the Read Across America program. Michael Sullivan (2003) describes one program that began in a school with reading aloud to students, then moved to the public library for more selections offered by community leaders in the late afternoon and evening. For more ideas on this nationwide celebration, go to www.nea.org/readacross.

School librarians and public librarians may be part of a larger organization in communities with established literary festivals. In the Miami Book Fair International, multiple opportunities are offered to students, educators, and all segments of the community to participate in literacy and cultural activities in several languages. Groups from some schools travel to the Book Fair to attend sessions with authors and illustrators, while in other schools, authors and illustrators visit classrooms and school auditoriums. Events occur in public libraries, college libraries, school libraries, and the streets of downtown Miami.

ACADEMIC LIBRARIES

Within the broader library community, academic institutions including their libraries offer a wide range of potential services and resources to school librarians and secondary students for the purpose of supporting literacies. AASL's *Empowering Learners: Guidelines for School Library Media Programs* (2009) encourages partnerships with academic libraries. The National Board for Professional Teaching Standards for Library Media also expects that highly qualified librarians will become part of an extended learning team with staff from college libraries (2001). In 2009, AASL published a *Position Statement on the School Library Media Specialist's Role in Reading*, which delineated various strategies to facilitate and promote reading. An online toolkit provides resources to implement the role, which includes a slide presentation titled What Every SLMS Should Know about Collaboration with Other Literacy Professionals, with academic librarians targeted as potential partners.

A 2006 national report, *A Test of Leadership: Charting the Future of U.S. Higher Education*, outlines the current state of higher education in this country and calls for improvements to ensure that students with college degrees are ready for the workplace. Recognizing the role of high schools in preparing students for college, the document urges collaboration "to create a seamless pathway between high school and college" (p. 2). Recommendations from the report include the alignment of K-12 graduation standards with college and employer expectations and the expansion of Advanced Placement, International Baccalaureate, and dual enrollment programs. Specifically, the report demands, "States should provide incentives for higher education institutions to make long-term commitments to working actively and collaboratively with K-12 schools and systems to help underserved students improve college preparation and persistence" (p. 17).

Miranda Bennett (2007) suggests that the goal of this report to improve higher education aligns with the Association of College & Research Libraries' (ACRL) *Strategic Plan 2020*, which also promotes the increase of outreach to the K-12 educational community and a focus on lifelong learning. The intent of ALA divisions to work together is carried out by ACRL's Liaisons Coordinating and Component Committees. Both divisions are represented in the Interdivisional Committee on Information Literacy.

The obvious link between school and academic libraries is the shared goals of preparing students to conduct research in college and to be lifelong learners. A key example of productive collaboration between academic librarians and school librarians is the TRAILS project to identify and address skills needed by high school students to succeed in college (Owen, 2010), which has been described in the library orientation section of this chapter. While the development of inquiry or information literacy skills is not the primary focus of this book, a close look at the READS curriculum reveals several common components that are also included in an information literacy curriculum. The characteristics and use of nonfiction as a genre of literature is an integral part of the READS curriculum, as are the important topics of intellectual freedom and ethical and legal use of information.

Kuhlthau, Maniotes, and Caspari (2007) discuss the interrelated nature of inquiry or information literacy skills and literary works, "In guided inquiry, we often begin with a compelling fiction story that raises many questions and leads to lots of 'tell me more' topics" (p. 65). In other situations, a teacher or librarian begins with research on a historical era, investigating the social context and arts before introducing a novel (e.g., *The Great Gatsby* or *Their Eyes Were Watching God*). Kuhlthau et al. emphasize:

This inquiry project sets the stage for making the required reading more relevant to the students' lives. Once these students begin to see similarities between the lives of current pop culture figures and the characters in the novel, they become more interested in reading and discussing this work of fiction. (p. 66)

From a broader perspective, the development of excellent reading skills will certainly enhance a student's ability to excel in an academic setting. In addition, both school and academic librarians proclaim the development of lifelong reading habits as goals for their work.

Visits to Academic Libraries

One traditional strategy still in use is the field trip from schools to nearby academic libraries. Michelle Visser (2006) from the University of Colorado at Boulder writes about her experiences in arranging visits to the library for students from elementary, middle, and high schools. She describes the positive impressions on students created by seeing original medieval manuscripts, prints, and books, including those owned by famous literary and world leaders. Visser (2005) reports, "After studying the horrors of World War II, for example, one high school class said the war was more tangible to them because they were able to touch a book that Adolf Hitler held and signed" (p. 33). In her article in *School Library Journal*, Visser (2005) encourages school librarians to inform the teachers in their schools about special collections available in academic libraries, which can spark students' interests in content area studies.

High school students are allowed to check out books during class visits to the Arlington Library at the University of Texas, according to Evelyn Barker (2009). For more than five years, she has worked with juniors in the International Baccalaureate (IB) Program who gather resources for a required 4,000-word extended essay. She conducts library instruction classes on catalog and database use, in addition to providing assistance with individual research topics. Students from other grades with assignments on state history also use the resources and services of this library.

In these articles, the academic librarians urge high school librarians to plan months in advance for such visits. Barker (2009) summarizes the advantages to the hosting library: outreach to the community is part of the academic library's mission; such visits provide opportunities to introduce potential students to research skills; and the library tours provide an introduction to the services of academic libraries (p. 23).

Other on-campus K-12 activities are as follows:

- Carr and Rockman (2003) report other two examples of projects providing services for K-12 students on college campuses. A two-week summer library camp was offered to middle schools students at the California State University at Fresno, sponsored by a federally funded Migrant Scholars program. These students conducted research projects and produced a slide presentation and created a webpage.

- Special education students in ninth and tenth grades attended a modified version of an information literacy course at Ohio State University in another project supported by federal funds (Carr & Rockman, 2003).

- At Kent State University, high school students enrolled in Upward Bound programs were brought on campus to attend classes for six weeks during the summer. Academic librarians worked with students on projects related to their coursework (Seeholzer, 2010).
- At California State University Northridge campus, high school groups in general education and the Advance Placement program are brought to the library for instructional sessions, including the use of the catalog and databases, the difference between Dewey Decimal and Library of Congress call numbers, and the location of periodical articles in databases (Garcia, 2009).

Academic Librarians in K-12 Schools

In some locations, academic librarians have visited schools to present research skill lessons to students. After hearing about college librarians visiting high schools at a library conference, Martha Ameika implemented the idea in a South Carolina school. She arranged for librarians from four area colleges to present sessions in her school to senior English classes. Topics covered included the use of online databases instead of the Internet, citing sources, evaluating resources, defining research problems, and academic integrity and plagiarism. In her article in *VOYA* in 2008, Ameika reports that one librarian told students that "most professors require students to use subscription databases rather than the open Internet" (p. 408). A college professor came to the high school with the academic librarian and told the groups "how critically the plagiarism issue could affect students' college and professional careers" (p. 408). Ameika reports that the majority of teachers in her school soon began to alter assignments, requiring students to use only state and school provided databases as sources for research papers.

After observing her middle-school daughter's use of Internet sites, Margaret Keys became aware of the need for research skill instruction early in the secondary school years. Representing two academic institutions in Sacramento, California, she went into the middle school to deliver instruction tailored to the science teacher's assignment, using a combination of print and online resources (Keys, 2010). She e-mailed both public and academic library reference desk personnel to inform them of the upcoming assignment. She also encouraged the teacher and students to contact her through e-mail with further questions on the research project.

Academic libraries also serve students and educators in K-12 schools and support literacies through other outreach strategies:

- Traveling trunks of educational materials are available for loan through some universities. The University of Texas at Arlington Library distributes primary source materials both through an educator loan kit program and through online digital collections.
- Calisphere is a collection of more than 150,000 digitized primary sources targeted at K-12 teachers and students by the University of California at Berkeley and the California Digital Library. The themed collections are aligned with California's State Board of Education Content Standards (Kunda, 2007). Check it out at http://www.calisphere.university ofcalifornia.edu.
- Academic librarians from several institutions have written about providing in-service training for K-12 educators. Delores Carlito from the University of Alabama at Birmingham provides training sessions both on campus and at school sites (Carlito, 2010). Topics include student research, technology tools, and the use of the state-provided Alabama Virtual Library. The first tip that she provides to fellow academic librarians wanting to du-

plicate her model of outreach is, "Get to know area media specialists and teachers. School media specialists are the best way for an academic librarian to connect with schools and teachers" (p. 116). Carlito (2010) also goes into schools to teach research methods, brings classes to the on-campus library, or combines the use of the two sites for an instructional unit, according to the needs of the teacher and the media specialist.

Academic Librarians' Involvement in Reading Promotion

An Edible Book Contest sponsored by a university library? This unusual project is an annual event at the University of Florida in Gainesville. Cakes have been created representing *Eragon, Cinderella, Charlotte's Web,* and *Who Moved My Cheese,* in addition to edible bookmarks and even an edible book truck (Malanchuk, 2010). The contest is part of the community's celebration of National Library Week, with collaboration among academics, the public, and public schools. The creations are displayed on tables under a covered walkway outside the main library. Culinary students from a local high school have contributed goodies to this contest. According to Malanchuk (2010), the "purpose of this joint venture by library staff, users, administrators, and other friends of libraries is to recognize and celebrate the necessary and valuable contributions that libraries make in their communities" (p. 4).

"One Book, One Community" projects have been implemented across the country with support from academics, the public, and school libraries. In Georgia, academic librarians from Valdosta State University worked with colleagues from other library institutions to secure funding from the National Endowment for the Arts (NEA) Big Read initiative (Hood & Rogers, 2009). These authors provide details about the community-wide event on the project's information page http://www.valdosta.edu/library/about/bigread.shtml.

An academic library joins a county reading association to stage a Children's Reading Celebration & Young Author's Fair at California State University Channel Islands (Hoffman, 2009). The Young Author's Fair showcases the writing of students in grades K-6. In addition to displays of students' books, the program includes storytelling and reading by college students, a make-your-own book station, reading therapy dogs, and an unusual "paint-by numbers" activity. Hoffman writes:

> *Each year, an artist is hired to create a large canvas filled with paint-by-numbers areas that children fill in with paint throughout the day. By the end of the event, a fully formed mural appears, usually the face of a famous literary character (past images have included Pippi Longstocking and Harry Potter). (p. 173)*

In a remarkable reading program implemented by academic librarians in a school setting, University of Florida library staff members assisted with a parent–student reading club in a middle school. This activity is reported by Iona R. Malanchuk (2006) in *Young Adult Library Services,* who writes,

> *Knowing that there are many compelling novels for youth available at the nearest public or school library, these UF academic librarians wanted to introduce middle school students to unforgettable stories and characters. . . . Parents participated in the monthly club meetings consistently and with gratitude. (p. 13)*

The middle school librarian hosted the meetings in the library and collected money from the students and parents in advance to buy paperback editions of the Newbery award-

READS Component	READS Indicator	AASL *Standards for the 21st-Century Learner**	Common Core State Standards—English Language Arts**
1. Read as a personal activity			
The student will:			
1.3 Use community resources for recreational and informational needs.	1.3.2 Visit museums, galleries, science centers, and parks virtually or in person (e.g., Smithsonian museums, Museum of Science and Industry).	• 1.2.2 Use prior and background knowledge as context for new learning. • 4.1.1 Read, view, and listen for pleasure and personal growth. • 4.1.2 Respond to literature and creative expressions of ideas in various formats and genres. • 4.1.4 Seek information for personal learning in a variety of formats and genres. • 4.2.1 Display curiosity by pursuing interests through multiple resources. • 4.2.2 Demonstrate motivation by seeking information to answer personal questions and interests . . . • 4.3.3 Seek opportunities for pursuing personal and aesthetic growth. • 4.4.1 Identify own areas of interest. • 4.4.2 Recognize the limits of own personal knowledge.	• Reading: Informational Text—10 Read and comprehend literary nonfiction in the grade text complexity band . . . • Reading: Literature—10 Read and comprehend literature in the grade text complexity band . . .

*Excerpted from *Standards for the 21st-Century Learner* by the American Association of School Librarians, a division of the American Library Association, copyright © 2007 American Library Association. Available for download at www.ala.org/aasl/standards. Used with permission.

**Excerpted from *Common Core State Standards for English Language Arts*. National Governors Association Center for Best Practices and Council of Chief State School Officers Commercial License. Copyright © 2010. Used with permission of NGA Center/CCSSO.

winning titles used for the project. Refreshments were provided for each meeting by the school administration. Concerning the motivation of the academic librarians to get involved with middle school students, Malanchuk explains,

> It seems logical to tap the inherent desire to promote reading for pleasure that exists among most librarians. In addition, academic librarians' involvement in outreach programs in support of public school students meets the service criteria of most university tenure and promotion requirements. (p. 13)

MUSEUMS AND OTHER COMMUNITY RESOURCES

Imagine the power of an authentic Native American headdress or a medieval suit of armor to bring alive curriculum units for students. Rich collections of learning materials housed in museums are available in many of our communities and online for all (Blaine, 2009; Byerly, 2008; Krueger, 2008). Such a headdress can be found in the National Museum of the American Indian in Washington, DC or viewed online at http://AmericanIndian. si.edu/searchcollections. The Metropolitan Museum of Art in New York offers examples of armor from various cultures and online at http://www.metmuseum.org/toah/works-of-art/27.177.1,2.

Museums share the designation of educational institution with schools and public libraries, zoos, aquariums, and other scientific facilities. Museums are also considered cultural institutions because of their mission to preserve and display collections of artifacts. The common attributes of libraries and museums were formally recognized in 1996, when the U.S. government merged both groups into the Institute of Museum and Library Services (IMLS). In the Museum and Library Services Act of 1996, museums were defined as "a public or private nonprofit agency or institution organized on a permanent basis for essentially educational or aesthetic purpose, which, utilizing a professional staff, owns or utilizes tangible objects, cares for them, and exhibits them to the public on a regular basis."

A 2009 report issued by IMLS titled *Museums, Libraries, and 21st Century Skills* provides new direction for public institutions that in the past were concerned primarily with displaying or circulating mostly tangible collections. These collections were usually selected by museum and library personnel acting independently. The new philosophies and processes for museums and libraries alike are collections with both tangible and digital objects, an increased focus on user engagement and active experiences, institutional personnel participating in collaborative partnerships, and determination to enhance the knowledge of users and contribute to the development of 21st century skills (*Museums, Libraries, and 21st Century Skills*, 2009). The creators of this document have embraced the work of the Partnership for 21st Century Skills, calling for museum and library personnel to carefully plan how their activities and collections will meet the needs of all users including young people to "build such skills as information, communications and technology literacy, critical thinking, problem solving, creativity, civic literacy, and global awareness" (p. 1). Strategic Council Members of the Partnership for 21st Century Skills include AASL, the National Education Association, and other corporate and educational organizations.

Museums and other cultural institutions offer informal or free-choice learning opportunities consistent with the principles of student-centered education (Callison, 2006). The concept of free-choice learning indicates that individuals decide if, when, and what experiences they will seek out. Callison (2006) describes free-choice learning as a part of lifelong learning, a primary goal of library programs. When school librarians work with teachers to introduce museum resources to students, this adds to their ongoing efforts to encourage students to become lifelong learners.

When visits to museums are planned as part of a unit of study in a school, connections are made between the cultural artifacts and curricular content. If in a physical museum, usually a guide provides commentary describing the link between the object and the curriculum. A museum educator explains,

> *Using objects in teaching provides opportunities for spatial understanding, bodily-kinesthetic ways of knowing, and other intelligences, depending on the object. Using an object engages the*

senses, which increases interest and leads to individuals creating a personal connection to the learning. When students manipulate the objects, they can use the physical information to inform and help develop abstract ideas.

(Kuhlthau et al., 2007, p. 70)

Visits to museums and other community resources contribute significantly to activating and building students' background knowledge, a major educational goal. The specific advantage of this strategy is the development of "the knowledge and experience that readers bring to the text" (p. 29), according to Harvey and Goudvis (2007). Encounters with museums, historic landmarks, and natural history sites expand vocabulary, provide information, add essential cultural context, and stimulate young people to learn more about the world through reading, listening, and viewing.

In the past, field trips to museums were planned as annual events tied to state curricula. However, in recent years, trips outside school buildings have been reduced for several reasons, including tight budgets, liability concerns, and time constraints related to intense testing preparation. On the positive side, the virtual resources made available for free from many museums offer a pathway to viewing the world's treasures. Fisher and Frey (2010) distinguish between direct and indirect methods for building background knowledge:

As the Internet continues to grow and more sites are interactive, teachers can build background knowledge in direct but virtual ways. For example, a history teacher uses the Louvre Museum Web site to show his students Islamic art that they have likely never seen in person, and a biology teacher has her students complete a number of virtual dissection labs as part of their practice work. (p. 62)

Tours of our national parks are available online and can be integrated into social studies and science classes directly or used as stimuli for writing in language arts classes. See our sidebar for some of the choices of virtual tours of national parks. A variety of technologies are used by the different parks, so previews of the sites are recommended. For a more complete listing of national parks, use the National Park Service website at the bottom of the table.

Hands-on manipulation of data is offered on some of the educational resources available on the Internet. Interactive learning environments are identified and described by Lamb and Johnson (2010) in *School Li-*

Museums and the Web 2010

Best of the Web

Education: Museum of Modern Art

Meet Me—The MoMA Alzheimer's Project: Making Art Accessible to People with Dementia (http://www.moma.org/meetme)

Exhibition: The Historical Society of Pennsylvania

Honorable Mention: PhilaPlace (http://www.philaplace.org/)

Innovative: Royal Observatory, Greenwich

Solar Stormwatch (http://solarstormwatch.com/)

Podcast: National Museum of Australia

National Museum of Australia's Audio on demand program (http://www.nma.gov.au/audio/)

Research: Victoria & Albert Museum

V&A Search the Collections (http://collections.vam.ac.uk/)

Social Media: Picasso Museum

Museum Picasso Online Community (http://www.bcn.cat/museupicasso/en/get-involved/online-community.html)

People's Choice: National 911 Memorial and Museum

(http://makehistory.national911memorial.org/)

Best Overall: Indianapolis Museum of Art

ArtBabble (http://www.artbabble.org)

brary Monthly. These authors characterize interactivities as providing "an engaging environment where learners can organize resources, manipulate information, and even create new content" (p. 41). Lamb and Johnson direct us to a variety of sources for interactive websites, including Thinkfinity, Media Awareness Network, and museums. See our READS Internet Resources list for some of these links appropriate for secondary schools.

School librarians can use a source from Lamb and Johnson's excellent article to search for appropriate sites for school projects and recreational use by students, staff, and parents. Museums and the web is an international consortium of museums, educators, webmasters and designers, librarians, supporters of science and the arts, and others, which provides a website and annual conference to identify and showcase the best offerings of educational institutions. The website is hosted by Archives & Museum Informatics and features an annual Best of the Web list in various categories.

> ## Virtual Field Trips
>
> ### U.S. National Park Service
>
> Carl Sandburg Home: http://www.nps.gov/carl/forteachers/distancelearning opportunities.htm
>
> Death Valley National Park: http://www.nps.gov/history/museum/exhibits/death_valley/index.html
>
> Don't let it loose! Invasive species of Everglades National Park: http://www.efieldtrips.org/EvergladesInvasives/index.htm
>
> Grand Canyon National Park: http://www.nps.gov/grca/forteachers/distancelearning opportunities.htm
>
> Great Smoky Mountains: http://www.nps.gov/grsm/forteachers/distancelearningopportunities.htm
>
> Sitka National Historical Park: http://www.nps.gov/sitk/forteachers/distancelearning opportunities.htm
>
> National Park Service. Distance Learning Opportunities: http://www.nps.gov/learn/distance.cfm

Many of these sites and their categories have been included in the Best of the Web 2010 chart. You can return to this site to check the archives of winners from past years and to watch for the announcement of the newest annual list.

Another innovative web offering is the Google Art Project, first revealed in February 2011 (O'Byrne, 2011). This project provides virtual access to more than 1,000 paintings from 17 American and European museums. Learn more about using this project with students in a resource from The Learning Network of *The New York Times*, "Real vs. Virtual: Examining Works of Art Online," which is part of our READS Lessons & Activities for this chapter.

This Google resource complements the widely used geography tool, Google Earth. An application of this tool that can be used to implement the READS Curriculum is the Mapping Literature activity described by Cavanaugh (2008). Early in 2011, GoogleLitTrips posted a new activity for middle schools featuring the book *Sugar Changed the World* by Marc Aronson and Marina Budhos. Check our Further Reading list and READS Internet Resources list for more details.

The virtual resources available on the Internet expand the possibilities of all students for experience with the riches of museums, science centers, historical sites, and nature for youth, providing more equitable learning conditions. School librarians can expand the reading, listening, and viewing worlds of students and teachers by calling attention to these resources and working with teachers to connect these tools and sites to the curriculum, thereby expanding their use in classrooms. More directly, school librarians can guide students to understanding how these educational sites can be used to continue learning throughout their lives, using the creations of nature and mankind around the globe.

READS LESSONS AND ACTIVITIES

Read as a Personal Activity

Select Listening and Viewing Resources for Enjoyment and Information

Audio listening practices: Exploring personal experiences with audio texts. By Traci Gardner. Includes interactive ReadWriteThink Notetaker. ReadWriteThink. (Gr. 9–12) http://www.readwrite think.org/classroom-resources/lesson-plans/audio-listening-practices-exploring-873. html

Out loud. By Shannon Doyle. Includes values of reading aloud and use of audiobooks. The Learning Network: *The New York Times.* (Gr. 6–12) http://learning.blogs.nytimes.com/2009/05/21/ out-loud/

Use Community Resources for Recreational and Informational Needs

Connecting past and present: A local research project. By Linda Templeton. Includes Tips for Interviews and Museum Exhibit Teacher Tips. ReadWriteThink. (Gr. 9–12) http://www. readwritethink.org/classroom-resources/lesson-plans/connecting-past-present- local-1027.html

Crossword puzzle: Museums. By Frank A. Longo. The Learning Network: *The New York Times.* (Gr. 9–12) http://www.nytimes.com/learning/teachers/xwords/print/20040101.html

Eruption and destruction: Curating an exhibition on Pompeii. By Sarah Kavanaugh and Holly Epstein Ojalvo. The Learning Network: *The New York Times.* (Gr. 8–12) http://learning.blogs.nytimes. com/2011/03/08/eruption-and-destruction-curating-an-exhibitio-on-pompeii/

An exploration of text sets: Supporting all readers. By Kathy Egawa. ReadWriteThink. Gr. 6–8) http://www.readwritethink.org/classroom-resources/lesson-plans/exploration-text-sets- supporting-305.html

Extraordinary evidence. (Virtual fieldtrip) Includes teachers' guide, student guide, and performance rubrics. Smithsonian. (Gr. 5–12) http://americanhistory.si.edu/exhibitions/resources/ lincoln/Lincoln_Extraordinary_Evidence.pdf

Heads up!: A checklist for transitioning to college. By Patricia Owen. (2010). *School Library Monthly, 26* (8), 8–9. (Gr. 12)

National library card month begins today. (Calendar activity) ReadWriteThink. (Gr. K-6 up) http:// www.readwritethink.org/classroom-resources/calendar-activities/national-library-card- month-20285.html

Not just books. By Michelle Sale and Yasmin Eisenhauer. The Learning Network: *The New York Times.* (Gr. 6–12) http://learning.blogs.nytimes.com/2006/04/21/not-just-books/

Playing curator: Designing a museum exhibition (into the curriculum). By Elisa M. Hansen. (2009). *School Library Media Activities Monthly, 25* (3), 18–20. (Gr. 6–8)

Real vs. virtual: Examining works of art online. (Resource) By Dinah Mack and Holly Epstein Ojalvo. The Learning Network: *The New York Times.* (Gr. 9–12) http://learning.blogs.nytimes. com/2011/02/07/real-vs-virtual-examining-works-of-art-online/

A trip to the museum: From picture to story. By Scott Filkins. Includes Qualities of Good Storytelling, Online Art Sources, and Timeline tool. ReadWriteThink. (Gr. 6–8) http://www.readwrite think.org/parent-afterschool-resources/activities-projects/trip-museum-from-picture-30302. html

A world of readers: Libraries around the world. By Helen Hoffner. ReadWriteThink. (Gr. 6–8) http:// www.readwritethink.org/classroom-resources/lesson-plans/world-readers-libraries- around-1057.html

READS INTERNET RESOURCES

Select Listening and Viewing Resources for Enjoyment and Information

Audiobooks

Lit2Go: An online service of Florida's educational technology clearinghouse. http://etc.usf.edu/lit2go/index.htm

Sync: Sync YA literature into your earphones. http://www.audiofilemagazine.com/sync/index.html

Talking the talk: An audiobook lexicon. Mary Burkey. http://www.audiofilemagazine.com/features/fea1007.html

Tune into teen listening. Books on tape. http://library.booksontape.com/2009-pdf/literacy/teenlistening.pdf

Podcasts

Book trailer resources. By Naomi Bates. http://livebinders.com/play/play_or_edit?id=13228

Book trailers for readers. By Michelle Harclerod. Lee County, FL. http://www.booktrailersforreaders.com/

Booktalks quick and simple. Podcasts by Nancy J. Keane. http://www.nancykeane.com/booktalks/mp3/ollestad_crazy.mp3

Digital booktalk. University of Central Florida. Book Trailers for K-12. http://digitalbooktalk.com/

National Public Radio Podcast Directory. http://www.npr.org/rss/podcast/podcast_directory.php

The New York Times: Book review podcast. http://www.nytimes.com/ref/books/books-podcast-archive.html

Scholastic—librarians—authors & books—booktalks. http://www.scholastic.com/librarians/ab/booktalks.htm

Use Community Resources for Recreational and Informational Needs

Public Libraries

AASL/ALSC/YALSA School/Public Library Cooperation. http://wikis.ala.org/readwriteconnect/index.php/AASL/ALSC/YALSA_School/Public_Library_Cooperation

Miami-Dade Public Library System (FL). http://www.mdpls.org/

Multnomah Public Library. http://www.multcolib.org/

New York Public Library. http://www.nypl.org/

Orange County Public Library (FL). http://www.ocls.info/Children/Teen/doit/doit.asp

Museums and Other Community Resources

Betwixt folly and fate. Colonial Williamsburg. http://www.history.org/history/teaching/dayinthelife/

Google art project. http://www.googleartproject.com/

Google lit trips. http://www.googlelittrips.org/

How do we know what we know? http://www.exploratorium.edu/evidence/

Interactives. Annenberg Media. http://www.learner.org/interactives/

Last extinction. Nova. http://www.pbs.org/wgbh/nova/clovis/prec-flash.html

Museum of Modern Art. Interactive activities for young adults. http://www.moma.org/learn/activities

Museums and the web. http://www.archimuse.com/mw2010/
Shakespeare: Subject to change. Interactive. http://broadband.ciconline.org/shakespeare/

Museum Databases Online

Dallas Museum of Art. http://www.dallasmuseumofart.org
Detoit Institute of Arts. http://www.dia.org
The Getty, Los Angeles. http://www.getty.edu
High Museum, Atlanta. http://www.high.org
Metropolitan Museum of Art, New York. http://www.metmuseum.org
Museum of Fine Arts, Boston. http://www.mfa.org
National Gallery, London. http://www.nationalgallery.org.uk
National Gallery of Art, Washington, DC. http://www.nga.gov
National Museum of Nuclear Science & History, Albuquerque, NM. Online museum. http://www.nuclearmuseum.org/online-museum/
Virtual Museum of Geology. http://skywalker.cochise.edu/wellerr/aawellerweb.htm

WORKS CITED: AUDIOBOOKS AND OTHER DIGITAL MEDIA

American Foundation for the Blind. (2005). *Talking books.* Retrieved from http://www.afb.org/Section.asp?SectionID=37

Audio Publishers Association. (2010). *Audiobook sales increase in 2009.* Retrieved from: http://www.audiopub.org/PDFs/SalesSurveyPR62810.pdf

Baker, R. B. (2004). *Reading or cheating? Using research to support audiobooks in the literacy landscape.* American Library Association Conference, Orlando, FL.

Beers, K. (1998). Listen while you read. *School Library Journal, 44* (4), 30–35.

Burkey, M. (2007). *Talking the talk: An audiobook lexicon.* Audiofile. Retrieved from http://audiofilemagazinw.com/features/fea1007.html

Burkey, M. (2008a). The audible art of poetry. *Book Links, 17* (5), 34–35.

Burkey, M. (2008b). Audiobooks alive with the sound of music. *Book Links, 18* (1), 24–25.

Cardillo, A., Coville, B., Ditlow, T., Myrick, E., & Lesesne, T. (2007). Tuning in to audiobooks: Why should kids listen? *Children & Libraries, 5* (3), 42–46.

Chance, R. (2008). *Young adult literature in action: A librarian's guide.* Westport, CT: Libraries Unlimited.

Eash, E. K. (2006). Podcasting 101 for K–12 librarians. *Computers in Libraries, 26* (4), 16–21.

Gardiner, H. (1983). *Multiple intelligences.* New York: Basic Books.

Grover, S., & Hannegan, L. (2005). Not just for listening; integrating audiobooks into the curriculum. *Book Links, 14* (5), 16–19.

Hew, K. F. (2009). Use of audio podcast in K–12 and higher education: A review of research topics and methodologies. *Educational Technology, Research and Development, 57* (3), 333–357.

Holley, P. S. (2009). Tune into Teen Listening. Books on tape. Retrieved from http://library.booksontape.com/2009-pdf/literacy/teenlistening.pdf

Lesesne, T. S. (2007). Purposeful listening. *Voice of Youth Advocates, 30* (5), 413–415.

Lesesne, T. S. (2009). Why listen at all? *Voice of Youth Advocates, 30* (3), 221–223.

Myrick, E. (2008). Say it with music: Audiobooks with pizzazz. *The Booklist, 105* (5), 64.

Warlick, D. (2009). *Redefining literacy 2.0.* Santa Barbara, CA: Libraries Unlimited.

Wilhelm, J. D. (2007). *Engaging readers & writers with inquiry.* New York: Scholastic.

Wolfson, G. (2008). Using audiobooks to meet the needs of adolescent readers. *American Secondary Education, 36* (2), 105–114.

FURTHER READING: AUDIOBOOKS AND OTHER DIGITAL MEDIA

Burkey, M. (2009). The future of audio formats. *Book Links, 18* (4), 50–51.

Burkey, M. (2010). Voices in my head: Audiobook book clubs. *The Booklist, 106* (9/10), 109.

Dresang, E. T., & Kotrla, M. B. (2011). *School libraries and the transformation of readers and reading*. New York: Routledge.

Jones, P., Hartman, M. L., & Taylor, P. (2006). *Connecting with reluctant teen readers*. New York: Neal-Schuman.

Quinones, D. (2010). Digital media (including video!) resources for the STEM classroom and collection. *Knowledge Quest, 39* (2), 28–32.

Swan, K. O., & Moder, M. (2009). Trend alert: A history teacher's guide to using podcasts in the classroom. *Social Education, 72* (2), 95–102.

WORKS CITED: LIBRARY ORIENTATION

American Association of School Librarians. (2007). *Standards for the 21st century learner*. Chicago, IL: American Library Association.

American Association of School Librarians. (2009). *Empowering learners: Guidelines for school library media programs*. Chicago, IL: American Library Association.

Behen, L. D. (2006). *Using pop culture to teach information literacy: Methods to engage a new generation*. Westport, CT: Libraries Unlimited.

Foote, C. (2010). Checking out the iPad: A pilot project tests the hot new tech tool. *Multimedia & Internet@schools, 17* (6), 17–19.

Gustafson, C. (2002). Can I borrow your id card? A play for reader's theater. *Book Report, 20* (5), 34–35.

Lamb, A., & Johnson, L. (2008). The virtual teacher-librarian: Establishing and maintaining an effective web presence. *Teacher Librarian, 35* (4), 69–72.

Owen, P. L. (2010). Using TRAILS to assess student learning: A step-by-step guide. *Library Media Connection, 28* (6), 36–38.

Schloman, B. F., & Gedeon, J. A. (2007). Creating TRAILS: Tool for real-time assessment of information literacy skills. *Knowledge Quest, 35* (5), 44–49.

Steward, A. (2008). Orientation rx: The cure for your common media center orientation. *Library Media Connection, 26* (7), 34–36.

Vrabel, T. (2008). So you think they'll roll their eyes: A new look at library orientation. *Library Media Connection, 26* (7,) 37.

FURTHER READING: LIBRARY ORIENTATION

Dando, P. M. (2005). First steps in online learning. *Knowledge Quest, 34* (1), 23–24.

Franklin, P., & Stephens, C. G. (2006). Jump start your year—planning. *School Library Media Activities Monthly, 23* (2,) 46–47.

Jones, P. S. (2007). Teaching students about locating resources @ your library. *Library Media Connection, 25* (5), 36–37.

Preddy, L. B. (2002). Student inquiry in the research process, Part 2: Inquiry research orientation. *School Library Media Activities Monthly 19* (4), 24–26.

Trinkle, C. (2009). Cross curriculum: Who has . . . library orientation? *School Library Monthly, 26* (1), 11.

WORKS CITED: PUBLIC LIBRARIES

Allington, R., & McGill-Franzen, A. (2008). Got books? *Educational Leadership, 65* (7), 20–23.
Boddy, B. (2006). Teen department: Columbus Public Library, Columbus, Georgia. *Voice of Youth Advocates, 29* (5), 412–413.
Brehm-Heeger, P. (2008). *Serving urban teens.* Westport, CT: Libraries Unlimited.
Burkey, M. (2008). Public libraries, digital media, & you. *Book Links, 18* (2), 51–52.
Bush, G. (2006). Walking the road between libraries: Best practices in school and public library co-operative activities. *School Library Media Activities Monthly, 22* (6), 25–28.
Gallagher, K. (2009). *Readicide: How schools are killing reading and what you can do about it.* Portland, ME: Stenhouse.
Gorman, L. (2010). Purposes behind summer reading lists. *Teacher Librarian, 37* (5), 52–55.
Mahood, K. (2006). *A passion for print: Promoting reading and books to teens.* Westport, CT: Libraries Unlimited.
Rutherford, D, & Shanks, B. (2004). A fantastic team: Schools and public libraries. *Voice of Youth Advocates, 27* (5), 357–359.
Squires, T. (2009). *Library partnerships: Making connections between school and public libraries.* Medford, NJ: Information Today.
Sullivan, M. (2003). *Connecting boys with books: What libraries can do.* Chicago, IL: American Library Association.
Valenza J. K. (2004). *Power tools recharged: 125+ forms and presentations for your school library information program.* Chicago, IL: American Library Association.
Van Linden Tol, P., Vasquez, C. G., & Westover, S. (2005). Reaching out to middle and high schools. *Public Libraries, 44* (2), 65–66.
Wepking, M. (2009). From communication to cooperation to collaboration: School and public librarians as partners for student success. *Library Media Connection, 28* (3), 24–26.

FURTHER READING: PUBLIC LIBRARIES

Bush, G. (2007). Be true to our school. In P. Monteil-Overall & D. C. Adcock (Eds.), *Collaboration.* Chicago, IL: American Library Association.
De Groot, J., & Branch, J. (2009). Solid foundations: A primer on the crucial, critical, and key roles of school and public libraries in children's development. *Library Trends, 58* (1), 51–62.
DelGuidice, M. (2009). Are you overlooking a valuable resource? A practical guide to collaborating with your greatest ally: The public library. *Library Media Connection, 27* (6), 38–39.
DelGuidice, M., Luna, R., & Zorn, M. G. (2010). Public librarian. *Knowledge Quest, 38* (5), 26–29.
Jones, P., Hartman, M. L., & Taylor, P. (2006*). Connecting with reluctant teen readers.* New York: Neal-Shuman.
MacRae, C. D. (2006). Teachers and librarians working together for teens and their reading. *Voice of Youth Advocates, 29* (5), 385.
Serving young teens and 'tweens. (2007). Westport, CT: Libraries Unlimited.

WORKS CITED: ACADEMIC LIBRARIES

Ameika, M. (2008). Introducing college research at the high school level: A jump start on success. *Voice of Youth Advocates, 31* (5), 408–409.
American Association of School Librarians. (2009). *Empowering learners: Guidelines for school library media programs.* Chicago, IL: American Library Association.

American Association of School Librarians. (n.d.). *Position statement on the school librarian's role in reading*. Retrieved from http://www.ala.org/ala/mgrps/divs/aasl/aaslissues/positionstatements/roleinreading.cfm

Barker, E. (2009). Making a difference to the K-12 community. *Louisiana Libraries, 72* (2), 21–23.

Bennett, M. (2007). Charting the same future? The ACRL strategic plan and the report of the commission on the future of higher education. *College & Research Libraries News, 68* (6), 370–2, 377.

Carlito, D. (2010). Secondary classroom instruction in Birmingham. In C. Smallwood (Ed.), *Librarians as community partners: An outreach handbook*. Chicago, IL: American Library Association.

Carr, J. S., & Rockman, I. F. (2003). Information-literacy collaboration: A shared responsibility. *American Libraries, 34* (8), 52–54.

Garcia, E. P. (2009). A new explosion in our intellectual commonwealth. In N. Courtney (Ed.), *Academic library outreach: Beyond the campus walls*. Westport, CT: Libraries Unlimited.

Hoffman, D. (2009). Children's reading celebration & young author's fair. In N. Courtney (Ed.), *Academic library outreach: Beyond the campus walls*. Westport, CT: Libraries Unlimited.

Hood, Y., & Rogers, E. (2009). The NEA big read comes to Valdosta! In N. Courtney (Ed.), *Academic library outreach: Beyond the campus walls*. Westport, CT: Libraries Unlimited.

Keys, M. (2010) Academic connections: A college librarian reaches out to a middle school. In C. Smallwood (Ed.), *Librarians as community partners: An outreach handbook*. Chicago, IL: American Library Association.

Kuhlthau, C. C., Maniotes, L. K, & Caspari, A. K. (2007). *Guided inquiry: Learning in the 21st century*. Westport, CT: Libraries Unlimited.

Kunda, S. (2007). What's a second grader doing in special collections? Academic libraries teach out to K-12 schools. *OLA Quarterly, 13* (1), 22–25.

Malanchuk, I. R. (2006). Academic librarians organize a sixth-grade reading club. *Young Adult Library Services, 4* (4), 13–17.

Malanchuk, I. R. (2010). Bake a book and they will come. In C. Smallwood (Ed.), *Librarians as community partners: An outreach handbook*. Chicago, IL: American Library Association.

National Board for Professional Teaching Standards. Retrieved from: http://www.nbpts.org/the_standards/standards_by_cert?ID=19&x=67&y=15

Owen, P. L. (2010). Using TRAILS to assess student learning: A step-by-step guide. *Library Media Connection, 28* (6), 36–38.

Seeholzer, J. (2010). Upward bound outreach to talented high school students. In C. Smallwood (Ed.), *Librarians as community partners: An outreach handbook*. Chicago, IL: American Library Association.

U.S. Department of Education. (2006). *A test of leadership: Charting the future of U.S. higher education*. Washington, DC.

Visser, M. (2005). The real McCoy. *School Library Journal, 51*(12), 33.

Visser, M. (2006). Special collections at ARL libraries and K-12 outreach: Current trends. *The Journal of Academic Librarianship, 32* (3), 313–319.

FURTHER READING: ACADEMIC LIBRARIES

American Association of School Librarians, (n.d.). *Position statement on the school librarian's role in reading*. Retrieved from http://www.ala.org/ala/mgrps/divs/aasl/aaslissues/positionstatements/roleinreading.cfm

Cahoy, E. S., & Moyo, L. (2009). K-16 outreach: Creating connections that matter. In N. Courtney (Ed.), *Academic library outreach: Beyond the campus walls*. Westport, CT: Libraries Unlimited.

Clement, G. (2009). Reading out through digital library programs: The Everglades digital library experience. In N. Courtney (Ed.), *Academic library outreach: Beyond the campus walls*. Westport, CT: Libraries Unlimited.

Coleman, T. L., & McCraw, J. E. (2009). Reaching out to future users: K-12 outreach at Kansas State Libraries. In N. Courtney (Ed.), *Academic library outreach: Beyond the campus walls*. Westport, CT: Libraries Unlimited.

Conley, D. T. (2005) *College knowledge: What it really takes for students to succeed and what we can do to get them ready*. San Francisco, CA: Jossey-Bass.

Hurst, S., & Magnuson, M. (2007). Chat, email, and IM reference: School libraries and academic libraries, what we can learn from each other. *Knowledge Quest Web, 35* (5). Retrieved from http://www.ala.org/ala/mgrps/divs/aasl/aaslpubsandjournals/knowledgequest/kqwe barchives/v35/355/355hurstmagnuson_.cfm

Johnson, A., & Pulford-Russell, T. (2009). Preparing our students to succeed. *OLA Quarterly, 15* (4), 10–12.

Macklin, A. S. (2007). iSkills and ICT literacy assessment: Building a case for collaboration between school and academic librarians. *Knowledge Quest Web 35* (5). Retrieved from http://www.ala.org/ala/mgrps/divs/aasl/aaslpubsandjournals/knowledgequest/kqwebarchives/v35/355/355macklin.cfm

Oakleaf, M., & Owen, P. L. (2010) Closing the 12–13 gap together: School and college librarians supporting 21st century learners. *Teacher Librarian, 37* (4), 52–58.

Smalley, T. N. (2004). College success: High school librarians make the difference. *The Journal of Academic Librarianship, 30* (3), 193–198.

WORKS CITED: MUSEUMS AND OTHER COMMUNITY RESOURCES

Blaine, A. S. (2009). 'Internet at the museum.' *Searcher, 17* (10), 10–15.

Byerly, G. (2008). Museum websites: Historical museums. *School Library Media Activities Monthly, 24* (8), 40–41.

Callison, D. (2006). Informal learning. In D. Callison & L. Preddy (Eds.), *The blue book: On information age inquiry, instruction and literacy*. Westport, CT: Libraries Unlimited.

Cavanaugh, T. W. (2008). Mapping literature: Integrating GIS and reading. *Knowledge Quest, 36* (4) Retrieved from http://www.ala.org/ala/mgrps/divs/aasl/aaslpubsandjournals/knowledgequest/kqwebarchives/v36/364/364cavanaugh.cfm

Fisher, D., & Frey, N. (2010). Building and activating background knowledge. *Principal Leadership, 11* (4), 62–64.

Harvey, S., & Goudvis, A. (2007). *Strategies that work: Teaching comprehension for understanding and engagement*. Portland, ME: Stenhouse.

Institute of Museum and Library Services. (2009). *Museums, libraries, and 21st century skills*. Washington, DC.

Krueger, K. (2008). Art museum image gallery: Visual literacy through the curriculum. *School Library Media Activities Monthly, 25* (3), 45–46.

Kuhlthau, C. C., Maniotes, L. K., & Caspari, A. K. (2007). *Guided inquiry: Learning in the 21st century*. Westport, CT: Libraries Unlimited.

Lamb, A., & Johnson, L. (2010). Interactives: Dynamic learning environments. *School Library Monthly, 26* (5), 41–44.

O'Byrne, R. (2011). From the archives: Horace Shipp extolled the virtues of print publishing in the December 1950 issue, and there are more books on art published now than ever before. But can they compete with the innovations of our digital age, such as Google"s Art Project? *Apollo, 98* (1), 98.

FURTHER READING: MUSEUMS AND OTHER COMMUNITY RESOURCES

Adam, A, & Mowers, H. (2007). Got the world on a screen; Google Earth serves up more than a geography lesson. *School Library Journal, 53* (4), 40–42.

Barack, L. (2009). Yes, they can: Google lit trips and games give kids a new perspective on social justice. *School Library Journal, 55* (11), 13.

Bomar, S. (2009). The genocide project. *Knowledge Quest, 37* (4), 11.

Brisco, S. (2007). Art museum image gallery is an eyeful. *School Library Journal, 53* (6), 77–78.

Brodie, C. S., Maldini, M., & Byerly, G. (2007). Institute for library and information literacy education. *School Library Media Activities Monthly, 23* (5), 23–25.

Byerly, B., & Brodie, C. S. (2005). Celebrating women: History, biographies, and museums. *School Library Media Activities Monthly, 21* (8), 30–32.

Eakle, A. J. (2009). Museum literacies and adolescents using multiple forms of texts "on their own." *Journal of Adolescent & Adult Literacy, 53* (3), 204–214.

Greenblatt, M. (2006). Reach out to riches: Collaborating with museums and cultural institutions to enhance learning. *Teacher Librarian, 33* (5), 30–33.

Hubel, J. S. (2009). A day at the museums. *Library Media Connection, 28* (2), 16–17.

Lamb, A., & Johnson, L. (2010). Virtual expeditions: Google Earth, GIS, and geovisualization technologies in teaching and learning. *Teacher Librarian, 37* (3), 81–85.

Lincoln, M. (2006). Witness to history. *School Library Journal, 52* (2), 54–57.

Sardone, N. B., and Devlin-Scherer, R. (2010). Keeping it current: Using technology to teach about social issues. *English Journal, 99* (4), 61–64.

Zaino, J. (2009). Field-tripping goes virtual. *Instructor, 119* (2), 34–36. http://www.ala.org/ala/mgrps/divs/aasl/aaslpubsandjournals/knowledgequest/kqwebarchives/v36/364/364cavanaugh.cfm

Part 3

Explore Creative Works

5

Identifying Literary Genres and Themes

This chapter of the book begins with essential questions for the profession: Why should school librarians teach and promote various genres of literature? Can the search for theme(s) connect students to literature? Can an increased understanding of themes in literature improve one's quality of life? In this chapter, these and other questions are addressed. An expanded group of genres will be explored and a literary genre framework will be introduced. The various genres are characterized, recent titles are highlighted, and activities are suggested for introducing them to students. Finally, the range of services related to literature provided by school librarians will be explored.

WORKING WITH GENRES

Focusing on genre from the perspective of the school librarian, the foremost reason to teach students about genre is to guide young people to develop their tastes or preferences in reading. By developing familiarity with a wide range of genres, students are more likely to find the type of reading that engages their interests and enables them to find more books "like this one or this author." This will be an early step in creating a lifelong reading habit, which is a recurring phrase and intention in the mission statements of many school library programs. Wilhelm (2008), a middle school teacher and author, captures this vital rationale in *You Gotta Be the Book.* "Part of encouraging adolescents to read is knowing a variety of materials and encouraging kids to read different genres and authors to learn the scope of what is available and the field of their own taste" (p. 48). Mike Cadden (2011) writes, "Genre distinctions are important to readers . . . genre also helps readers find what they like, which is no small consideration if the goal is to encourage lifelong reading for pleasure as well as information" (p. 302).

Finding a reading comfort zone creates an enjoyment of reading that, hopefully, will be expanded and extended with further exposure to various types of reading and connections with people, educators, family, and peers, who articulate their own pleasure in reading. In the English Language Arts Standards (1996) from NCTE/IRA, Standard 1 states: "Students read a wide range of print and nonprint texts . . . for personal fulfillment" (p. 19). Wilhelm (2008) emphasizes the value of broad reading, "Readers will develop the interests, willingness, and abilities to dive and swim in more challenging literary currents if they have first learned the pleasures of the swim in waters that are meaningful, safe, and engaging for them" (p. 49).

READS Component	READS Indicator	AASL *Standards for the 21st-Century Learner**	Common Core State Standards—English Language Arts**
2. Explore characteristics, history, and awards of creative works			
The student will:			
2.1 Identify and critically analyze literary and media genres and themes.	2.1.1 Demonstrate knowledge of the distinguishing characteristics of literary and media genres (e.g., historical fiction, biography, documentary).	• 2.3.2 Consider diverse and global perspectives in drawing conclusions. • 3.3.2 Respect the differing interests and experiences of others, and seek a variety of viewpoints. • 4.1.2 Read widely and fluently to make connections with self, the world, and previous reading. • 4.1.3 Respond to literature and creative expressions of ideas in various formats and genres. • 4.1.4 Seek information for personal learning in a variety of formats and genres. • 4.1.5 Connect ideas to own interests and previous knowledge and experience. • 4.2.2 Demonstrate motivation by seeking information to answer personal questions and interests . . . • 4.2.4 Show an appreciation for literature . . .	• Reading: Literature—6 Analyze a case in which grasping point of view requires distinguishing what is directly stated in a text from what is really meant . . . • Reading: Literature—7 Analyze multiple interpretations of a story, drama, or poem . . . • Reading: Literature—9 Demonstrate knowledge of foundational works of American literature . . . • Reading: Literature—10 Read and comprehend literature in the grade text complexity band . . . • Writing—9 Draw evidence from literary or informational texts to support analysis . . .

*Excerpted from *Standards for the 21st-Century Learner* by the American Association of School Librarians, a division of the American Library Association, copyright © 2007 American Library Association. Available for download at www.ala.org/aasl/standards. Used with permission.
**Excerpted from *Common Core State Standards for English Language Arts*. National Governors Association Center for Best Practices and Council of Chief State School Officers Commercial License. Copyright © 2010. Used with permission of NGA Center/CCSSO.

From a broader educational perspective, school librarians teach genre to help students develop knowledge of text types, which will not only heighten enjoyment of reading, but also promote success in classroom studies, testing situations (Harvey & Goudvis, 2007), and workplace experiences. Understanding various generic distinctions among texts builds schema (Fisher & Frey, 2009; Smith, 1991). Judi Moreillon (2007) explains,

Schema theory suggests that knowledge is stored in abstract structures called schemas. People organize and retain information in their memories based on a hierarchy of characteristics. . . . When applied to reading comprehension, schema theory postulates that readers have preconceived concepts that influence their understandings of text. (p. 138)

As students read and participate in discussions of the characteristics of various genres, they build a framework to help them understand current and future reading selections. As students advance through secondary schools, they encounter more complex texts in various content areas, which creates problems for many. Though content area teachers have been encouraged to teach reading, all are not yet proficient in this area, according to Marilyn Jager Adams, research professor in Cognitive and Linguistic Sciences at Brown University.

Dr. Adams was interviewed by Rebecca Hill in an article titled "Common Core Curriculum and Complex Text," published in *Teacher Librarian* in February, 2011. Dr. Adams suggests that language is sometimes used differently in various fields, requiring additional training for teachers. "It depends on how words are used, verbal stress, or the syntax of the words. The reader has to be able to put it into context. So you have to understand the genre structures to unpack it," said Dr. Adams, as reported by Hill (2011).

A third reason for teaching a variety of genres is to provide an opportunity for students to practice reading and language skills that are essential to literacy. Harvey and Goudvis (2007) offer details on teaching reading comprehension:

Certain genres and forms lend themselves to teaching certain strategies. Realistic fiction and memoirs often spur connections and questions in readers. Poetry often stimulates visualizing and inferential thinking. We frequently choose nonfiction pieces to teach determining importance and synthesizing information. (p. 64)

Moreillon (2007) advocates the use of both fiction and nonfiction literature selections to teach synthesis. She explains, "When choosing texts for the purpose of synthesizing ideas and information, educators can provide students with carefully selected text sets of resources at various reading levels, in multiple genres, and in a variety of formats, including websites and other technology sources" (p. 136).

Through wide reading, listening, and viewing, students have exposure to new information and vocabulary, a fourth reason for teaching genres. Nonfiction reading, including biographies and memoirs, is an obvious choice for gaining new information, but readers also learn from fiction genres, including realistic, historical, fantasy, and so on. Contemporary media sources, including television, radio, and the Internet, are valid sources of new information, though students must develop evaluative skills to sort out reliable facts. In their book, *Background Knowledge*, Fisher and Frey (2009) point out, "As teachers, we have to help students negotiate the Internet in ways that allow them to harness its power as the ultimate background knowledge builder and activator" (p. 142). These authors also emphasize the interconnection between background knowledge and vocabulary. They suggest that teachers can model the use of inferring to discover the meaning of unfamiliar words. Reading extensively from various genres has long been promoted as one of the best ways to develop vocabulary (Krashen, 2004; Marzano & Pickering, 2005).

Reading and using a wide range of literary genres provide students with multiple models for writing. This fifth reason for teaching genres reflects the close relationship between reading and writing. Dutro and McIver (2011) comment on this connection: "The explicit use of literature as a model for writing makes the interconnections of reading and writing visible, offering young writers insight into what can too often appear to be a mysteriously crafted whole" (p. 104). Bomer (1995) points out the advantages of exposing students to various genres, which prepares them for future writing and reading assignments, emphasizing that he doesn't teach poetry expecting students to write it all their lives, but so that they develop the habit of working with new genres.

The use of literature as models for writing is a common practice of classroom teachers; however, Dutro and McIver (2011) caution that students' favorite texts may not necessarily be used as examples. They highlight the role of librarians in expanding the range of literary examples featured in library activities and used in classrooms: "Toward this end, library and media specialists are in a unique position to bridge the potential gap between the texts that students admire and the examples that classroom teachers rely on to illustrate the panoply of literary devices and decisions that published authors use and make" (p. 98).

A helpful definition of genre is provided by Moreillon (2007), which reflects the common usage in the school library field: "A genre is a particular category of book, one with a typical style, form, or content. Examples include realistic fiction, historical fiction, science fiction, fantasy, tradition literature . . . biography, and informational texts" (p. 156). Another definition is included in the glossary of the NCTE/IRA Standards for the English Language Arts (1996): "A category used to classify literary and other works, usually by form, technique, or content. Categories of fiction such as mystery, science fiction, romance, or adventure are considered genres" (p. 49). Saricks (2009) refers to a more limited definition sometimes used in public libraries: "In *Readers' Advisory Service in the Public Library*, genre is defined as 'any sizable group of fiction authors and/or specific titles that have similar characteristics or appeal; these are books written to a particular, specific pattern'" (p. 6). While we will begin our discussion of genre with the traditional fiction and nonfiction categories, we will expand it to other types of reading, listening, and viewing materials in use today.

When planning how to cover the topic of genre in library program activities, a school librarian will find opportunities to fulfill the entire range of essential services to students and staff, including guiding individual and groups of readers, supporting classroom teaching, collaborating on activities, directly teaching literature concepts, developing collections, and promoting resources through displays on websites and in the library. If new in a school, the first step is to find out how genre is covered in the curriculum standards used in the school and how various teachers cover genres in actuality. It is also helpful to know which specific titles are used in a classroom before organizing activities for the group. For example, if a teacher uses *Hatchet* in the classroom, as many do, you would not want to include it in a booktalk on adventure stories.

A traditional way that librarians support classroom teaching is by gathering class collections of resources on a topic under study. In secondary schools, these resources may be placed on reserved status in the library, so they may be used by various classes covering the topic at the same time. When one of the authors first made the move to secondary school from elementary, she heard the term "text set" used in a meeting of teachers of remedial reading with the reading coach. While it was simple to infer a meaning from the context of the usage of the term, nonetheless, it was not familiar and somewhat confusing. In a later conversation with a reading teacher, it was confirmed that a text set is a collection of materials on a particular theme, topic, author, or genre. This is one of many situations in which school librarians need to understand the terminology, curriculum, and requirements of various departments in the school. In elementary schools, librarians refer to these as class collections and regularly provide these sets of materials to teachers. Secondary teachers have been receptive, though sometimes surprised, when offered the same service.

Activities Introducing Various Genres

In addition to the typical literary genres used in schools and public libraries (e.g., realistic fiction, fantasy, science fiction, etc.), discussions of types of books should include a broader perspective. Formats of books may be picture books, short stories, dramatic forms, or graphic novels. To promote understanding of this concept and to meet the needs of more students, displays and teaching activities should include all available formats on the featured topic. Further, the delivery system of the work may be audiobook, e-book, or print. Finally, many books cross over genre boundaries and a variety of names are used to describe these hybrid literary genres including mash-ups, transmedia, interactive storytelling, or participatory media (Lamb & Johnson, Part 2, 2010).

The Literary Genre Framework found in this book is based on the works of Fountas and Pinnell (2001), Wilhelm (2001), and Williams (2009), among others, which integrate recent innovations in the delivery of text in digital and auditory formats. It was difficult to make some choices when categorizing genres and formats, but this chart can assist newcomers to libraries and classrooms in understanding and teaching the many ways of accessing, enjoying, and learning from texts. The decisions on genre categories is an ongoing project and the authors would like to have input from colleagues on this framework.

When working with sixth graders in a middle school, it is appropriate to use a basic approach to major genres, which provides an opportunity to ensure that all students in the class or grade level have a framework for understanding the concept. School librarian Joann Vergona Krapp wrote a series of articles in 2004 and 2005 in *School Libraries Media Activities Monthly*, describing and giving examples of the most often-cited genres, realistic fiction (problem novels), historical fiction, fantasy, science fiction, mystery and adventure, and folk and fairy tales. For a school librarian new to teaching genres, this series would be helpful, beginning with the overview article, "So Many Books: Genres of Children's Fiction" from the October 2004 issue of *School Library Media Activities Monthly*. In the June 2005 issue of *School Library Media Activities Monthly*, Krapp added the genre of humorous fiction, including school, family, and friendship stories, which delights many adolescents making the sometimes difficult transition to middle school.

Another excellent source for ideas is the ReadWriteThink series of lessons and materials. A baseline unit offering many possibilities, "Genre Study: A Collaborative Approach", may be appropriate for classes of ELL and special education students; this unit is recommended for grades 3–5 but can certainly be used above those grades. See the list of READS Lessons and Activities in this chapter for the direct link to this lesson and many others on genres. In the overview to this unit, ReadWriteThink staffer Lisa Storm Fink writes, "Genre studies are an opportunity for classroom teachers to collaborate with the school library media specialist and make multiple connections in literacy instructions. A genre study can take the form of a literary lunch bunch, co-teaching, or collaborative planning." After an introduction to the term genre, this lesson begins with students identifying what they know about specific genres, augmented by the instructor as appropriate. The characteristics of the genres can be recorded on charts or shared on prepared handouts. The ReadWriteThink lesson resources include bookmark masters for each of the various genres. Sixth grade

Literary Genre Framework

Genre	Definition	Subgenre or Types	Appeal	Uses	Text Features
Realistic Fiction	Imaginative writing that reflects the experiences and lives of people today	Problem novel; Adventure; Sports; Mystery; Humor; Romance; Magical realism	Focuses on concerns and interests of this age group	Character development; development of conflict and plot; inferring themes; connection of self to text; text to world (e.g., how problem in novel impacts family, peers, society); develops understanding of the realities of peers and societal issues	Narrative structure; characters; setting; theme; plot; conflict
Historical Fiction	Imaginative writing that creates stories of people living in the past, integrating information about the historical period			Settings; activating background knowledge; visualizing; character and plot development; inferring themes; frequently selected for use with social studies unit on a particular era	Narrative structure; characters; setting; theme; plot; conflict
Fantasy	Imaginative writing with at least one element not found in the real world	Low fantasy / Magical realism; Urban fantasy; High fantasy; Supernatural	Alternative universe; ideal societies; quest for honor, self-fulfillment, or power	Narrative structure; characters; setting; theme; plot; conflict; visualization skills; critical thinking;	Narrative structure; characters; setting; theme; plot; conflict

Science Fiction	Fantasy in which some aspects of the story involve advanced technological knowledge	Alien encounters; Time travel; Space travel; Space opera; Dystopia; Steampunk; Cyberpunk; Biopunk	Alternative worlds; speculation on the future; impact of mankind's treatment of environment	Narrative structure; characters; setting; theme; plot; conflict; identifying writing strategies used to create believability	Narrative structure; characters; setting; theme; plot; conflict
Folklore		Folktales, Fables, Myths, Legends, Epics			Narrative structure; characters; setting; theme; plot; conflict
Poetry	Distillation of experience using language to create meaning and emotional response	Lyrical; Narrative; Free verse; Concrete; Limericks; Found; Haiku; Cinquain; Novels in verse	Power of spoken word; figurative language	Models of language; inferences; visualization; theme; figurative language	Lines; breaks; white space; stanzas; text placement in concrete poetry
Nonfiction	Text about the realities of people, events, ideas, emotions, and things	Expository / Narrative; Persuasive; Opinion / Editorial; Reference texts; Textbooks; Journalism; Picture books; Photo essay; Tests; Promotional materials/ advertising; Websites	Information for practical or aesthetic needs; Intellectual curiosity; information about world and others	Personal information; curriculum support; to meet practical life needs; establishes background knowledge; pairing fiction and nonfiction to understand topics; determining importance; summarizing; vocabulary development	Expository, narrative, and descriptive writing; headings and subheadings; illustrations of many types; facts inserted in boxes; sequence (numerical or chronological); text organizers (indexes, tables of content, glossaries, bibliographies, and web links); use of signal words (e.g., most important, in conclusion, etc.); text structures (compare / contrast; cause / effect; problem/solution/ question/ answer; description/sequence)

(Continued)

Literary Genre Framework

Genre	Definition	Subgenre or Types	Appeal	Uses	Text Features
Biography	Narrative of a person's life		Range of people from contemporary and historical eras	Information on individuals; writing model; background knowledge; text to self connections	Narrative structure; use of quotations; sometimes chronological order and/or flashbacks; may contain photos, drawings, maps, or other documents
Autobiography	Narrative of a person's own life		Models for how to live; allows vicarious preview of own future and of various career paths	First person "I"; writing model; background knowledge; text to self connections; writing model	First-person point of view in narrative structure; sometimes chronological order and/or flashbacks; may contain photos, drawings, maps, or other documents
Memoir	Personal recollection of a significant event or series of events in a person's life		Accessible language; vivid materials; emotional description of life events	Text to self connections; writing model; background knowledge; stimulates discussion	First-person point of view; memories; reflection on meaning of life experiences

Literary Genre Framework					
Forms	**Definition**	**Subgenre**	**Appeal**	**Uses**	**Text Features**
Picture Books	Books in which a story told in images, or in an interaction between text and images, or a topic is explored using images or a combination of text and images	Storybook Wordless Concept Realistic fiction Fantasy Science fiction Nonfiction Biographies Folklore Post-modern	Visuals; short text; increases emotional impact of text	Entertainment; information; examples of genres; examples of literary elements and figurative language; models of writing; content knowledge; styles of art; to stimulate thinking about difficult topics (e.g., prejudice; injustice, racism) and character traits	Images; images combined with text; features vary by subgenre
Graphic Literature	Fiction and nonfiction sequential art narratives of book length, usually combining text and visuals	Graphic novels Graphic nonfiction Graphic biographies Manga	Integration of visuals and text; similarity to comics and other visual media	Introduction to genre or classic literature; bridge to novel study; analysis of story elements; literary terms; visual literacy; analysis of art style	Sequential art; narrative or expository text; manga (right to left sequence)
Short Stories	Fictional prose tales of brief length	All fiction subgenres	Brevity; immediate engagement; range of genres	Genre study; character analysis; plot and style analysis; literary terms and elements of fiction; mentor text for writing; bridge to novel study	Narrative structure; characters; setting; theme; plot; conflict
Drama	A fiction, nonfiction, or poetic composition intended to be performed	Plays; Skits; One-act plays; Monologues; Readers' theatre; Classics; Tragedies; Comedies; Screenplay; Teleplay	Oral tradition; emotional connection; expressive art	Genre study; literary history; entertainment	Dialogue Stage directions

(Continued)

Literary Genre Framework					
Forms	**Definition**	**Subgenre**	**Appeal**	**Uses**	**Text Features**
Multiplatform Works (Transmedia Storytelling)	Extended reading experience, combining genre hybrids with varied media types	e-Book; Book apps; Printed book; Audiobook; Virtual game; Cards; Music; Websites; Simulations; Student input	Blend of audio and print genres and virtual technologies (videos; social interactions, gaming); reluctant readers; ELL	Independent reading; genre study; response to literature; special education	Narrative structure; digital images, oral elements; game cards; interactive text
Film	Art form with fiction or nonfiction narratives conveyed with sound and moving images	Fiction Documentary Educational videos/ DVDs Television programs	Mainstream media; perceived relevance to young people; thematic connections to novels and curriculum	Introduction or extension of literature study; examples of literary elements; visual literacy; content area support	Screenplay; characters; dialogue; sets; costumes; props; musical lyrics; camera angles

teacher Donalyn Miller requires her students to enter the characteristics in a genre notebook, describing her lesson procedure in *The Book Whisperer* (2009). In Miller's classroom, she introduced the genres one at a time, using the genre notes throughout the year. For a librarian with an assigned class, this process could be adapted for a set period of time.

Consider the use of a booktalk to introduce students to various genres, one of your own or a podcast, *Books Worth Owning*, from ReadWriteThink: http://www.readwrite think.org/parent-afterschool-resources/podcast-episodes/books-worth-owning-30334. html. This booktalk includes adventure, historical fiction, realistic fiction, and story collections and features *The Hunger Games* by Suzanne Collins, among other titles. A new podcast on literature for young people is published monthly by ReadWriteThink. These programs may be automatically received as a text message on your computer. Check out the options at http://www.readwritethink.org/rss/text-messages.xml.

Student Genre Activities

Once the basics of the genres are established, students can practice placing books in appropriate genres in several ways:

- Genre booktalk using state contest titles: A follow-up strategy is to booktalk titles from the current year's state reading program, inserting genre clues within the description of each book. Students would identify the genre, and place a prepared sentence strip with the title and a small image of the cover on large genre signs.

- Student-created genre displays: For classes with experience in identifying genres, or perhaps as a review for seventh or eighth grade classes, the hands-on activity could be working in groups with stacks of books (mixed genres) to identify genres. After the class reconvened, students could describe the genre and book, placing it in an appropriate genre display with signs provided by the media specialist or teacher.

- Genre clues: Another variation on this strategy is for a small group of students to be assigned to a stack of books of the same genre. The group will develop a list of clues to the genre, from easy to more difficult; these clues will be presented to the entire class or another small group, rotating through all genres covered in the lesson. Part of the clues could be an oral reading from a section of the book blurb from the flyleaf or back cover. Instructions to students for the activity could include offering verbal clues initially, without showing the book, followed by showing the book cover.

- Genre location and display: In an activity combining genre, the use of the library catalog, library location skills, and graphic art skills, pairs or groups of students draw a genre name card from a basket, use the catalog to identify titles, and find the books on the shelves to create a display with a genre sign. The librarian would need to provide card stock and markers and also plan out the genre name cards, making sure that sufficient titles are available in the catalog and on the shelves. For example, realistic fiction signs would have a subgenre listed (e.g., sports, mysteries, adventure, school stories, romance, etc.). For the nonfiction genre cards, specific subjects could be added (e.g., soccer, music, World War II, etc.). For the genre of biography, the terms individual biography or autobiography with a specific name could be used.

If time and computers are available, pairs or groups of students could create genre bookmarks, signs, or multimedia presentations to be shared with the class. If using images from the Internet, it would be appropriate to have students provide evidence of copyright permission to use the image for educational purposes. See the Analyze section of this book for specific directions and additional ideas on responding to literature.

Which Literary Selections?

As school librarians, the role with literature is viewed from two broad perspectives: making it accessible to students and supporting the teaching of literature in classrooms. The issue of physical access to students is covered in the chapters on Read as a personal activity, and the process of addressing intellectual access and understanding for students by illuminating the literary genres is found in Explore. In supporting the use of literature in classrooms, school librarians need to understand an underlying issue that teachers deal with each year. Which literary selections will they teach? Will it be classical literature, the canon, or contemporary young adult literature? While this issue exists in middle schools, it is discussed more often in high schools (Gilmore, 2011).

Chris Baldrick (2008) in *The Oxford Dictionary of Literary Terms* defines the canon as "a body of works recognized by authority. . . . The canon of a national literature is a body of writings especially approved by critics or anthologists and deemed suitable for academic study" (p. 47). Donelson and Nilsen (2005) characterize two primary positions on classroom literary selections, with many shades of gray in between. On one side are those who want all students to be familiar with certain classics, so that they are acculturated into a more unified society, with similar values and attitudes. On the other hand, some believe that the traditional literary canon lacks cultural diversity and students deserve to have their own values and attitudes present in the materials they are required to read. Some authors refer to this as a division between classics and young adult literature, though this is an oversimplification of the issues. In reality, many adults today declare that the intense examination and dissection of classics in high schools left them with a negative impression of literature.

In 2010, in *Reading Ladders: Leading Students from Where They Are to Where We'd Like Them to Be*, Teri S. Lesesne addresses this issue by describing the need to use literature that is both rigorous and relevant. Concerning the term rigorous, she declares, "This term is often code for the work of classic authors who have been a part of the literary canon for decades. The works of Hawthorne and Hemingway, of Faulkner and Fitzgerald, of Cooper and Dickens possess sufficient rigor to make them worthwhile for study in the English classroom" (pp. 1–2). To document her assessment of use of the classics, Lesesne writes:

> YA literature has made little if any progress in terms of being studied in the English curriculum, especially past middle school. Applebee's 1991 study examined the most frequently studied anthologies used in English classrooms and concluded that 86 percent of the selections were written by white authors, fewer that 25 percent of the authors were female, and almost 70 percent of the authors were from North America. (p. 2)

Lesesne (2010) advocates the use of literature in classrooms that is relevant to today's students, young adult literature perhaps combined with the classics. In the introduction to *Reading Ladders: Leading Students from Where They Are to Where We'd Like Them to Be*, Jim Blasingame offers insight into Lesesne's valuation of relevance, "A book that has characters, locations, and situations (i.e., conflicts) that readers may struggle with in their own daily lives can facilitate a connection" (p. ix), which is crucial for engagement. He continues, "Young adult literature provides opportunities for readers to develop relationships with books and to respond to books in ways that are often impossible when they read canonical literature" (p. ix).

It is essential for school librarians to understand that teachers may or may not have complete control over which works are taught in classrooms. In some states and districts, a formal curriculum mandates the selections used. No question, the nature of required testing used locally has a major impact on what is covered. If particular novels, dramas, and poetry are covered in examinations, there may be little room in the school year for other works. In this second decade of the 21st century, changes to the literary curriculum are underway. As of early 2011, more than 40 states have adopted the Common Core State Standards for English Language Arts & Literacy in History/Social Studies, Science, and Technical Subjects developed by the Common Core State Standards Initiative. While this curriculum encompasses goals and expectations of students, it does not prescribe what to teach, leaving those decisions to state and local officials. However, the intention is to standardize the national curriculum, which could lead to sharing tests across states and possibly the selection of common texts. Appendix B of the Common Core State Standards for English Language Arts & Literacy in History/Social Studies, Science, and Technical Subjects does list text exemplars but states clearly that the titles are intended only as guideposts to the types of texts that may be selected by educators.

In order to comprehend the conflicts that many English or language arts teachers experience, it is essential for school librarians to understand the background issues about the selection of materials for classroom use. Librarians often serve on curriculum or literacy councils in schools and may be involved in discussions about which books will be taught. Teachers may come to seek advice from the school librarian on the selection of books on a certain theme or genre to provide choices to students concerning the books they will read. Based on their extensive knowledge of books and of students' interests, school librarians will be able to recommend books for consideration.

Fiction: Realistic Fiction

Fiction collections in secondary school libraries are dominated by young adult literature, books written specifically for this age group. Though these collections include many books written for adults, most tweens and teens prefer to read stories about people like themselves, experiencing the same problems, joys, and sorrows, and struggling to become independent. The tone of realistic fiction varies from bleak and intense, through many shades of gray, to humorous.

The term problem novel is used for the many books dealing with the most serious issues of abuse, deprivation, inequities, teen pregnancies, and other difficult topics. Comparing the plots in these books to headlines from current newspapers, Rosemary Chance (2008) calls these books dark modern realistic fiction. Unfortunately, suicide and bullying are two of the recent topics from the headlines. Two high school titles on suicide are *Thirteen Reasons Why* by Jay Asher (2007) and *By the Time You Read This, I'll Be Dead* by Julie Anne Peters (2010). Bullying is the theme of *Jumped* by Rita Williams-Garcia (2009) for high school readers. Middle school titles on bullying are *Bystander* by James Preller (2009) and *The Truth about Truman School* by Dori Hillestad Butler (2008) on cyberbullying. Nonfiction titles on bullying to pair with these fiction works in discussions are *We Want You to Know: Kids Talk about Bullying* by Deborah Ellis (2010) and *Teen Cyberbullying Investigated: Where Do Your Rights End and Consequences Begin* by Tom Jacobs (2010).

Romance

While sets of genre labels purchased for the library still includes one for romance fiction, this subgenre is far different from the past. Certainly, books of this type meet the developmental needs of students in secondary schools as they read to understand the changing roles they are or hope to be experiencing. Some reviewers link romance and chick lit, though the terms are far from synonymous. Relationships with vampires also qualify for romance, though not within the realistic fiction genre. To confuse the issue further, books written for adult women may also be tagged as chick lit in reviews, public libraries, and book stores.

School librarian Christine Meloni has been writing about chick lit for teens for years and describes it this way, "These fun books are about boys, friendship, family, fitting in, and growing up. . . . Although these are not the issue-driven type of novels considered for the Newbery Award, they are often traditional coming-of-age stories that girls can identify with" (2006, p. 18). Meloni identifies two categories of chick lit, the original humorous stories and the novels of privileged girls. According to Meloni (2006, 2010), among the authors of the entertaining, beach-type light-hearted books are Louise Rennison, Carolyn Mackler, and Meg Cabot. On the other hand, she points out that

Although privileged chick-lit books have similar plots, they are exclusively about wealthy beautiful girls who live in exciting places, wear trendy clothes, and date hot guys. . . . To stay queen bee, the ladies of The Clique by Lisi Harrison, Gossip Girls by Cecily von Ziegesar, and The A-List often deceive their friends or are cruel to outsiders.

(Meloni, 2006, p. 18)

The characters in the books in these series are often called mean girls (Cart, 2010). In another article, Meloni (2011) declares, "Romantic comedies are not just for girls! Many male readers . . . enjoy funny, male-centered comic fiction about dating, high school, growing up, and family. Welcome to lad lit" (p. 1). Titles she places in this subgenre of lad lit include *Slam* (2007) by Nick Hornby, *Carter Finally Gets It* (2009) by Brent Crawford, and *What My Girlfriend Doesn't Know* (2007) by Sonya Sones. Meloni (2011) assures us that girls will read these books because they are curious about the male perspective on dating and friendship.

Other young adult authors combining romance and a more realistic tone are Sarah Dessen, Maureen Johnson, Lauren Myracle, and Catherine Gilbert Murdock. However, Dessen's work is identified as chick lit by some. In an interview, Roger Sutton (2009) asked Sarah Dessen about her opinion of the term chick lit: "I'm not as offended by it as others are. But I also think it's become too wide a term. We sort of throw anything with a pink cover into it. It used to be targeted very specifically, and now anything that isn't Literature and has women in it is chick lit" (p. 48).

Humor

Middle school students love to laugh when they read and appreciate the books from Lemony Snicket, A Series of Unfortunate Events. Though danger lurks in these novels, humor also helps the stories to move along. Jack Gantos's Joey Pigza books also include many funny lines. Other middle school titles include *Surviving the Applewhites* (Tolan, 2002), *Flipped* (Van Drannen, 2001), and *The Schwa Was Here* (Shusterman, 2004). Rosemary Chance (2008) writes about the types of humor for secondary students, "Sarcasm, teasing, grossness, lewd jokes, exaggeration, word play, plus humor at the expense of adults are staples of humor for grades 6 through 10. In the last years of high school teens begin to appreciate satire and parody, while some continue to prefer more infantile devices" (p. 50). One title that transitions from eighth grade to high school is *Sleeping Freshmen Never Lie* by David Lubar (2005). For sixth graders, Lubar (2009, 2010) has published five titles so far in a mixed genre (humor and horror) series, Nathan Abercrombie, Accidental Zombie, which will fill the need for lower reading level, with high humor appeal.

YALSA's theme for Teen Read Week in 2007 was LOL@your library, which was a pleasure to implement. At one school, the reading coach was cosponsor of the event and volunteered to research humorous quotes from various public figures including Mark Twain, and then to create large signs, and post them around the school. YALSA has posted a list of books titled *What's So Funny?*, which is available at this website http://www.ala.org/yalsa/booklistsawards/booklists/popularpaperback/07ppya. Scroll down the page to locate this list.

Mysteries

Solving puzzles is the engaging hook of mysteries, and many young people enjoy this process. Students willingly play detective, searching for inferences (clues) leading to the culprit in the story. Authors frequently create series based on one character, encouraging readers to move on to another case. Television mystery series featuring forensic experts have led to requests for books like CIS or NCIS. Good responses are Alane Ferguson's *Forensic Mystery* series or Christopher Golden's *Body of Evidence* series (Clark, 2008). The covers of these books add to the appeal for teens, such as the toe tag on the foot of the corpse from Ferguson's *The Angel of Death* (2006). Story lines dominate this genre, though mysteries for tweens do not usually involve a corpse. Public librarian Joyce G. Saricks (2009), describing them as one of the intellect genres, writes, "The mood of mysteries ranges from dark and gritty to lighthearted and witty with a multitude of variations in between" (p. 198).

Crime-infested novels exhibiting high levels of suspense are sometimes called thrillers, overlapping the mystery genre. Author Nancy Werlin (2010) insists thrillers differ from mysteries. "Thrillers tend to be about nasty people doing bad, illegal, and/or unethical things, although usually there's also a blameless individual around as protagonist who is endangered body and soul by these bad people and their immoral plans", she discloses. Werlin insists, "Readers of thrillers are . . . consorting with people who are no better than they should be, people who are doing things that shock us, make us afraid, and . . . excite us. Thrillers are a guilty-pleasure type of reading. Mysteries are almost respectable, but thrillers? No" (p. 302). Her mystery, *The Killer's Cousin*, first published in 1998, was reissued in 2009.

Recently published mysteries for middle school libraries include *The Adventures of Jack Lime* by James Leek (2010), *Trash* by Andy Mulligan (2010), *The Red Blazer Girls: The Ring of Rocamador* by Michael Beil, and *The Unknowns* by Bendict Carey (2009), which features mathematical clues. Mysteries appropriate for high school students are *The Morgue and Me* by John C. Ford, *I Am the Messenger* by Marcus Zusak (2005), *Eye of the Crow* by Shane Peacock (2007) from the series *The Boy Sherlock Holmes*, and a recent reissue of *The A.B.C. Murder* by Agatha Christie (2006, 1936).

Sports

This type of realistic fiction is a traditional favorite of boys, though some sports titles feature girls as main characters, expanding the appeal of the genre. Recently, sports books have often focused on the reality of the use of steroids and other drugs by athletes. Teri Lesesne (2010) identifies other connections: "Most novels that feature athletes and sports deal with other themes and issues such as power, competition, accomplishment, and dedication" (p. 116). Authors known for their books of sports fiction include Chris Crutcher, Carl Deuker, Bruce Brooks, Robert Lipsyte, and Dan Gutman. Recent sports reads are from Deuker, *Runner* (2005), *Gym Candy* (2007), and *Payback Time* (2010), and two titles focusing on competitive girls, *Boost* (Mackel, 2008) and *Shutout* (Halpin, 2010).

Adventure

Librarians and teachers frequently turn to adventure stories to entice reluctant students into reading. Book reviewer Vicky Smith (2010) describes the appeal of this genre, "The fast pace, the concentration on physicality, and the frequent how-to element of the tales can often seduce children who would rather be out engaging in adventures of their own (or finding them in video games)" (p. 173). Action, plot, and believable characters are essential elements of adventure. Donelson and Nilsen (2005) declare, "The most important literary device found in adventure stories is verisimilitude. With so much emphasis on danger, writers must provide realistic details galore to assure us, despite some inner misgivings, that the tale is possible and believable" (p. 174). Outstanding authors in this area are Gary Paulsen, Will Hobbs, Jean Craighead George, and Roland Smith. Current contemporary adventure stories include *Take Me to the River* (Hobbs, 2011), *Storm Mountain* (Birdseye, 2010), and *As Easy as Falling Off the Face of the Earth* (Perkins, 2010).

Fiction: Historical Fiction

For some, historical fiction represents the best reading, blending an interest in history with other beloved story lines. However, it has not been high on the popularity lists with students (Carter, 2010; Krapp, 2005). *Booklist* columnist and author Michael Cart (2010) reports an increased presence for historical fiction titles in young adult literature beginning in the mid-1990s, citing his choice of 21 historical fiction titles out of a total 61 fiction titles for his 2000 best of the year list. He points to Scholastic's series *Dear America*, first introduced in 1996, as a major influence on the increase of historical fiction titles. Cart (2010) credits Scholastic's use of the diary format and the commissioning of outstanding authors to create the books, including Walter Dean Myers, Joseph Bruchac, Karen Hess, Carolyn Meyers, Jim Murphy, and Ann Rinaldi (p. 105), among others.

A second contributing factor to the increased popularity is the recent trend toward genre mash-ups (Rabey, 2010) or genre blending. Because some librarians and many teachers (Miller, 2009) assign students to read from a specified list of genres each year, students may show up in the library to ask for a historical fiction title with a sense of dread. Betty Carter (2010) explains that underneath the historical fiction genre label exist multiple subgenres including historical mystery, adventure, and romance. She maintains, "If we want our kids to read historical fiction, the best approach is first to consider the types of books they already know and like, and then expand those tastes by recommending similar tales with a historical setting . . . they are willing to venture backward in time within the constraints of already beloved genres" (p. 139). Other subgenre additions to historical fiction mix are historical fantasies (Saricks, 2008) and science fiction (Rabey, 2010).

A compelling educational value of historical fiction is the development of background knowledge for students and the examples of well-crafted settings. Carter (2010) describes the difficult tasks of writing historical fiction for authors, "First, they have to create a story that catches the attention of readers; second, they must interest these readers in a particular time period; and third, they must ensure that the story suits the setting" (p. 138). Critic Anne Scott MacLeod (2010) maintains that, in an effort to accommodate today's feminist sensibilities, many contemporary authors of historical fiction distort the truth about women's roles in the past, creating female characters that rise above the restraints of the time period of the story. "They evade the common realities of the societies they write about. . . . To do that, they set aside the social mores of the past as though they were minor afflictions, small obstacles, easy—and painless, for an independent mind to overcome" (p. 150), MacLeod explains. Perhaps this issue suggests an interesting follow-up to the reading of a historical fiction title, comparing and contrasting the role of women in the novel and in historical sources of the time period.

From this discussion, we can recommend appropriate activities for use with historical fiction.

- Bibliographies and booktalks centered around historical fiction should include subgenres to increase appeal to students in language arts classes or social studies classes, who may be assigned to read books from particular historical periods;

- MacLeod's (2010) concern about historical revisionism suggests an interesting follow-up to the reading of a historical fiction title, comparing and contrasting the role of women in the novel and in historical sources of the time period. In the October 2009 issue of *The Reading Teacher*, Mary Taylor Rycik and Brenda Rosler offer an interesting selection of historical fiction and nonfiction titles for use in middle schools.

- Among the reader response strategies recommended by Rycik and Rosler (2009) for use with historical fiction are: writing letters from the point of view of a character in a book, creating a timeline of events during a historical period, creating and performing a skit about an event in a book, contrasting the lives of two diverse characters in a book in a Venn diagram, creating a scene for an existing or a new character for a book, developing a newspaper for a period of history from a book, locating websites about a historical event.

- Expand the fact and fiction combination by assigning students to locate a variety of types of information on the historical period of the novel, including primary source documents as images, audio, and video that are available. For documents issued in the past, such as the Magna Carta or Gettysberg Address, students could create an audio or video version.

- Student presentations on historical novels could also include a geographical component using maps from the era of the book and current day maps including Google Earth images.

Fiction: Fantasy

The tide of popularity has swept higher for fantasy fiction since the late 1990s because of the publishing phenomena of three series of books, *Harry Potter*, *Twilight*, and more recently, *The Hunger Games*. *Harry Potter* led the way, chronologically, in terms of international impact, and spin-off marketing, including a delightful theme park. Movies have followed for all three series, though the planning for *The Hunger Games* movie is in the early stages as this book goes to press.

As a genre, fantasy traces its roots to traditional literature, sharing heroes, magical characters and objects, frequent references to ancient myths and legends, and themes of good and evil or right and wrong. However, in modern fantasies, characters show growth and change in contrast to traditional literature, renowned for its flat characters (Fuhler & Walther, 2007; Kurkjian, Livingston, Young, & Avi, 2006). Recent novels with strong connections to specific traditional stories include *Rose Daughter* (McKinley, 1997) from *Beauty and the Beast*, *Ugly* (Napoli, 2006) from *The Ugly Duckling*, and *East* (Pattou, 2003) from *East of the Sun and West of the Moon* (Fuhler & Walther, 2007).

More than other fiction genre, fantasy develops the imagination of readers and encourages critical thinking (Fuhler & Walther, 2007). These authors also suggest that fantasy can be read on various levels, offering thoughtful readers a look at personal and societal problems. Fuhler and Walther (2007) explain, "Fantasy teaches its perceptive readers about life in general and themselves personally while taking them out of this world and allowing them to travel much farther afield" (p. 98). Author Avi (Kurkjian et al., 2006) comments on the connection between reality and fantasy: "Let me suggest that when it comes to fantasy, the task is to find the truth, then write about it as if it were imagined. In short, in a world where the truth is often hidden, fantasy reveals reality" (p. 496).

Fantasy also offers the advantage of appealing to young people and adults alike. In an essay on fantasy titled "Your Journey Is Inward, But It Will Seem Outward", Deirdre F. Baker (2010) encourages adult and child conversations on a book both have read. She points out, "It is in fantasy that adult and child readers are most likely to converge: witness the crossover success of J. K. Rowling's Harry Potter series and of Philip Pullman's His Dark Materials, trilogy, for example" (p. 125).

Wrapped into the broad genre of fantasy are the works sometimes referred to as horror or scary stories by tweens. With its vampires and werewolves, *Twilight* fits right into this category. After moving from elementary to middle school, one school librarian was surprised to learn that students were still asking for scary stories or, more specifically, *Scary Stories to Read in the Dark*. Knowing that the library catalog does not include the term "scary stories", only horror or ghost stories could be offered as search terms. Recently, Neal Gaiman's *The Graveyard Book* has been published, which could be just right for those middle school students; one subject heading for this title is supernatural fiction. One public librarian, Diana Tixier Herald, prefers the term paranormal fiction to horror, offering many titles in *Teen Genreflecting* (2003).

Science Fiction

This subgenre of fantasy is distinguished by the additional criteria of including technological advances that could, in fact, happen in the future. To explain this type of fiction, the typical example is Jules Verne's *Twenty Thousand Leagues Under the Sea* published in 1870, which features undersea vehicles similar to the 20th century's submarines. Joyce G. Saricks (2009) defines science fiction as "speculative fiction that appeals to the reader's intellect" (p. 245). She considers the setting to be the dominant element in this genre, "Setting is crucial and invokes otherness of time, place, and/or reality. Both the physical setting of the story and the inherent technical and scientific detail create this essential frame" (p. 245). Fuhler and Walther (2007) identify the themes of science fiction as mind control, genetic engineering, space technologies and travel, visitors from outer space, future political and social systems, life in the future, and survival (p. 105).

Much of science fiction has a dark and serious tone and is also called dystopian fiction; it has been represented in middle and high schools for years by Lois Lowry's *The Giver*, a Newbery Medal winner. The punks are another subgenre of science fiction which are admittedly weird and abnormal. Meet the steampunk, cyberpunk, and biopunk novels! After reading the article "The Punks of Science Fiction" by Rebecca Hill from the October 2010 issue of *VOYA*, one of the book's authors realized she had seen some of these titles but didn't realize what to make of them at the time. One of the first of this group of novels to emerge from science fiction ranks was steampunk, which Hill describes as "an amalgam of old and new that often features technology in an antiquated setting" (p. 335). The contemporary example is Scott Westerfeld's *Leviathan* (2009), which already has a follow-up title, *Behemoth* (2010), with both set during World War I. Hill explains, "In steampunk, readers will find characters in a subculture that embraces this technology in an alternative history, taking old ideas and using them in new technological ways that are not relevant for the historical age as we know it" (p. 335).

In a parallel subgenre to steampunk, cyberpunk novelists use current technology and imagine new applications in an outlaw culture. Hill (2010) lists William Gibson's *Neuromancer* (1984) as an early example of cyberpunk and Cory Doctorow's *Little Brother* (2008), *Maker* (2010), and *For the Win* (2010) as current examples.

The third of the punk subgenres are biopunk novels, which, according to Hill (2010), includes Mary Shelley's *Frankenstein*. Hill points out, "Dealing with themes of human experimentation, misused biotechnologies, and synthetic biology, biopunk looks at the human body from a genetic and molecular level" (p. 336). Recent titles of this type are Scott Westerfeld's *Uglies* (2005), *Pretties* (2005), *Specials* (2006), and *Extras* (2007), as well as *The Clone Codes* (2010) by Patricia C., Fredrick L. and Frank McKissack.

If you think your students would like science fiction or one of these hybrids, READS Lessons for this chapter includes a terrific teaching plan and resources titled "Finding the Science behind Science Fiction through Paired Readings" by Lisa Storm Fink for Read-WriteThink. Very interestingly, Fink is quoted in Hill's (2010) article on science fiction, which also mentions school librarians! Hill (2010) promotes collaboration between school librarians and teachers, writing:

> Since science fiction is not often found in the classroom, a multitude of opportunities exist to use it. To encourage cross curriculum uses, school media specialists can point at these options to teachers through book talks or "walk and talk". Then teachers might give it more of a chance, says Storm Fink, especially "if they saw how it could fit into their curriculum and maybe meet multiple goals/standards/indicators that would help motivate the teacher." Finally, it also provides the school library media specialist, as well as the classroom teacher, a unique chance to introduce their students to a genre that is not often assigned in the classroom. (p. 336)

The ReadWriteThink lesson includes a list of science fiction titles along with science titles for paired readings. Updated examples of titles for comparisons include *Leviathan* and *Behemoth* by Scott Westerfeld, *The Technology of World War I* by Stewart Ross (2003), and *Decades of the 20th Century* by Stephen Feinstein (2006).

The list of activities for use with the range of fantastic genres includes great variety:

- Begin with artistic connections because of the rich settings in these books, asking students to respond to a book with an art project or to identify the style of art used in the book's illustrations.
- For Harry Potter fans, have them explore Harry Potter's World virtually and write about which area they would most like to visit.
- Have groups of students debate the merits of two fantasy titles, comparing the characters, settings, magical persons or objects, and themes of the books.
- Assign students to compare and contrast fantasy and science fiction, showing characteristics and examples, using a freehand Venn diagram or ReadWriteThink Student Interactive: Venn Diagram, 2 Circles, http://www.readwritethink.org/classroom-resources/student-interactives/venn-diagram-circles-30006.html.
- Have students identify fantasy and science fiction books made into motion pictures and create a display showing their work.
- In a science fiction title, have students identify evidence that the author used nonfiction sources when writing the novel. and
- Assign students to match science fiction books with nonfiction titles or websites on the same area of science.

Fiction: Short Stories

Short stories are being selected for leisure reading by teens more than in the past. Now with flashy jacket art and collections available by theme, genre, and favored authors, young people are finding the fiction subgenre more appealing. Many teachers are now using not only short stories by traditional authors but are pulling stories from contemporary young adult authors for classroom use. As many librarians find themselves with scheduled classes, the use of short stories as read alouds or texts for group or independent reading activities makes sense and offers potential for integrating reading and writing strategies into activities in the library program.

The list of advantages of using short stories begins, of course, with brevity. Students can hear or read a short story in a single class period, perhaps with time for discussion or activities. Other advantages of using short stories are offered by teachers Kimberly Hill Campbell (2007) and Heather Lattimer (2003), and school librarian Lynn Rashid (2008):

- The use of short stories instead of novels provides additional exposure to authors, whether classical, multicultural, or contemporary.
- In-class reading of a short story allows teachers to observe students reading and to provide individualization and intervention as needed.
- The focus on a single story encourages deep reading and analysis of literary elements.
- Literature circles work well with short stories and foster active discussions and sharing of ideas about the stories.
- Short stories can serve as manageable mentor texts for writing activities.
- Some stories are available on audiotape or in translated foreign language versions to accommodate the needs and preferences of all students.

Rashid also points out a bonus feature of this literary form: "Educators challenged to find high-interest/low-reading-level materials will find that the short story can be a perfect match for struggling and/or disinterested students" (p. 17). Take a look at the list of short story collections and use them to recommend titles to teachers, to suggest to students, to feature in displays, or to use in a reading forum session in the library. Among the READS Lessons and Activities for this chapter is a lesson on organizing a short story fair as a culminating activity after reading and writing about stories in class. ReadWriteThink offers a podcast titled "Sampling Short Stories," which could be used as introduction to short stories for students or to update staff on more recent additions in this literary genre.

Poetry

The publishing of poetry in its various forms has been expanding in recent years, including the genre-blending novels in verse. Other reasons for the recent improvement in popularity of poetry include its brevity and increased accessibility, as books of poetry have been published targeting the lived experiences of young people (Lesesne, 2003), expanded notions of what constitutes poetry (e.g., song lyrics, hip-hop, rap, and found poetry), ease of locating poetry through many websites, and opportunities to participate in poetry through writing and performing, often on the Internet (Chatton, 2010).

Novels in verse written specifically for teens began in the 1990s. Karen Hesse's *Out of the Dust* won the Newbery Award in 1998 and is considered one of the finest examples of this genre. Other notable authors of novels in verse are Sonya Sones, Virginia Euwer Wolff, and Ron Koertge. Wolff published the final title, *This Full House*, in the Make Lemonade Trilogy in 2009. Walter Dean Myers, master of multiple genres, wrote *Amiri and Odette: A Love Story* in 2009 (Pure Poetry: *VOYA*'s Poetry Picks, 2009, 2010).

Values of Poetry

The values of using poetry in its many variations in secondary schools begin with supporting reading through exposure to the sounds of language and vocabulary, use of inferences in interpretation, and development of fluency in speaking poetry individually and through choral readings (Campbell, 2007; Fuhler & Walther, 2007). Speaking poetry in various ways also promotes the development of oral speaking skills, essential in the academic world and throughout life. Further, through exposure to poetry, students learn to observe the world around them more clearly, find their voices in expressing the meaning of poems, and eventually craft their own works (Campbell, 2007). In addition, continual exposure to developmentally suitable poetry through the grades gradually builds the skills needed in high school to interpret the traditional poetry required in the curriculum. Finally, the use of poetry can lead to an appreciation of language and its potential to enrich lives. Poet Naomi Shihab Nye (2010) describes how poetry impacted her as a child, "Poetry wasn't worrying about anything. It was contemplating. . . . Poetry wasn't trying to get us to do anything, it was simply inviting us to think, and feel, and see" (p. 235).

By using poetry throughout the curriculum, teachers can promote students' understanding of literature and content area topics. High school English teacher James Carlson (2010) used song-poems and his guitar to "challenge students to think critically about the issues being raised by the literature and the song. . . . We studied artists such as Neil Young, Bob Dylan, and Johnny Cash for social, cultural, historical, and literary purposes" (pp. 55–56). See the lesson "Stairway to Heaven: Examining Metaphor in Popular Music" listed in Chapter 9.

Librarian Barbara Chatton (2010) has gathered a wealth of poetic resources for use in elementary and middle school content areas in her book *Using Poetry across the Curriculum*. The book features thorough coverage of curricula areas including expansive topics for science, social studies, mathematics, physical and health education, the arts, and more with specific poems and their sources. Selections for holidays and occasions are included as well as examples of the many types of poetry. A bonus is the connection of the lists of poetry to national standards for each of the disciplines.

When poet Marilyn Singer was asked to arrange a presentation on poetry for the ALA Conference in 2010, she knew that her dominant message would be that poetry must be heard. She decided to ask other poets what they thought librarians need to know about poetry. Singer (2010) reports in an article in *School Library Journal* that Charles R. Smith, Jr., exclaimed, "Poetry must be taken off the pedestal. While poetry month is a good idea in theory, it ultimately confines poetry to that one month" (p. 28). The message from Laura Purdie Salas to Singer encourages wide variety, "The most important concept I'd love to see librarians and media specialists embrace is that poetry is available for everyone—from the rainbow-unicorn-loving kids to the goth kids. . . . Let them read silly and serious, escapist and thought-provoking, rural and urban poetry" (p. 28). Poet Julie Larios urged Singer to convey to librarians the importance of integrating poetry into book lists and celebrations of all types so that poetry and prose are side by side.

An excellent source for ideas for poetry celebrations is The Learning Network: *The New York Times*. In addition to this list for National Poetry Month, http://learning.blogs. nytimes.com/?s=11+ways+to+celebrate+national+poetry+month, Poetry Pairings are a weekly feature of the educational blog. Also, see our Lessons list for other poetry teaching resources.

Nonfiction

Nonfiction is a vital genre for students, in terms of usefulness for school work, testing, and value in postsecondary endeavors, and is a favored type of reading for some individuals. It provides the content of most curricular areas, including many primary source documents in secondary schools. Nonfiction is also the literary genre that has undergone the most change in recent years because of rapid technological advances; students and educators alike need to develop expertise in locating and evaluating various types of nonfiction available on the Internet. This is also the real-world genre, which will be used more by adults than any other.

Perceptions of educators about nonfiction have changed in recent years, shifting from utilitarian only to acknowledgement of the literary aspects of the genre. Kristo, Colman, and Wilson (2008) point to the use of narrative, author's voice, and artistic design in many nonfiction works. In 1989, NCTE established the Orbis Pictus Award for nonfiction to highlight the qualities of the best nonfiction for children and young people. Lehman (2009) asserts, "Texts such as those chosen for this award have moved nonfiction literature beyond merely the presenting of information and into the realm of stimulating aesthetic experiences" (p. 199). Nonfiction is also being used extensively in the classroom as models for various types of writing.

For school librarians, nonfiction is the nexus of reading promotion and inquiry or information literacy skills instruction. For struggling and ELL middle school students, a school librarian can collaborate with teachers to provide instruction and practice with identifying keywords in research questions, using an index to locate appropriate search terms, and locating required facts using text features. Targeting state testing objectives, a school librarian worked with intensive reading teachers in middle school on these essential skills using the *World Almanac for Kids* and other reference sources. Surprisingly, students were reluctant to close the almanacs once they discovered music awards and other biographical data on their pop favorites. The culminating activity was a research contest on a current topic (e.g., the Olympics, other sporting event, or topic of teacher choice).

Another excellent opportunity to present a nonfiction framework to students is the beginning of a major research project, when students will need to locate a variety of information sources on a topic. For example, the National History Fair competition is part of coursework in many school districts. With a changing theme each year, this academic event offers an authentic situation providing a teachable moment for describing the types of informational sources. School librarians can collaboratively plan in advance with teachers to bring students into the library, or the librarian to present in classrooms, so that students will be prepared for the research experience. Learn more about this event and the potential value it offers to your students on the organization's website http://www.nhd. org/GettingStarted.htm. As part of the planning process, the teacher's requirements need to be considered. For example, some teachers designate numbers and types of sources, including how many sources may be from the free web. A certain number of primary sources may be required. In some schools, students are required to complete a form for any source from the Internet, except for subscription databases, describing the scope, authority, validity, and so on of the site.

When preparing for the overview session on nonfiction sources for students, it is helpful for a school librarian to select a sample topic within the scope of the History Fair or other assignment and use a think-aloud strategy to model the process of critiquing print or digital sources for appropriateness for the topic and assignment guidelines, authority, validity, currency, and so on. It may be appropriate to model the use of key vocabulary terms specific to the topic or era, as well as search terms typically used in catalogs or online databases, which may not be obvious to teens.

Reference Resources

The subgenre of reference materials is certainly in a state of flux in school libraries. The current recommendation is to purchase reference materials in e-book form or as online services. However, it will take a transition period and considerable funds to convert to a totally online environment for reference, though new libraries may have such collections. Most existing libraries will spend many years in a transitional phase with reference. The reality is that many teachers still prefer their students to use authoritative print reference sources, perhaps indicating their lack of comfort with the online environment. Sometimes, teachers perceive that they have more control over students' work when they insist that print sources only are acceptable for a research project. While it is within the school librarians' range of responsibilities to provide training for staff on the use of online resources, they still need to meet teachers' expectations for resources to support a classroom unit of study whenever possible. They must provide teachers with models of research assignments with various requirements regarding acceptable sources (e.g., at least two of your five sources must be print; at least two of your online sources must be from our subscription databases; for any online sources other than our subscription databases, you must complete our form on Online Information Sources, including authority, bias, relevance, validity, etc.). Offer to provide training for students on locating and evaluating informational websites.

Nonfiction Activities

When presenting the genre framework for nonfiction, it will be beneficial to students for the school librarian to discuss possible sources, including available subscription databases, for each type of appropriate nonfiction (e.g., biographical sources, journalistic texts, and expository or narrative nonfiction). Some school librarians choose to create pathfinders for the topic, frequently posted on the school library's website, which is convenient for student use. An outstanding example is school librarian Joyce Valenza's site for Springfield High School, http://springfieldpathfinders.wikispaces.com/. In early 2011, among numerous pathfinders are ones on documentaries, biographies, primary sources, and court cases.

Teachers have been reporting the use of essays in classrooms and requesting collections from school librarians to use with their students. The advantage of this type of nonfiction is its brevity as well as the great variety of topics. Kimberly Hill Campbell (2010) reveals her motives:

> *I want students to discover that essays can be humorous, cynical, poignant, intimate, informative, persuasive, flexible, and literary—and typically need more than five paragraphs to do so. I want students to know that essays are not just a high school assignment or part of a college application: essays are written and read because we need to share our thoughts, our experiences, our voices.* (p. 50)

Campbell likes to begin with Dave Barry's and Stephen King's humorous essays. Another source of her essays for classroom use is National Public Radio's *This I Believe* website (http:thisibelieve.org), which she uses as mentor texts. Recent titles appropriate for school libraries include *The Best American Essays, 2010* (Houston Mifflin Harcourt), *The Best American Science and Nature Writing 2010* (Houghton Mifflin Harcourt), and *Best African American Essays, 2010* (One World/Ballantine). Essays by Dave Barry, Carl Hiassen, another political humorist, and many other writers can also be accessed through periodical databases.

Another approach to introducing nonfiction sources to middle or high school students is to present a basic lesson on the genre, followed by more specific instruction and practice with related procedures and topics, as described in the Lesson Approach box.

Pairing a fiction book with a nonfiction title is a strategy with great potential for engaging students and extending their background knowledge. Since some students have a strong preference for either fiction or nonfiction, combining the two in a library or classroom activity could provide increased student appeal. This approach could be used in libraries for booktalks, with scheduled library classes, or in book club situations. Teachers may chose this strategy and call on the school librarian to suggest titles or to involve students in research on a nonfiction topic related to a fiction work. In October, 2010, *Fort*

LESSON APPROACH

Planning

Prepare area for lesson by placing examples of nonfiction materials on each table including books (personal experience, procedural, informational, and persuasive); magazines; newspapers; real-world genres (travel or career brochures, real-estate guides, movie schedules, etc.); video/DVDs; cards with informational website titles and URLs (online newspapers, Library of Congress website, state website, political speeches, subscription databases, etc.).

Direct Instruction

1. Open session by asking students to identify the broad genre of literature represented on the tables.
2. Lead discussion on the types of nonfiction. Point out an article in a magazine and project the same article from a subscription database.
3. Distribute Nonfiction Genre Chart, describing any examples not previously discussed. Explain chart divisions as needed.
4. Describe four subgenres of nonfiction determined by purpose (personal experience, procedural, informational, and persuasive). Ask students to sort materials by subgenre at each table and select one or two tables to describe materials to class.
5. Direct students at each table to decide on a group nonfiction topic. Instruct groups to collect at least four types of resources on the topic using the library collection, catalog and the Internet . The group will create a poster listing the nonfiction topic with titles and types of resources. Allow groups to present to the class.
6. Proceed with classroom assignment or with library activity.

Extensions

- Link to location of nonfiction materials in the library.
- Extend lesson to include text structure discussion of materials: expository, narrative, or mix.
- Expand lesson to primary source documents.
- Explore biographical materials (reference, biographies, autobiographies, memoirs).
- Expand lesson to evaluative criteria for selecting nonfiction sources (scope, authority, accuracy, relevance, currency, validity).

Mose: And the Story of the Man Who Built the First Free Black Settlement in Colonial America by Glennette Tilley Turner was published by Abrams Books for Young Readers. This book received outstanding reviews and was placed on *Booklist's* 2010 Books for Older Readers list. The first thought on reading these reviews is to pair this book with *Copper Sun* by Sharon M. Draper (2006). *Copper Sun* is a historical fiction novel telling the story of 15-year-old Amari who was kidnapped from her African home in 1738 and sent to South Carolina as a slave. She was purchased by the owner of a rice plantation and was forced to serve as a companion to his son. She became friends with a white girl who was an indentured servant on the plantation. Eventually, the two girls fled the plantation together and made their way south to a place they had been told offered freedom, Fort Mose in northern Florida. Though Draper (2006) included factual information on Fort Mose in the back of *Copper Sun*, the book does not offer the detail and illustrations including original primary source documents that are provided in *Fort Mose: And the Story of the Man Who Built the First Free Black Settlement in Colonial America*. Used together, these books offer many curriculum possibilities, including historical and geographical studies; a focus on the various settings in the novel; comparisons of the life histories, economic influences, and social conditions of the two girls; the character traits of the girls, including perseverance and resourcefulness, two of the dispositions described in AASL's *Standards for the 21st-Century Learner* (2007), and more. *Copper Sun* is generally recommended for use with students in senior high schools because of the nature of the treatment Amari was forced to endure.

Another method for pairing fiction and nonfiction can be linking a novel with informational text available on the Internet. For example, a novel dealing with a health condition could be paired with online sites on health information. Students may get interested in the health facts after becoming emotionally involved with a character in the novel and, along the way, gain useful knowledge about the medical condition. Birch and McGee (2007) write about turning to the Internet for health information when she could not afford a specialized database on health. Fortunately for Birch and the students in her school, her sister was involved with the National Library of Medicine and was able to provide here with a free, useful site, MedlinePlus (http://medlineplus.gov). This versatile resource offers a virtual tour introduction for students, a printable brochure, and an option for viewing much of the site in Spanish (Birch & Magee, 2007). Another option is TeensHealth (www.teenshealth. org). On the topic of obesity, for middle school libraries, link the novel *Models Don't Eat Chocolate Cookies* by Erin Dionne with the health websites; if you would like to add a print nonfiction title, use *Talking about Your Weight* by Hazel Edwards and Goldie Alexander (2010). Upper middle or high school novels on obesity are *Fat Cat* by Robin Brande (2009) or *Looks* by Madeleine George (2008), which deals with both obesity and anorexia. On the health topic of diabetes, try *Sweetblood* by Pete Hautman (2003), which could be used with the health websites, and *Investigating Diabetes: Real Facts for Real Lives* (2010). For more variety, add back issues of the *Current Health* magazine.

Here is a roundup of additional brief ideas for using nonfiction in library work:

- Implement activities introducing nonfiction titles that highlight the text structures (compare/contrast, cause/effect, problem solution/question/answer, or description/sequence). See the READS Lessons and Activities list for a recent article by Michael Stencil, Sr., which provides several forms for use with students. We suggest adding magazine and newspaper articles and Internet sites to the selection of resources.
- Work with students in developing nonfiction readers' theater presentations for library programs and classroom projects.

- Feature nonfiction materials in displays in the library for Arbor Day, Hispanic Heritage Month, Black History Month, international events such as the Olympics or World Cup Soccer championships, and so on.
- Maintain ongoing lists of nonfiction materials frequently used in the curriculum (e.g., immigration, photography, Holocaust, ancient civilizations, Hispanic art and artists, etc.)
- Serve on curriculum and/or classroom selection committees. With a growing trend to use online sources instead of traditional print textbooks, we can offer our experience as information specialists. Read more about this in the article by Mardis in our nonfiction bibliography.

Nonfiction: Biography

This subgenre of nonfiction is valued for personal information about individuals and is used many ways in the curriculum. Teachers may request a text set of biographies in various formats to serve as models for writing or as information sources in the classroom (e.g., inventors or artists). If a teacher wants a class to locate information on individuals on a broad topic, a mini-lesson on sources could include print reference sources (biographical dictionaries and general and specialized encyclopedias), books on historical periods, individual biographies, collective biographies, autobiographies, and memoirs, and virtual resources (websites, newspapers, subscription databases, among others). Ask teachers during the planning process about the purpose of the research, how much information students need, and how much time is available before determining which sources to recommend.

Individual biographies are the broadest and most impersonal of the several types of works in this category. Covering the subject's entire life, biographies are impartial and may represent varying points of view on the person, supported by source material. Autobiographies are written on a complete life by the subject themselves, often with the assistance of a coauthor, and cover the entire life of the individual. Memoirs present a reflective snapshot (Fraser, 2008) of a period in one's own life, focusing on an event and place.

Middle schools widely use *Anne Frank: The Diary of a Young Girl* in English and language arts classrooms, often to prepare students for Holocaust studies in social studies. The Common Core Curriculum Mapping Project (2010) calls for the use of this autobiography in seventh grade in a unit titled "Determination in Life and in Literature." The essential question set for this unit is "How does real-world determination inform the depiction of determined literary characters?" This project identifies many other resources to be used with this text as well as a lesson plan. See the READS Internet Resources list for the link to the Common Core Curriculum Mapping Project.

Kimberly Hill Campbell (2007) suggests that memoirs are particularly well-suited for use in middle schools as a genre study linked with writing craft activities, explaining, "It's been my experience that memoir is a genre that appeals to adolescents. Memoirs grab readers and draw them in. The 'stuff of one's life' is fascinating, particularly to adolescents who in the work of figuring out their own life stuff" (p. 116). Lattimer (2003), another middle school educator, is also a proponent of the use of memoir, pointing out,

> By bringing memoirs into the classroom, we provide students with the opportunity to grow as readers and to become more reflective and grounded individuals. . . . By asking them to recognize the learning that is often revealed in memoirs, we lead them toward wisdom that can help them make sense of their own experiences and prepare them to deal with future situations. (p. 25)

Campbell (2007) reads aloud excerpts of memoirs in her classroom to familiarize her students with features of the genre and to serve as models for their own writing. She often selects the memoirs of authors, both because of the quality of the memoir and to create interest in their books. For middle school students, she recommends *Hole in My Life* by Jack Gantos, *Bad Boy: A Memoir* by Walter Dean Myers, as well as *Dispatches from the Edge: A Memoir of War* by journalist and television personality Anderson Cooper.

Some high school teachers are now working with the subgenre of contemporary memoir as part of their reading and writing program. Two English teachers describe their experiences using contemporary memoirs in their classrooms in an article in *English Journal*. Kirby and Kirby (2010) explain, "Looking for texts . . . that lead students to improve their abilities in sophisticated reading, writing, critical thinking, and inquiry strategies, we found CM to be a genre ideally suited for teens of the 21st century" (p. 22). These authors traced the emergence of what they call contemporary memoir from autobiography as part of experimentation with the nonfiction genre in the 1970s associated with Truman Capote, Joan Didion, Annie Dillard, and John Hersey, among others. Terms used for these variations on nonfiction include literary nonfiction, creative nonfiction, and documentary narrative (Kirby & Kirby, 2010). The distinguishing features of contemporary memoir, according to these authors, are use of brief episodes of events and places, use of conventional narrative structures, frequent inclusion of postmodern structures (e.g., leaving out transitions, leaving blanks in the text, use of white space and symbols), and reflective writing emphasizing perceived truth. Kirby and Kirby believe that their students benefit from reading and writing contemporary memoir by analyzing the thoughts of others as expressed in their memoirs, reflecting on and writing about their own lives, and exploring the elements of narration to improve their own writing.

From a collection development perspective, memoirs are usually shelved as part of biography and autobiography collections, often without a distinguishing subject heading. This is a situation in which use of the category feature of at least one major online catalog, *Destiny*, will be very helpful. By creating a category for memoirs, you will be prepared to respond quickly to a teacher's request for memoirs for the classroom. Also, remember to check nonfiction and reference titles for short memoirs. Examples include *The Portable Harlem Renaissance Reader*, Viking, 1994; *Voices of the Holocaust*, UXL, 1997; and *Growing Up Latino: Memoirs and Stories*, Houghton Mifflin, 1993.

Activities for Biographies

To encourage students to move beyond typical book reports, check out the lessons in the READS Explore section or try one of these ideas:

- Have students work in pairs to choose two individuals from the same historical period, career field, geographical area, and so on, as appropriate. After completing research independently, have students compare and contrast the individuals in visuals and an oral presentation.
- Direct students to consider the impact of the biographee's contribution to another person living during the same time period (Fontichiaro, 2009).
- Assign students to conduct an interview with the person in the style of a self-selected television host of today, working with another class member. and
- Assign students researching a person from the past to create a cultural profile for the biographee, including place, economic class, time period, and so on and answer the

question "Would this person make a significant contribution in today's world? Why or why not?"

In addition to supporting classroom activities by providing texts, school librarians may choose to work with memoirs in other ways. Selections from memoirs make compelling read-alouds, which could be used to introduce the genre or as an opening for a research project. If used as a genre study, the personal nature of memoirs stimulates discussion among students. In *Thinking through Genre: Units of Study in Reading and Writing Workshops, Grades 4–12*, Heather Lattimer (2003) recommends questions to stimulate thinking by students:

- What is happening in the memoir: how does the author feel about what is happening?
- Have you experienced similar emotions or reactions? How does your connection help you to better understand the memoir?
- What did the author learn from his/her experience? About himself or herself? Other people? The world?
- Reflect on your connection. Does the author's learning apply to your own experience?
- Do you agree with the conclusions that the author came to? Why or why not? (p. 28)

Drama

Projects with dramatic works offer the potential for significant engagement for both actors and audiences. For schools with dramatic arts programs, this genre takes a more prominent place than in most secondary schools, as few materials for middle school and high schools are published. From a collection development perspective, classical plays and collections of short selections for tryouts in dramatic productions in the school and community theater are appropriate. These resources may also be of interest to teachers wanting to incorporate drama into their curriculum. Recent titles include: *Comedy Scenes for Student Actors: Short Sketches for Young Performers* by Laurie Allen (2009); *Actor's Choice: Monologues for Teens* (2008); and *More Short Scenes and Monologues for Middle School Students: Inspired by Literature, Social Studies, and Real Life* by Mary Hall Surface (2007). Full-length plays written especially for teens are featured in this title for high schools: *Fierce & True: Plays for Teen Audiences* (2010), commissioned by the Children's Theatre Company in Minneapolis, Minnesota. A title appropriate for all secondary schools is *Acting Out: Six one-act Plays! Six Newbery Stars!* (2008). This is an especially intriguing title, as each of these outstanding authors (Patricia MacLachlan, Sharon Creech, Katherine Paterson, Susan Cooper, Richard Peck, and Avi) started with a single word to create a play.

Another approach to drama is the use of reader's theatre in library programs and classrooms. A recent title in this area is *Readers Theatre for Middle School Boys: Investigating the Strange and Mysterious* by Ann N. Black (2008). Also, see the bibliography of Readers' Theatre resources in the Analyze section of this book. Even better, have your students (or yourself) create the scripts from fiction or nonfiction titles for a more complex experience with drama. In many books, the dialogue in the book works as a script. Middle school teacher and *Book Links* columnist Dean Schneider (2010) highly recommends this process, describing his work with two novels by Walter Dean Myers that are, in fact, written as scripts, *Monster* (1999) and *Riot* (2009), and therefore ideal for readers' theatre activities. "I keep readers' theater casual, simply putting desks in a big oval, taking volunteers (or selecting students I think would be especially good for certain roles), reading through the text, and stopping often to discuss the story" (p. 22), Scheider (2010) writes. Other works that Scheider suggests for dramatic activities include *Acting Out: Six One-Out Plays! Six Newbery Stars; Day of Tears* by Julius Lester; and *Bat 6* by Virginia Euwer Wolff.

The school librarian's role with drama will range from collection development and supporting teachers with resources, collaborating with teachers in working together with dramatic activities, teaching literature if working with classes independent of teachers, to reading promotion if developing dramatic activities for school-wide celebrations.

Picture Books

Picture books in secondary classrooms? How can you justify this for older students? Let's count the ways! First, a definition is in order. Picture books are those books in which a story is told in images or in an interaction between text and images or a topic is explored using images or a combination of text and images. In other words, picture books may be fiction or nonfiction, wordless or a combination of text and images. They vary from simple stories or concept books for young children to sophisticated works with multiple layers of meaning. Picture books can be used in secondary schools for pleasurable moments, to teach and practice literary craft and reading concepts, and to provide examples of content area knowledge. The challenge to educators in secondary schools is to capture the attention of students; picture books automatically bring a smile to the faces of most students. The combination of visuals and text in picture books also tends to create an emotional response to the story or topic. Burke and Peterson (2007) explain, "Drawing on their extensive visual knowledge, readers have the potential to gain a deeper sensitivity to the character's emotions and intentions, and greater insight into the issues and struggles portrayed in the books, than may be possible when reading the text alone" (p. 74). In addition to these sound reasons, picture books are short, allowing a read-aloud session and discussion or activity in a single class period.

Picture books are categorized in various ways by their illustrations, text, or physical parts. Concept books explore different aspects of an idea, object, or group of objects, which could be the alphabet, color, size, vegetables, love, or money. Toy and movable books have moving parts, which can be quite sophisticated and engaging (e.g., medieval castles and mythological gods). Wordless books depend completely on the illustrations to convey a story, which work well for writing activities. Most books are in the picture storybook category, in which the text and illustrations function interdependently to convey a fiction story or folklore selection. All of the fiction genres are represented in picture books, creating many opportunities for integrating them into library, language arts, and content area programs. Nonfiction picture books are another large category with many uses in secondary schools.

The form of picture books has been influenced by the new ways of displaying, interpreting, and using ideas and information that are part of the digital age, contributing to increasingly sophisticated books. A groundbreaking title is David Macaulay's *Black and White* (1990), which has been described as a postmodern picture book. This book features four stories in one, with visuals on each double page spread divided into four parts, each with its own illustrative style. After finishing the book, a reader begins to recognize how the stories fit together. To make sense of this book, a reader uses advanced interpretative techniques and skills, which have been described as new literacies or multiliteracies (Anstey, 2002). A single reading of such texts is usually not sufficient; readers may need to move back and forth in a nonlinear fashion to process the interactions of the story lines and illustrations.

Picture books meet the needs of all adolescent learners, including struggling, special education, and second language learners (for accessible, vocabulary rich material). Kimberly Hill Campbell (2007), a language arts teacher, believes "Reconnecting students with the literature of their childhood allows them to reconnect with why they like to read" (p. 176). Through examples of how to use picture books in secondary schools, further advantages of this literary form will be evident.

- Use a picture book at the beginning of a semester to create a literate environment in the room, to reveal to students your pleasure in books, and to model fluent reading. Campbell (2007) suggests, "letting students know that the purpose in reading this book is to take them back to their earlier memories of elementary school. Our task will be to listen to the story and then list memories of school that come to mind through the use of the writing prompt 'I remember'" (p. 187). Before a holiday, when students are restless, is another excellent time for a picture book reading. When students are tired, perhaps after half a day of intensive testing, picture book sessions can break the tension and provide a relaxing yet beneficial experience. See the Picture Books for Secondary Students list for titles on the Reads Resources wiki (http://readsresources.wikispaces.com/).

- Introduce literary elements with picture books, selecting titles with outstanding characters, plots, settings, or dialogue as appropriate. After modeling the literary element through a real-aloud, students can work with other titles in pairs or groups to practice the skill. A picture book can also serve as a mentoring text to prepare students for their own writing. Students working with one book in a pair or group can prepare character or setting descriptions to be used with specific pages from their book, then meet with another group to exchange their book projects. Another option would be to describe a character using a Venn diagram or other graphic organizer to share with others.

- When teaching theme, read a picture book aloud and guide students in discovering the meaning of the work. As a follow-up, students can work in pairs or groups with another picture book title to apply the process of determining theme. An alternative would be to provide a group of students with various books on the same or similar theme. Each student could read the book and record their thinking on the theme. After at least two students read and determine the theme of each book, the group members could discuss their thinking and compare the development of the theme in each book. Another option is for students to work in pairs on a book to prepare anticipation guides to be used before and after reading a book. See the anticipation guides links in READS Lessons and Activities under Explore—Genre.

- Collaboratively plan with a science or social studies teacher to bring students to the library (or school librarian will go to the classroom) to use picture books on a classroom topic. Pairs of students will read the book and prepare anticipation guides to be used by others before and after reading a book. On subsequent days, students will continue learning about the topic by using the anticipation guides and reading the books.

- Provide picture book biographies of individuals (or a combination of picture books and collective biographies with short, illustrated profiles) to students. Assign students to read the biographical selection and create a biographical poem using these directions: http://www.readwritethink.org/files/resources/lesson_images/lesson398/biopoem.pdf.

- In response to teacher request, provide text sets of resources including picture books on topics being studied for use in the library classroom. Offer to co-teach reader response strategies for the art and texts of the picture books, such as creating a reader's theatre presentation based on a book, literature circle discussions on the theme or the relationship of the book to the curriculum topic, or the styles of art used in the books.

- Promote the use of picture books and novels at departmental meetings by creating a sample reading ladder (Lesesne, 2010) on genres or other topics of interest to the group. Discuss the various reading and interest levels and gradual increase of text complexity of books selected for the ladder. Offer to create custom reading ladders with teachers.

Magazines and Newspapers

Many students enter the library and head straight for the magazine section. Maybe it is the brevity of each issue that appeals to them. Some students find their personal interests covered in the colorful pages of *Transworld Skateboarding*, *Cycle World*, *Florida Sportsman*, or *Seventeen*. Others find their cultural heritage validated in *Jet* or *Latina*. Certain teens follow their academic interests in *Science World* or *Scientific American*. Newspapers attract the most attention the morning after an important sporting events or when the school is featured in the news coverage.

While many school and public librarians have reported that young people like magazines through the years, in 2006 Sandra Hughes-Hassell conducted a research study in an urban middle school that produced data on the preference of students for magazines as their favorite leisure reading. More than 700 students in this low-income middle school located in a large northeastern U.S. city completed the survey consisting of 16 multiple choice and 4 open-ended questions. Both males (68%) and females (76%) picked magazines as their top leisure reading choice (Hughes-Hassell & Rodge, 2007). Among the appeals of magazines for these adolescents are the many quality pictures, the reading level, and the ease of gaining information, according to Hughes-Hassell and Rodge (2007). A question emerging from this research is which specific magazines are preferred by this group of adolescents. In another article on this leisure reading study in *School Library Media Activities Monthly*, Hughes-Hassell and Cox (2008) comment on the magazine titles preferred by these teens, "The surveys show . . . that many urban teens read magazines that have not been part of [a] traditional periodicals collection such as *Black Beat*, *Latina*, *Low Rider*, *Sister to Sister*, *Slam*, *Urban Latino*, and *Word Up*. Not all of these titles have an obvious or immediate connection to curriculum, but they are a vital part of the literacy support system" (pp. 56–57).

Since many periodicals are now available free online, some school librarians are rethinking the purchase of print subscriptions. Some magazines have the identical content available free online while others have only print subscription information online (e.g., the educational journals from Carus: *Calliope*, *Cobblestone*, *Faces*, *Cricket*, *Dig*, *Muse*, and *Cicada*). The determining factors in purchasing print magazines and newspapers are the purposes of a periodical collection and local conditions including the budget available, educational programs offered in the school and teachers' use of the collection. Purposes of providing a print periodical collection are:

- Magazine articles are short, current, and often accompanied by colorful and appealing illustrations including charts and graphs.
- Newspapers offer current news and feature coverage of news events at local, national, and international levels.
- Students can find current reading material on topics of personal interest.
- Some magazines and newspapers are available free online while others require subscriptions for online use (e.g., *The New York Times* and *U.S.A. Today*).
- Reading local newspapers provides a link to the community and encourages voting and other participation in civic activities.

- Periodical articles are often used as selections on standardized tests and provide excellent practice with reading and content area skills.
- Periodical collections bring many students and teachers into libraries.
- Teachers and students benefit by having older magazine volumes in classrooms.
- Developing a habit of reading periodicals is a valuable lifelong reading skill.

Magazines for Middle Schools		Magazines for Senior High Schools
World History and News		
Calliope: http://www.cobblestonepub.com/magazine/CA		Cicada: http://www.cobblestonepub.com/magazine/CIC
Time for Kids: http://www.timeforkids.com/TFK/kids		Smithsonian: http://www.smithsonianmag.com/
		Time: http://www.time.com/time/
United States History		
Cobblestone: http://www.cobblestonepub.com		Consumer Reports: http://www.consumerreports.org/cro/a-to-z-index/products/index.htm
World Cultures		
Faces: http://www.cobblestonepub.com/magazine/FAC/		Discover: http://discovermagazine.com/
Teen Culture		
Girls' Life: http://www.girlslife.com		Ebony: http://www.ebonyjet.com/
		Seventeen: http://www.seventeen.com/
		Slam: http://www.slamonline.com/
		Tiger Beat: http://www.bopandtigerbeat.com/
		Teen Ink: http://www.teenink.com/
		Teen Voices: http://www.teenvoices.com
		Word Up: http://www.wordupmag.com/
African American Interests		
Jet		Jet
Hispanic Interests		
Latina: http://www.latina.com/		Latina: http://www.latina.com/
Science, Art, History		
Muse: http://www.cobblestonepub.com/magazine/MUS/		Mad: http://www.dccomics.com/mad/

Magazines for Middle Schools		Magazines for Senior High Schools	
World History and News			
Science			
National Wildlife Federation		P.C. World: http://www.pcworld.com/	
Popular Science: http://www.popsci.com/		Popular Mechanics: http://popularmechanics.com	
Science World		Popular Science: http://www.popsci.com/	
		Scientific American: http://www.scientificamerican.com/	
Sports			
Sports Illustrated for Kids: http://www.sikids.com/		Sports Illustrated: http://sportsillustrated.cnn.com/	
Transworld Skateboarding: http://skateboarding.transworld.net/		Transworld Skateboarding: http://skateboarding.transworld.net/	

For these reasons, print periodical collections are still needed in school libraries, depending on local conditions and usage patterns. The policy of keeping back volumes of magazines for one year and then offering them to teachers is a rewarding practice. At the middle school and high school levels, it brings teachers into the library and opens doors to future collaborative teaching projects. An exception to this policy can be made for the excellent curriculum magazines from Carus Publishing because the content often matches curriculum objects and is not available online. Keep them in the library and occasionally lend them out for classroom use. Choose a mix of titles appealing to students and matching general curriculum needs for middle and high schools. These lists are not expansive because library budgets are currently lean across the country and many titles are available online. School librarians will want to select titles to match the interests of students and staff and to meet the needs of the local curriculum. The web address for titles is included where appropriate.

Take a look at two lessons using periodicals. They are in the READS Lessons and Activity list under the subheading of nonfiction—Magazine Redux: An Exercise in Critical Literacy from The Learning Network of *The New York Times* and That's a Wrap! News Reporting Using Online Periodicals, from *School Library Monthly*.

Sources used in compiling the lists of periodical titles are Cole (2009), Hochadel (2010), Lattimer (2003), and Webber (2009).

Graphic Literature

With this literary form, we may have students in our schools with more knowledge about the books than we have ourselves! Many secondary students are big fans of graphic novels and could very well serve as advisers on collection development, after you set out the guidelines for appropriateness for your school communities. With roots in comic books of the past, this form is now recognized as a viable choice for use in school classrooms. Michele Gorman (2003) describes graphic novels as "award-winning, creative works that have as much literary merit as they do artistic credence" (p. 136). Significant events in the acceptance of graphic novels in the literature mainstream occurred when Art Spiegelman's *Maus* earned a special Pulitzer Prize in 1986, followed by a Caldecott Honor Book Award in 2007 for *The Wall: Growing Up Behind the Iron Curtain* by Peter Sis, and the Printz Award in 2008 for *American Born Chinese* by Gene Luen Yang. Beginning in 2007, YALSA issues an annual list of Great Graphic Novels for Teens. Note the use of the term "form" when discussing graphic literature. This is not a separate genre of literature, but an alternative form, similar in this respect to picture books. Graphic literature is available in a range of fiction and nonfiction genres, providing a great way for librarians to promote other works to students who prefer only graphic novels (e.g., if you like _____ type of graphic novels, then try _____ novels). From the other perspective, guide readers who prefer traditional books to graphic novels by suggesting titles in their favorite genres.

Activities with graphic novels can begin with an informative display, bulletin board, or booktalk presentation covering the various types of graphic literature. Though the most frequently used term is graphic novels, it is somewhat problematic in that it implies all examples are fiction, which is not the case. Students may be familiar with only their favored types, such as manga or superheroes. Other activities include:

- Develop and implement a presentation called Graphics Galore, covering comic books, newspaper cartoons, political cartoons, graphic novels and nonfiction, manga, and hybrid products. Provide students and teachers with a list/pathfinder of websites for each type of graphic literature. Bring in a technology teacher, if appropriate, to work with students in creating a graphic project, using the Comic Life software or websites. (Use Lamb and Johnson, 2010, Parts 1 and 2, for ideas and websites.)
- Consult with department heads and teachers about expanding the graphic literature collection in the library. Show reviews and articles on outstanding titles including classics.

Multiplatform Works

An example of evolving reading experiences made possible by the features of the Internet is the creation of multiplatform or transmedia products, combining hand-held books with web-based elements including videos, gaming options, reader response opportunities, and more. Lamb and Johnson (2010) explain, "In transmedia storytelling, integral elements of the story are told through different media and each media type provides distinct contributions to the participant's understanding of the story" (p. 64). Examples of such mixed media products include *The 39 Clues* series (2008) and *Skelton Creek* (2009) by Scholastic, *The Amanda Project* series (2009) by HarperTeen, and the *Cathy Vickers* trilogy (2006) by Running Press. In these products, story lines may begin in the book and/or audiobook and expand in a virtual game or video, providing an engaging experience for learners. Groenke and Maples (2010) recommend that teachers consider these new products because "young adult digi-novels may provide opportunities for teachers to transform the use of literature in English classrooms in such a way that adolescents will see relevance between the classroom, the technological world they inhabit, and their literacy futures" (p. 43). Teachers and school librarians are developing various ways of using these products in schools, ranging from read-alouds before online activities to use in independent literacy work stations.

WORKING WITH THEMES

As we consider strategies to guide students in exploring literature and forging connections to their own lives, the identification of theme in a book or other media can offer a thoughtful and unifying approach to deriving meaning from what is read, heard, and/or viewed. Theme is the message or abstract concept that remains with a reader after completing a book. Various readers may reach different conclusions about the meaning of a story, based on their own life experiences. After thinking through the story elements of character, plot, conflict, resolution, and setting, readers make inferences combining evidence in the

READS Component	READS Indicator	AASL *Standards for the 21st-Century Learner**	Common Core State Standards—English Language Arts**
2. Explore characteristics, history, and awards of creative works			
The student will:			
2.1 Identify and critically analyze literary and media genres and themes.	2.1.2 Analyze universal themes in text, visual, and digital resources (e.g., alienation from society).	• 2.3.2 Consider diverse and global perspectives in drawing conclusions. • 3.3.2 Respect the differing interests and experiences of others, and seek a variety of viewpoints. • 4.1.2 Read widely and fluently to make connections with self, the world, and previous reading. • 4.1.3 Respond to literature and creative expressions of ideas in various formats and genres. • 4.1.5 Connect ideas to own interests and previous knowledge and experience. • 4.2.2 Demonstrate motivation by seeking information to answer personal questions and interests . . . • 4.2.4 Show an appreciation for literature . . .	• Reading: Literature—6 Analyze a case in which grasping point of view requires distinguishing what is directly stated in a text from what is really meant . . . • Reading: Literature—7 Analyze multiple interpretations of a story, drama, or poem . . . • Reading: Literature—9 Demonstrate knowledge of foundational works of American literature . . . • Speaking and Listening—1c Initiate and participate effectively in a range of collaborative discussions: Propel conversations by posing and responding to questions . . . • Writing—9 Draw evidence from literary or informational texts to support analysis . . .

*Excerpted from *Standards for the 21st-Century Learner* by the American Association of School Librarians, a division of the American Library Association, copyright © 2007 American Library Association. Available for download at www.ala.org/aasl/standards. Used with permission.

**Excerpted from *Common Core State Standards for English Language Arts*. National Governors Association Center for Best Practices and Council of Chief State School Officers Commercial License. Copyright © 2010. Used with permission of NGA Center/CCSSO.

text and their personal background knowledge to reach a conclusion about the central idea or ideas of the book (Lesesne, 2003; Moreillon, 2007).

For her middle school students, Campbell (2007) describes theme as the "so what" of the story, the message. But one could argue that theme is more than just the message. It is the "why" readers read. Although I hope my students will be engaged, even entertained, as they read, I want them to see how stories help them understand their own lives and the world . . . how this message or theme reflects larger themes or messages (p. 52).

While themes are usually expressed as universal truths about humanity and life, certain themes may be more relevant to the lives of young people. Through the selection of novels with relatable themes for use in classrooms, educators can improve students' experiences with literature. Teri Lesesne (2003) explains,

> When evaluating the theme of a story, it is important to consider several questions: Is the theme of substance/value to the reader? Is the theme delivered in such a way as to avoid being didactic? Are multiple themes possible and accessible to the reader? The very best [books] that YA literature has to offer . . . present themes applicable to reader's own lives. (p. 61)

Examples of themes identified by Lesesne as appealing to young people are "love conquers all," "power corrupts," "exploration of the inner self," "you can't judge a book by its cover," "betrayal," and "sometimes bad things happen to good people."

The identification of theme in literary selections is a required reading and writing skill on standardized tests in many states and can present a significant challenge for struggling readers and ELL students. Judi Moreillon (2007) recommends that school librarians and teachers begin with recalling familiar stories or fables and guide students in brainstorming possible themes with students. In the advanced lesson titled "Making Predictions and Inferences" from her book *Collaborative Strategies for Teaching Reading Comprehension* (2007), she suggests the use of an anticipation guide providing possible themes to assist students learning to identify theme. An example of an anticipation guide she created for the picture book *Freedom Summer* is available online: http://www.ala.org/ala/aboutala/offices/publishing/editions/webextras/moreillon09294/moreillon_supplement6j.doc. She also includes an "Evidence-Background Knowledge-Inference Category Matrix" as well as an example at this site.

Detailed information about the processes involved in interpretive reading and analytical writing, which are required to master test items on theme, is provided by Olson, Land, Anselmi, and AuBuchon in the December 2010/January 2011 issue of the *Journal of Adolescent & Adult Literacy*. These academic researchers at the University of California, Irvine, partnered with a local school district to address the academic needs of ELL students in a professional development effort and research study called the Pathway Project. These students are required to identify, analyze, and interpret theme in the California High School Exit Exam. These researchers provide valuable insights for use by school librarians and teachers on the cognitive strategies required in identifying and expressing theme, including cognitive strategic sentence starters. For example, the recommended sentence starters for forming interpretations are: "What this means to me is . . .; I think this represents . . .; or The idea I'm getting is . . ." (p. 251). The use of short stories for interpretation is recommended by these researchers, so that students can concentrate on interpretation and writing skills. A school librarian could use these sentence starters and other strategies recommended in the article with classes in the library or could recommend them to teachers in collaborative planning sessions. Another role for a librarian is to locate engaging short stories to be used with identifying theme. This article is highly recommended to librarians and teachers for the valuable academic strategies that are essential for all students.

Depending on the individual literacy needs of students in each class, teachers designing instructional sequences may choose to have students work in small groups, with materials on the same theme to encourage participation by all. The collection of works on various reading levels may include novels, poetry, films, nonfiction, or graphic novels. The unit often begins with a shorter and more accessible selection, such as a picture book, short story, film clip, song, or article before moving on to more complex works.

Richison, Hernandez, and Carter (2002) provide rationales for using what they call a "theme basket" process in secondary schools. The combination of resources on the same theme, including picture books, beginning and mid-level chapter books, young adult novels, required classics, nonfiction, popular texts like songs and raps, nonfiction, websites, and others, offer appeal to all

> **Bib in a Box**
>
> **Theme: Transforming Value of Culture**
>
> Abdel-Fattah, R. (2005). *Does my head look big in this?* [Realistic Fiction] New York: Orchard Books Audiobook.
>
> Hesse, K. (2003). *Aleutian sparrow.* [Historical Fiction] New York: Margaret K. McElderry Books.
>
> Park, I. S. (2002). *When my name was Keoko.* [Historical Fiction] New York: Clarion Audiobook/e-Book.
>
> Polak, M. (2009). *The middle of everywhere.* [Realistic Fiction] Custer, WA: Orca.
>
> Pratchett, R. (2008). *Nation.* [Historical Fiction] New York: HarperCollins Audiobook/e-Book.
>
> Sullivan, P. (2003). *Maata's journal: A novel.* [Historical Fiction] New York: Atheneum Books for Young Readers.
>
> Veciana-Suarez, A. (2002). *Flight to freedom.* [Realistic Fiction] New York: Orchard.

students and multiple pathways to the intended meanings of authors and creators. By encouraging visual imagery of the various texts, teachers provide access to all students, whatever their reading level. The authors of this article discuss how the theme basket approach allows the use of a variety of activities and assessment tools addressing the multiple intelligences of individuals and cite the work of Howard Gardner in describing this theory of human capacities. Richison et al. (2002) summarize the benefits of a theme basket approach combined with instruction on visualizing and expressing responses to literature in multiple ways:

> *Including multigenre selections in the supplemental literature assists those less proficient readers in accessing the ideas and themes we expect all students in our classes to understand. Theme baskets also provide a natural progression to the themes and issues in more sophisticated adult literature, and young readers are able to bridge that gap, thus enabling them to actually enjoy their reading as more mature readers. (p. 81)*

Schools librarians are perfect partners to teachers in assembling a rich array of resources for such thematic units. In addition to gathering resources, librarians may participate as discussion leaders in a co-teaching role to provide appropriate differentiated learning experiences for students. When planning these discussions, refer to the list of questions offered by Kylene Beers (2003) in her book, *When Kids Can't Read, What Teachers Can Do.*

The process of gathering resources on a single theme may be an enjoyable experience or it can be a challenge for librarians, depending on how the theme is expressed. The term theme is used in a variety of ways by educators, often denoting the topic of a curriculum. A teacher may refer to a curricular theme of the Holocaust or the history of a state. Since the theme of a literary work is defined as "the writer's message or main idea . . . what

Bib in a Box

Theme: Alienation from Society

Anderson, L. H. (1999). *Speak.* [Realistic Fiction/Audiobook/e-Book] New York: Farrar, Straus, Giroux.

Camus, A. (1993). *The stranger.* [Realistic Fiction/Audiobook] New York: Knopf.

Gallo, D. R. (2001). *On the fringe.* [Short Stories] New York: Dial.

The outsiders. (2008). Directed by F. Coppola. [Nonprint/DVD] Burbank, CA: Warner Home Video.

Picoult, J. (2007). *Nineteen minutes.* [Realistic Fiction] New York: Atria.

Satraphi, M. (2004). *Persepolis 2.* [Memoir/Graphic Novel] New York: Pantheon.

Wright, R. (2008, c1993). *The outsider.* [Realistic Fiction] New York: Harper Perennial.

Bib in a Box

Theme: Ability of Human Experience to Rise above Grief and Loss

Belton, S. (2006). *Store bought baby.* [Realistic Fiction] New York: Greenwillow.

Bingham, Kelly. (2007). *Shark girl.* [Realistic Fiction] Cambridge, MA: Candlewick. e-Book

Hoffman, A. (2003). *Green angel.* [Fantasy] New York: Scholastic.

Howe, J. (Ed.) (2001). *The color of absence: 12 stories about loss and hope.* [Short Stories] New York: Atheneum.

Kor, E. M., & Rojany, L. (2010). *Surviving the angel of death: The story of a Mengele twin in Auschwitz.* [Biography] Terre Haute, IN: Tanglewood.

Myers, E. (2004). *When will I stop hurting?: Teens, loss, and grief.* [Nonfiction] Lanham, MD: Scarecrow.

Naik, A. (2009). *Coping with loss: The life changes handbook.* [Nonfiction] New York: Crabtree.

Rabb, M. (2007). *Cures for heartbreak.* [Realistic Fiction] New York: Delacorte.

Turner, A. (2006). *Hard hit.* [Realistic Fiction] New York: Scholastic.

the writer wants you to remember most" (Olson et al., 2011), all readers may not express a theme in identical language. The expression of a theme may vary by an individual's background knowledge, previous instruction, experience with reading literature, or personal point of view. When planning a unit of instruction with teachers or discussing a request for resources, an essential task is developing a clear understanding of how the teacher interprets the theme selected and plans to use the materials in the classroom. Some expressions of a theme are single words with others formed as phrases or brief statements. For example, the theme of family is common; it is expressed as a single word by Grimes (2006); as a statement "When you're family, you take care of your own" by Olson et al. (2011); or as "importance of family and home," "family isolation," or "family values" by Herz and Gallo (2005) in various books. Often a theme is more abstract and is expressed in different ways. For example, Moreillon (2007) provides a one sentence theme for the topic of perseverance: "No matter how difficult your life seems, never give up trying to improve your situation" (p. 83). Herz and Gallo (2005) offer "survival of the fittest" or "overcoming odds" on the same theme and Teri Lesesne (2010) suggests "sometimes bad things happen to good people."

Locating materials on a theme depends on the term itself. For example, some themes are standard subject headings (e.g., good vs. evil—fiction). Others have to be researched as keywords in catalogs or online sources (e.g., betrayal, alienation, abuse of power). For the most useful online sources for themes, search through reviews of books as well as descriptions including the *Wilson Core Collections* online, and the *Children's Literature Comprehensive Database*, both subscription services. If these sources are not available in your school, try the public library or local colleges and universities. A particularly helpful professional journal is *Book Links*, which specializes in curricular uses of books. A direct search of *Book Links* using the ProQuest database has been most productive (e.g., click on *Book Links* in the list of publications tab). Other free online sources for locating books are listed on our READS Internet Resources under the Read as a Personal Activity section. Traditional print sources for locating titles on topics are sometimes helpful in theme searches: *Best Books for Middle School and Junior High School Readers* (2009) and *Best Books for High School Readers* (2009). Herz and Gallo's *From Hinton to Hamlet: Building Bridges between Young Adult Literature and the Classics* (2005) is also useful for locating titles on certain themes. Of course, a well-read school librarian is the best source, supported by colleagues and online groups such as LM_NET. Usually, at least once each day, someone will ask for assistance locating materials on a theme or topic on LM_NET. Throughout this section of Chapter 5, brief bibliographies are included on theme examples in the READS curriculum.

Another application of the theme searching approach is to involve students in exploring a single theme across multiple genres and forms, which can encourage understanding from a variety of perspectives (Kettel & Douglas, 2003). Prepare students for the assignment by creating displays of materials on a single theme. Provide a think-aloud on the process of gathering various sources on a theme, including a discussion of search strategies including standard subject headings, the use of keywords in searching, and the use of specialized tools for locating theme materials. Tweens and teens will be especially skilled at finding songs to add to theme lists!

Frequently, students are provided opportunities to respond to the literary works individually or in groups by sharing themes on sentence strips or posters, by creating symbols or collages to represent the theme, or by creating a theme in bottle (Van Zile, 2001). Jago (2004) suggests allowing students to choose three literary selections such as poems and complete a Goldilocks assignment. Students will write an essay in which they categorize one selection as too easy, one as too hard, and one as just right. For the just right selection, the theme will be discussed in the essay.

Other opportunities for school librarians to work with theme with students include organizing booktalks or book discussion groups by theme, providing a themed list of new ma-

---

Bib in a Box

Theme: Good vs. Evil (Sixth Grade)

Chabon, M. (2002). *Summerland.* [Fantasy/e-Book/Audiobook] New York: Hyperion.

Colfer, E. (2003). *The wish list.* [Fantasy/e-Book] New York: Hyperion.

Delaney, J. (2008). *Attack of the fiend.* [Fantasy/e-Book/Audiobook] New York: Greenwillow.

Grant, M. (2008). *Gone.* [Supernatural] New York: Hyperion..

Jacques, B. (1997). *Pearls of Lutra.* [Fantasy] New York: Philomel.

Pullman, P. (1998). *Clockwork, or all wound up.* [Fantasy] New York: Scholastic.

Singer, I. S. (1996). *The topsy-turvy emperor of China.* [Folklore/Audiobook] Prince Frederick, MD: Recorded Books.

Stevenson, R. L. (2009). *The strange case of Dr. Jekyll and Mr. Hyde.* [Horror/Graphic Novel] Mankato, MN: Stone Arch Books.

Bib in a Box

Theme: Good vs. Evil (Seventh Grade)

Almond, D. (2008). *Clay.* [Science Fiction/e-Book] New York: Random House.

Clare, C. (2009). *City of bones.* [Fantasy/e-Book/Audiobook] New York: Walker.

Eisner, W. (Adapter). (2003). *Sundiata: A legend of Africa.* [Legend/Graphic Novel] New York: NBM.

Funke, C. (2003). *Inkheart.* [Fantasy/-Book/Audiobook/DVD] New York: Scholastic.

Horowitz, A. (2005). *Raven's gate.* [Fantasy/Audiobook] New York: Scholastic.

Jinks, C. (2005). *Evil genius.* [Science Fiction] Orlando, FL: Harcourt.

Langrish, K. (2010). *The shadow hunt.* [Fantasy] New York: HarperCollins.

Rowling, J. K. (1998). *Harry Potter and the sorcerer's stone.* [Fantasy/DVD/Audiobook] New York: Scholastic.

Bib in a Box

Theme: Man vs. Nature (Sixth Grade)

Butts, E. (2007). *SOS: Stories of survival.* [Short Stories] Toronto: Tundra Books.

Hiaasen, C. (2005). *Flush.* [Realistic Fiction/ e-Book/Audiobook] New York: Knopf.

Hobbs, W. (2002*). Wild man island.* [Realistic Fiction/e-Book/Audiobook] New York: HarperCollins.

Jordon, R. (2008). *The last wild place.* [Realistic Fiction] Atlanta, GA: Peachtree.

Philbrick, W. R. (2004). *The young man and the sea.* [Realistic Fiction] New York: Scholastic.

Stuff happens with Bill Nye: Backyard. (2009). [Nonprint/DVD] Discovery Education.

Taylor, T. (2004). *Ice drift.* [Realistic Fiction] San Diego, CA: Harcourt.

Van Draanen, W. (2007). *Sammy Keys and the wild things.* [Realistic Fiction/e-Book/Audiobook] New York: Knopf.

Bib in a Box

Theme: Man vs. Nature (Seventh Grade)

Collard, S. B. (2006). *Flash point.* [Realistic Fiction] Atlanta, GA: Peachtree.

Hiaasen, C. (2002). *Hoot.* [Realistic Fiction/ e-Book/DVD] New York: Knopf.

Hobbs, W. (2011). *Take me to the river.* [Realistic Fiction/e-Book] New York: HarperCollins.

Hokenson, T. (2006). *The winter road.* [Realistic Fiction/e-Book] Asheville, NC: Front St.

Kaye, B. (2010). *Going blue: A teen's guide to saving our oceans & waterways.* [Nonfiction] Minneapolis, MN: Free Spirit Press.

Paulsen, G, (2006/1988). *The island.* [Realistic Fiction/Audiobook] New York: Scholastic.

Smith, R. (2007). *Peak.* [Realistic Fiction/ e-Book/Audiobook] Orlando, FL: Harcourt.

Vaupel, R. (2003). *My contract with Henry.* [Realistic Fiction] New York: Holiday House.

terials for teachers in a newsletter or in-service session, or creating reading ladders (Lesesne, 2010) of resources on teacher request. Lesesne (2010) defines reading ladders as "a series or set of books that are related in some way (e.g., thematically) and that demonstrate a slow gradual development from simple to more complex" (p. 48). These sets of titles may include a single type of book (e.g., horror fiction) on different levels or various genre and media on many topics or themes.

READS LESSONS AND ACTIVITIES

Explore Characteristics, History, and Awards of creative Works

Identify and Critically Analyze Literary and Media Genres and Themes

10 ways to use The New York Times for teaching literature. (Resource) By Katherine Schulten and Holly Epstein Ojalvo. The Learning Network: *The New York Times.* http://learning.blogs.nytimes.com/2010/08/06/10-ways-to-use-the-new-york-times-for-teaching-literature/?pagemode=print

Anticipation guide. http://www.greece.k12.ny.us/academics.cfm?subpage=935

Anticipation guide. (Resource) ReadWriteThink. (6–12) http://www.readwritethink.org/files/resources/lesson_images/lesson226/anticipation.pdf

Cover to cover: Comparing books to movies. By Sharon Roth. ReadWriteThink. (Gr. 6–8 up) http://www.readwritethink.org/classroom-resources/lesson-plans/cover-cover-comparing-books-1098.html

Get visual with genres. By Nancy Hobbs, Myra Oleynik, and Kristen Sacco. *School Library Monthly, 27* (6), 15–17. (Gr. 2–12)

Kid lit crit. By Annissa Hambouz and Yasmin Chin Eisenhauer. Includes article "Why Teachers Love Depressing Books." The Learning Network: *The New York Times.* (Gr. 6–12) http://learning.blogs.nytimes.com/2004/08/23/kid-lit-crit/

Literature's leaders. (Resource) Discusses use of fictional literary characters as leaders. Colorado Youth Leadership Network. (Gr. 6–12) http://www.youthleadership.com/literature.html

Podcast: Sampling short stories. (Resource) Includes lists of stories. ReadWriteThink. http://www.readwritethink.org/parent-afterschool-resources/podcast-episodes/sampling-short-stories-30590.html

Short story fair: Responding to short stories in multiple media and genres. By Patricia Schulze. ReadWrite Think. (Gr. 9–12) http://www.readwritethink.org/classroom-resources/lesson-plans/short-story-fair-responding-418.html

Unlocking the underlying symbolism and themes of a dramatic work. By Traci Gardner. Includes Inter active Drama Map. ReadWriteThink. (Gr. 9–12) http://www.readwritethink.org/classroom-resources/lesson-plans/unlocking-underlying-symbolism-themes-272.html

Genres

Biography

Animated museum of famous revolutionary war heroes. By Sydney Minter. (2007) Includes Five-Square Format worksheet. *School Library Media Activities Monthly, 23* (9), 15–17. (Gr. 4–8)

Biography project: Research and class presentation. By Loraine Woodard and Kathleen Benson Quinn. ReadWriteThink. (Gr. 6–8) http://www.readwritethink.org/classroom-resources/lesson-plans/biography-project-research-class-243.html

A biography study: Using role-play to explore author's lives. By Carol S. Anderson and Debra J. Cof fey. Includes Interactives ReadWriteThink Timeline Tool and K-W-L-S Chart. ReadWriteThink. (Gr. 9–12) http://www.readwritethink.org/classroom-resources/lesson-plans/biography-study-using-role-398.html

Guided comprehension in action: Teaching summarizing with the bio-cube. By Alexandria Gibb and Dani ella Bevilacqua. ReadWriteThink. (Gr. 6–8) http://www.readwritethink.org/classroom-resources/lesson-plans/guided-comprehension-action-teaching-1028.html

How to write a biopoem. (Resource) ReadWriteThink. (6–12) http://www.readwritethink.org/files/resources/lesson_images/lesson398/biopoem.pdf

Power pointing biographies. By Dawn Adams. (2007). *School Library Media Activities Monthly, 23* (9), 18–20. (Gr. 5 up)

What would Cleopatra do? Drawing lessons from history or literature. By Sarah Kavanagh and Holly Epstein Ojalvo. The Learning Network: *The New York Times* (Gr. 9–12) http://learning.blogs.nytimes.com/2010/12/07/what-would-cleopatra-do-drawing-lessons-from-history-or-lit erature/

Graphic Literature

Graphic novel/Comics terms and concepts. (Resource) ReadWriteThink. (Gr. 9–12) http://www.read writethink.org/files/resources/lesson_images/lesson1102/terms.pdf

Making it visual for ELL students: Teaching history using Maus. By Christian W. Chun and Martha At well. ReadWriteThink. (ESL Gr. 9–12) http://www.readwritethink.org/classroom-resources/lesson-plans/making-visual-students-teaching-1178.html

Pictures tell the story: Improving comprehension with Persepolis. By Janet M. Ankiel. Includes handout Graphic Novel/Comics Terms and Concepts. ReadWriteThink. (Gr. 9–12) http://www.read writethink.org/classroom-resources/lesson-plans/pictures-tell-story-improving-1102.html

That's the story of my life. By Holly Epstein Ojalvo. Includes storyboard form to create a graphic novel. The Learning Network: *The New York Times*. (Gr. 9–12) http://learning.blogs.nytimes.com/2008/11/13/thats-the-story-of-my-life/?pagemode=print

Historical Fiction

Looking for the history in historical fiction: An epidemic for reading. By Lisa Storm Fink. Includes Historical Fiction definition and Questions to Consider While Reading Historical Fiction. ReadWrite Think. (Gr. 3–5 up) http://www.readwritethink.org/classroom-resources/lesson-plans/looking-history-historical-fiction-404.html

Mixed Genres

Genre detectives (into the curriculum). By Katie Baynor. (2009). *School Library Monthly, 25* (2), 7–9. (Gr. 4 up)

Genre study: A collaborative approach. By Lisa Storm Fink. Includes Genre Characteristics and Mystery Bookmark. ReadWriteThink. (Gr. 3–5 up) http://www.readwritethink.org/classroom-resources/lesson-plans/genre-study-collaborative-approach-270.html

Imagine that! Playing with genre through newspapers and short stories. By Jacqueline Podolski. Includes Qualities of Newspaper Articles chart. ReadWriteThink. (Gr. 6–8) http://www.readwritethink.org/classroom-resources/lesson-plans/imagine-that-playing-with-311.html

Reading and analyzing multigenre texts. By Traci Gardner. ReadWriteThink. (Gr. 6–8) http://www.readwritethink.org/classroom-resources/lesson-plans/reading-analyzing-multigenre-texts-293.html?tab=1#tabs

Mystery

Everyone loves a mystery: A genre study. By Che-Mai Gray. Includes Words You Should Know and Mystery Cube interactive. ReadWriteThink. (Gr. 6–8 up) http://www.readwritethink.org/classroom-resources/lesson-plans/everyone-loves-mystery-genre-796.html

Investigating genre: The case of the classic detective story. By Scott Filkins. ReadWriteThink. (Gr. 9–12) http://www.readwritethink.org/classroom-resources/lesson-plans/investigating-genre-case-classic-30596.html

What's in a mystery? Exploring and identifying mystery elements. By Betsy Brindza. Includes Mystery Graphic Organizer. ReadWriteThink. (Gr. 3–5 up) http://www.readwritethink.org/classroom-resources/lesson-plans/what-mystery-exploring-identifying-865.html

"Who done it?" (into the curriculum). By Aimee Barham. (2009). *School Library Media Activities Monthly, 25* (4), 19–21. (Gr. 6 up)

Nonfiction

Beyond "what I did on vacation": Exploring the genre of travel writing. By Drew Schrader. Includes Elements of Good Travel Writing and Suggested Reading in the Travel Writing Genre. ReadWriteThink. (Gr. 9–12) http://www.readwritethink.org/classroom-resources/lesson-plans/beyond-what-vacation-exploring-1086.html

Connecting The New York Times to your world. (Resource) Tool for text to self, to text, and to world. The Learning Network: *The New York Times.* (Gr. 6–12) http://graphics8.nytimes.com/images/blogs/learning/pdf/activities/ConnectWorld_NYTLN.pdf

Fact/Question/Response. (Resource) Tool for analyzing nonfiction selection or news article. The Learning Network: *The New York Times.* (Gr. 6–12) http://graphics8.nytimes.com/images/blogs/learning/pdf/activities/FactQuestResponse_NYTLN.pdf

Identifying cause and effect. (Resource) Tool for locating cause and effect. The Learning Network: *The New York Times*. (Gr. 6–8) http://graphics8.nytimes.com/images/blogs/learning/pdf/activities/CauseEffect_NYTLN.pdf

Identifying nonfiction text structure. By Michael Stencil Sr. *School Library Monthly, 27* (6), 13–15. (Gr. 6–8).

K/W/L chart. (Resource) Tool for analyzing topic or news article. The Learning Network: *The New York Times*. (Gr. 6–12) http://graphics8.nytimes.com/images/blogs/learning/pdf/activities/KWL_NYTLN.pdf

Magazine redux: An exercise in critical literacy. By Valerie A. Stokes. Includes Online Magazine list. ReadWriteThink. (Gr. 9–12) http://www.readwritethink.org/classroom-resources/lesson-plans/magazine-redux-exercise-critical-214.html

Podcast: New and noteworthy nonfiction. (Resource) ReadWriteThink. (Gr. 6–12) http://www.readwritethink.org/parent-afterschool-resources/podcast-episodes/noteworthy-nonfiction-30755.html

Postcards. (Resource) Tool for creating a postcard to or from people in a newspaper article. The Learning Network: *The New York Times.* (Gr. 6–12) http://graphics8.nytimes.com/images/blogs/learning/pdf/activities/Postcards_NYTLN.pdf

Telling a Times story: Reinterpreting news through a storyboard. (Resource) The Learning Network: *The New York Times.* (Gr. 6–12) http://graphics8.nytimes.com/images/blogs/learning/pdf/activities/Storyboard_NYTLN.pdf

That's a wrap! News reporting using online periodicals. By Maureen Tannetta. (2011) *School Library Monthly, 27* (8) 15–16. (Gr. 5 up)

Using THIEVES to preview nonfiction texts. By Cynthia A. Lassonde. Includes The Elements of THIEVES. ReadWriteThink. (Gr. 6–8 up) http://www.readwritethink.org/classroom-resources/lesson-plans/using-thieves-preview-nonfiction-112.html

Viewing vocabulary: Building word knowledge through informational websites. Includes Vocabulary Prompts and Find the Word! Worksheets. By Hallie Kay Yopp and Ruth Helen Yopp. ReadWriteThink. (Gr. 6–8 up) http://www.readwritethink.org/classroom-resources/lesson-plans/viewing-vocabulary-building-word-1081.html

Poetry

Enhancing a poetry unit with American Memory. By Alison Westfall and Laura Mitchell. American Memory: The Learning Page. (Gr. 7–9) http://memory.loc.gov/learn/lessons/98/poetry/poem.html

Latino poetry blog: Blogging as a forum for open discussion. By Tiia Kunnapas. Includes Poetry Analysis Sheet. ReadWriteThink. (Gr. 8–12) http://www.readwritethink.org/classroom-resources/lesson-plans/latino-poetry-blog-blogging-1160.html

Musical poetry. By Elizabeth Ramos. Includes Poetic Devices handout. Scholastic. (Gr. 10–12) http://www2.scholastic.com/browse/lessonplan.jsp?id=159&FullBreadCrumb=%3Ca+href%3D%22http%3A%2F%2Fwww2.scholastic.com%2Fbrowse%2Fsearch%2F%3Fntx%3Dmode%2Bmatchallpartial%26_N%3Dfff%26Ntk%3DSCHL30_SI%26query%3Dmusical%2520poetry%26Nr%3DOR%28Resource_Type%3ALesson%2520Plan%2CResource_Type%3AInformal%2520Lesson%2520Article%2CResource_Type%3AUnit%2520Plan%29%26N%3D0%26Ntt%3Dmusical%2Bpoetry%22+class%3D%22endecaAll%22%3EAll+Results%3C%2Fa%3E

Pairing fiction with poetry and performance. By Susan Ruckdeschel. Includes Inquiry Questions Guide and Interactive Novel/Poem Compare and Contrast Frame ReadWriteThink. (Gr. 9–12) http://www.readwritethink.org/classroom-resources/lesson-plans/pairing-fiction-with-poetry-1001.html

Poetry pairings. (Resource) Includes weekly feature, *Poetry Pairings,* providing poems and other resources sometimes connected to current events or seasons. The Learning Network: *The New York Times.* (Gr. 6–12) http://learning.blogs.nytimes.com/

Visual interpretations of poetry. By Constance Vidor. *School Library Media Activities Monthly, 25* (8), 11. (Gr. 6–8)

Realistic Fiction

Finding comfort in books by using realistic fiction. By Sharon Hall. (2006). *School Library Media Activities Monthly, 22* (10), 13–15. (Gr. 6)

High-interest novel helps struggling readers confront bullying in schools. By Kathleen Benson. Features The Bully by Paul Langan. ReadWriteThink. (Gr. 8–12) http://www.readwritethink.org/classroom-resources/lesson-plans/high-interest-novel-helps-390.html?tab=1#tabs

Science Fiction

Dark materials: Reflecting on dystopian themes in young adult literature. By Annissa Hambouz and Katherine Schulten. The Learning Network: *The New York Times.* (Gr. 9–12) http://learning.blogs.nytimes.com/2011/01/06/dark-materials-reflecting-on-dystopian-themes-in-young-adult-literature/?pagemode=print

Dystopian Booktalks. By Terri Snethen and Abby Cornelius. *From the creative minds of 21st century librarians:* e-book (pp. 190–193). (Gr. 10) http://digital-literacy.syr.edu/page/view/221

Finding the science behind science fiction through paired readings. By Lisa Storm Fink. Includes Suggested Science Fiction Texts list. ReadWriteThink. (Gr. 6–8) http://www.readwritethink.org/classroom-resources/lesson-plans/finding-science-behind-science-927.html

Space: The familiar frontier (science fiction). By Shannon Doyle. Includes Past, Present and Future handout. The Learning Network: *The New York Times.* (Gr. 9–12) http://learning.blogs.nytimes.com/?s=space%3A+the+familiar+frontier&search.x=25&search.y=13

Literary Themes

Anticipation guide: Possible one-sentence themes. (Resource) By Judi Moreillon. (Gr. 6–12) http://www.ala.org/ala/aboutala/offices/publishing/editions/webextras/moreillon09294/moreillon_supplement6j.doc

Boys read: Considering courage in novels. By Helen Hoffner. ReadWriteThink. (Gr. 6–8) http://www.readwritethink.org/classroom-resources/lesson-plans/boys-read-considering-courage-997.html

Exploring setting: Constructing character, point of view, atmosphere, and theme. ReadWriteThink. (Gr. 9–12) http://www.readwritethink.org/search/partner.html?sort_order=relevance&q=exploring+setting&old_q=pictures+tell+the+story&srchgo.x=16&srchgo.y=8

Finding the story in the song. PBS Teachers: American Roots Music. (Gr. 8–12) http://www.pbs.org/teachers/connect/resources/976/preview/

The history behind song lyrics. ReadWriteThink. (Gr. 6–8) http://www.readwritethink.org/classroom-resources/lesson-plans/history-behind-song-lyrics-812.html

I've got the literacy blues. By Maureen Carroll. Includes The Blues Graphic Organizer. ReadWriteThink. (Gr. 9–12) http://www.readwritethink.org/classroom-resources/lesson-plans/literacy-blues-266.html

The literary element of theme. (Resource) ReadWriteThink. (Gr. 9–12) http://www.readwritethink.org/files/resources/lesson_images/lesson800/theme.pdf

Pink Floyd and the carpe diem theme. By Joe Knap. The Rock and Roll Hall of Fame & Museum. (Gr. 8–12) http://rockhall.com/education/resources/lesson-plans/sti-lesson-6/

Teacher resource: Evidence—background knowledge—inference category matrix. (Resource) By Judi Moreillon. Use with *Anticipation Guide* in this section. (Gr. 6–12) http://www.ala.org/ala/aboutala/of fices/publishing/editions/webextras/moreillon09294/moreillon_supplement6k.pdf

Unlocking the underlying symbolism and themes of a dramatic work. Includes Drama Map. The Learning Network: *The New York Times.* (Gr. 9–12) http://www.readwritethink.org/classroom-re sources/lesson-plans/unlocking-underlying-symbolism-themes-272.html

Viewer, she marries him: Comparing "Jane Eyre" in literature and film. By Shannon Doyle and Holly Epstein. The Learning Network: *The New York Times.* (Gr. 9–12) http://learning.blogs.nytimes. com/2011/03/10/viewer-she-marries-him-comparing-jane-eyre-in-literature-and-film/

READS INTERNET RESOURCES

Explore Characteristics, History, and Awards of creative Works

Identify and Critically Analyze Literary and Media Genres and Themes

Literature learning ladders. http://eduscapes.com/ladders/index.htm

Teaching literature. http://www.teachingliterature.org/teachingliterature/index.htm

VirtuaLit interactive tutorials: Poetry, Fiction, Drama. http://bcs.bedfordstmartins.com/virtualit/de fault.asp?uid=0&rau=0

Web English teacher. http://www.webenglishteacher.com/index.html

Genres

Genre characteristics chart. Scholastic. http://www2.scholastic.com/content/collateral_resources/ pdf/r/reading_bestpractices_comprehension_genrechart.pdf

Literary genres. California Department of Education. http://www.filmsite.org/filmnoir.html

Graphic Novels

Graphic novel/Comics. http://www.comicsbeat.com/category/twilight/

Internet public library for teens: Graphic Novels. http://www.ipl.org/div/graphicnovels/

Nonfiction

National Council for the Social Studies: Notable trade books for young people. http://www.ncss.org/ resources/notable/

National Science Teachers Association: Outstanding science trade books for students K-12. http://www. nsta.org/ostbc

Biography

Biographical dictionary. http://www.s9.com/

Biography.com. http://www.biography.com/

The biography maker. Jamie McKenzie. http://fno.org/bio/QUEST.HTM

Information please: People. http://www.infoplease.com/people.html

Multnomah County Library homework center. http://www.multcolib.org/homework/biohc.html

Folklore

Folklinks: Folk- and fairy-tale sites. http://www.pitt.edu/~dash/folklinks.html#generalfairytale

Minneapolis Institute of the Arts: World myths and legends in art. http://www.artsmia.org/world-myths/

Native American Myths. http://americanfolklore.net/folklore/native-american-myths/

Poetry

Academy of American Poets. http://www.poets.org/

Glossary of poetic devices. http://www.kyrene.org/schools/brisas/sunda/poets/poetry2.htm

Poetry 180: A poem a day for American high schools. The Library of Congress. http://www.read.gov/poetry/180/

Poetry foundation. (Includes search feature for poems, poets, and videos and About This Poem, offering context and related poetry.) http://www.poetryfoundation.org/

Poetry resources for teens: The Academy of American Poets. http://www.poets.org/page.php/prmID/394

Teen ink: A teen literary magazine and website. http://www.teenink.com/

Writing with writers: Poetry. http://teacher.scholastic.com/writewit/poetry/

Films

Documentary films. The greatest films. http://www.filmsite.org/docfilms.html

Motion pictures/Film study. http://www.frankwbaker.com/motion_pictures.htm

Using documentaries in the classroom. http://www.frankwbaker.com/using_docs_in_the_classroom.htm

Theme

ATN reading lists: Themes. (ATN—All Together Now) http://atn-reading-lists.wikispaces.com/Themes

VirtuaLit: Elements of fiction: Theme. http://bcs.bedfordstmartins.com/virtualit/fiction/elements.asp

WORKS CITED: GENRES

Baldrick, C. (2008). *Oxford dictionary of literary terms.* New York: Oxford University.

Bomer, R. (1995). *Time for meaning: Crafting literate lives in middle and high school.* Portsmouth, NH: Heinemann.

Cadden, M. (2011). Genre as nexus: The novel for children and young adults. In S. A. Wolf, K. Coats, P. Enciso & C. A. Jenkins (Eds.), *Handbook of research on children's and young adult literature* (pp. 302–313). New York: Routledge.

Chance, R. (2008). *Young adult literature in action: A librarian's guide.* Westport, CT: Libraries Unlimited.

Common Core State Standards Initiative. (2010). Common core state standards. Retrieved from http://www.corestandards.org/

Donelson, K. L., & Nilsen, A. P. (2005). *Literature for today's young adults.* Boston, MA: Pearson Education.

Dutro, E., & McIver, M. C. (2011). Imaging a writer's life: Extending the connection between readers and books. In S. A. Wolf, K. Coats, P. Enciso & C. A. Jenkins (Eds.), *Handbook of research on children's and young adult literature* (pp. 92–107). New York: Routledge.

Fink, L. S. (n.d.). *Genre study: A collaborative approach.* ReadWriteThink. Retrieved from http://www.readwritethink.org/classroom-resources/lesson-plans/genre-study-collaborative-approach-270.html

Fisher, D., & Frey, D. (2009). *Background knowledge; the missing piece of the comprehension puzzle.* Portsmouth, NH: Heinemann.

Fountas, I. C., & Pinnell, G. S. (2001). *Guiding readers and writers grades 3–6: Teaching comprehension, genre, and content literacy.* Portland, ME: Stenhouse.

Gilmore, B. (2011). Worthy texts: Who decides? *Educational Leadership, 68* (6), 46–50.

Harvey, S., & Goudvis, A. (2007). *Strategies that work: Teaching comprehension for understanding and engagement* (2nd ed.). Portland, ME: Stenhouse.

Hill, R. (2011). Common Core Curriculum and complex texts. *Teacher Librarian, 38* (3), 42–46.

Krapp, J. V. (2004). So many books: Genres of children's fiction. *School Library Media Activities Monthly, 21* (2), 44–45.

Krapp, J. V. (2005). Just for fun. *School Library Media Activities Monthly, 21* (10), 41–42.

Krashen, S. (2004). *The power of reading: Insights from the research.* Westport, CT: Libraries Unlimited.

Lamb, A., & Johnson, L. (2010). Divergent convergence. Part I: Cross-genre, multi-platform, transmedia experiences in school libraries. *Teacher Librarian, 37* (5), 76–81.

Lamb, A., & Johnson, L. (2010). Divergent convergence. Part 2: Teaching and learning in a transmedia world. *Teacher Librarian, 38* (1), 64–69.

Lesesne, T. S. (2010). *Reading ladders: Leading students from where they are to where we'd like them to be.* Portsmouth, NH: Heinemann.

Marzano, R. J., & Pickering, D. J. (2005). *Building academic vocabulary: Teacher's manual.* Alexandria, VA: Association for Supervision and Curriculum Development.

Miller, D. (2009). *The book whisperer: Awakening the inner reader in every child.* San Francisco, CA: Jossey-Bass.

Moreillon, J. (2007). *Collaborative strategies for teaching reading comprehension: Maximizing your impact.* Chicago, IL: American Library Association.

Saricks, J. G. (2009). *The readers' advisory guide to genre fiction* (2nd ed.). Chicago, IL: American Library Association.

Smith, C. B. (1991). The role of different literary genres. *The Reading Teacher, 44* (6), 440.

Wilhelm, J. S. (2001). *Improving comprehension with think-aloud strategies.* New York: Scholastic.

Wilhelm, J. D. (2008). *"You gotta be the book"; teaching engaged and reflective reading with adolescents.* New York: Teachers College Press.

Williams, T. L. (2009). A framework for nonfiction in the elementary grades. *Literacy Research and Instruction, 48* (3), 247–263.

WORKS CITED: LITERARY GENRE FRAMEWORK

Campbell, K. H. (2007). *Less is more: Teaching literature with short texts—grades 6–12.* Portland, ME: Stenhouse.

Fountas, I. C., & Pinnell, G. S. (2001). *Guiding readers and writers grades 3–6: Teaching comprehension, genre, and content literacy.* Portland, ME: Stenhouse.

Harvey, S., & Goudvis, A. (2007). *Strategies that work: Teaching comprehension for understanding and engagement* (2nd ed.). Portland, ME: Stenhouse.

Lamb, A., & Johnson, L. (2010). Divergent convergence. Part I: Cross-genre, multi-platform, transmedia experiences in school libraries. *Teacher Librarian, 37* (5), 76–81.

Lamb, A., & Johnson, L. (2010). Divergent convergence. Part 2: Teaching and learning in a transmedia world. *Teacher Librarian, 38* (1), 64–69.

Lattimer, H. (2003). *Thinking through genre: Units of study in reading and writing workshops 4–12.* Portland, ME: Stenhouse.

Wilhelm, J. D. (2001). *Improving comprehension with think-aloud strategies: Modeling what good readers do.* New York: Scholastic.

Williams, T. L. (2009). A framework for nonfiction in the elementary grades. *Literacy Research and Instruction, 48* (3), 247–263.

FURTHER READING: LITERARY GENRE FRAMEWORK

Bluestein, N. A. (2010). Unlocking text features for determining importance in expository text: A strategy for struggling readers. *The Reading Teacher, 63* (7), 597–600.

Hesse, D. (2009). Imagining a place for creative nonfiction. *English Journal, 99* (2), 18–24.

Huck, C. S., Hepler, S., Hickman, J., & Kiefer, B. Z. (2001). *Children's literature in the elementary school.* Boston, MA: McGraw-Hill.

Keene, E. O., & Zimmerman, S. (1997). *Mosaic of thought: Teaching comprehension in a reader's workshop.* Portsmouth, NH: Heinemann.

WORKS CITED: REALISTIC FICTION

Cart, Michael. (2010). A literature of risk. *American Libraries, 41* (5), 32–35.

Chance, R. (2008). *Young adult literature in action: A librarian's guide.* Westport, CT: Libraries Unlimited.

Meloni, C. (2006). Teen chick lit. *Library Media Connection, 25* (2), 18–19.

Meloni, C. (2010). Chickalicious: Want to woo reluctant female readers? Chick lit may be the ticket. *School Library Journal, 56* (6) 32–35.

Meloni, C. (2011). Lad lit. *Voice of Youth Advocates, 33* (6), 508–509.

Saricks, J. G. (2009). *The readers' advisory guide to genre fiction* (2nd ed.). Chicago, IL: American Library Association.

Sutton, R. (2009). An interview with Sarah Dessen. *The Horn Book Magazine, 85* (3), 243–250.

Mysteries

Cart, M. (2010). *Young adult literature: From romance to realism.* Chicago, IL: American Library Association.

Clark, R. C. (2008). Older teens are serious about their series: Forensic mysteries, graphic novels, horror, supernatural, and chick lit series. *Library Media Connection, 27* (3), 22.

Saricks, J. G. (2009). *The readers' advisory guide to genre fiction* (2nd ed.). Chicago, IL: American Library Association.

Werlin, N. (2010). What makes a good thriller? In R. Sutton & M. V. Parravano (Eds.), *A family of readers: The book lover's guide to children's and young adult literature* (pp. 145–151). Somerville, MA: Candlewick.

Historical Fiction

Cart, M. (2010). *Young adult literature: From romance to realism.* Chicago, IL: American Library Association.

Carter, B. (2010). When dinosaurs watched black-and-white TV. In R. Sutton & M. V. Parravano (Eds.), *A family of readers: The book lover's guide to children's and young adult literature* (pp. 138–144). Somerville, MA: Candlewick.

Krapp, J. V. (2005). Historical fiction. *School Library Media Activities Monthly, 21* (6), 42–43.

MacLeod, A. S. (2010). Writing backward. In R. Sutton & M. V. Parravano (Eds.), *A family of readers: The book lover's guide to children's and young adult literature* (pp. 145–151). Somerville, MA: Candlewick.

Miller, D. (2009). *The book whisperer: Awakening the inner reader in every child.* San Francisco, CA: Jossey-Bass.

Rabey, M. (2010). Historical fiction mash-ups: Broadening appeal by mixing genres. *Young Adult Library Services, 9* (1) 38–41.

Rycik, M. T., & Rosler, B. (2009). The return of historical fiction. *The Reading Teacher, 63* (2), 163–166.

Saricks, J. (2008). Revisiting historical fiction. *Booklist, 104* (16), 33.

Smith, V. (2010). "Know-how and guts." In R. Sutton & M. V. Parravano (Eds.), *A family of readers: The book lover's guide to children's and young adult literature* (pp. 172–179). Summerville, MA: Candlewick.

WORKS CITED: FANTASY

Baker, D. F. (2010), "Your journey is inward, but will seem outward." In R. Sutton & M. V. Parravano (Eds.), *A family of readers: The book lover's guide to children's and young adult literature* (pp. 124–132). Somerville, MA: Candlewick.

Cart, M. (2010). *Young adult literature: From romance to realism.* Chicago, IL: American Library Association.

Fuhler, C. J., & Walther, M. P. (2007). *Literature is back! Using the best books for teaching readers and writers across genres.* New York: Scholastic.

Herald, D. T. (2003). *Teen genreflecting: A guide to reading interests* (2nd ed.). Westport, CT: Libraries Unlimited.

Kurkjian, C., Livingston, N., Young, T., & Avi. (2006). Children's books: Worlds of fantasy. *The Reading Teacher, 59* (5), 492–503.

Science Fiction

Cart, M. (2010). *Young adult literature: From romance to realism.* Chicago, IL: American Library Association.

Fuhler, C. J., & Walther, M. P. (2007). *Literature is back! Using the best books for teaching readers and writers across genres.* New York: Scholastic.

Hill, R. (2010). The punks of science fiction. *Voice of Youth Advocates, 33* (4), 335–357.

Saricks, J. G. (2009). *The readers' advisory guide to genre fiction* (2nd ed.). Chicago, IL: American Library Association.

WORKS CITED: SHORT STORIES

Campbell, K. H. (2007). *Less is more: Teaching literature with short texts—grades 6–12.* Portland, ME: Stenhouse.

Lattimer, H. (2003). *Thinking through genre: Units of study in reading and writing workshops 4–12.* Portland, ME: Stenhouse.

Rashid, L. (2008). When less is more: New short story collections to get teens reading. *School Library Journal, 5* (1), 16–19.

WORKS CITED: POETRY

Campbell, K. H. (2007). *Less is more: Teaching literature with short texts—Grades 6–12.* Portland, ME: Stenhouse.
Carlson, J. R. (2010). Songs that teach: Using song-poems to teach critically. *English Journal, 99* (4), 65–71.
Cart, M. (2010). *Young adult literature: From romance to realism.* Chicago, IL: American Library Association.
Chatton, B. (2010). *Using poetry across the curriculum. Learning to love language* (2nd ed.). Santa Barbara, CA: Libraries Unlimited.
Fuhler, C. J., & Walther, M. P. (2007). *Literature is back! Using the best books for teaching readers and writers across genres.* New York: Scholastic.
Lesesne, T. R. (2003). *Making the match: The right book for the right reader at the right time, grades 4–12.* Portland, ME: Stenhouse.
Nye, N. S. (2010). Gazing at things. In R. Sutton & M. V. Parravano (Eds.), *A family of readers: The book lover's guide to children's and young adult literature* (pp. 233–235). Somerville, MA: Candlewick.
Pure poetry: VOYA's poetry picks 2007 (2008). *VOYA, 31* (1), 13.
Pure poetry: VOYA's poetry picks 2009 (2010). *VOYA, 33* (1), 113.
Singer, M. (2010). Knock poetry off the pedestal. *School Library Journal, 56* (4), 28–31.

WORKS CITED: NONFICTION

Birch, P., & Magee, M. (2007). It's not Grey's Anatomy or Gray's Anatomy; it's much more! *School Library Media Activities Monthly, 24* (4), 17–19.
Campbell, K. H. (2010). Eavesdropping on contemporary minds: Why we need more essays in our high school classrooms. *English Journal, 99* (4), 50–54.
Kristo, J. V., Colman, P., & Wilson, S. (2008). Bold new perspectives: Issues in selecting and using nonfiction. In S. S. Lehr (Ed.), *Shattering the looking glass: Challenge, risk, and controversy in children's literature* (pp. 339–360). Norwood, MA: Christopher-Gordon.
Lehman, B. A. (2009). *Children's literature and learning: Literary study across the curriculum.* New York: Teacher's College Press.

Biography/Memoir

Campbell, K. H. (2007). *Less is more: Teaching literature with short texts—Grades 6–12.* Portland, ME: Stenhouse.
Fontichiaro, K. (2009). Re-envisioning the biography report. *School Library Monthly, 26* (1), 5.
Fraser, E. (2008). *Reality rules: A guide to teen nonfiction reading interests.* Westport, CT: Libraries Unlimited.
Kirby, D. L., & Kirby, D. (2010). Contemporary memoir: A 21st century genre ideal for teens. *English Journal, 99* (4), 22—29.
Lattimer, H. (2003). *Thinking through genre: Units of study in reading and woritng workshops 4–12.* Portland, ME: Stenhouse.

WORKS CITED: DRAMA

Black, A. N. (2008). *Readers' theatre for middle school boys: Investigating the strange and mysterious.* Westport, CT: Libraries Unlimited.

Lesesne, T. S. (2003). *Making the match: The right book for the right reader at the right time, grades 4–12.* Portland, ME: Stenhouse.

Schneider, D. (2010). The novel as screenplay: Monster and *Riot* by Walter Dean Myers. *Book Links, 19* (2), 20–21.

WORKS CITED: PICTURE BOOKS

Anstey, M. (2002). "It's not all black and white": Postmodern picture books and new literacies. *Journal of Adolescent & Adult Literacy, 45* (6), 444–457.

Burke, A., & Peterson, S. S. (2007). A multidisciplinary approach to literacy through picture books and drama. *English Journal, 96* (3), 74–77.

Campbell, K. H. (2007). *Less is more: Teaching literature with short texts—grades 6–12.* Portland, ME: Stenhouse.

Lesesne, T. S. (2010). *Reading ladders: Leading students from where they are to where we'd like them to be.* Portsmouth, NH: Heinemann.

WORKS CITED: GRAPHIC LITERATURE

Gorman, M. (2003). *Getting graphic!: Using graphic novels to promote literacy with preteens and teens.* Worthington, OH: Linworth.

Groenke, S. L., & Maples, J. (2010). Young adult literature goes digital: Will teen reading ever be the same? *The ALAN Review, 37* (3), 42–46.

Lamb, A., & Johnson, L. (2010). Divergent convergence. Part I: Cross-genre, multi-platform, transmedia experiences in school libraries. *Teacher Librarian, 37* (5), 76–81.

WORKS CITED: MAGAZINES

Chance, R. (2008). *Young adult literature in action: A librarian's guide.* Westport, CT: Libraries Unlimited.

Cole, P. B. (2009). *Young adult literature in the 21st century.* Boston, MA: McGraw-Hill Higher Education.

Donelson, K. L., & Nilsen, A. P. (2005). *Literature for today's young adults* (7th ed.). Boston, MA: Pearson Education.

Harvey, S., & Goudvis, A. (2007). *Strategies that work: Teaching comprehension for understanding and engagement* (2nd ed.). Portland, ME: Stenhouse.

Hochadel, C. (2010). Who's hot and who's not in teen magazines. *VOYA, 33* (5), 404–408.

Hughes-Hassell, S., & Cox, E. J. (2008). Urban teenagers, leisure reading, and the library media program. *School Library Media Activities Monthly, 25* (1), 56–58.

Hughes-Hassell, S., & Rodge, P. (2007). The leisure reading habits of urban adolescents. *Journal of Adolescent & Adult Literacy, 51* (1), 22–33.

Lattimer, H. (2003). *Thinking through genre: Units of study in reading and writing workshops 4–12.* Portland, ME: Stenhouse.

Webber. C. (2009). The original handhelds: Forget about iPods. Here are 11 magazines that teens can't resist. *School Library Journal, 55* (5), 30–32.

WORKS CITED: LITERARY THEME

Barr, C., & Gillespie, J. T. (2009). *Best books for high school readers: Grades 9–12.* Westport, CT: Libraries Unlimited.

Barr, C., & Gillespie, J. T. (2009). *Best books for middle school and junior high school readers: Grades 6–9*. Westport, CT: Libraries Unlimited.

Beers, K. (2003). *When kids can't read, what teachers can do: A guide for teachers 6–12*. Portsmouth, NH: Heinemann.

Campbell, K. H. (2007). *Less is more: Teaching literature with short texts—Grades 6–12*. Portland, ME: Stenhouse.

Grimes, S. (2006). *Reading is our business: How libraries can foster reading comprehension*. Chicago, IL: American Library Association.

Herz, S. K., & Gallo, D. R. (2005). *From Hinton to Hamlet: Building bridges between young adult literature and the classics* (2nd ed.). Westport, CT: Greenwood Press.

Jago, C. (2004). The heart and soul of literature. *Voices from the Middle, 11* (3), 60–61.

Kettel, R. P., & Douglas, N. L. (2003). Comprehending multiple texts: A theme approach incorporating the best of children's literature. *Voices from the Middle, 11* (1), 43–48.

Lesesne, T. S. (2003). *Making the match: The right book for the right reader at the right time, Grades 4–12*. Portland, ME: Stenhouse.

Lesesne, T. S. (2010). *Reading ladders: Leading students from where they are to where we'd like them to be*. Portmouth, NH: Heinemann.

Moreillon, J. (2007). *Collaborative strategies for teaching reading comprehension: Maximizing your impact*. Chicago, IL: American Library Association.

Olson, C. B., Land, R., Anselmi, T., & AuBuchon, C. (2011). Teaching secondary English learners to understand, analyze, and write interpretive essays about theme. *Journal of Adolescent & Adult Literacy, 54* (4), 245–256.

Richison, J. D., Hernandez, A. C., & Carter, M. (2002). Blending multiple genres in theme baskets. *English Journal, 92* (2), 76–81.

Van Zile, S. (2001). *Awesome hands-on activities for teaching literary elements*. New York: Scholastic.

FURTHER READING: LITERARY THEMES

Alley, K. M. (2008). *Teaching integrated reading strategies in the middle school library media center*. Westport, CT: Libraries Unlimited.

Beach, R., Appleman, D., Hynds, S., & Wilhelm, J. (2011). *Teaching literature to adolescents* (2nd ed.). New York: Routledge.

Cole, P. B. (2009). *Young adult literature in the 21st century*. Boston, MA: McGraw-Hill Higher Education.

Evans, J. (2004). From Sheryl Crow to Home Simpson: Literature and composition through pop culture. *English Journal, 93* (3), 32–36.

Fuhler, C. J., & Walther, M. P. (2007). *Literature is back! Using the best books for teaching readers and writers across genres*. New York: Scholastic.

Harvey, S., & Goudvis, A. (2007). *Strategies that work: Teaching comprehension for understanding and engagement* (2nd ed.). Portland, ME: Stenhouse.

Mahood, K. (2006). *A passion for print: Promoting reading and books to teens*. Westport, CT: Libraries Unlimited.

Moreillon, J., & Fontichiaro, K. (2008). Teaching and assessing the dispositions: A garden of opportunities. *Knowledge Quest, 37* (2), 64–67.

Santoli, S. P., & Wagner, M. E. (2004). Promoting young adult literature: The other "real" literature. *American Secondary Education, 33* (1), 65–75.

Schneider, D. (2010). The novel as screenplay. *Book Links, 19* (2), 20–22.

Ward, A. A., & Young, T. A. (2009). Compassion through friendship. *Book Links, 19* (1), 31–33.

Zambo, D. (2007). Using picture books to provide archetypes to young boys: Extending the ideas of William Brozo. *The Reading Teacher, 61* (2), 124–131.

6

Exploring Social, Cultural, and Historical Contexts

In this section of Explore, the focus is on guiding students to literature that reflects their own selves, societal issues, history, and cultures around the globe. Multiple genres of literature can be employed to explore students' interests, curiosity, and curricular requirements to learn in these contexts. While expository works will provide current, historical, and cultural specifics, narrative selections will address the aesthetic aspects of emotions and attitudes, enabling readers to walk in the shoes of others and view life from various perspectives.

PERSONAL IDENTITY

Students in the stage of early adolescence are consciously or unconsciously involved in the process of discovering their own identity, within their own families, communities, and society. The *National Curriculum Standards for Social Studies* (2010) establishes 10 themes worthy of study. The fourth theme is individual development and identity; this theme states, in part, "Questions related to identity and development, which are important in psychology, sociology, and anthropology, are central to the understanding of who we are" (2010). The standards further specify, "In the middle grades, issues of personal identity are refocused as the individual begins to explain his or her unique qualities in relation to others, collaborates with peers and with others, and studies how individuals develop in different societies and cultures" (2010). In the professional writings on children's and young adult literature, stages of literature appreciation are described, roughly corresponding to age groups, with middle school students experiencing the task of finding themselves in literature (Donelson & Nilsen, 2005). Middle school teacher Jeffrey Wilhelm (2008) summarizes how literature met the needs of his students: "reading was an important way to get to know yourself, who you are, what you believe, and what you should or might do in different situations" (p. 49).

When African American author Christopher Paul Curtis visits classrooms, he reports that students tend to ask similar questions in all schools. However, he was once asked what books had touched him when he was a kid. This question deviated from the usual list and he was temporarily at a loss to respond to the student. He writes (Curtis, 2008) that he finally provided a vague answer to the student's question, but later gave it serious thought. Though he came from a home with many books and parents who read constantly,

READS Component	READS Indicator	AASL *Standards for the 21st-Century Learner**	Common Core State Standards—English Language Arts**
2. Explore characteristics, history, and awards of creative works			
The student will:			
2.2 Recognize that social, cultural, political and historical events influence ideas and information.	2.2.1 Analyze and compare a variety of historically and culturally significant works in various formats (e.g., film noir, Greek plays).	• 2.3.2 Consider diverse and global perspectives in drawing conclusions. • 3.3.2 Respect the differing interests and experiences of others, and seek a variety of viewpoints. • 4.1.2 Read widely and fluently to make connections with self, the world, and previous reading. • 4.1.3 Respond to literature and creative expressions of ideas in various formats and genres. • 4.1.5 Connect ideas to own interests and previous knowledge and experience. • 4.2.2 Demonstrate motivation by seeking information to answer personal questions and interests . . . • 4.2.3 Maintain openness to new ideas . . . • 4.4.4 Interpret new information based on cultural and social context.	• Reading: Informational Text—7 Integrate and evaluate multiple sources of information presented in different media or formats. . . • Reading: Informational Text—8 Delineate and evaluate the reasoning in texts . . . • Reading: Literature—6 Analyze a case in which grasping point of view requires distinguishing what is directly stated in a text from what is really meant . . . • Reading: Literature—7 Analyze multiple interpretations of a story, drama, or poem . . . • Reading: Literature—9 Demonstrate knowledge of foundational works of American literature . . . • Writing—9 Draw evidence from literary or informational texts to support analysis . . .
	2.2.2 Demonstrate an appreciation for cultural and ethnic diversity by selecting appropriate creative and literary works.	• 4.1.2 Read widely and fluently to make connections with self, the world, and previous reading.	• Reading: Informational Text—7 Integrate and evaluate multiple sources of information presented in different media or formats . . .

READS Component	READS Indicator	AASL *Standards for the 21st-Century Learner**	Common Core State Standards—English Language Arts**
		• 4.1.3 Respond to literature and creative expressions of ideas in various formats and genres. • 4.1.4 Seek information for personal learning in a variety of formats and genres. • 4.1.5 Connect ideas to own interests and previous knowledge and experience. • 4.2.1 Display curiosity by pursuing interests through multiple resources. • 4.2.2 Demonstrate motivation by seeking information to answer personal questions and interests . . . • 4.2.3 Maintain openness to new ideas . . . • 4.3.3 Seek opportunities for pursuing personal and aesthetic growth. • 4.4.4 Interpret new information based on cultural and social context.	• Reading: Informational Text—8 Delineate and evaluate the reasoning in texts . . . • Reading: Literature—6 Analyze a case in which grasping point of view requires distinguishing what is directly stated in a text from what is really meant . . . • Reading: Literature—7 Analyze multiple interpretations of a story, drama, or poem . . . • Reading: Literature—9 Demonstrate knowledge of foundational works of American literature . . . • Writing—9 Draw evidence from literary or informational texts to support analysis . . .

*Excerpted from *Standards for the 21st-Century Learner* by the American Association of School Librarians, a division of the American Library Association, copyright © 2007 American Library Association. Available for download at www.ala.org/aasl/standards. Used with permission.

**Excerpted from *Common Core State Standards for English Language Arts*. National Governors Association Center for Best Practices and Council of Chief State School Officers Commercial License. Copyright © 2010. Used with permission of NGA Center/CCSSO.

he couldn't recall a favorite book. He scored well on reading tests and enjoyed reading comics and magazines, but not books. Finally, he writes, "I think I've hit on at least one very important reason. I believe that there were no books that really touched me as a child because there were no books that were written for, by, or about me. There were no books from an African-American perspective" (2008, p. 158).

Walter Dean Myers, another prominent African American author, has written many books in multiple genres with African American characters. However, he writes that he did not read a book with characters like himself until he was an adult. He vividly describes the frustrating experience of not finding characters like himself in books, "Books transmit values. And if you're not in the books, what does that tell you? That tells you you're no longer valuable" (Italie, 2011). These poignant reflections show how these authors view the limitations of the literature selections available to them as young people and also reveal their commitment to creating stories to meet the developmental needs of students. These same stories also serve as windows into the lives of their peers for students of other ethnic groups, leading to an understanding of the common developmental stages of youth in all cultures.

The need for books reflecting various cultures is a societal issue as well as a personal need. Alfred Tatum is a university professor specializing in the literacy needs of African American males. He describes the continuing literacy gap for African American males, especially in urban areas where many students live in difficult home situations (Tatum, 2008). He contends that when schools use the culturally authentic books of Myers, Christopher, Sharon Flake, Angela Johnson, Jacqueline Woodson, and others, opportunities for students to find success in school and to develop strategies for dealing with life outside of school are increased. Tatum (2008) writes, "Literature can lead young men to engage in self-correcting tendencies that they might not imagine for themselves if they are not exposed to literature that connects to their multiple backdrops—personal, community, economic, gender, and cultural—through which they filter their lives experiences" (p. 151).

Finding authentic characters in fiction and nonfiction is a major concern for Native Americans, according to Metzger and Kelleher (2008), adding to "the identity crisis children and teens already face" (p. 36). In addition, this group works to counteract the stereotyped images of American Indians found in books and the visual media. Debbie Reese, Native American and assistant professor of American Indian Studies at the University of Illinois at Urbana, works proactively to provide educators with quality materials through publishing articles and maintaining a blog, http://americanindiansinchildrensliterature. blogspot.com/. Reese (2008) recommends many titles appropriate for seasonal displays and programs but encourages librarians and teachers to integrate materials by and about Native Americans into the curriculum throughout the year. She also is a frequent contributor to LM_NET, keeping her message fresh for school librarians.

The major roles that school librarians will play in this area of diversity in literature will be selection, promotion, and recommending titles to teachers. It is essential to examine your own biases and preferences as you carry out these roles. Author Mitali Perkins provides an insightful look at the issue of ethnicity and culture in an article titled "Straight Talk on Race: Challenging the Stereotypes in Kids' Books" in *School Library Journal* in 2009. She relates her own experiences growing up in California but living in a home smelling and looking like a traditional Bengali one. Perkins offers five questions for our consideration when working with materials on ethnicity and culture: "Are the nonwhite characters too good to be true? How and why does the author define race? Is the cover art true to the story? Who are the change agents? How is beauty defined?" (pp. 28–32). You should read her article in full to experience her revealing examples and powerful ideas about the value of discussing literature. She concludes, "Our calling as educators and authors is to pay attention, both to the young people we serve and to the books they're reading, and to ask questions with them. Great stories, like their human counterparts, are beautiful yet flawed, and discussing them in community can strengthen their power to enlighten, inspire, and let justice roll down" (p. 32).

Perkins (2009) suggests that discussions of the events and themes in books can increase the value of the stories. Among the ways that school librarians can provide this conversational link is through reader advisory encounters, through participation in literature activities with teachers, through readers' forum sessions in library classes, or in book club activities with students.

Though books representing all cultures from around the world are essential in school library collections, it is especially important to provide books about the ethnic groups attending your schools. A primary task of a librarian new to a school must be to examine the student demographics and assess the library collection, so that all students can find themselves in literature. Middle school librarian and storyteller Walter Mayes calls on librarians to adapt their libraries as students change to "mirror the school population" (p. 26), as reported by Marcoux (2009) in *Teacher Librarian*. Mayes also states "Right now the most underrepresented group in literature is South American teens. Latino authors are Mexican American, Cuban American, etc., but I am not seeing a lot of South American authors" (p. 24). This assessment is accurate, as increasing numbers of students from South and Central America are attending schools here in Florida and other states, but few books are available to meet the needs of this group. At this point, libraries primarily offer only nonfiction books on the countries.

Another group of young people who sometimes feel alienated from the mainstream are those with disabilities. They also seek to find themselves in the books they read and to experience acceptance among their peer group. Emily Wopperer (2011) writes,

> *Literature portraying characters with disabilities can help children and young adults develop the habit of reading about characters like themselves, and it can support the development of personal power by portraying these characters as strong and believable. This literature can also assist children and young adults with disabilities in developing self-esteem and sense of purpose. (p. 26)*

Recently, the character of Artie Abrams in the television show Glee has been providing a role model of a young person with a disability participating in the high school scene and experiencing both the highs and lows of teen life. Wopperer (2011) also informs educators that it is important to include books featuring individuals with disabilities into all types of displays and collections, to demonstrate the potential of leading normal lives.

Young people seeking to find characters like themselves in books include those with strong religious values and others with alternative lifestyles (Koss & Teale, 2009). More titles featuring characters with strong Christian values are being published and made available in libraries. However, librarians are continuing to search for fiction books on Muslim culture, as news events here and abroad keep this culture clash on the front burner. Baer and Glasgow (2010) report that a high percent of Americans have negative views about this religious group, creating conflicts for Muslim people living here. The wearing of the *hijab*, head scarf, outside the home by Muslim girls and women has become symbolic of this cultural conflict and is a central part of the novel *Does My Head Look Big in This?* by Randa Abdel-Fattsh (2007), offering opportunities for class discussions of this topic.

Books featuring characters who are gay, lesbian, bisexual, transgender (GLBT), or questioning have increased in numbers in recent years. Banks and Gardner (2009) describe the books published from 1980 to 1995 as featuring GLBT characters primarily in secondary roles, intended to elicit sympathy from readers. In recent books, GLBT youth are cast as multidimensional main characters sharing many interests and concerns of all young people. According to Banks, "These books present adolescent characters . . . as smart, interesting, and often complex individuals in search of themselves and a place in the world that will let them develop as full human beings" (p. 35). Writing about why GLBT literature matters, Haydee Camacho (2011) emphasizes the potential of creating tolerance for others in the community and the need to provide books on a variety of life experiences. She writes, "It's important to have a wide range of GLBT characters so that one character doesn't have to represent the entire range of experience" (p. 138).

These books should be displayed and featured in booktalks and other promotions to validate the lifestyles, belief systems, family patterns, and cultures represented in the community. Author Neesha Meminger (2011) urges librarians to try many avenues to put diverse books into students' hands. She believes "If diverse reading choices are normalized . . . it becomes a safe space to bring up issues . . . to discuss differences" (p. 12). Appealing to school and public librarians in *Young Adult Library Services*, Meminger advises us to focus on the universality of these stories rather than how characters are different from others. She contends that "books about marginalized teens are books about all teens. The themes in all these books—identity, fitting in, belonging, family, dating, relationships, faith—are absolutely universal" (p. 12).

SOCIAL ISSUES

Literature not only serves the needs of students to find characters like themselves, but also provides stimuli for examining issues of concern in society. For starters, consider the points emerging from a single broad question: Do all young people in our country and around the world have an equal opportunity to learn? Why or why not? Several reasons come to mind, such as poverty and class struggles, family abuse, role of women, discrimination resulting from race, religious preferences, gender, sexual orientation, and more. Many of these topics were raised in our discussion about individual identity issues, but also need to be confronted at a societal level. The recent series of natural and man-made disasters in Japan make us conscious of the impact of nature on society and the impact of man on nature, through the failures of the nuclear power plants. Will this change the way nations think about energy use and dangers? The resilience shown through the caring responses of the Japanese people to each other throughout the difficulties should be noted. A political cartoon by Chan Lowe published in the *South Florida Sun Sentinel* on March 15, 2011, provides a telling commentary: A man watching coverage of the disaster on television says "Don't worry . . . it couldn't happen here." A woman responds, "What couldn't?" A third person answers, " A major disaster with absolutely no looting" (Lowe, 2011). What about the crime and violence in the United States and many other countries? Why didn't that happen in Japan?

Considering the enormity of these concerns, the pertinent question becomes how can school librarians contribute to the process of educating students on these issues? When an economics teacher came into the library office and asked to discuss an upcoming project with her class, the librarian had no idea how complex and rewarding the collaborative experience would turn out to be. The teacher wanted her students to read fiction books about economic and social issues around the world before conducting research on the economic condition raised in the fiction book. Since the high school was in the process of applying to become part of the International Baccalaureate program, global issues and displays had been promoted in various ways that school year. Fortunately, the teacher initiated the planning process six to eight weeks in advance of the implementation date. The teacher had noticed the display of books in the library for the annual state reading program and was interested in *Sold* by Patricia McCormick, which told the story of a young girl in Nepal who was sold into the prostitution trade by her stepfather. She was already reading *A Long Way Gone: Memoirs of a Boy Soldier* (2007) to the class. Through discussion of the read-aloud, she was preparing students to analyze issues in the book that each would read independently.

After beginning the search for materials and thinking over the project for several days, the librarian proposed to the teacher that they could apply for a local public education fund grant to purchase new materials for the project. She enthusiastically agreed to cosponsor the grant and promptly filled out the required forms with the instructional goals and plans for the unit. Since she was already scheduled to attend an AASL Conference, it was convenient to search for current economics reference sources in the vendor hall, expediting the completion of the list of products and prices for the grant.

Bib in a Box

Fiction and Informational Texts on Poverty

Booth, C. (2006). *Tyrell*. New York: PUSH.

Darrow, S. (2003). *The painters of Lexieville*. Somerville, MA: Candlewick.

Deuker, C. (2005). *Runner*. Orlando, FL: Houghton Mifflin.

Flake, S. (2003). *Begging for change*. New York: Hyperion.

Flake, S. (2003). *Money hungry*. New York: Hyperion.

Ghent, N. (2005). *No small thing*. Somerville, MA: Candlewick.

Kephart, B. (2010). *The heart is not a size*. New York: HarperTeen.

Lelami, L. (2009). *Secret son*. Chapel Hill, NC: Algonquin.

McKay, S. (2010). *Thunder over Kandahar*. Toronto: Annick.

Mulligan, A. (2010). *Trash*. Oxford: David Fickling.

Paterson, K. (1991). *Lyddie*. New York: Puffin.

Qamar, A. (2008). *Beneath my mother's feet*. New York: Atheneum.

Ryan, P. M. (2001). *Esperanza rising*. New York: Scholastic.

Schroeder, M. (2010). *Saraswati's way*. New York: Farrar, Straus, Giroux.

Steinbeck. J. (1986). *Tortilla flat*. New York: Penguin.

Strasser, R. (2009). *If I grow up*. New York: Simon.

Walls, J. (2005). *The glass castle: A memoir*. New York: Scribner.

Wolff, V. E. (1993). *Make lemonade*. New York: Holt.

Woodson, J. (2000). *Miracle's boys*. New York: Putnam.

Finding books on the topic was not as straightforward as expected as catalog records did not necessarily use poverty-fiction or economic conditions-fiction subject headings for books. However, with the use of wildcard searches and consultations with library colleagues, a list of books was created and made accessible to the teacher. Additional fiction and biography titles as well as reference materials including e-books on economics were ordered with grant funds. Books were also borrowed from other libraries in the district so that students could have a choice of titles. After the materials were received, the teacher brought each class to the library for booktalks and selection of a title for the project.

Upon reflection, the librarian would add several elements to the planning process and implementation. First, she would share several lesson plans from ReadWriteThink with the teacher: she would also accept the teacher's invitation to come to the classroom to view students' completed projects. Though it is often difficult to get away from tasks and classes waiting in the library, observing the students working in the classroom provides a more complete understanding of the insights gained by students from their readings and could provide useful information for future projects.

This economics teacher had a clear understanding of the value of using a critical literacy approach with students. Through modeling and the posing of questions about the impact of economics and other social and political influences in the book she read aloud, *A Long Way Gone: Memoirs of a Boy Soldier*, the teacher opened her students' minds to looking at a story in a broader perspective. When needed, she brought in other materials to provide background knowledge for students, so that they could understand the forces behind the civil war in Sierra Leone. She encouraged her students to look beyond the plot events of the memoir and recognize the social and political forces at work and how they impacted the characters in the story.

Fisher and Frey (2009) define critical literacy as "the practice of challenging texts through an analysis of the role that power, culture, class, and gender play in the message" (p. 119). These authors suggest that it is beneficial for students to take a questioning or critical approach to whatever they read, hear, and view. McLaughlin and DeVoogd (2004) offer a series of questions to use when reading books, newspapers, magazines, song lyrics, or online text:

- Whose viewpoint is expressed?
- What does the author want us to think?
- Whose voices are missing, silenced, or discounted?
- How might alternative perspectives be represented?
- How would that contribute to your understanding the text from a critical stance?
- What action might you take on the basis of what you have learned? (p. 53)

High school English teacher Kiran Subhani Qureshi (2006) provides insight into the lived experience of a person who stands out from the norm, relating the reaction she received as a Muslin woman wearing a head scarf to school. She summarizes the potential of a critical approach to creating compassion in students:

In the post-9/11 world, it is no longer sufficient for students to read literature that affirms their circumstance, values, or lifestyle. This generation is inundated with mixed messages by media on the threat of terror and the ideals of freedom. . . . Instead of passively looking at mirror images of their experiences, students must actively engage in looking through many and varied windows so they can make informed choices as global citizens. (p. 35)

APPRECIATION OF CULTURAL AND ETHNIC DIVERSITY

Staging multicultural fairs and events in schools is a popular strategy for exposing students to other cultures, frequently featuring guest speakers, food, costumes, craft displays, and musical performances. If a librarian is involved in this program, display books, non-print items, maps, and websites as a part of any multicultural event and contact teachers to encourage them to use these rich materials in the classroom, as well as using them in library classes. Electronic messages to teachers can highlight opportunities to integrate multicultural materials into all areas of the curriculum. While this approach will certainly build background knowledge, may create an awareness of other cultures, and may be efficient in exposing multiple classes to speakers and artifacts, it does have limitations for secondary students and should be considered a starting point for learning about cultures. Elise Begler (1998) refers to such events as the "'five Fs', food, fashion, fiestas, folklore, and famous people" (p. 272). She suggests that exploring a culture involves learning about the values and beliefs of the people and the social, economic, and political systems of the country.

A major rationale for creating opportunities for students to learn about other cultures is to show the common bonds among all people and to create understanding of the differences among individuals. This diversity is a natural outcome of living in other places, participating in different family patterns, customs, languages, and religions, and contributes

READS Component	READS Indicator	AASL *Standards for the 21st-Century Learner**	Common Core State Standards—English Language Arts**
2. Explore characteristics, history, and awards of creative works			
The student will:			
2.2 Recognize that social, cultural, political and historical events influence ideas and information.	2.2.2 Demonstrate an appreciation for cultural and ethnic diversity by selecting appropriate creative and literary works.	• 4.1.2 Read widely and fluently to make connections with self, the world, and previous reading. • 4.1.3 Respond to literature and creative expressions of ideas in various formats and genres. • 4.1.4 Seek information for personal learning in a variety of formats and genres. • 4.1.5 Connect ideas to own interests and previous knowledge and experience. • 4.2.1 Display curiosity by pursuing interests through multiple resources. • 4.2.2 Demonstrate motivation by seeking information to answer personal questions and interests . . . • 4.2.3 Maintain openness to new ideas . . . • 4.3.3 Seek opportunities for pursuing personal and aesthetic growth. • 4.4.4 Interpret new information based on cultural and social context.	• Reading: Informational Text—7 Integrate and evaluate multiple sources of information presented in different media or formats. . . • Reading: Informational Text—8 Delineate and evaluate the reasoning in texts . . . • Reading: Literature—6 Analyze a case in which grasping point of view requires distinguishing what is directly stated in a text from what is really meant . . . • Reading: Literature—7 Analyze multiple interpretations of a story, drama, or poem . . . • Reading: Literature—9 Demonstrate knowledge of foundational works of American literature . . . • Writing—9 Draw evidence from literary or informational texts to support analysis . . .

*Excerpted from *Standards for the 21st-Century Learner* by the American Association of School Librarians, a division of the American Library Association, copyright © 2007 American Library Association. Available for download at www.ala.org/aasl/standards. Used with permission.

**Excerpted from *Common Core State Standards for English Language Arts*. National Governors Association Center for Best Practices and Council of Chief State School Officers Commercial License. Copyright © 2010. Used with permission of NGA Center/CCSSO.

Websites for Multicultural Resources

Annotated bibliography of children's literature focusing on Latino people, history, and culture: http://clnet.ucla.edu/Latino_Bibliography.html

Celebrating cultural diversity through children's literature: http://www.multiculturalchildrenslit.com/

Cynthia Leitich Smith: http://www.cynthialeitichsmith.com/lit_ resources/diversity/diversity.html

American Indians in children's literature. Debbie Reese: http://americanindiansinchildrensliterature.blogspot.com/

LUCY (Librarianship Upgrades for Children and Youth Services): http://education.odu.edu/eci/lucy/

Multicultural literature. Cooperative children's book center: http://www.education.wisc.edu/ccbc/books/multicultural.asp

Multicultural review: http://www.mcreview.com/current issue/pdf/REVIEWS.pdf

Teaching tolerance: http://www.tolerance.org/resources?keys=&level=6&subject=15

WOW review: Reading across cultures: http://wowlit.org/on-line-publications/review/

to the global mosaic. However, these differences can also be a source of much divisiveness and strife in our schools, communities, and nation. By using multicultural literature with secondary students, combined with discussions and opportunities to examine personal values and stereotypes, educators can create meaningful experiences that lead to acceptance of others and an appreciation of cultures around the globe.

A first response to the need to connect students with high quality multicultural materials is to evaluate the library collection and add or borrow titles as needed. As part of the process of gathering a wide range of resources on countries and cultures, taking a careful look at local, state, and national curricular goals and objectives, as well as the demographics of the school and community, is essential. In addition to the usual book and media review resources, several websites specialize in multicultural materials and are listed in our sidebar.

A second step is to consider the curriculum and likely areas to connect with multicultural resources. Foreign language classes frequently conduct research on countries speaking the native language taught in the class and may be open to using folklore and fiction with settings in the target countries. Some schools have multicultural social studies classes and these teachers may welcome collaboration with the librarian. Teachers of ELL students are also potential partners for collaboration.

The ideal strategy for engaging students with multicultural literature is to collaborate with a teacher to address curricular content at the same time that librarians provide experiences called for in this section of the READS Curriculum and in AASL's *Standards for the 21st Century Learner*.

Many teachers involve school librarians in selecting materials for a curricular unit, though too often the request comes in a short note or comment with only the briefest indication of the goals or plans for the instructional sequence. To provide the most appropriate collection for instruction, one requires an understanding of the characteristics of the students, the time allowed to the unit, the scope and nature of materials needed, as well as the intended use of the resources. However, the reality is that not all teachers show willingness to collaborate with school librarians in depth.

Fortunately, the online literature provides an illuminating example in which a school librarian participated in a year-long series of curricular units using a variety of genres including multicultural literature dealing with social issues. In this unit, which she calls Multicultural Conversations: Online Literature Circles Focusing on Social Issues, school librarian Judi Moreillon (2010) responds to a middle school teacher's request for booktalks on multicultural titles and enters into collaborative co-teaching experience, which offers us many points for discussion. Her role in this unit was to gather materials, co-plan the instructional sequence with the teacher including jointly designing a rubric for assessing students' discussion postings, booktalk the titles for each of the four literature explorations, teach students how to use websites and several Web 2.0 tools, teach ethical use of information, respond to students' posts on their literature selection, assess student responses, detect problems with some groups, arrange for additional input from high school library aides, and reflect on the success of the project with the teacher.

The school librarian and the classroom teacher were joined during part of the year by a teacher intern, facilitating the high level of interaction with students and their response to the literary selections. For the final project of the year, centering on the books of author Jacqueline Woodson, the senior high library aides contributed to the learning process by posting questions for students online, leading them to connect the issues of race and prejudice emerging from the books to local situations. Moreillon reports about this teaching experience in an article on the WOW Stories: Connections from the Classroom website at the University of Arizona: http://wowlit.org/on-line-publications/stories/storiesiii1/3/. This article is from Volume III, Issue 1, with the theme Exploring the Diversity that Surrounds Us.

In the article, she comments on the challenges for a single classroom teacher to manage a unit using multiple literature selections with three classes of students. However, she acknowledges that the multiple responsibilities and time constraints of school librarians, especially in this era of reduced clerical and professional staffing in libraries, makes it hard to devote so much time to projects with one teacher. Yet, she also recognizes the need for students to engage in extended conversations concerning their own attitudes and their perceptions of the underlying issues in the books in order to create the desired change in their worldview. Moreillon continues:

> *The ongoing nature of literature circles makes it difficult for school librarians to participate . . .*
> *where the time commitment restricts them from interacting with students in other classes at*

Bib in a Box

Hispanic Poetry

Argueta, J. (2001). *A movie in my pillow:* una pelicula en mi almohada: Poemas. [Poems] San Francisco, CA: Children's Book Press. (Gr. 6–8)

Cool salsa: Bilingual poems on growing up Latino in the United States. (1994). New York: Holt. (Gr. 6–10)

De veras?: Young voices from the national Hispanic cultural center. (2008). Albuquerque, NM: University of New Mexico Press. (Gr. 9–12)

The FSG book of twentieth-century Latin American poetry. (2011). Edited by Ilan Stavans. New York: Farrar, Straus, Giroux. (Gr. 6–12)

Mora, P. (2000). *My own true name: New and selected poems for young adults, 1984–1999.* Houston, TX: Arte Publico. (Gr. 6–12)

Mora, P. (2010). *Dizzy in your eyes: Poems about love.* New York: Knopf. (Gr. 7–12)

Paper dance: 55 Latino poets. (1995). New York: Persea Books. (Gr. 11–12)

Red Hot Salsa: Bilingual poems on being young and Latino in the United States. (2005). New York: Holt. (Gr. 7–12)

Soto, G. (1992). *Neighborhood odes.* New York: Harcourt Brace Jovanovich. (Gr. 6–8)

Soto, G. (1995). *New and selected poems.* San Francisco, CA: Chronicle. (Gr. 9–12)

Soto, G. (2006). *A fire in my hands* (rev. ed.). New York: Harcourt. (Gr. 6–8)

Wachale! Poetry and prose about growing up Latino in America. (2001). Peterborough, NH: Cricket. (Gr. 6–8)

The wind shifts: New Latino poetry. (2007). Tucson, AR: University of Arizona. (Gr. 9–12) *regular times over a period of several weeks. The fact that these discussions occurred online allowed the classroom teachers and me to monitor the conversations and interject thought-provoking comments and questions as needed to push the students to more critical responses and interactions. (n.p.)*

In addition to providing resources for student use, school librarians can also impact instruction in classrooms by offering teachers professional resources and ideas for using them. In the section on READS Lessons and Resources, you will find several other lessons on the topics of cultural and ethnic diversity. One lesson for use in middle school emphasizes vocabulary development, "Using Picture Books to Explore Identity, Stereotyping, and Discrimination." An easy way to update this lesson is by adding newer titles to the list of picture books. Another title to consider is *Saltypie: A Choctaw Journey from Darkness into Light* (2010) by Native American author Tim Tingle.

To maximize the effectiveness of lessons on social and cultural issues, suggest that teachers offer choice of selections to students, to encourage engagement in the project. Kathy Short (2011) recommends that teachers and school librarians pair books to be examined by students, so that similarities and differences in perspectives can be compared. The pairing could be fiction and nonfiction about the same place and culture; views of landmark life stages and events in different cultures (schooling, marriage, child care); or both historical and contemporary stories from the same culture.

Within the library itself, students from all cultural situations deserve to be welcomed and shown respect. Consider these suggestions:

- Honor the cultural and linguistic heritage of students by taking time to learn to pronounce their names correctly.
- Provide books and magazines in the native language of students whenever available. Place displays of books in other languages in a convenient location and provide attractive signage. Integrate books in other languages in displays to offer choice to students.
- Encourage students to check out books in both languages.
- Make available a subscription database with periodicals and multimedia data from other countries, which can meet the needs of both newcomers and the general population to compare points of view on current and historical issues (e.g., Gale's *Global Issues in Context*).
- Demonstrate the foreign language search features of Google and other available search engines.
- Integrate examples relevant to the cultures and learning styles of all cultures into individual and group discussions and instruction (e.g., if students are from South or Central America, use books about soccer, Latino/Latina authors and artists when demonstrating the catalog or location of materials).
- Include students from minority cultures on library advisory committees or task forces and listen to their opinions on materials to add to the library collection.
- Recruit students speaking the language of newcomers as library aides. Multiple benefits result from this simple action. First, students speaking the minority language are viewed as role models and mentors for the ELL population and can assist in orienting students to the library and school. Second, the multilingual library aide can serve as an interpreter for the librarian if needed.
- Organize student activity groups so that ELL students have a mentor student in the group, planning in advance with teachers who know the students well.
- Create a safe environment for learning by asking open-ended questions, allowing multiple answers and/or by arranging for pairs of students to confer on questions before responding.

- Team with a classroom or ELL teacher to offer a book club for ELL students or a mix of ELL and other interested students after school or during lunch, incorporating vocabulary activities into book discussions.
- Provide audiobooks of texts used in classroom activities and for pleasure listening.
- Create an international zone in the library by placing objects representing various cultures around the facility.

If it is December, the Tree of the Continents should be front and center in the library. Featuring ornaments representing the culture or wildlife of one of the continents, the tree will be the center of attention for several weeks. In the elementary and middle school, a contest activity can be open to students, one in which any student could be a winner. Using an entry form prepared by the librarian, students identify each continent and name at least two ornaments from each continent. Several atlases can be displayed handy nearby for anyone needing a refresher on the continent names. In one library, a candy cane was the seasonal prize for winners. An origami bird, maple leaf, gingerbread man, panda bear, lion, toucan, Uncle Sam, penguin, fortune cookie, giraffe, and Beefeater were among the ornaments on the tree. For a period of eight years, in an elementary, middle, and high school in South Florida, the Tree of the Continents was a seasonal centerpiece in the library, celebrating cultures and geography around the globe. Some years the tree was a six-foot fake fir, provided by the PTA, and other years it was a stylized metal framework found in a home garden shop. The ornaments were collected during trips to Canada and various countries in Europe, as well as from catalogs and holiday shops. The dose of geography went down well under the guise of holiday fun!

HISTORICALLY AND CULTURALLY SIGNIFICANT WORKS

A school librarian may become involved with locating and possibly using historically and culturally significant selections in a variety of ways. In the first scenario, a language arts, English, or reading teacher requests resources to use with a unit on a literary period or specific novel study. A second scenario is a curriculum planning project by a language arts, English, or reading department that is establishing a curriculum for a new school or undertaking a major curriculum revision in an existing school. A third possibility is a social studies teacher or department that is looking for resources for a particular course or time period. A fourth scenario is a science or math teacher wanting historical and biographical information on individuals or inventions related to their content. A fifth area is a school-wide project, perhaps focusing on a local or national celebration or event (e.g., statehood, war commemoration, or national election). A final possibility could be a lesson or unit to be taught by the librarian (e.g., short stories or poetry written by state authors from different eras; travel writing from various decades; comparison of historical and current newspapers and magazines; historical approach to recreational activities such as sports, dancing, games, needlework; or analysis of current event articles from newspapers, magazines, and online publications).

The values of a historical approach to learning have been described by many organizations and individuals. The second of nine themes of the *National Curriculum Standards for Social Studies* from the National Council of Social Studies is time, continuity, and change. According to this organization, "Studying the past makes it possible for us to understand the human story across time" (n.p., 2010). This document stresses the importance of students' use of both primary and secondary historical sources. After describing the development of social studies skills in elementary grades, the Standards specify expectations of students in secondary schools:

> *Through a more formal study of history, students . . . develop a deeper understanding and appreciation for difference perspectives on historical events and developments, recognizing that interpretations are influenced by individual experiences, sources selected, society values, and cultural traditions. They are increasingly able to use multiple sources to build interpretations of past events and eras. High school students . . . build and defend interpretations that reconstruct the past and draw on their knowledge of history to make informed choices and decisions in the present. (n.p.)*

The *National Curriculum Standards for Social Studies* also emphasize the role of geography in historical studies in the third theme, People, Places, and Environments. The Standards specify:

> *Students learn where people and places are located and why they are there . . . [and] address questions such as: Why do people decide to live where they do or move to other places? . . . How do people interact with the environment and what are some of the consequences of those interactions? . . . How do maps, globes, geographic tools and geospacial technologies contribute to the understanding of people, places, and environments? (n.p., 2010)*

These concepts are essential to developing the background knowledge required for comprehending both historical prose and historical fiction.

The American Historical Association provides an online document by Peter N. Stearns (2008) titled "Why Study History?" Stearns identifies two fundamental reasons for learning about history: "History helps us understand people and societies . . . [and] helps us understand change and how the society we live in came to be" (n.p., 2008). He also asserts that studying history contributes to moral understanding, prepares students for becoming good citizens, and provides self, family, and cultural identity. He also maintains that historical study trains students to assess evidence, to develop useful habits of mind, and to acquire essential job skills.

The English Language Arts Standard for History/Social Studies from the *Common Core State Standards Initiative* also integrates social studies concepts with reading and literature. In the section on Integration of Knowledge and Ideas, secondary students are expected to work with and analyze several primary and secondary sources, comparing and contrasting treatments of the same topic. For school librarians, this is another area where reading objectives and inquiry or information literacy skills overlap. School librarians will be able to approach teachers with an offer to introduce or reinforce understanding of primary source materials.

As language arts and English teachers plan instruction, they consider the settings of the literary selection, among other characteristics. If the work is set in another historical period and place, plans are made to assist students in understanding the historical, cultural, and geographical context of the literary selection. For advanced placement students in high schools, this step is especially important. The AP Literature and Composition examination includes high level reading passages from several different historical periods (Beach, Appleman, Hynds, & Wilhelm, 2011). These authors identify several important advantages of understanding historical context for students. First, students are prepared to make a judgment about the actions of the fictional characters if they are familiar with the typical behavior for the time period of the book. Next, if students grasp the cultural perspectives of an era, such as Puritan New England, the Civil War, or Elizabethan England, they are more likely to "know what is possible or impossible, acceptable or unacceptable, purposeful or futile within a character's scope of choice because they will comprehend the cultural constraints under which that character is operating" (p. 66). Finally, referring to *The Scarlet Letter*, Beach et al. (2011) point out,

A historical framework supplies readers with a set of plausibility measures for possible interpretations. Knowing about the physical isolation and scarcity of resources among the Puritans, readers know better than to suggest, even to themselves, that Hester ought to leave Salem in favor of a more accepting community. (p. 66)

Multiple methods may be employed by educators to provide historical, social, and geographical context for students. Often, during an introductory or pre-reading activity, teachers choose to use a film clip, artifact, political cartoon, intriguing question, picture book, dramatic scene, song, or other item to engage student interest in the new topic or literary work and to begin the process of activating or adding background knowledge. Jeffrey Wilhelm (2007) refers to this process as frontloading before beginning a literary or historical study. In *Teaching Literature to Adolescents* by Beach et al. (2011), purposes and possibilities for the initial activity are explained:

Consider a text you will be teaching. What kind of introductory "frontloading" activity would you use that would: 1) motivate students for reading and inquiry; 2) activate or build on students' prior knowledge or background information regarding the essential question and unit theme; and 3) work to organize inquiry, set purposes and consolidate learning about the theme throughout the unit, i.e. how will it help students set purposes for their reading, focus their learning, clarify what they are coming to know, and help them to monitor their learning progress. Simple brainstorming is the simplest kind of frontloads, but there are hundreds of other activities that can fulfill these purposes: rankings, surveys, K-W-L, etc. (p. 121)

Once the unit of study is underway, teachers can build students' understanding of the historical context of the literary selection by creating an assignment in which students research certain aspects of the topic and then share their findings with the class. Another method for adding background knowledge is to use a video, film clip, or guest speaker to contribute facts about the topic. School librarians will be able to suggest resources on the topic for teachers to use in providing historical context or can assist in organizing a research experience for students. A particularly valuable strategy to involve students in analyzing data is a compare and contrast model, which encourages higher order thinking and learning.

The READS Curriculum suggests sample resources for building historical understanding. In sixth grade, Greek and Roman mythology is the example, which can be used to develop understanding of ancient Greece and Rome civilizations or as a significant form of early literature. Students can compare two myths from either Greek or Roman literature or compare the Greek version of the same story in Roman mythology (e.g., Zeus and Jupiter). Another angle is to assign students to locate artistic versions of a single myth and compare the art forms. Students could also research a mythological figure such as Apollo and describe how that name and figure is used today in commerce and art.

Useful resources for mythology at the middle school level include the *Lincoln Library of World Mythology* and the *UXL Encyclopedia of World Mythology*. Several audiobooks are available for related readings and projects: *The Last Olympian* (Listening Library, 2009), *Theseus* (Full Cast Audio, 2009), and *Hercules* (Full Cast Audio, 2009). Two recent DVD productions featuring mythological characters are *Percy Jackson & the Olympians: The Lightening Thief* (20th Century Fox, 2010) and *Green Lantern: First Flight* (Warner, 2009).

In seventh grade, two examples are included: political cartoons and African American handmade quilts. Political cartoons have been used as a form of political comment and

Bib in a Box

Quilts

Dobard, R. G. *The secret story of quilts and the underground railroad.* [Text]

Hopkinson, D. *Sweet Clara and the freedom quilt.* [Picture Book]

Latham, I. *Leaving Gees Bend.* [Fiction]

Raven, M. *Night boat to freedom.* [Picture Book]

Tobin, J. L., Dobard, R. G., & Wahlman, M. S. *Hidden in plain view: A secret story of quilts and the Underground Railroad.* [Informational]

Woodson, J. *Show way.* [Picture Book]

satire for hundreds of years and are readily available in books, newspapers, magazines, and commercial databases. In the READS Lessons and Activities section, you will find several lessons on political cartoons.

African American handmade quilts were part of the story of slavery and the underground railroad that provided a way out of the South for slaves during the Civil War era. The stories of these quilts have been told in fiction and folklore for many years. Several recommended titles on quilts in the African American community are included in the Bib in a Box. *Hidden in Plain View* (1999) relates the theory of the role of quilts in communicating hidden messages as part of underground railroad activities. The authors interviewed an African American woman who shared the oral stories from her family history. This book was well-reviewed by the *New York Times* and recommended for grades 10 up in *The Wilson Core Collection*. Quilt-making was also a part of the utilitarian crafts created by African Americans and other cultural groups in our country and around the world. Through the use and recommendations to teachers of materials about cultural artifacts such as quilts, school librarians can contribute to lively literary and historical discussions and validate the cultural heritage of students in our schools.

For eighth graders, historical and multicultural resource examples include Hispanic poetry and situation comedies. Titles of poetry concentrating on the Hispanic experience are included in the bibliography and are typical of the literature available for all cultural groups.

Situation comedies are representative of the many cultural literary and artistic creations that characterize the various decades of history in America and other countries. Beginning in the early days of television programming in the 1950s, situation comedies depict many social conditions and situations. *I Love Lucy* featured a wide-eyed red-haired comedian with a Cuban musician for a husband, though viewers couldn't see her hair color in the black and white television era. PBS offers a lesson on Lucille Ball, on the READS Lessons and Activities list. Students could compare today's comedies to *I Love Lucy*, *All in the Family*, or *M*A*S*H*, focusing on issues from the news events and issues addressed in the comedies.

The cultural examples for 9th or 10th grades are from the fine arts. Many resources are available in school library collections and on the Internet for Shakespeare's plays and sonnets. The examples for 11th and 12th grades are from the ancient and modern worlds. From the motion picture community, film noir refers to primarily black and white movies, usually bleak in tone. Background information and terminology for units on film are provided by Carolyn Fortuna in an article from *Knowledge Quest* in 2010. Check the READS Internet Resources list for a lesson from PBS on Billy Wilder, who created the prominent films in this genre. Greek plays were one of the entertainment forms of the historical period, containing clear references to political and social issues of the time.

READS LESSONS AND ACTIVITIES

Explore Characteristics, History, and Awards of Creative Works

Recognize that Social, Cultural, Political and Historical Events Influence Ideas and Information

Accountable book clubs: Focused discussions. By Darla Salay. Includes Critical Thinking Map, social issues questions, and Books about Social Issues list. ReadWriteThink. (Gr. 7–8) http://www.readwritethink.org/classroom-resources/lesson-plans/accountable-book-clubs-focused-1163.html

American masters: Billy Wilder: Film noir inventor and genius. PBS. (Gr. 9–12) www.pbs.org/wnet/americanmasters/lessons/billy-wilder-film-noir-inventor-and-genious/lesson-overview/1289

American masters: Lucille Ball: What's so funny? PBS. (Gr. 5–8) www.pbs.org/wnet/americanmasters/lessons/lucille-ball-what's-so-funny/lesson-overview/1285

An ancient Odyssey. By Deborah Lerman and Javaid Khan. Includes activity on history and geography of ancient Greece. The Learning Network: *The New York Times.* (Gr. 6–12). http://learning.blogs.nytimes.com/2002/10/23/an-ancient-odyssey/

Assessing cultural relevance: Exploring personal connections to a text. By Traci Gardner. Includes Cultural Relevance Review Guidelines and Gathering Evidence of Cultural Relevance. ReadWriteThink. (Gr. 9–12) http://www.readwritethink.org/classroom-resources/lesson-plans/assessing-cultural-relevance-exploring-1003.html

Behind the masks: Exploring culture through art and poetry. By Judi Moreillon and Diana Roderick. Includes Cultural Mask Research Graphic Organizer. ReadWriteThink. (Gr. 9–12) http://www.readwritethink.org/classroom-resources/lesson-plans/behind-masks-exploring-culture-395.html

Breaking barriers, building bridges: Critical discussion of social issues. By Joy F. Moss. ReadWriteThink. (Gr. 6–8) http://www.readwritethink.org/classroom-resources/lesson-plans/breaking-barriers-building-bridges-86.html

Building background knowledge. Includes activities using *Sing Down the Rain.* In *Collaborative Strategies for Teaching Reading Comprehension* by Judi Moreillon. (Advanced) Resources available online: Choral Reading Transcript—http://storytrail.com/pages/choral.pdf; Tohono O'dham Path finder—http://storytrail.com/pages/TOK.html

Collaborative homework questions. (Resource) Includes questions on fairness, gender, race, class, power. These questions also work well with the topic of poverty. From lesson Accountable book clubs. ReadWriteThink. (Gr. 6–12) http://www.readwritethink.org/files/resources/lesson_images/lesson1163/questions.pdf

Critical media literacy: TV programs. By Laurie A. Henry. ReadWriteThink. Includes Media Observation Sheet. (Gr. 6–8) http://www.readwritethink.org/classroom-resources/lesson-plans/critical-media-literacy-programs-96.html?tab=1#tabs

Debunking stereotypes about Muslims and Islam. Includes Debunking Misconceptions about Muslims and Islam handout. Teaching Tolerance. (Gr. 6–12) http://www.tolerance.org/print/activity/debunking-muslim-myths

Exploring satire with the Simpsons. By Junius Wright. ReadWriteThink. Includes Analyzing Characters from The Simpsons and Analyzing an Episode of The Simpsons worksheets useful with any show. (Gr. 9–12) http://www.readwritethink.org/classroom-resources/lesson-plans/exploring-satire-with-simpsons-811.html

The freedom riders and the popular music of the Civil Rights Movement. EdSITEment. (Gr. 9–12) http://edsitement.neh.gov/lesson-plan/freedom-rides-and-role-popular-music-civil-rights-movement#sect-activities

Immigration: Our changing voices. By Susan Cassata and Mary Reiman. Includes Primary Source Analysis Tool. The Library of Congress. (Gr. 6–12) http://www.loc.gov/teachers/classroommaterials/lessons/voice/

It's no laughing matter: Analyzing political cartoons. (Resource) Includes Cartoon Analysis Guide. Library of Congress. http://www.loc.gov/teachers/classroommaterials/presentationsandac tivities/activities/political-cartoon/resources.html

Making personal and cultural connections using A Girl Named Disaster. By Kathleen Benson Quinn. ReadWriteThink. (Gr. 6–8) http://www.readwritethink.org/classroom-resources/lesson-plans/making-personal-cultural-connections-166.html

Mexican culture and history through its national holidays. By Teresa Madden and Brenda Agilar. EdSITEment. (Gr. 6–8) http://edsitement.neh.gov/view_lesson_plan.asp?id=740

National Archives document analysis worksheets. (Resource) Includes written document, photograph, cartoon, poster, map. National Archives. (Gr. 6–12) http://www.archives.gov/education/les sons/worksheets/

Power ballads. By Amanda Christy Brown and Kristin McGinn Mahoney. The Learning Network: *The New York Times.* (Gr. 6–12). http://learning.blogs.nytimes.com/2009/05/08/power-ballads/

Promoting diversity in the classroom and school library through social action. By Michelle Ota. Includes Interactive ReadWriteThink Printing Press. ReadWriteThink. (Gr. 6–8). http://www.read writethink.org/resources/resource-print.html?id=317&tab=1

Seuss and Silverstein: Posting questions, presenting points. By Helen Hoffner. Examines social issues through literature; lesson targeted at struggling readers. ReadWriteThink. (Gr. 9–12). http://www.readwritethink.org/classroom-resources/lesson-plans/seuss-silverstein-posing-questions-283.html

Using picture books to explore identity, stereotyping, and discrimination. By Loraine Woodard. ReadWriteThink. (Gr. 6–8) http://www.readwritethink.org/classroom-resources/lesson-plans/using-picture-books-explore-952.html?tab=1#tabs

Why study history? (Resource). By Peter N. Stearns. American Historical Association. (Gr. 6–12) http://www.historians.org/pubs/free/WhyStudyHistory.htm

Young adult literature about the Middle East: A cultural response perspective. By Scott Filkins. ReadWriteThink. (Gr. 6–8) http://www.readwritethink.org/classroom-resources/lesson-plans/young-adult-literature-about-1136.html

Folklore

American folklore: A jigsaw character study. By Renee Goularte. Includes Jigsaw Group Discussion Worksheet and Character Study Matrix Sample. ReadWriteThink. (Gr. 3–6) http://www.readwrite think.org/classroom-resources/lesson-plans/american-folklore-jigsaw-character-30524.html

Analyzing and comparing medieval and modern ballads. By Susan Spangler. Includes Checklist for Ballads. ReadWriteThink. (Gr. 9–12) http://www.readwritethink.org/classroom-resources/les son-plans/analyzing-comparing-medieval-modern-1097.html?tab=4#tabs

Elements of folktales. By Kathy Cook. Includes Folktale Links. ArtsEdge. (Gr. 5–8) http://artsedge.kennedy-center.org/content/2212/

Elements of myths. By Kathy Cook. Includes vocabulary list. ArtsEdge. (Gr. 5–8) http://artsedge.kennedy-center.org/content/2232/

Exploring American tall tales. By Diane Messina. Includes vocabulary list and assignment sheet. ArtsEdge. (Gr. 5–8) http://artsedge.kennedy-center.org/content/2216/

Exploring Arthurian legend. EdSITEment. (Gr. 9–12) http://edsitement.neh.gov/view_lesson_plan.asp?id=235

Fables and trickster tales around the world. EdSITEment. (Gr. 3–5 up). http://edsitement.neh.gov/view_lesson_plan.asp?id=237

Fairy tale autobiographies. By Patricia Schulze. Includes Interactive Literary Elements. ReadWriteThink. (Gr. 5–9) http://www.readwritethink.org/classroom-resources/lesson-plans/fairy-tale-autobiographies-1.html

Folklore: Some useful terminology. (Resource) EdSITEment. http://edsitement.neh.gov/lesson_images/lesson407/folkloreterms.pdf

Funky fables. By Kevin Humphrey. (2005). Includes Funky Fable Rubric. *School Library Media Activities Monthly*, 22 (4) 15–16. (Gr. 5–8)

Heroes and legends. By Jennifer Chandler. Includes Mythological Hero Chart. Scholastic. (Gr. 6–8) http://www2.scholastic.com/browse/lessonplan.jsp?id=113&FullBreadCrumb=%3Ca+href%3D%22http%3A%2F%2Fwww2.scholastic.com%2Fbrowse%2Fsearch%2F%3FNtx%3Dmode%2Bmatchallpartial%26_N%3Dfff%26Ntk%3DSCHL30_SI%26query%3Dheroes%2520and%2520legends%26N%3D0%26Ntt%3Dheroes%2Band%2Blegends%22+class%3D%22endecaAll%22%3EAll+Results%3C%2Fa%3E

It came from Greek mythology. EdSITEment. (Gr. 3–5 up) http://edsitement.neh.gov/printable_lesson_plan.asp?id=234

King Arthur: Man or legend? Includes Symbolism in the Legend of King Arthur. ArtsEdge. (Gr. 5–8 up) http://www.artsedge.kennedy-center.org/content/3700/

Myths, folktales, & fairy tales for Grades 7–9. Scholastic. (Gr. 7–9) http://www2.scholastic.com/browse/lessonplan.jsp?id=580&FullBreadCrumb=%3Ca+href%3D%22http%3A%2F%2Fwww2.scholastic.com%2Fbrowse%2Fsearch%2F%3FNtx%3Dmode%2Bmatchallpartial%26_N%3Dfff%26Ntk%3DSCHL30_SI%26query%3Dmyths%2C%2520folktales%2C%2520and%2520fairy%2520tales%2520for%2520grades%25207–9%26N%3D0%26Ntt%3Dmyths%252c%2Bfolktales%252c%2Band%2Bfairy%2Btales%2Bfor%2Bgrades%2B7–9%22+class%3D%22endecaAll%22%3EAll+Results%3C%2Fa%3E

Myths, folktales, & fairy tales for Grades 10–12. Scholastic. (Gr. 10–12) http://www2.scholastic.com/browse/lessonplan.jsp?id=581&FullBreadCrumb=%3Ca+href%3D%22http%3A%2F%2Fwww2.scholastic.com%2Fbrowse%2Fsearch%2F%3FNtx%3Dmode%2Bmatchallpartial%26_N%3Dfff%26Ntk%3DSCHL30_SI%26query%3Dmyths%2C%2520folktales%2C%2520and%2520fairy%2520tales%2520for%2520grades%252010–12%26N%3D0%26Ntt%3Dmyths%252c%2Bfolktales%252c%2Band%2Bfairy%2Btales%2Bfor%2Bgrades%2B10–12%22+class%3D%22endecaAll%22%3EAll+Results%3C%2Fa%3E

One story, many tales. By Phyllis Gron. Includes What Is a Folktale? ArtsEdge. (ESL 9–12) http://www.artsedge.kennedy-center.org/content/2390/

Sundiata, Mali's lion king. By Rebecca Jones. ArtsEdge. (Gr. 5–8) http://artsedge.kennedy-center.org/content/2352/

Tall tales today. By Kathy Cook. Includes vocabulary and Tall Tale Checklist. ArtsEdge. (Gr. 5–8) http://artsedge.kennedy-center.org/content/2267/

To tell the tale. By Rachel Klein and Yasmin Chin Eisenhauer. Includes identification of themes in world folktales. The Learning Network: *The New York Times.* (Gr. 6–12). http://learning.blogs.nytimes.com/2003/07/18/to-tell-the-tale/

Walk through the 20th century. By Tammy Bunton. (Includes history, culture, literature) Education World. (Gr. 6–12) http://www.educationworld.com/a_tsl/archives/00–1/lesson0010.shtml

Weaving words: The art of storytelling (Includes tips on storytelling and series of lessons on folklore). ArtsEdge. (Gr. 5–8 up) http://artsedge.kennedy-center.org/content/3481/

World of myths. ArtsEdge. By Kathy Cook. (Gr. 5–8) http://artsedge.kennedy-center.org/content/2226/

READS INTERNET RESOURCES

Explore Characteristics, History, and Awards of Creative Works

Recognize that Social, Cultural, Political and Historical Events Influence Ideas and Information

American Indians in children's literature. Debbie Reese. http://americanindiansinchildrensliterature.blogspot.com/

Celebrate diversity with dream in color/African American heritage. http://www.scholastic.com/dream
incolor/africanamericanheritage/

Celebrate diversity with dream in color/Asian Pacific American culture. http://www.scholastic.com/
dreamincolor/asianpacificheritage/

Celebrate diversity with dream in color/Hispanic American culture. http://www.scholastic.com/dream
incolor/latinoheritage/

Curriculum trunks. Holocaust Museum Houston. Free. http://www.hmh.org/ed_cur_trunk.shtml

EconoKids: Rutgers University project on economics and children. Includes reviews of picture books
and books for older children and teens. http://econkids.rutgers.edu/econkids-home-econ
menu-154

Film noir. The greatest films. http://www.filmsite.org/filmnoir.html

Lyrics.Time. http://www.lyricstime.com/

Multicultural literacy. Reading is fundamental (RIF). http://www.rif.org/us/literacy-resources/mul
ticultural.htm

The New Americans. PBS. http://www.pbs.org/independentlens/newamericans/

The Smithsonian Center folklife and oral history interviewing guide. By Marjorie Hunt. The Smithsonian
Center for Folklife and Cultural Heritage. http://www.folklife.si.edu/education_exhibits/re
sources/guide/introduction.aspx

Strange fruit: Protest music. Independent Lens / PBS. http://www.pbs.org/independentlens/
strangefruit/protest.html

Teaching tolerance. http://www.tolerance.org/?source=redirect&url=teachingtolerance

WOW review: Reading across cultures. http://wowlit.org/on-line-publications/review/

Folklore

Ancient Greek literature & mythology. http://www.infoplease.com/spot/ancientgreece-litmyth.html

Encyclopedia mythica. http://www.pantheon.org/

Folklore and mythology electronic texts. E. L. Ashliman. University of Pittsburgh. http://www.pitt.
edu/~dash/folktexts.html

Grimm Brothers' home page. http://www.pitt.edu/~dash/grimm.html

Mythology. Web English teacher. http://www.webenglishteacher.com/myth2.html

Native American lore index page. http://www.ilhawaii.net/~stony/loreindx.html

Tales online. http://talesunlimited.com

World myths & legends in art. The Minneapolis Institute of Arts. http://www.artsmia.org/world-
myths/index.html

WORKS CITED: CULTURAL, SOCIAL, & HISTORICAL CONTEXTS

Baer, A. L., & Glasgow, J. N. (2010). Negotiating understanding through the young adult literature
of Muslim cultures. *Journal of Adolescent & Adult Literacy, 54* (1), 23–32.

Banks, W. P., & Gardner, T. (2009). Literacy, sexuality, and the value(s) of queer young adult litera-
tures. *English Journal, 98* (4), 33–36.

Beach, R., Appleman, D., Hynds, S., & Wilhelm, J. (2011). *Teaching literature to adolescents* (2nd ed.).
New York: Routledge.

Begler, E. (1998). Global cultures: The first steps toward understanding. *Social Education, 62* (5),
272–275.

Camacho, H. (2011). Where GLBT literature is going and why it matters. *VOYA, 34* (2), 138.

Common Core State Standard. (2010). English Language Arts Standards: History/Social Studies.
Retrieved from http://www.corestandards.org/the-standards/english-language-arts-stan
dards/history-social-studies/grades-11–12/

Curtis, C. P. (2008). The literary world of Bud, Kenny, Luther, and Christopher: Finding books for me. In S. S. Lehr (Ed.), *Shattering the looking glass; challenge, risk & controversy in children's literature* (pp. 155–159). Norwood, MA: Christopher-Gordon.

Donelson, K. L., & Nilsen, A. P. (2005). *Literature for today's young adults*. Boston, MA: Pearson Education.

Fisher, D., & Frey, N. (2009). *Background knowledge: The missing piece of the comprehension puzzle*. Portsmouth, NH: Heinemann.

Fortuna, C. (2010). Lights! Camera! Action!: A grammar of film for media literacy. *Knowledge Quest, 38* (4), 10–23.

Italie, H. (2011). Walter Dean Myers, 73, a hero to young readers. Yahoo! News. Retrieved from http://yahoo.com/s/ap/20110304/ap_en_ot/us_books_walter_dean_myers/

Koss, M. D., & Teale, W. H. (2009). What's happening in YA literature? Trends in books for adolescents. *Journal of Adolescent & Adult Literacy, 52* (7), 263–272.

Lowe, Chan. (2011). Japan earthquake aftermath: Political cartoon. *South Florida Sun Sentinel*. Retrieved from http://blogs.trb.com/news/opinion/chanlowe/blog/2011/03/

Marcoux, E. (2009). Diverse yet universal: Two men with similar perspectives. *Teacher Librarian, 36* (3), 22–27.

McLaughlin, M., & DeVoogd, G. (2004). Critical literacy as comprehension: Expanding reader response. *Journal of Adolescent & Adult Literacy, 48* (1), 52–62.

Meminger, N. (2011). Getting diverse books into the hands of teen readers: How do we do it? *Young Adult Library Services, 9* (3), 12.

Metzger, K., & Kelleher, W. (2008). The dearth of native voices in young adult literature: A call for more young adult literature by and for indigenous peoples. *ALAN Review, 35* (2), 36–42.

Moreillon, J. (2010). Multicultural conversations: Online literature circles focused on social issues. *WOW Stories, 3* (1). Retrieved from http://wowlit.org/on-line-publications/stories/storiesiii1/3/

National Council for the Social Studies. (2010). *National Curriculum Standards for Social Studies*. Retrieved from http://www.socialstudies.org/standards

National Council for the Social Studies. (2010). *National Curriculum Standards for Social Studies: Chapter 2—The themes of social studies*. Retrieved from http://www.socialstudies.org/standards/strands

Perkins, M. (2009). Straight talk on race: Challenging the stereotypes in kids' books. *School Library Journal, 55* (4), 28–32.

Qureshi, K. S. (2006). Beyond mirrored worlds: Teaching world literature to challenge students' perception of "other." *English Journal, 96* (2), 34–40.

Reese, D. (2008). Native voices. *School Library Journal, 54* (11), 56–60.

Short, K. (2011). Paired books: Reading a book in the context of another book. WOW Currents. Retrieved from http://wowlit.org/blog/2011/02/14/paired-books-reading-a-book-in-the-context-of-another-book/

Stearn, P. N. (2008). Why study history? American Historical Association. Retrieved from http://www.historians.org/pubs/free/WhyStudyHistory.htm

Tatum, A. W. (2008). African-American males at risk: A researcher's study of endangered males and literature that works. In S. S. Lehr (Ed.), *Shattering the looking glass; challenge, risk & controversy in children's literature* (pp. 137–153). Norwood, MA: Christopher-Gordon.

Wilhelm, J. D. (2007). *Engaging readers & writers with inquiry*. New York: Scholastic.

Wilhelm, J. D. (2008). *"You gotta be the book"; Teaching engaged and reflective reading with adolescents*. New York: Teachers College Press.

Wopperer, E. (2011). Inclusive literature in the library and classroom. *Knowledge Quest, 39* (3), 26–34.

FURTHER READING

Agosto, D. E. (2007). Building a multicultural school library: Issues and challenges. *Teacher Librarian, 34* (3), 27–31.

Bush, G. One indivisible day: Teaching social justice through literature. *School Library Media Activities Monthly, 24* (8), 24–27.

Cohen, A. (March 27, 2011). Muslim-Americans try to "write" Hollywood's wrongs. National Public Radio. [Podcast] Retrieved from http://www.npr.org/2011/03/27/134621891/muslim-americans-try-to-write-hollywoods-wrongs

Collins, J. (2010). Transform global literature circles with Web 2.0. *Library Media Connections, 29* (2), 24–25.

Devoogd, G. (2006). Question authority. *School Library Journal, 52* (4), 48–52.

Hancock, M. R. (2008). The status of reader response research: Sustaining the reader's voice in challenging times. In S. S. Lehr (Ed.), *Shattering the looking glass; challenge, risk & controversy in children's literature* (pp. 91–108). Norwood, MA: Christopher-Gordon.

Hunt, T. J., & Hunt, B. (2005). Learning by teaching multicultural literature. *English Journal, 94* (3), 76–80.

Kaplan, J. S. (2007). Recent research in young adult literature: Three predominant strands of study. *ALAN Review, 34* (3), 53–60.

Kern, D. (2007). Flying with critical literacy wings. *New England Reading Association Journal, 43* (2), 87–89.

Knowles, L., & Smith, M. (2007). *Understanding diversity through novels and picture books.* Westport, CT: Libraries Unlimited.

Lehman, B. A., Freeman, E. B., & Scharer, P. L. (2010). *Reading globally, K-8.* Thousand Oaks, CA: Corwin.

Loh, C. E. (2010). Reading nation and world: Cultivating culturally and critically reflexive readers. *English Journal, 100* (1), 108–112.

Maples, J., & Groenke, S. (2009). Who is an American? Challenging middle school students' assumptions through critical literacy. *Voices from the Middle, 17* (2), 28–35.

McPherson, K. (2008). Shaping global criticality with school libraries. *School Libraries Worldwide, 14* (2), 35–44.

Mestre, L. S. (2009). Culturally responsive instruction for teacher librarians. *Teacher Librarian, 36* (3), 8–12.

Moreillon, J., & Cahill, M. (2010). When cultures meet. *School Library Monthly, 27* (2), 27–29.

Sardone, N. B., & Devlin-Scherer, R. (2010). Keeping it current: Using technology to teach about social issues. *English Journal, 99* (4), 61–64.

Steiner, S. F., Nash, C. P., & Chase, M. (2008). Multicultural literature that brings people together. *The Reading Teacher, 62* (1), 88–92.

Taliaferro, C. (2009). Using picture books to expand adolescents' imaginings of themselves and others. *English Journal, 99* (2), 30–36.

Wolk, S. (2009). Reading for a better world. Teaching for social responsibility with young adult literature. *Journal of Adolescent & Adult Literacy, 52* (8), 664–673.

7

Appreciating Literary and Artistic Excellence

All young people deserve the opportunity to read, view, and hear a broad range of resources, including high quality literary and artistic materials. To ensure positive interactions with excellent materials, students must have exposure and free access to use them. Through displays, promotions, and programs, school librarians introduce students to award-winning books and media. In secondary schools, the range of appropriate awards and lists of outstanding materials expands significantly from the elementary level and includes titles geared to adults. This wide selection of materials provides many opportunities for marketing library collections and connecting with classroom agendas.

Informational books are now taking more space on our shelves dedicated to award-winning titles. In the past, fiction was the dominate genre represented in the awards. Recently, new awards for nonfiction have been established, reflecting an increased emphasis on encouraging the use of informational materials other than textbooks in classrooms. The Young Adult Library Services Association (YALSA) Award for Excellence in Nonfiction for Young Adults was first presented in 2010 to Deborah Heiligman for *Charles and Emma: The Darwins' Leap of Faith*. In 2000, the Robert F. Sibert Medal was created by the Association of Library Service for Children (ALSC) for nonfiction, to be awarded to an author and illustrator for the most distinguished informational book for children published in English. The first Sibert Medal went to Marc Aronson for *Sir Walter Raleigh and the Quest for El Dorado* in 2001. Also, both fiction and nonfiction books are eligible for the Printz Award, sponsored by YALSA and first presented in 2000.

In addition, as other formats for reading, listening, and viewing have expanded, new awards for media have become available. For example, the Odyssey Award, established in 2006 by YALSA and ALSC and first presented in 2008, honors excellence in audiobook production (Cart, 2010). An industry group, the Audio Publishers Association, was established in 1986 and created a platform to promote its products, the Audie Awards, in 1996. Though librarians recognize the limitations of an award from a for-profit organization, the Audie Awards focus attention on new products available to meet collection needs. The Amazing Audiobooks for Young Adults list by YALSA also identifies quality audiobooks each year.

The topic of book awards and lists is a major one in libraries of all types, in schools of all levels, for authors and illustrators, and for many readers, as well as for publishers of books and journals. Writing from the perspective of a judge for several book awards and

READS Component	READS Indicator	AASL *Standards for the 21st-Century Learner**	Common Core State Standards—English Language Arts**
2. Explore characteristics, history, and awards of creative works			
The student will:			
2.3 Appreciate literary and artistic excellence.	2.3.1 Identify award-winning authors, illustrators, and producers of literary and creative works (e.g., Pulitzer Prize winners).	• 4.1.3 Respond to literature and creative expressions of ideas in various formats and genres. • 4.2.4 Show an appreciation for literature . . .	• Reading: Literature—10 Read and comprehend literature in the grade text complexity band . . . • Writing—9 Draw evidence from literary or informational texts to support analysis . . . .

*Excerpted from *Standards for the 21st-Century Learner* by the American Association of School Librarians, a division of the American Library Association, copyright © 2007 American Library Association. Available for download at www.ala.org/aasl/standards. Used with permission.

**Excerpted from *Common Core State Standards for English Language Arts*. National Governors Association Center for Best Practices and Council of Chief State School Officers Commercial License. Copyright © 2010. Used with permission of NGA Center/CCSSO.

a university researcher, Junko Yokota (2011) points out, "Children are often required to read award-winning literature, adults often view award winners as credentials determining worth, publishers see them as moneymakers, and authors and illustrators bask in the recognition" (p. 467).

When, and even before, books are published, they are examined by reviewers, who influence their success with comments and assigned age and grade levels. As books are put to use in schools, public libraries, and homes, children and young adults begin to form opinions about them. Judges of book and media awards and compilers of lists apply a variety of criteria to select their favorites, which continue to impact choices made by librarians, parents, and other purchasers. Bestseller lists also influence many readers who want to be ready to enter conversations about the latest literary hit.

The intent or purpose varies among the award or reading list committees or professional journal staff members. Some intend to select only one best title meeting the stated criteria related to literary quality, with several honor books or media. For the big name awards, this is the situation (e.g., the Caldecott Medal, the Newbery Medal, the Printz Award, etc.). In the case of the book lists, the intent is to identify multiple outstanding titles, often within a date of publication range (e.g., Best Fiction for Young Adults, Booklist Editor's Choice, Notable Children's Books, among others). The creators of some reading lists do not intend to select the best of the year, but to pull together lists of books with appeal to the interests of young people (e.g., Quick Picks for Reluctant Young Adult Readers).

Within schools, books and other media are viewed through several lenses, including those of the librarian, reading experts, language arts or English teachers, and other content area teachers. The school librarian considers the perspectives of all groups when evaluating reviews, awards, and lists for selection purposes. In addition, the periodical collection for the school should include the professional journals of the major educational groups and made readily available to teachers. Though some book and media awards are available free online, other organizations require a member's password to access the most recent list (e.g., National Council for the Social Studies). The older resource lists are available to all online.

An ideal situation occurs when teachers and the school librarian read reviews and consider awards and lists, then collaborate in making final selections for purchase. In this current period of limited funds for materials, the wise course is to create a database or other list of desired titles and add notes of recognition and merit received by each title. When a title appears on several notable and best lists, receives awards, and meets curricular needs, and has high student appeal, it becomes clear that it is a priority item for purchase.

The selection of outstanding resources for secondary students is organized first by awards for literary and artistic quality, both from the American Library Association (ALA) and its divisions, and from other professional organizations and groups. The next section is comprised of lists of resources with multiple titles, most published annually, from library professional organizations and from other professional organizations, journals, newspapers, and publishers. The final section is popularity awards, voted by students and organized by professional groups of educators.

AWARDS FOR LITERARY QUALITY

American Library Association and Divisions

Alex Awards. Named for Margaret Alexander Edwards, young adult librarian. Ten books written for adults with special appeal to young adults. YALSA

Andrew Carnegie Medal for Excellence in Children's Video. ALSC

Coretta Scott King Book Award. Given to an African American author and illustrator. Ethnic and Multicultural Information Exchange Round Table / ALA

Coretta Scott King—John Steptoe Award for New Talent. Intended to encourage new authors and illustrators. Ethnic and Multicultural Information Exchange Round Table/ALA

John Newbery Medal. Awarded to American author for distinguished writing for children. Fiction or nonfiction. ALSC

Laura Ingalls Wilder Medal. Honors author or illustrator for substantial and lasting contribution to literature for children. ALSC

Michael L. Printz Award. Book exemplifying literary excellence in young adult literature for ages 12 to 18. Fiction or nonfiction. YALSA

Mildred L. Batchelder Award. Goes to American publisher for children's book considered outstanding in foreign language in a foreign country and subsequently translated and published in the United States. ALSC

Odyssey Award for Excellence in Audiobook Production. For children's or young adult audiobook. ALSC/*Booklist*/YALSA

Pura Belpre Award. Presented to a Latino or Latina writer and illustrator whose work best portrays, affirms, and celebrates the Latino cultural experience in an outstanding work of literature for children and youth. ALSC and REFORMA, the National Association to Promote Library and Information Services to Latinos and the Spanish Speaking

Randolph Caldecott Medal. Awarded to illustrator of distinguished American picture book. ALSC

Robert F. Sibert Informational Book Medal. Award goes to author and illustrator. ALSC

Schneider Family Book Award. Goes to author or illustrator of a book with artistic expression of the disability experience intended for children and adolescents. ALA

William C. Morris YA Debut Award. Honors a first-time author writing for teens. YALSA

YALSA Award for Excellence in Nonfiction. New in 2010. YALSA

Other Professional Organizations and Groups

Amelia Elizabeth Walden Book Award for Young Adult Fiction. Assembly on Literature for Adolescents (ALAN)

American Indian Youth Literature Award. Given for writing and illustrating by and about American Indians. Awarded for a picture book, middle school book, and young adult book. American Indian Library Association

Americas Award for Children's and Young Literature. Features works from the United States in English or Spanish that portrays Latin American, the Caribbean, or Latinos in the U.S. Consortium of Latin American Studies Programs (CLASP)

Asian/Pacific American Award for Literature. Given to authors of books about Asian/Pacific Americans and their heritage. Picture book, children's literature, literature for young adults, adult fiction, adult nonfiction. Asian/Pacific American Librarians

Astrid Lindgren Memorial Award. Goes to author, illustrator, oral storyteller, or those active in promoting reading. Swedish Arts Council

Audie Award. Provides multiple awards including audiobook of the year, children and teen audiobooks, and fiction and nonfiction works in various genres. Audio Publishers Association

Boston Globe—Horn Book Award. Honors picture books, fiction and poetry, and nonfiction books published in the United States. *Boston Globe, The Horn Book Magazine*

Carter Woodson Book Award. Honors social science books for young readers that depict ethnicity in the U.S. National Council for the Social Studies

Edgar Award. Honors mystery writers in various categories including short story, novel, juvenile, young adult, play, crime fact, and TV episode. Mystery Writers of America

Eisner Award. Honors creators of graphic novels in more than 20 categories including best publications for kids and teens. Comic Convention, Inc.

Hans Christian Andersen Award. To encourage international understanding given on biennial basis to an international author and illustrator whose body of work has made a lasting contribution to children's literature. International Board on Books for Young People (IBBY)

Jane Addams Book Award. Honors books for younger children and older children promoting cause of peace, social justice, world community, and the equality of the sexes and all races. Women's International League for Peace and Freedom and Jane Addams Peace Association

Middle East Book Awards. Given for picture books, youth literature, and youth nonfiction. Middle East Outreach Council/Middle East Studies Association

National Book Award. Winners selected by writers in these categories: fiction, nonfiction, poetry, and young people's literature. National Book Foundation

NCTE Award for Excellence in Poetry for Children. Given every two years for excellence in poetry for ages 3–13. National Council of Teachers of English

Nobel Prizes. International awards in literature, physics, chemistry, medicine, economic sciences, and peace. Nobel Foundation

Orbis Pictus Award for Outstanding Nonfiction for Children. Book judged on accuracy, organization, design, style. For K-8. National Council of Teachers of English

Pulitzer Prizes. Awards excellence in journalism, including editorial cartoons, photography, reporting, and writing; and letters, drama, and music. Pulitzer Prize Board/Columbia University

Lists of Resources

Lists from Library Professional Organizations

Amazing Audiobooks for Young Adults. Includes top 10 selections. Fiction and nonfiction. YALSA

The Amelia Bloomer Book List. Books with significant feminist content for ages birth through 18. Fiction and nonfiction. Selected by a committee of the Feminist Task Force of the Social Responsibilities Round Table/YALSA

Best Fiction for Young Adults. Name change for 2011 list from Best Books for Young Adults. Includes top 10. YALSA

Fabulous Films for Young Adults. Group of films relating to a theme with appeal to young adults. Selection criteria consistent with the Library Bill of Rights. Includes documentaries. YALSA

Great Graphic Novels for Teens. Graphic novels published in past 16 months. Includes top 10. Fiction and nonfiction. YALSA

Great Interactive Software for Kids List. Exemplary computer software and multi-platform media. ALSC

Great Web Sites for Kids. Websites for prekindergarten through middle school on selected topics: animals, the arts; history and biography; literature and languages; reference desk; mathematics and computers; sciences; social sciences; sites for parents, caregivers, teachers, and others. ALSC and ALA

Notable Children's Books. Preschool through middle school. ALSC

Notable Children's Recordings. Preschool through middle school. ALSC

Notable Children's Videos. Preschool through middle school. ALSC

Notable Videos for Adults. 15 outstanding programs released with past two years. Video Round Table/American Library Association

Outstanding Books for the College Bound and Lifelong Learners. 2009; revised every five years. Arts and humanities; history and culture; literature and language; arts; science and technology; and social sciences. YALSA and Association of College and Research Libraries

Outstanding Reference Sources. For small and medium-sized libraries. Reference and User Services Association

Popular Paperbacks for Young Adults. Popular or topical titles. Includes top 10 selections. Fiction and nonfiction. Topics vary from year to year. YALSA

Quick Picks for Reluctant Young Adult Readers. Intended for recreational use, not curricular or remedial use. Includes top 10 selections. Fiction and nonfiction. YALSA

Rainbow Project Book List. Recommended books deal with lesbian, bisexual, transgendered and questioning issues and situations for children up to age 18. Includes top ten selections. Fiction and nonfiction. Gay, Lesbian, Bisexual, and Transgender Round Table and Social Responsibility Round Table/ALA

Lists by Professional Organizations, Journals, Newspapers, and Publishers

Best Books. In December issue. School Library Journal

Booklist Editors' Choice: Adult Books for Young Adults. The year's best personal reading for teens. ALA Publishing

Booklist Editors' Choice: Books for Youth. ALA Publishing

Booklist Editors' Choice: Media. ALA Publishing

READS Component	READS Indicator	AASL *Standards for the 21st-Century Learner**	Common Core State Standards—English Language Arts**
2. Explore characteristics, history, and awards of creative works			
The student will:			
2.3 Appreciate literary and artistic excellence.	2.3.2 Demonstrate a knowledge of and respect for the concept of intellectual freedom.	• 3.3.1 Solicit and respect diverse perspectives . . . • 3.3.7 Respect the principles of intellectual freedom. • 4.1.2 Read widely and fluently to make connections with self, the world, and previous reading. • 4.1.3 Respond to literature and creative expressions of ideas in various formats and genres. • 4.2.3 Maintain openness to new ideas . . . • 4.3.1 Participate in the social exchange of ideas, both electronically and in person.	• Reading: Informational Text—7 Integrate and evaluate multiple sources of information presented in different media or formats . . . • Reading: Informational Text—8 Delineate and evaluate the reasoning in texts . . . • Reading: Informational Text—9 Analyze foundational U.S. documents of historical and literary significance (including the Bill of Rights) . . . • Reading: Literature—6 Analyze a case in which grasping point of view requires distinguishing what is directly stated in a text from what is really meant . . . • Reading: Literature—9 Demonstrate knowledge of foundational works of American literature . . . • Reading: Literature—10 Read and comprehend literature in the grade text complexity band . . . • Speaking and Listening—1 Initiate and participate effectively in a range of collaborative discussions . . . • Writing—9 Draw evidence from literary or informational texts to support analysis . . .

Booklist Editors' Choice: Reference Sources. ALA Publishing

Booklist's Top of the List. The single best title of the year in adult fiction, adult nonfiction, youth picture book, reference source, video/DVD, and audiobook. ALA Publishing

IBBY Honour List. Recognizes international writers, illustrators, and translators from IBBY member countries. Issued on biennial basis for multilingual works. International Board for Young People (IBBY)

Notable Books for a Global Society. Children's Literature & Reading Special Interest Group/International Reading Association

Notable Children's Books in the English Language Arts. Gr. K-8. Children's Literature Assembly/National Council of Teachers of English

Notable Social Studies Trade Books for Young People. National Council for the Social Studies and Children's Book Council

Outstanding Science Trade Books for Students K-12. Supplemental materials provided for most titles. List published online and in science journals. National Science Teachers Association, Children's Book Council

Popularity Awards

Children's Choices Reading List. K-Gr. 6. Published in the October issue of *The Reading Teacher.* International Reading Association and The Children's Book Council

Teens Top Ten. YALSA

Young Adults' Choices Reading List. Gr. 7–12. Published in the November issue of the *Journal of Adolescent & Adult Literacy.* International Reading Association

State Readers' Choice Awards (See chart and discussion in Chapter 11)

INTELLECTUAL FREEDOM

One of the challenges and responsibilities of a school librarian is informing students, teachers, administrators, parents, and community groups about intellectual freedom. Providing free access to reading and learning materials is a vital aspect of the work of a school librarian in implementing the READS curriculum. Though a bounty of appealing and outstanding resources is available in school libraries, a few people believe that students should not be allowed to read, view, or hear certain items. From the perspective of young people, information about intellectual freedom is crucial as current students, citizens, and future parents. For teachers, this topic impacts their choice of materials for classroom use, strategies for enabling critical thinking in their classes, relationships with parents and the community, and possibly their ability to retain their jobs. For administrators, this area is a potential public relations nightmare if a complaint goes to the school board and creates negative press for the school and the district. However, it is also an opportunity to show support for the rights of students and teachers. Parents can be involved as staunch supporters of school libraries and the freedom to read or the one who makes a complaint against a particular book.

Intellectual freedom means using one's mind to read, listen, view, create, or speak in a free and open manner. This right is a cornerstone of American society and is guaranteed in the First Amendment to the U.S. Constitution. The First Amendment begins: "Congress shall make no law . . . abridging the freedom of speech, or of the press" (1791). However, the First Amendment was not formally linked to libraries until 1939, when the first version of the Library Bill of Rights was approved by the American Library Association

List in a Box

Banned Books Week Taglines

2011 Free Your Mind: Read a Banned Book
2010 Think for Yourself and Let Others Do the Same
2009 Speak. Read. Know.
2008 Closing Books Shuts Out Ideas
2007 Banned Books Ahoy! Treasure Your Freedom to Read
2006 Read Banned Books: They're Your Ticket to Freedom
2005 Read Banned Books: It's Your Freedom We Are Talking About
2004 Campaign for the Freedom to Read: Elect to Read a Banned Book
2003 Can the Ban on Books!
2002 Let Freedom Read: Read a Banned Book
2001 Develop Yourself: Explore Your Mind to a Banned Book
2000 Fish in the River of Knowledge: Celebrate Your Freedom to Read

Source: Banned Books Week: Celebrating the Freedom to Read. http://ala.org.

(Stripling, Williams, Johnston, & Anderton, 2010). It seems reasonable that, as library users, young people would enjoy these same privileges. However, it was not until 1943 that the U.S. Supreme Court ruled that minors were entitled to First Amendment rights in the case of *West Virginia State Board of Education v. Barnette* (Stripling et al., 2010).

Though not stated explicitly in the First Amendment, the right to read is derived from the freedom of speech and is a foundational element of school library documents. After the Library Bill of Rights was first established in 1939, the companion document, *Access to Resources and Services in the School Library Media Program: An Interpretation of the Library Bill of Rights*, was adopted by the ALA Council in 1986 and last amended in 2008. This document states:

School library media specialists assume a leadership role in promoting the principles of intellectual freedom within the school by providing resources and services that create and sustain an atmosphere of free inquiry. . . . Intellectual freedom is fostered by educating students in the use of critical thinking skills to empower them to pursue free inquiry responsibly and independently.

The recent rapid development of online technologies has prompted the establishment of two additional interpretations of *The Library Bill of Rights*, *Access to Digital Information, Services, and Networks: An Interpretation of the Library Bill of Rights*, adopted in 1996 and last amended in 2009, and *Minors and Internet Interactivity: An Interpretation of the Library Bill of Rights*, adopted in 2009. A timeline is provided for selected documents on intellectual freedom to show the expansion over the years of the original *Library Bill of Rights*. These statements impact the work of school librarians in multiple ways, including collection development; establishment of appropriate practices and facilities; support of teachers and reading programs; teaching literature, the research process, and production skills; and provision of Internet access and policies. When implementing the intent of these professional documents, school librarians will fulfill the five roles outlined in *Empowering Learners: Guidelines for School Library Media Programs*: leader, instructional partner, information specialist, teacher, and program specialist.

In 2004, Doug Johnson, a leader, author, and frequent presenter on school libraries and technology, wrote that school librarians need to be involved in championing students' rights to information in a filtered network environment, to help write and monitor district acceptable use policies, to protect students' and educators' privacy online, to teach evaluation of resources and ethical use practices, and to work to close the digital divide, ensuring access to technology for all. Five years later, he coauthored an article with Joyce Kasman Valenza in *School Library Journal* (October, 2009), exhorting school librarians to

Timeline of Selected Documents on Intellectual Freedom		
Original Date/Last Amended	**Document**	**Organization**
1791	Bill of Rights to United States Constitution	United States Congress
1939	Library Bill of Rights	ALA Council
1971/2009	Challenged Materials: An Interpretation of the Library Bill of Rights	ALA Council
1972/2008	Free Access to Libraries for Minors: An Interpretation of the Library Bill of Rights	ALA Council
1981/2009	Guideline on The Students' Right to Read	National Council of Teachers of English
1986/2008	Access to Resources and Services in the School Library Media Program: An Interpretation of the Library Bill of Rights	ALA Council
1989/2004	Access for Children and Young Adults to Nonprint Materials: An Interpretation of the Library Bill of Rights	ALA Council
1993/2008	Access to Library Resources and Services Regardless of Sex, Gender Identity, Gender Expression, or Sexual Orientation: An Interpretation of the Library Bill of Rights	ALA Council
1996/2009	Access to Digital Information, Services, and Networks: An Interpretation of the Library Bill of Rights	ALA Council
2002	Privacy: An Interpretation of the Library Bill of Rights	ALA Council
2009	Services to People with Disabilities: An Interpretation of the Library Bill of Rights	ALA Council
2009	Importance of Education to Intellectual Freedom: An Interpretation of the Library Bill of Rights	ALA Council
2009	Minors and Internet Interactivity: An Interpretation of the Library Bill of Rights	ALA Council
2010	Prisoners Right to Read: An Interpretation of the Library Bill of Rights	ALA Council

embrace the responsibilities required to ensure that all students have equitable access to the Internet:

Enough with the "yeah, buts," opting out of the intellectual freedom battle by saying things like: but my IT people block that, the principal will never approve that, the board has a policy, or the parents will get upset. Intellectual freedom is our banner to wave and to wave now. If a parent or administrator tells us to remove a book from our collections, we fight. But many of the new communication tools . . . which are used effectively in some schools and libraries are blocked in too many others. Are we willing to take the fight for open access to information and tools to the same level that we've fought for in the past . . . for materials in written form? Are we helping develop good Internet filtering policies? Are we demonstrating and showing models of the effective use of online tools to our policy makers? And are we bringing the technology department onboard with the concept of intellectual freedom? It is time for librarians who get intellectual freedom to be heroes and fight. (p. 30)

The instructional responsibilities of school librarians related to intellectual freedom and censorship are clear in the *Standards for the 21st-Century Learner* (2007). Strategies for providing information on intellectual freedom are lessons and staff training, displays in the library, broadcasts to the school, the library website, and outreach to the community including local media outlets and the public library.

Practices within the Library

A frontline opportunity to model intellectual freedom exists in the practices and attitudes of the school librarian and staff when selecting materials on many viewpoints and topics, making ideas and information freely available to students in multiple formats, and by interacting with students in positive and sensitive ways, opening the door to discussion of materials and issues, but respecting the privacy of students when necessary. When in discussions with students about the use of materials, using the terms access or connections to information may be more understandable than referring to intellectual property rights (Adams, 2009). However, we suggest that in some situations, it is appropriate to equate access and intellectual property rights in conversations with senior high students, to elevate their understanding of academic language. Other applicable terms are "right to read" or "freedom to read."

Another issue related to access to materials and personal freedom is the right to privacy, which is covered in the Fourth and Fifth Amendments as well as state and federal laws. If a student needs an item from the library collection that is not on the shelf and is checked out by another individual, the student often asks who has the item. This is the teachable moment to explain that the identity of a person using a book is confidential, protected by library policy in addition to state and federal laws, specifically the Bill of Rights. Whenever new clerical staff is hired, it is crucial to provide training on this issue immediately, as many kind people initially view providing information on the location of a book as being helpful to patrons. It will be useful to share the language of *Privacy: An Interpretation of the Library Bill of Rights* during training: "Everyone (paid or unpaid) who provides governance, administration, or service in libraries has a responsibility to maintain an environment respectful and protective of the privacy of all users" (ALA, 2002).

Another practice within the library that models intellectual freedom is providing opportunities for students to suggest items for consideration for the library collection. This can be managed through the use of a traditional or online suggestion box or by including students on a library advisory committee. Helen R. Adams (2009), school librarian and vocal advocate for intellectual freedom, writes, "Use selection policy criteria such as 'reflect the pluralistic nature of a global society' and/or 'free of bias and stereotyping' to teach students about the right of all members of a democratic society, including minors, to view, listen to, and read materials with diverse perspectives" (p. 55). A brief synopsis of such criteria for selection could be posted beside a suggestion box in the library or online as part of a website to take advantage of the moment to connect the concept of intellectual freedom and choice of reading/viewing/listening materials.

Examples of school libraries with online materials suggestion features include Lalor Library Media Center in Tenafly High School in New Jersey (http://www.librarymedia.net/index.html, David Di Gregorio, library media supervisor). This site provides a link for patrons to e-mail a suggestion to the library staff. Another site is The Unquiet Library at Creekview High School in Canton, Georgia. An online form for suggested library materials is linked to the home page at https://sites.google.com/site/theunquietlibrary/home. This form is targeted at both students and staff and provides multiple categories for describing the desired items. Media specialists at Creekview High School are Buffy Hamilton and Roxanne Johnson.

An inherent aspect of the right to read is equal access to materials and resources. This topic is addressed in *Free Access to Libraries for Minors: An Interpretation of the Library Bill of Right (2008)*. Within the library setting, school librarians need to be cognizant of the reality that not all students have computer and printer access in their homes. Many teachers are now giving outside of class assignments, requiring students to word process or create other documents. School librarians can provide opportunities within the school day and extended hours of the library for students to use computers and software to access information online, create documents, and e-mail assignments to teachers. Students can still be found waiting at the door of the library in the morning to use resources to prepare for the school day. Another concern is the need for facilities and furniture that allow students with physical disabilities to access books, computers, and all other resources in the library.

The celebration of Banned Books Week is probably the most frequently used strategy for promoting intellectual freedom in school libraries. A major aspect of the celebration is displays within and outside the library. A multitude of suggestions for Banned Books Week is available at the ALA website under the Office of Intellectual Freedom. The READS Internet Resources list provides specific URLs leading to resources. Some of the slogans used over the past 10 years are placed in a sidebar. The slogan selected for a particular year may not appeal to you, so choose another one offered in the past. Recycling good ideas and display materials is a great thing to do!

Direct Instruction and Collaboration

Opportunities abound for collaborating with teachers on units in language arts, social studies, science, and other areas incorporating intellection freedom concepts. In 2009, ALA issued a new directive on the need for instruction, *Importance of Education to Intellectual Freedom: An Interpretation of the Library Bill of Rights*. Whether through collaborative units based on content area objectives or in sessions inviting teachers to bring classes for sessions built around Banned Book Week, Constitution Day, or other commemorative events, school librarians need to find ways to communicate with students on these important issues.

The broad term intellectual freedom encompasses numerous other more specific meanings, as indicated by the language choices used in articles and books about this concept. Rosemary Chance (2008) explains:

> *Think of the term "intellectual freedom" as a large umbrella. Underneath that umbrella we find both negative actions (censoring, banning, challenging, labeling) and positive actions (reconsideration, selecting, reading freely). Each of these actions has a direct relationship to books published, written, and read by young adults. (p. 136)*

Chance's quote provides us with an approach and the beginning of a word bank of terms to be used in instructional activities with students and others. When creating an initial awareness of intellectual freedom concepts, the use of positive terms is appropriate: freedom to read, right to choose, respect for the perspectives of others, variety of opinions, multiple viewpoints, or tolerance of others. When explaining the restrictive actions sometimes taken by individuals or groups, the negative terms are introduced: banned books, censorship, violation of rights of others, challenging a book, restriction of ideas, or imposition of moral views on others.

Several lessons on intellectual freedom are found on the READS Lessons and Activities list. Another option is implementing a session opening with a short story from the collection edited by Judy Blume, *Places I Never Meant to Be*, followed by a discussion of intellectual freedom, incorporating appropriate vocabulary terms, which could be highlighted in a word wall display. You may want to follow up one of these lessons or your own lesson with the Intellectual Freedom Word Sorts included in this chapter. This activity is developed for advanced students and includes vocabulary terms in a word bank. It could be adapted for use at the middle school level.

Another approach, which could be coordinated with a language arts or reading teacher, is using novels featuring intellectual freedom themes such as censorship, free speech, or free press in literature circles or a book club activity. Pat Scales (2001) provides teaching

Intellectual Freedom Word Sort			
freedom	opinion	First Amendment	ideas
appropriate	protect	censorship	U.S. Constitution
"right to read"	values	reality	parents
obscenity	control	tolerance	educators
authors	respect	morals	violation
teenagers	challenge	viewpoint	choices
learning	rights	citizens	"freedom of speech"
choices	intellectual	removal of book	banned
restrict	perspective	complaint	book challenge

1. Conduct lesson on intellectual freedom/book banning from READS Lessons and Activities list or own lesson. Include use of all terms in word bank.
2. Divide students into groups of four and distribute the Intellectual Freedom Word Sort.
3. Instruct students to think about the words and how they could be sorted in a variety of ways. Encourage students to analyze the words and consider the perspectives of various people impacted by a book challenge. Each table of students will decide on at least four ways to cluster the words. The goal is to use all words at least once. A word could be used more than once by labeling the second use of the word (e.g., protect 2). Provide an example not likely to be used by students (e.g., words an author would prefer: "right to read," ideas, choices, learning, freedom, First Amendment, etc.).
4. Distribute poster board or large sheets of paper and pens. Direct students to create charts of word groups and prepare to share and justify their use of the words to the class.

guides to 12 books that are often used in classrooms. In addition, activities are included on the READS Lessons and Activity list, which can be used during Banned Book Week. One offering is an audio broadcast, "Podcast: Censorship and Your Freedom to Read" from the ReadWriteThink website. This is a booktalk by host and teacher Jennifer Buehler created for Banned Book Week 2010 and appropriate for continued use in other years. Links to many organizations providing information as well as book display themes and ideas are found on the READS Internet Resources list. The top 10 titles on the 2010 Most Frequently Challenged Books list from ALA's Office of Intellectual Freedom are provided.

Language Arts Ideas

- Discuss the importance of the right to read in society and check out books from the Banned Book Week displays in the library.
- Discuss the differences between challenged and banned books with older students. After reading a banned book, have students research book reviews on the book, press coverage of the community controversy, and the results of the challenge process (Stephens, 2008), reporting back to the class. Alternatively, instead of reading an entire book, have students choose one of the books from the current list of banned books and implement the same activities. A longer list of banned books is included on the ALA Office of Intellectual Freedom site.
- Locate video or online interviews with authors on intellectual freedom topics.
- Have students respond to a quotation on First Amendment issues using the ALA resource Notable Quotations on the First Amendment, Censorship and the Freedom to Read on our READS Internet Resources list.
- Assign students to write letters to editors in newspapers and magazine during Banned Book Week.

Social Studies Ideas

- Connect intellectual freedom activities to study of the Constitution and establishment of the American government.
- Examine the role of intellectual freedom concepts in current events (e.g., recent political events in the Middle East, China's refusal to allow the winner of the Nobel Peace Prize to travel to receive the prize).
- Discuss Supreme Court cases related to free speech, intellectual freedom, and rights of minors. Use mock trial drama scenarios to engage students in issues. Johns (2008) suggests, "Students take the role of parents, reading a 'banned book,' filling out the reconsideration form and writing a letter to the editor about their disapproval or, most often, support for the book" (p. 7).
- Observe Bill of Rights Day on December 15 with a presentation by the school librarian; assign middle school students to play the interactive Bill of Rights Game (see READS Internet Resources list).
- Check The Learning Network blog on the *New York Times* website for current offerings. On October 26, 2010, a word activity was posted, Fill-In: First Amendment, based on a recent political news story, accompanied by an attention-grabbing graphic of the First Amendment tattooed on a man's arm. Follow the link on our READS Lessons and Activities list.
- Select a film to use with social studies classes from the First Amendment Film Festival offerings on our READS Internet Resources list.

Teacher Support and Training on Intellectual Freedom Issues

List in a Box

2010 Most Frequently Challenged Books

1. *And Tango Makes Three.* By Peter Parnell and Justin Richardson
2. *The Absolutely True Diary of a Part-Time Indian.* By Sherman Alexie
3. *Brave New World.* By Aldous Huxley
4. *Crank.* By Ellen Hopkins
5. *The Hunger Games.* By Suzanne Collins
6. *Lush.* By Natasha Friend
7. *What My Mother Doesn't Know.* By Sonya Sones
8. *Nickel and Dimed.* By Barbara Ehrenreich
9. *Revolutionary Voices.* Edited by Amy Sonnie
10. *Twilight.* By Stephanie Meyer

Source: The Office for Intellectual Freedom of the American Library Association. http://www.ala.org.

School librarians may be called on by teachers or administrators when books are challenged within a school. Hopefully, a process for reconsideration of materials is already established in the school, so that the request will be for location of reviews on the book in question. If such a protocol is not part of the school or library handbook, then the librarian should assume a leadership role and plan with the administration to form a staff committee to create a plan that should include selection guidelines for library and classroom resources. Start with appropriate professional statements from the Timeline of Selected Documents on Intellectual Freedom Issues. The website for the National Council of Teachers of English also has several useful resources at the Anti-Censorship Center, including a template for creating a rationale for teaching a book. The site also sells CDs with rationales for more than 300 books. See the READS Internet Resources for the link. In *Knowledge Quest* 2007, Principal Jeffrey Gibson suggests that the best approach to managing censorship challenges is to partner with the school librarian to champion the rights of students. What a powerful message this would be for teachers!

The materials discussed here may also be used in providing an in-service for the teaching staff on dealing with potential censorship issues. Consider using these dramatic metaphors: "censorship as a barbed wire fence . . . censorship as a patina . . . censorship as a dangerous tightrope" (pp. 654–656). These thought-provoking phrases were written by Fenice B. Boyd and Nancy C. Bailey in an article in *Journal of Adolescent & Adult Literacy* published in May 2009. These skilled authors address censorship challenges in classrooms and libraries using young adult literature as examples and offer rich language patterns to illuminate this difficult topic, which will be appreciated by other teachers.

Community Advocacy for Intellectual Freedom

Another means of protecting the intellectual freedom of students is to address school boards and other community educational and civic groups with positive messages about the efforts of the school staff. If possible, work with administrators and teachers in developing a common message for these community organizations about various aspects of intellectual freedom including the right to read classroom selections and to use the resources of the school library; the need to support the learning needs of low income, special education, and English language learners; and the advantages of having access to current online information.

Involving students in presentations to the community is a good practice. For example, the Florida Association for Media in Education (FAME) sponsors an annual Intellectual Freedom Scholarship. High school seniors write essays on "The Importance of

Intellectual Freedom" and compete for the scholarship from the organization. This student could read the winning essay to a community group and participate in a panel discussion with the principal, teachers, and librarian on intellectual freedom issues. Any school could sponsor a local contest to encourage understanding of these concepts by teens. To learn more about organizing this program, check the FAME website http://www.floridamedia.org/?page=IF_Award.

Connecting parents and young adult literature is another valuable strategy that is used by some reading advocates. Former school librarian and lifetime advocate for intellectual freedom, Pat Scales, invited parents to come to school and discuss young adult novels being read by their children. She had read widely as a teen, including adult novels given to her by her father, who discussed them with her (Scales, 2007). She used her discussion skills with groups of parents that she called "Communicate through Literature". Scales reports on this successful parent book group in a *Knowledge Quest Web Edition* in 2007. She recalls:

> *Fifty parents gathered in the school library once a month to learn about books their young adolescents were reading, and to develop skills for discussing the books with them. No one seemed to shy away from the issues. In fact the books provided a bridge that allowed them to deal with tough issues like suicide, teenage sexuality, death, bullying, and drug and alcohol abuse. Before long parents and students were reading together. Then Judy Blume read about the program and contacted me. She is the person who helped me see how this program actually promoted the principles of intellectual freedom. . . . Before I realized it, I became a spokesperson for intellectual freedom and, in a pro-active way, I began fighting the censorships wars across the nation.*

A final suggestion for promoting intellectual freedom is to cast light on the role of school librarians in protecting the rights of students in your school district. In 2011, Helen R. Adams expressed concern about the impact of the loss of school library positions on the First Amendment rights of students. She asserts: "There is an app for protecting intellectual freedom in school libraries; it is a school librarian! Students will not learn about the principles of intellectual freedom unless a full-time school librarian is in place" (p. 53). Imagine the power of this message when presented by a team of teachers, the principal, and the librarian to the school board and other community groups!

READS LESSONS AND ACTIVITIES

Explore Characteristics, History, and Awards of Creative Works

Appreciate Literary and Artistic Excellence

Introducing authors. Haeffner, C. (2006). Includes note-taking sheet and rubric. *School Library Media Activity Monthly, 22* (8) 29–31.

Nobel Prize games. Nobelprize.org. (Gr. 11–12) http://nobel.org/educational_games/

The 'Nobel'est people. By Alison Zimbalist. The Learning Network: The *New York Times*. (Gr. 6–12) http://learning.blogs.nytimes.com/1998/10/09/the-nobelest-people/?

Podcast: Teen book awards revisited. (Resource) 2/02/2010. ReadWriteThink. (Gr. 6–12) http://www.readwritethink.org/parent-afterschool-resources/podcast-episodes/teen-book-awards-revisited-30496.html

Today, the American Library Association announces its annual book award winners. (Calendar activity). ReadWriteThink. (Gr. 3–12) http://www.readwritethink.org/classroom-resources/calendar-activities/today-american-library-association-20625.html

Intellectual Freedom

Do students have the right to read? First Amendment Center. (Gr. 8–12) http://www.firstamend mentschools.org/resources/lesson.aspx?id=13963

A case for reading—examining challenged and banned books. By Lisa Storm Fink. ReadWriteThink. (Gr. 3–5 and up) http://www.readwritethink.org/classroom-resources/lesson-plans/case-read ing-examining-challenged-410.html

Censorship in the classroom: Understanding controversial issues. By Beth O'Connor. Includes Self-Reflection on Censorship and Propaganda. ReadWriteThink. (Gr. 9–12) http://www.read writethink.org/classroom-resources/lesson-plans/censorship-classroom-understanding-controversial-203.html

Fill-In: First Amendment. (Activity) By Katherine Schulten. The Learning Network: *The New York Times.* (Gr. 8–12) http://learning.blogs.nytimes.com/2010/10/26/fill-in-first-amendment/

First amendment first aid kit. (Resource) Random House. (Gr. 6–12) http://www.randomhouse.com/teens/firstamendment/

First amendment rights. ALA Privacy Web. (Gr. 6–8) http://www.privacyrevolution.org/images/uploads/SchoolLibraryLessons.pdf

Get ready to celebrate banned books week! (Calendar activity). ReadWriteThink. (Gr. 7–12) http://www.readwritethink.org/classroom-resources/calendar-activities/ready-celebrate-banned-books-20295.html

Notable First Amendment court cases. (Resource) Office of Intellectual Freedom. American Library Association. http://www.ala.org/ala/aboutala/offices/oif/firstamendment/courtcases/courtcases.cfm

Notable quotations on the First Amendment, censorship and the freedom to read. (Resource) Office of Intellectual Freedom. American Library Association. http://www.ala.org/ala/aboutala/offices/oif/ifissues/issuesrelatedlinks/quotations.cfm

Podcast: Censorship and your freedom to read. (Resource) Includes most frequently challenged books and YA authors' perspectives on being censored. ReadWriteThink. (Gr. 6–12) http://www.readwritethink.org/parent-afterschool-resources/podcast-episodes/censorship-your-freedom-read-30634.html

Privacy matters. ALA Privacy Web. (Gr. 9–12) http://www.privacyrevolution.org/images/uploads/SchoolLibraryLessons.pdf

Recommended reading? By Jennifer Rittner and Yasmin Chin Eisenhauer. Includes article on book banning. The Learning Network: *The New York Times.* (Gr. 6–12) http://learning.blogs.nytimes.com/2006/06/19/recommended-reading/

Talking about banned books. (Resource) Random House. (Gr. 6–12) http://www.randomhouse.com/teens/firstamendment/talking.html

READS INTERNET RESOURCES

Explore Characteristics, History, and Awards of Creative Works

Appreciate Literary and Artistic Excellence

Awards

Alex Awards. http://www.ala.org/yalsa/booklists/alex

Excellence in Nonfiction for Young Adults. http://www.ala.org/ala/mgrps/divs/yalsa/booklist sawards/nonfiction/nonfiction.cfm

Margaret A. Edward Award (YALSA). http://www.ala.org/yalsa/edwards

Michael L. Printz Award. http://www.ala.org/yalsa/printz

Newbery Medal (ALSC). http://www.ala.org/ala/mgrps/divs/alsc/awardsgrants/bookmedia/newberymedal/newberymedal.cfm

Nobel Prize Winners in Literature: Winners 2010–1901. http://almaz.com/nobel/literature/literature.html

Odyssey Award (ALSA). http://www.ala.org/ala/mgrps/divs/alsc/awardsgrants/bookmedia/odysseyaward/index.cfm

The Pulitzer Prizes. http://www.pulitzer.org/

William C. Morris Debut YA Award. http://www.ala.org/yalsa/morris

Intellectual Freedom

Anti-Censorship Center. National Council of Teachers of English. (Offers CDs for sale with rationales for teaching more than 300 books). http://www.ncte.org/action/anti-censorship

Banned Books Week. ALA Store. http://www.alastore.ala.org/SearchResult.aspx?CategoryID=269

Banned Books Week: Celebrating the freedom to read. http://www.ala.org/ala/issuesadvocacy/banned/bannedbooksweek/

Bill of Rights game. National Constitution Center. http://www.constitutioncenter.org/billofrightsgame/

Censorship and freedom of the press. Web English Teacher. http://www.webenglishteacher.com/censor.html

Censorship creates blindness poster. Random House. http://www.randomhouse.com/teens/firstamendment/FirstAmend.Poster.pdf

Defining Internet freedom. U.S. Department of State. http://www.america.gov/media/pdf/ejs/defining-internet-freedom.pdf

First Amendment Film Festival. American Library Association. http://www.ala.org/ala/issuesadvocacy/banned/bannedbooksweek/ideasandresources/first_amendment_film_festival/filmfestival.cfm

Freedom to Read Foundation timeline. American Library Association. http://www.ala.org/ala/mgrps/affiliates/relatedgroups/freedomtoreadfoundation/ftrfinaction/timeline/timeline.cfm

Intellectual freedom: From AASL essential links. http://aasl.ala.org/essentiallinks/index.php?title=Intellectual_Freedom

"Kids, know your rights! A young person's guide to intellectual freedom". http://www.ala.org/ala/mgrps/divs/alsc/issuesadv/intellectualfreedom/kidsknowyourrights.pdf

Lessons school librarians teach others: Class: The subject is integrity. By Doug Johnson. American Libraries, December 2004. http://www.ala.org/ala/aboutala/offices/oif/iftoolkits/ifmanual/lessonsschoollibrariansteachothers.pdf

Library Bill of Rights. American Library Association. http://www.ala.org/ala/issuesadvocacy/intfreedom/librarybill/index.cfm

Multnomah County Library: Banned books. http://www.multcolib.org/homework/banned.html

National coalition against censorship. http://www.ncac.org/

Rationales for teaching challenged books. National Council of Teachers of English. http://www.ncte.org/action/anti-censorship/rationales

What IF? Questions and answers on intellectual freedom. http://www.education.wisc.edu/ccbc/freedom/whatif/

BIBLIOGRAPHY: AWARDS

Cart, M. (2010). *Young adult literature: From romance to realism.* Chicago, IL: American Library Association.

Yokota, J. (2011). Awards in literature for children and adolescents. In S. A. Wolf, K. Coats, P. Enciso, & C. A. Jenkins (Eds.), *Handbook of research on children's and young adult literature* (pp. 467–478). New York: Routledge.

WORKS CITED: INTELLECTUAL FREEDOM

Adams, H. R. (2009). Citizens in training: Twelve ways to teach students about intellectual freedom. *School Library Media Activities Monthly, 25* (8), 55.

Adams, H. R. (2011). Fewer school librarians: The effect on students' intellectual freedom. *School Library Monthly, 27* (6), 52–53.

American Association of School Librarians. (2007). *Standards for the 21st-century learner.* Chicago, IL: American Library Association.

American Association of School Librarians. (2009). *Empowering learners: Guidelines for school library media programs.* Chicago, IL: American Library Association.

American Library Association. (1996). Library Bill of Rights. Retrieved from http://www.ala.org/ala/issuesadvocacy/intfreedom/librarybill/lbor.pdf

American Library Association. (2002). Privacy: An interpretation of the Library Bill of Rights. Retrieved from http://ala.org/ala/issuesadvocacy/intfreedom/librarybill/interpretations/privacy.cfm

American Library Association. (2008). Access to resources and services: An interpretation of the Library Bill of Rights. Retrieved from http://www.ala.org/ala/issuesadvocacy/intfreedom/librarybill/interpretations/accessresources.cfm

American Library Association. (2008). Free access to libraries for minors: An interpretation of the Library Bill of Rights. Retrieved from http://www.ala.org/ala/issuesadvocacy/intfreedom/librarybill/interpretations/freeaccesslibraries.cfm

American Library Association. (2009). Access to digital information, services, and networks: An interpretation of the Library Bill of rights. Retrieved from http://www.ala.org/ala/issuesadvocacy/intfreedom/librarybill/interpretations/accessdigital.cfm

American Library Association. (2009). Importance of education to intellectual freedom. Retrieved from http://ala.org/ala/issuesadvocacy/intfreedom/librarybill/interpretations/importanceofeducation.cfm

American Library Association. (2009). Minors and Internet interactivity: An interpretation of the Library Bill of Rights. Retrieved from http://www.ala.org/ala/issuesadvocacy/intfreedom/librarybill/interpretations/minorsinternetinteractivity.cfm

Boyd, F. B., & Bailey, N. M. (2009). Censorship in three metaphors. *Journal of Adolescent & Adult Literacy, 52* (8), 653–661.

Buehler, J. (2010). Censorship and your freedom to read. [Podcast] ReadWriteThink. Retrieved from http://www.readwritethink.org/parent-afterschool-resources/podcast-episodes/censorship-your-freedom-read-30634.html

Chance, R. (2008). *Young adult literature in action: A librarian's guide.* Westport, CT: Libraries Unlim ited.

Florida Association for Media in Education. (2011). Intellectual freedom scholarship. Retrieved from http://www.floridamedia.org/?page=IF_Award

Gibson, J. (2007). Championing intellectual freedom: A school administrator's guide. *Knowledge Quest, 36* (2), 46–48.

Johns, S. K. (2008). Intellectual freedom: Walking on a balance beam. *Florida Media Quarterly, 34* (1), 5–7.

Johnson, D. (2004). Lessons school librarians teach others. *American Libraries, 35* (11), 46–48.

Scales, P. (2007). It's about conversation. *Knowledge Quest Web Edition, 36* (2). Retrieved from http://www.ala.org/ala/mgrps/divs/aasl/aaslpubsandjournals/knowledgequest/kqwebarchives/v36/362/362scales.cfm

Stephens, W. (2008). Evidence of student voices finding meaning in intellectual freedom. *Knowledge Quest, 37* (2), 44–48.

Stripling, B., Williams, C., Johnston, M., & Anderton, H. (2010). Minors & Internet interactivity: A new interpretation of the LBOR. *Knowledge Quest, 39* (1), 38–45.

Valenza, J. K., & Johnson, D. (2009). Things that keep us up at night. *School Library Journal, 55* (10), 29–32.

FURTHER READING

Adams, H. R. (2008). The Library Bill of Rights and intellectual freedom. *School Library Media Activities Monthly*, 24 (5), 32.

Adams, H. R. (2010). Intellectual freedom online: The new battleground for minor's first amendment rights. *Knowledge Quest, 39* (1), 10–15.

Adams, H. R. (2010). Who are our friends? The community of the book. *School Library Monthly, 27* (2), 52–53.

Adams, H. R. (2011). The intellectual freedom calendar: Another advocacy plan for the school library. *School Library Monthly, 27* (7), 52–53.

Cole, P. B. (2010). *Young adult literature in the 21st century*. Boston, MA: McGraw-Hill Higher Education.

Doyle, R. P. (2010). *2010 Banned Book Week resource guide*. Chicago, IL: American Library Association.

Franklin, P., & Stephens, C. G. (2006). Banned Books Week and facing challenges. *School Library Media Activities Monthly, 23* (1). 44–45.

Lamb, A. (2007). Intellectual freedom for youth: Social technology and social networks. *Knowledge Quest, 36* (2), 38–45.

Lent, R. C. (2008). Facing the issues: Challenges, censorship, and reflection through dialogue. *English Journal, 97* (3), 61–66.

Lesesne, T. E. (2005). Censorship: The mind you close may be your own. *Voices from the Middle, 13* (1), 72–77.

McNicol, S. (2007). An open letter: Teenagers' views of censorship in libraries. *Knowledge Quest Web Edition, 36* (2). Retrieved from http://www.ala.org/ala/mgrps/divs/aasl/aaslpubsandjourn als/knowledgequest/kqwebarchives/v36/362/362mcnichol.cfm

Scales, P. (2001). *Teaching banned books: 12 guides for young readers*. Chicago, IL: American Library Association.

Scales, P. (2006). Fighting for the freedom to read. *Book Links,16* (1), 22–23.

Scales, P. (2007). Understanding the first amendment: Celebrating banned books week. *Book Links, 17* (1), 12–14.

Scales, P. R. (2009). *Protecting intellectual freedom in your school library*. Chicago, IL: American Library Association.

Scales, P. (2010). The blame game. *School Library Journal, 56* (1),16.

Youse, C. (2007). Banned books: Engaging students and teachers. *Knowledge Quest Web Edition, 36* (2). Retrieved from http://www.ala.org/ala/mgrps/divs/aasl/aaslpubsandjournals/ knowledgequest/kqwebarchives/v36/362/362_Youse.cfm

Part 4

Analyze Creative Works

8

Identifying and Analyzing Details of a Work

The *School Library Media Specialist's Role in Reading Toolkit* states that "School librarians are in a critical and unique position to partner with other educators to elevate the reading development of our nation's youth" through teaching and co-teaching reading comprehension strategies (Reading toolkit online). The READS Analyze component focuses on reading comprehension skills and strategies, blending research and best practices of language arts, reading, and library professionals with practical suggestions for ways to integrate them into the school library program.

IMPORTANCE OF BACKGROUND KNOWLEDGE

Reading is a dynamic process in which the reader must be fully engaged in order to maximize comprehension. During the reading experience, a good reader brings their individual schema and past experiences to the content in order to make the connections necessary to deepen comprehension. Harp (2006) explains that "reading is a meaning-making process in which there is a transaction between the thought and language of the author and the background knowledge of the reader" (p. 11). Moreillon (2007) observes that "background knowledge is what the reader brings to the reading event. Each reader's interpretation and each reading of the text are potentially unique" (p. 19). Consequently, school librarians need to nurture the uniqueness of each reader's interaction with the text. "Providing children with rich, diverse learning experiences through field trips (virtual and real), hands-on experimentation, role-playing, readers' theater, assemblies, and access to complex, multifaceted, and multicultural texts will help to address gaps in their schema" (Grimes, 2006, p. 94). In other words, "The reading of a text is an active event that necessarily entails the reader's bringing prior knowledge to bear on what is read" (Ross, McKechnie, & Rothbauer, 2006, p. 52).

To illustrate this point, create a mental picture of mountains topped with snow. What does your mind's visual image look like? What color are the mountains and the snow? Where on the mountain is the snow located? To construct this mind's image requires background knowledge. You need to have some knowledge of what a mountain and snow are in order to form this image. You may have gained this knowledge by traveling in the mountains, viewing movies or travelogues, or reading fiction or nonfiction texts. From this knowledge, you created a schema that you can call on when confronted with mountains

READS Component	READS Indicator	AASL *Standards for the 21st-Century Learner* *	Common Core State Standards—English Language Arts**
Analyze structure and aesthetic features of creative works			
The student will:			
3.1 Identify and analyze key ideas and details of a work.	3.1.1 Connect prior and background knowledge to textual or visual clues to understand a literary work (e.g., inferring, predicting).	• 1.1.2 Use prior and background knowledge as context for new learning. • 1.1.6 Read, view, and listen for information presented in any format . . . in order to make inferences and gather meaning. • 2.1.3 Use strategies to draw conclusions from information and apply knowledge to curricular areas, real-world situations, and further investigations. • 4.1.5 Connect ideas to own interests and previous knowledge and experience. • 4.1.6 Organize personal knowledge in a way that can be called upon easily. • 4.4.2 Recognize the limits of own personal knowledge.	• Language—3 Apply knowledge of language to understand how language functions in different contexts . . . • Language—6 Acquire and use accurately general academic and domain-specific words and phrases . . . • Reading: Informational Text—1 Cite strong and thorough textual evidence to support analysis . . . • Reading: Informational Text—4 Determine the meaning of words and phrases . . . • Reading: Literature—1 Cite strong and thorough textual evidence to support analysis of text . . . • Reading: Literature—4 Determine the meaning of words and phrases . . . • Writing—8 Gather relevant information from multiple authoritative print and digital sources . . .

*Excerpted from *Standards for the 21st-Century Learner* by the American Association of School Librarians, a division of the American Library Association, copyright © 2007 American Library Association. Available for download at www.ala.org/aasl/standards. Used with permission.

**Excerpted from *Common Core State Standards for English Language Arts*. National Governors Association Center for Best Practices and Council of Chief State School Officers Commercial License. Copyright © 2010. Used with permission of NGA Center/CCSSO.

and snow in a text. You have the contextual background with which to create your mind's visual image.

For other students, this may be a challenge. For instance, for students in South Florida who have not traveled more than five miles from their homes, creating a schema of mountains and snow may depend on acquiring background knowledge through reading a variety of texts, viewing television programs, or surfing the Internet. By providing these vicarious experiences for students through a wide variety of resources, the school librarian can be an integral part of the learning experience that will ultimately lead to more engaged and knowledgeable readers.

BACKGROUND KNOWLEDGE STRATEGIES

According to Harp (2006), "determining the understandings, attitudes, biases, and beliefs" of a reader is essential to enhancing reading comprehension. Consequently, the background knowledge or schema that a reader brings to the text needs to be relevant and meaningful. School librarians can facilitate those connections across the curriculum using a variety of strategies for determining and enhancing the background knowledge that students bring to the learning situation.

Sharing background stories with students can increase students' understanding of a particular concept or setting. By combining a personal story with a text passage, the school librarian can model for the students the process of mining their own personal schema to enrich the reading experience. For example, during a booktalk on *Peak* by Roland Smith, one of this book's authors briefly mentioned that on a trip to visit family in Colorado, she had difficulty breathing in enough oxygen at 10,000 feet up and recounted how that experience made her feel. She then related this experience to the following passage from *Peak* by Roland Smith, "I didn't think a thousand feet would make that much difference, but at that altitude even a hundred feet made a difference. . . . At this stage, my hope of getting to the summit, a mile and a half above where I was currently suffocating, seemed about as likely as me flying a Gamow bag to Jupiter" (p. 101).

"Visualizing, or forming a mental image, is what writers hope their readers do with the texts they create" (Fisher, 2009, p. 47). To assist students with building background knowledge and the ability to create a mental picture from the text, school librarians can combine more than one strategy to enrich the learning situation. In addition to the background story and the text passage, images of the setting could also be projected (e.g., Mt. Everest or mountains for *Peak*), with a brief oral description of the setting. In this example, the images help the students build a more concrete mental image or schema of mountains and snow.

Layered on to this learning situation, the school librarian can also engage students in the dialogue by eliciting comments from follow-up questions. Fisher states that "regardless of the approach, it is important that students learn to ask questions and not simply to answer questions posed by the teacher" (Fisher, 2009, p. 46). For the aforementioned example, the school librarian could follow up the personal story and reading of the passage from *Peak* by asking the following questions: (1) What mental image do you have of mountains and snow based on the personal story and the text passage? (2) What kinds of equipment and clothing do you think you would need to climb a mountain and why? (3) What happens to the amount of oxygen at higher altitudes and why? (4) Why is there snow at the higher altitudes and not below?

Incorporating questioning strategies into book presentations or discussions, as well as through research projects and creative projects, are methods for assessing and enhancing students' background knowledge. According to Grimes (2006), students who actively generate questions as they read increase comprehension (p. 43). Questioning strategies, such as asking fact-based or open-ended questions, will serve to elicit responses that can be expanded on with further discussion or clarified for misconceptions either in the library or classroom follow-up. The school librarian can nurture a questioning learning environment by consistently weaving these techniques throughout the library program.

Integrating questioning strategies into the library program can also include the following:

- "What do you think?" bulletin board: Post student-generated questions about books on display. The displayed books may be theme or topic related. To facilitate this project, the school librarian could collaborate with a teacher in any subject area whose students are working on a reading assignment (e.g., World War II fiction and informational texts).
- Think-aloud sessions: Modeling questioning strategies during a class discussion or literature circle (e.g., While I was reading this passage, I asked myself how I would feel if I were in the same situation and were lost in the wilderness. What kind of skills would I need to survive in this situation?)
- Bloom's Taxonomy display: In the library on a bulletin board, poster, or link from the library media web page, display Bloom's Taxonomy with related types of questions (e.g., What do I know about this topic? What can I infer from this passage?). Additionally, the display could be enhanced with book-related questions posed in each of Bloom's areas.
- "Question of the Day" segment in opening announcements: A literature-based question contest could be initiated with students dropping their responses into a fish bowl in the library. The next day's announcements could feature the winners. To further engage the faculty and students, their submitted questions based on their favorite books could be used during the segment.
- "Question" book trailers: Students could write brief book trailers on their favorite books, using only questions to spark interest in their selection (e.g., What is the purpose of digging all those holes in the middle of nowhere? Will I ever get out of this mess? Would anyone come to my rescue if things get worse around here? Find out the plight of this character in *Holes*!)

VOCABULARY DEVELOPMENT STRATEGIES

Before leaving the topic of background knowledge and its importance for reading comprehension, vocabulary development strategies and their role in reading comprehension and, ultimately to lifelong learning is discussed. Several years ago, Betty Hart and Todd Risley (1995) at the University of Kansas conducted a longitudinal seminal study on the impact of language and vocabulary development and its long-term impact on student achievement. They stated that "vocabulary growth reflects a child's rate of language learning in terms of how often the child is adding new words to the vocabulary that make distinctions among old words or that represent new concepts" (p. 142). The Hart and Risley research centered on families from three socio-economic incomes: professional, working class, and poverty levels.

According to the findings of Hart and Risley (1995), the average child in a poverty level home heard about 620 words an hour while a child in a professional home heard 2,150 (p. 132). Consequently, Hart and Risley estimated that by the age of four, children of professional families had heard an average of 48 million words addressed to them, while children in poverty level families had heard only 13 million, resulting in more than a 30 million word discrepancy between professional families and poverty level families (p. 132).

The long-term repercussions of this vocabulary deficit results in a more challenging learning environment for these children that is very difficult to overcome as they move through school. Marzano and Pickering (2005) emphasize this growing discrepancy by comparing the two types of students, those academically advantaged and those who "enter school with significant discrepancies in terms of their chances for academic success" (p. 3). Marzano and Pickering emphasize that the importance of acquiring academic background knowledge that includes an understanding of academic vocabulary is crucial to long-term educational success. The importance of vocabulary is further emphasized in Cynthia Anderson's (2009) article that highlights the five pillars of reading identified in the National Reading Panel's *Report on the Nation Teaching Children to Read.* Vocabulary shares its place with the four other pillars of reading including, phonics, phonological awareness, comprehension, and fluency. Her article discusses the importance of the school librarian's role in supporting students' acquisition of vocabulary.

Consequently, vocabulary development should be one of the linchpins in the school library's instructional program. As noted previously, lower socioeconomic students are at a disadvantage, but this situation also applies to English Language Learners (ELLs). Although school librarians do not necessarily explicitly teach vocabulary, they should incorporate an awareness of words and their importance to reading comprehension throughout their instructional program. School librarians are in a unique position to build an exciting, interesting culture around the importance of and a love of words.

Ideas for integrating vocabulary development may include traditional classroom approaches, but with a library twist. This approach may be particularly relevant if the school librarian has scheduled classes. Strategies that are frequently used include graphic organizers (e.g., semantic maps, Venn diagrams, compare or contrast charts) that help students understand relationships and concepts for a selected group of words. Figurative language examples (e.g., similes, metaphors, idioms, personifications, euphemisms) can be seamlessly woven into read-alouds, book discussions, or other literary activities. Bush (2005) offers additional tips for including vocabulary development in the library program in *Every Student Reads: Collaboration and Reading to Learn.* Integrating vocabulary development strategies into the library instructional program could include the following:

- School-wide vocabulary initiative: Collaborate with the content area teachers and share Marzano and Pickering's book on academic vocabulary (2005) or other subject specific sources. Initiate a school-wide agenda to teach and reinforce the use of content area vocabulary, using methods such as word walls, word sorts, word cards, word pyramids, or concept circles.
- Award-winning words: Prepare lists of challenging words from award-winning books. The lists may be used in displays, fixed to the book jackets, or projected before a booktalk or book discussion. For ideas of words to select, refer to the Sunshine State Young Reader's Award instructional activities on the Florida Association for Media in Education site at http://www.myssyra.org/archive/archive.html.
- Award-winning words follow-up: Introduce the list of words for a selected book to the students, eliciting ideas for definitions, synonyms, antonyms, and so on. Read the book or selected passages from the book, having the students give a thumbs-up when they hear one of the words. (For more challenged students, project words throughout reading.)

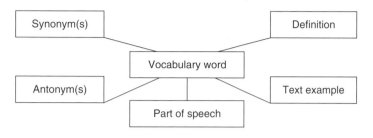

- Word-rich book trailers: Have students select and read a book from which they will create a book trailer. As students read their selection, instruct them to note challenging or descriptive words that could be used in their script. For added impact, the words could be incorporated into the trailer's visuals.

- Graphic organizer project: Organize a learning center in which pairs of students will use a dictionary (online or print) and/or a thesaurus to complete a graphic organizer based on academic or story related words. A generic graphic organizer that could be used includes the following components:

- Virtual art field trip: Collaborate with an art or social studies teacher to virtually visit an art museum (e.g., The Metropolitan Museum of Art in New York at http://www. metmuseum.org/ or Le Louvre in Paris, France, at http://www.louvre.fr/llv/commun/ home.jsp?bmLocale=en) and choose art or artifacts from a particular historical period or famous paintings to project to the students. (Additional visual literacy content could also be included in the lesson.) Have the students work in pairs to list ten descriptive words. Choose a student to record all of the descriptive words, using a spreadsheet or database program. Tally the frequency of each word used and then brainstorm with the class other descriptive word possibilities. As a follow-up, have the students write a paragraph in which they use as many of the descriptive words as possible. Have students share their paragraphs.

- Word origins: Use the *Oxford English Dictionary* (http://www.oed.com/—subscription required) to have students determine the origins of words and create a timeline on when the words entered the English language. Create a bulletin board with the timeline using commonly used words today or science/technology specific words, if collaborating with science, business education, or computer science teachers.

- Word games learning center: Have students rotate through several centers that are focused on developing vocabulary. Introduce students to the variety of word games (e.g., Dictionary Devil, Jumble Solitaire, Word Sudoku) on the Merriam-Webster Dictionary Online site (http://www.merriam-webster.com/game/index.htm). If multiple computers or wireless laptops are available, several centers with different games could be provided.

- Word of the Day: Subscribe to the "Word of the Day" feature on the Merriam-Webster Dictionary Online site (http://www.merriam-webster.com/word-of-the-day/) and feature the word in opening announcements and televised looping announcements throughout the day. As a monthly follow-up, list all the words featured in the past weeks as a regular feature in the school newspaper.

- Synonyms and antonyms: Prepare lists of words for which the students will have to write either the synonyms or antonyms. (Lists of words can be accessed at sites such as the Michigan Proficiency Exams site at http://www.michigan-proficiency-exams.com/ synonym-antonyms.html.) Depending on the academic level, instruct the students to complete the list, working individually or with a partner.

- Name That Thing: Access the Merriam-Webster Dictionary Online site and choose the Name That Thing feature (http://www.merriam-webster.com/namethatthing/index. htm#quiz-top). Project the game for the entire class to view and have students name the object before the time lapses. An alternative activity is to use a print visual dictionary and project the images. An advantage of this method is that the teacher or librarian can preselect the images to enhance vocabulary development related to the curriculum.

- Word relationships: Have students access (or project for the entire class) a visual dictionary such as *Visuwords Online* (http://www.visuwords.com/) or *ThinkMap Visual Thesaurus* (http://www.visualthesaurus.com/) and ask students for suggestions to enter and then review the word relationships with the students. Alternately, collaborate with a teacher and use vocabulary words being taught in the classroom. This would be particularly effective with science or technology vocabulary.

- Picturesque destination: Choose a geographical location that is either related to a book's or film's setting or that relates to a curriculum topic. Project images captured from a website and ask students for words that describe the setting. If a book or film is being referenced, then have students scan through the text or script to identify descriptive words and to determine if the words generated by the class are duplicated in the original text. Ideas for sites include the following: Hawaii at http://www.gohawaii.com/, BBC's London at http://www.bbc.co.uk/london/in_pictures/viewsoflondon/aerial_photos/, Google's images of China at: http://www.google.com/search?q=china+photos&hl=en&qscrl=1&nord=1&rlz=1T4SNYR_enUS328US330&biw=1280&bih=628&site=webhp&prmd=imvnsu&tbm=isch&tbo=u&source=univ&sa=X&ei=q8bDTqjLAZKitgempdDUDQ&sqi=2&ved=0CD0QsAQ, or the U.S. Department of the Interior's Rocky Mountain National Park at http://www.nps.gov/romo/index.htm (also includes live webcams of strategic locations).

- Picturesque destination word wall: As a follow-up to the picturesque destination activity, create a thematic word wall with several captured images and the lists of words generated by the students. Displays of related informational and fiction titles could also be included.

- Disposition words: Collaborate with a business education teacher or social studies teacher to deliver a lesson on the metacognitive and behavioral characteristics of a life-long learner, using words from the *AASL Standards for the 21st Century Learner*. A list of words and phrases that could be used includes the following: initiator, engaged, confident, self-directed, creative, questioner, adaptable, emotional resilient, persistent, flexible, divergent/convergent thinker, personally productive, capable leader, socially responsible, collaborative team member, curious, self-motivated, and/or open minded. Ask students to work in pairs or triads to define the terms in their own words. Then have students identify how these characteristics would be displayed in school and/or work.

The preceding list is a summary of methods for integrating vocabulary development activities into the school library program. Although the optimum scenario involves collaborating with other teachers, the school librarian can also independently integrate vocabulary development into promotional and instructional activities with the ultimate goal of positively impacting student achievement.

INFERENCES AND PREDICTIONS

In February 2011, on a well-publicized *Jeopardy* television game, IBM's Big Blue computer went head to head with the two top all-time *Jeopardy* winners. News reports on this event detailed Big Blue's difficulty in understanding the nuances of language, including the use of figurative language (e.g., metaphors, similes) and making inferences about the underlying meaning of the question. The human brain, on the other hand, computes these inferences based on preconstructed schema, as well as visual and/or contextual clues. According to Grimes (2006), the human brain's ability to make inferences is "the cornerstone of communication in all its forms" (p. 90). Grimes further states that "modeling how to make connections, create visualizations, and ask questions are essential first steps in teaching children to infer" (p. 92).

Making correct inferences depends on several factors: background knowledge, reading skills, and metacomprehension strategies. Harp (2006) further explains that making inferences is particularly difficult when cultural and/or historic references are alluded to in the text (p. 13). To aid students in developing the background knowledge necessary to make these connections and inferences, the school librarian can present meaningful activities located in the READS Explore section.

According to Grimes (2006), "predicting is inferring plus; the plus is an educated guess" (p. 95). The importance of making inferences and predictions in the reading, listening, viewing process is that it causes the student to become more engaged during the experience. It sparks curiosity in readers so that they want to read, view, or listen to the resource to find out if their inferences and predictions are correct.

In particular, by sparking students' curiosity to read selected titles through meaningful pre-reading techniques, the school librarian can reinforce a student's ability to make inferences and predictions. Armed with these skills, students can progress to more complex texts that require making inferences from implied relationships or information. Additionally, school librarians are in a unique position to assist students in developing these skills using connections across the curriculum. The following activities are not intended to teach these strategies, but rather to collaboratively work with teachers to reinforce them.

- Reading the fist line or paragraph or the last paragraph: Arrange the students into small groups or pairs. Have the students use either a prepared worksheet or have them fold a piece of notebook paper in half lengthwise. Instruct a student recorder to write the first or last sentence or paragraph of a selected book on one side of the worksheet. On the other side of the paper, each group will record their inferences and predictions about the book during a brainstorming session. Explain to the students that they also need to justify their responses. This activity may be modified depending on the curriculum area and the selection of books. For instance, historical fiction titles for social studies classes or science fiction for science classes could be used to reinforce the content being taught. A follow-up activity could have the students report on whether their inferences and predictions were correct after reading the book.

- Evaluating book jacket art: Place books with colorful, eye-catching covers on several tables. Arrange a small group of students around each table and have students make inferences and predictions based on the cover art, titles, and authors. Have a recorder jot down comments on the students' predictions on sticky notes and place these inside the front covers. Have students check books out from the selections on the tables. In a follow-up session, have students share whether or not the predictions aligned with the story's plot, characters, and other story elements.

- Providing a quote-for-the-day segment in opening announcements: Have the announcer read a quote from a book, mentioning the author and title if desired. Encourage students to submit their suggestions for the book title to the library either physically or virtually (e.g., e-mail, Twitter). Announce the winner on the next days' telecast and add the book to an ongoing display. In this exercise, students will either be using their background knowledge of fictional characters, recognizing setting or plot, or identifying an author's writing style. Based on their background knowledge, the students infer or suggest the title of the work.

- Using graphic novels or comics: According to Fisher, Frey, and Lapp (2009), "graphic novels are especially helpful in modeling elaborative inferences" (pp. 40–42). In this mini-lesson, visual sequential art from graphic novels or comic books are used to help students practice the ability to make inferences based on the actions portrayed and to also make relevant and informed predictions about what will be occurring next in the story. For the activity, project two frames of the novel and have students make inferences about the setting, characters, and plot. Then, have students predict what they think will happen next in the story. As a follow-up activity, distribute graphic novels or comic books to pairs of students and have one student select two frames from the story, covering other frames with sheets of paper. The other student will make inferences about the story and make predictions about the plot based on those two images. Both students can then read the remainder of the story to determine if they were correct.

- Planning backward: Read the ending of a short piece of literature and ask students to predict what happened in the plot of a short story, or the topic, or hypothesis covered in an essay. Either read the selection aloud or have the students read it silently to determine if their predictions were accurate. Follow up this activity with a discussion on what triggers (e.g., words, descriptions, phrases) influenced their predictions.

- Poetic inferences: Project a short poem that describes a person, place, or thing and read it aloud to the class. Give students a few minutes to note what they are thinking related to specific lines in the poem. Ask the students what or who they think is described in the poem and the specific language on which they based their decisions. If this activity was modeled in a think-aloud by the librarian, then have students repeat the activity individually using another poem.

- Visual contexts: Project a thought-provoking image that lends itself to further discussion. If collaborating with science or social studies teachers, then appropriate images could be projected. For instance, if working with social studies teachers, images from the Library of Congress Memory project could be used, such as the photographs in the Farm Security Administration—Office of War Information Photograph Collection at http://www.loc.gov/pictures/item/fsa1998021539/PP/ or the Berkeley Digital Library SunSITE collections at http://sunsite.berkeley.edu/Collections/. If collaborating with science teachers, images from the National Aeronautics and Space Administration at http://search.nasa.gov/search/edFilterSearch.jsp?empty=true, the Audubon Society at http://www.audubon.org/, or the National Wildlife Federation at http://www.nwf.org/ could be used. Initiate a discussion of the image, having the students note, either orally or in writing, the visual clues they are using to make inferences about the image. This activity could be enhanced by preceding it with a visual literacy lesson. Further reflective thinking could be elicited by asking questions such as the following: (1) How would the visual message be changed if the image were perceived from a different point of view (e.g., overhead, wide angle)? (2) How would the image's message be altered if the composition of the subjects was changed?

In conclusion, students need opportunities for expanding their background and language knowledge in order to become more skillful consumers of information. Additionally, they need to combine this knowledge with strategies for making predictions and inferences. School librarians can provide students, as they progress through the grades, opportunities for acquiring and practicing these skills by thoughtfully scaffolding texts, visuals, and activities. The resulting impact for students as they blend and use this knowledge is that they will become more successful, independent readers and learners.

CENTRAL IDEAS AND SUPPORTING DETAILS

Determining the main idea and supporting details in a text selection is essential to performing well on standardized tests and, in general, for academic success. Consequently, many instructional hours are devoted to teaching students strategies for determining the

READS Component	READS Indicator	AASL *Standards for the 21st-Century Learner**	Common Core State Standards—English Language Arts**
Analyze structure and aesthetic features of creative works			
The student will:			
3.1 Identify and analyze key ideas and details of a work.	3.1.2 Determine central ideas and supporting details of a work (e.g., paraphrasing, summarizing).	• 1.1.7 Make sense of information gathered from diverse sources by identifying . . . main and supporting ideas . . . • 2.1.2 Organize knowledge so that it is useful. • 4.2.3 Maintain openness to new ideas . . .	• Reading: Informational Text—3 Analyze a complex set of ideas or sequence of events and explain how specific individuals, ideas, or events interact and develop over the course of the text. • Reading: Literature—1 Cite strong and thorough textual evidence to support analysis of text . . . • Reading: Literature—3 Analyze the impact of the author's choices . . . • Reading: Literature—6 Analyze a case in which grasping point of view requires distinguishing what is directly stated in a text from what is really meant . . . • Reading: Literature—9 Demonstrate knowledge of foundational works of American literature . . .

*Excerpted from *Standards for the 21st-Century Learner* by the American Association of School Librarians, a division of the American Library Association, copyright © 2007 American Library Association. Available for download at www.ala.org/aasl/standards. Used with permission.

**Excerpted from *Common Core State Standards for English Language Arts*. National Governors Association Center for Best Practices and Council of Chief State School Officers Commercial License. Copyright © 2010. Used with permission of NGA Center/CCSSO.

main idea, which can be explicitly stated in a topic sentence or implied throughout the passage, and the reader must infer it from textual clues. Although most of these instructional activities are conducted in the classroom, the school librarian can also collaborate with teachers and integrate these activities into the library program. A few ideas are in the following list and additional ideas may be gathered from books listed in the reference list or from the readwritethink.org website.

- Examining topic sentences: Work with a middle school social studies teacher to reinforce the main idea and supporting details concepts before launching a civics research project. Choose a graphic organizer such as a fishbone graphic organizer or use Prevatte's (2007, p. 31) "Examining Topic Sentences and Main Idea in a Paragraph" graphic organizer to have students dissect a topic sentence. Practice with informational text passages on their research topics. Also gather ideas for informational text passages from Daniels and Steineke's (2011) *Texts and Lessons for Content-Area Reading*.

- Teasing out the main idea: Collaboratively work with an intensive reading teacher. Choose a paragraph from a short narrative to project or distribute to the class. Explain to students that they will be using a graphic organizer to determine the main idea of the passage. Read aloud or have the students read silently and then complete the graphic organizer. To end the activity, project the passage and conduct a think-aloud session while modeling the topic sentence and the supporting details, highlighting each in different colors. Continue the activity by reading aloud the entire narrative.

- Step it up: Work collaboratively with an English teacher to review reading multiple texts before beginning an author study. Choose a poem and a short narrative or two magazine articles dealing with the same topic and distribute or project them for the class to read. Have students use a graphic organizer to tease out the main idea and supporting details. Complete the activity by leading a compare or contrast discussion on the approaches of the two authors for presenting the main idea.

SUMMARIZING AND PARAPHRASING

One method for readers to make sense of what they are reading is summarizing. By using this strategy, students deepen their understanding of text information and are able to connect the details presented into a cohesive overarching idea. According to Frey, Fisher, and Berkin (2009), "Summarizing is an *ongoing* strategy—it's when you periodically pause as you are reading to restate what you just read" (p. 29). Good readers silently practice this strategy as they read by blending important details into the big idea presented. In this way, good readers engage in this cognitive process and monitor their comprehension of the overall meaning of the text, assimilating new information or concepts. However, struggling readers may get lost in the supporting details and, consequently, need guidance in developing this comprehension strategy.

Wormeli (2005) offers numerous approaches to help students hone this skill. He states that "summarization is a real-world skill" (p. 6) and should be practiced throughout the instructional program to facilitate retention of information in long-term memory. He states that students should be taught "to summarize with the awareness that it is a strategy that will open their minds and will make the content stick. It leads students to comprehension and retention that is the learning goal" (p. 6). Wormeli (2005) also suggests that summarization can be completed "in writing, but also orally, dramatically, artistically, visually, physically, musically, in groups, or individually" (p. 2).

Summarizing—Lesson Ideas

For the school librarian, there are many opportunities for reinforcing summarization skills, particularly during research and production activities. Integrating these skills into the library instructional program could include the following:

- Putting it back together: Collaboratively work with social studies teachers on a research project about the Renaissance or other historical period. Start with a brief review of the definition of a summary and the strategies for creating it, as well as a review of the resources that will be used. Explain that the class will be using a jigsaw method in which small groups will be researching one aspect of the historical period (e.g., dress, food, art, music, homes, businesses, etc.), summarizing their findings, and then reporting back to the entire class. Groups could produce a word processed handout, enter their findings on a wiki, or give a mediated oral report using presentation software. At the conclusion, a broad sweep of the historical period will be available for the class.

- Assessing the summary: Work with a biology teacher to reinforce the use of summarizing content area text to facilitate comprehension. Distribute or project a journal article on a biology topic (e.g., infectious diseases or cloning). If time permits, briefly review with the class how the article was searched for and retrieved from one of the science periodical databases. Highlight and discuss vocabulary that may be new to the students. Have the students silently read the article or, depending on the level of the students, read the article aloud. Review strategies for writing a quality summary and project or distribute a rubric that the students will use to analyze their work. Instruct the students to summarize the article, rereading as necessary, and complete the session with the students using the rubric to assess their work. Hoyt, Mooney, and Parkes (2003) offer a comprehensive rubric in *Exploring Informational Texts: From Theory to Practice.*

- Visual interpretation: Collaborate with the art teacher and/or a content area teacher. Explain to the students that they will be summarizing a literary passage using a visual medium. Choose an action-packed or intense passage from a young adult novel to read to the class (e.g., the lottery scene from *The Hunger Games.*). Then, have the students work with a partner to visually summarize in one image the essence of the passage. An alternative to the fiction passage is to give the students a concept (e.g., cloning with corresponding vocabulary) to visually summarize.

Paraphrasing—Lesson Ideas

Paraphrasing is producing your own interpretation of the important information and ideas that you have gleaned from another source. It may be more detailed than a summary and it will require a critical reinterpretation of the original thoughts. According to Wormeli (2005), paraphrasing is a critical skill needed to produce quality summaries, but it can be difficult for students to practice due to a limited vocabulary, particularly synonyms. This fact reinforces the need to continually integrate vocabulary development activities throughout the school library program.

- Wise notes from OWL: Reinforce techniques for paraphrasing by using the *6 Steps to Effective Paraphrasing* on the *Purdue Online Writing Lab* (OWL) at http://owl.english.purdue.edu/owl/resource/619/01/ that include the following:

  1. "Reread the original passage until you understand its full meaning.
  2. Set the original aside, and write your paraphrase on a note card.
  3. Jot down a few words below your paraphrase to remind you later how you envision using this material. At the top of the note card, write a key word or phrase to indicate the subject of your paraphrase.
  4. Check your rendition with the original to make sure that your version accurately expresses all the essential information in a new form.
  5. Use quotation marks to identify any unique term or phraseology you have borrowed exactly from the source.
  6. Record the source (including the page) on your note card so that you can credit it easily if you decide to incorporate the material into your paper."

Project the website and discuss the steps. If working with a language arts or social studies teacher, selections from a literary work or primary source document can be projected and used to model the process. Additionally, selections can be distributed or projected on which the students can practice.

• Wrap it up: Culminate a research project with students creating a presentation, giving them several product choices. Review the legal use of text, audio, and visuals in their finished product, including the bibliographic format. Review paraphrasing, quoting, and summarizing guidelines before research and product completion.

In conclusion, the READS Analyze component presents opportunities for the school library program to reinforce classroom instruction on reading comprehension strategies. By integrating instructional activities that address these skills across the content areas, the library instructional program will positively impact student achievement.

READS LESSONS AND ACTIVITIES

Analyze Structure and Aesthetic features of Creative Works

Identify and Analyze Key Ideas and Details of a Work

Critical literacy in action: Multimodal texts on global warming. By Amy Alexandria Wilson. Involves students in making inferences from informational text. ReadWriteThink. (Gr. 6–8)

Crossword puzzles student interactive. (Resource) ReadWriteThink. (Gr. K-12)

Elements of fiction. (Resource) virtuaLit. http://bcs.bedfordstmartins.com/virtualit/fiction/elements.asp

Flowchart for determining comprehension. (Resource) Scholastic/Teachers.

Focus on first lines: Increasing comprehension through prediction strategies. By Jacqueline Podolski. Includes lists of "first lines" of novels. ReadWriteThink. (Gr. 9–12) http://www.readwritethink.org/classroom-resources/lesson-plans/focus-first-lines-increasing-834.html?tab=1#tabs

Get the gist: A summarizing strategy for any content area. By Che-Mai Gray. ReadWriteThink. (Gr. 6–8) http://www.readwritethink.org/classroom-resources/lesson-plans/gist-summarizing-strategy-content-290.html

Guidelines for determining an author's main idea. (Resource) Scholastic/Teachers. http://www2.scholastic.com/content/collateral_resources/pdf/r/reading_bestpractices_comprehension_authorsmainidea.pdf

I've got it covered: Creating magazine covers to summarize texts. By Helen Hoffner. ReadWriteThink. (Gr. 6–8) http://www.readwritethink.org/classroom-resources/lesson-plans/covered-creating-magazine-covers-1092.html

Prereading strategy: Using the vocabulary, language, prediction (VLP) approach. By Valerie A. Adair. Includes vocabulary activities using informational magazine article. ReadWriteThink. (Gr. 6–8) http://www.readwritethink.org/classroom-resources/lesson-plans/prereading-strategy-using-vocabulary-30726.html

Prompts that guide students to use the general reading strategies. Scholastic/Teachers. http://www2.scholastic.com/content/collateral_resources/pdf/r/reading_bestpractices_comprehension_promptsthatguide.pdf

Scaling back to essentials: Scaffolding summarization with fishbone mapping. By Kathleen Donovan-Snavely. ReadWriteThink. (Gr. 6–8)

S.C.O.R.E language arts cyberguides. http://www.sdcoe.k12.ca.us/score/cyberguide.html

Starting points: General processes of reading. (Resource) Scholastic/Teachers. http://www2.scholastic.com/content/collateral_resources/pdf/r/reading_bestpractices_comprehension_startingpoints.pdf

Stop, ask, fix: Student checklist. (Resource) Scholastic/Teachers. http://www2.scholastic.com/content/collateral_resources/pdf/r/reading_bestpractices_comprehension_stopaskfixchecklist.pdf

Summarizing with scratch. By Lindsay Cesari. *From the creative minds of 21st century librarians: E-book.* p. 135–137. http://digital-literacy.syr.edu/page/view/221

Synthesis. (Resource) Compiled by Kristin Fontichiaro. *School Library Monthly, 27* (5), 11–12.

Techniques for visualizing across text. (Resource) Scholastic/Teachers. http://teacher.scholastic.com/ products/scholasticprofessional/authors/pdfs/wilhelm_readseeing_sample_pages.pdf

Viewing vocabulary: Building word knowledge through informational websites. By Hallie K. Yopp and Ruth Helen Yopp. ReadWriteThink. (Gr. 6–8) http://www.readwritethink.org/classroom-re sources/lesson-plans/viewing-vocabulary-building-word-1081.html

Visualization check sheet for readers. (Resource) Scholastic/Teachers. http://www2.scholastic.com/ content/collateral_resources/pdf/r/reading_bestpractices_comprehension_visualization. pdf

What lies ahead? Predicting the future of computing. By Jennifer Cutraro and Holly Epstein Ojalvo. The Learning Network: *The New York Times.* (Gr. 9–12) http://learning.blogs.nytimes. com/2011/12/14/what-lies-ahead-predicting-the-future-of-computing/

What think-alouds can do for students. Opening the window on reading strategies. (Resource) Scholastic/ Teachers.   http://www2.scholastic.com/content/collateral_resources/pdf/r/reading_best- practices_comprehension_thinkaloudscando.pdf

What to watch for: Questions to help assess reading (using think-alouds). Scholastic/Teachers.

Authors

Conversing with the author check sheet. (Resource) Scholastic Teachers. http://www2.scholastic.com/ content/collateral_resources/pdf/r/reading_bestpractices_comprehension_authorcheck- sheet.pdf

Meet the authors. (Resource) Includes YA authors. Barnes & Noble Studio. http://www.barnesand- noble.com/bn-studio/videos-podcasts/index.asp?

Understand the Literary Techniques and Complexities of a Work

Internet Public Library: Literary Criticism. http://www.ipl.org/div/litcrit/

Rules of Notice for Character. http://www2.scholastic.com/content/collateral_resources/pdf/r/ reading_bestpractices_comprehension_rulesofnoticechart.pdf

Web English Teacher. http://www.webenglishteacher.com/index.html

READS INTERNET RESOURCES

Analyze Structure and Aesthetic features of Creative Works

Identify and Analyze a Creator's Purpose and Style

Reading Online. *Teaching vocabulary to adolescents to improve comprehension.* http://www.readingon- line.org/articles/art_index.asp?HREF=curtis/index.html

Reading Rockets. http://www.readingrockets.org/

TeachingBooks.net. Subscription-based service. teachingbooks.net

VirtualLit: Elements of Fiction. http://bcs.bedfordstmartins.com/virtualit/fiction/elements.asp

Word Central. Merriam-Webster. http://www.wordcentral.com/

Authors

Authors4teens.com. http://www.authors4teens.com/links.asp

Barnes & Noble Studio. *Meet the authors.* Includes YA authors. http://www.barnesandnoble.com/ bn-studio/videos-podcasts/index.asp?

Conversing with the author check sheet. Scholastic Teachers. http://www2.scholastic.com/content/ collateral_resources/pdf/r/reading_bestpractices_comprehension_authorchecksheet.pdf

James Patterson's READKIDDOREAD.COM. http://www.readkiddoread.com/home
Literary History.com. *Literary criticism.* http://www.literaryhistory.com/
Multnomah County Public Library Homework Center. *High school literature.* http://www.multco
    lib.org/homework/hslit.html
Multnomah County Public Library Homework Center. *Literature & authors.* http://www.multcolib.
    org/homework/lithc.html
YA author blogs. http://bookleads.wikispaces.com/YA+author+blogs
Young adult literature. Web English Teacher. http://www.webenglishteacher.com/ya.html

WORKS CITED

American Association of School Librarians. *School librarian's role in reading toolkit.* Retrieved from
    http://www.ala.org/ala/mgrps/divs/aasl/aaslissues/toolkits/slroleinreading.cfm
American Association of School Librarians. (2007). *Standards for the 21st-century learner.* Chicago, IL:
    American Library Association.
Anderson, C. (2009). The five pillars of reading. *Library Media Connection, 28* (2), 22–25.
Bush, G. (2005). *Every student reads: Collaboration and reading to learn.* Chicago, IL: American Associa-
    tion of School Librarians.
Daniels, H., & Steineke, N. (2011). *Texts and lessons for content-area reading.* Portsmouth, NH: Heine-
    mann.
Fisher, D., Frey, N., & Lapp, D. (2009). *In a reading state of mind: Brain research, teacher modeling, and
    comprehension instruction.* Newark, DE: International Reading Association.
Frey, N., Fisher, D., & Berkin, A. (2009). *Good habits, great readers: Building the literacy community.*
    Boston, MA: Pearson.
Grimes, S. (2006). *Reading is our business: How libraries can foster reading comprehension.* Chicago, IL:
    American Library Association.
Harp, B. (2006). *The handbook of literacy assessment and evaluation* (3rd ed.). Norwood, MA: Christo-
    pher-Gordon.
Hart, B., & Risley, T. R. (1995). *Meaningful differences in the everday experiences of young American chil-
    dren.* Baltimore, MD: Paul H. Brookes.
Hoyt, L., Mooney, M., & Parkes, B. (2003). *Exploring informational texts: From theory to practice.* Ports-
    mouth, NH: Heinemann.
Marzano, R. J., & Pickering, D. J. (2005). *Building academic vocabulary: Teacher's manual.* Alexandria,
    VA: Association for Supervision and Curriculum Development.
Moreillon, J. (2007). *Collaborative strategies for teaching reading comprehension: Maximizing your impact.*
    Chicago, IL: American Library Association.
"Paraphrase: Write it in your own words." *Purdue Online Writing Lab* (OWL). Retrieved from http://
    owl.english.purdue.edu/owl/resource/619/01/
Prevatte, L. (2007). *Middle school literacy centers: Connecting struggling readers to literature.* Gainesville,
    FL: Maupin House.
Ross, C. S., McKechnie, L.E.F., & Rothbauer, P. M. (2006). *Reading matters: What the research reveals
    about reading, libraries, and community.* Westport, CT: Libraries Unlimited.
Wormeli, R. (2005). *Summarization in any subject: 50 techniques to improve student learning.* Alexandria,
    VA: Association for Supervision and Curriculum Development.

FURTHER READING

Alley, K. M. (2008). *Teaching integrated reading strategies in the middle school library media center.* West-
    port, CT: Libraries Unlimited.
Bernadowski, C., & Kolencik, P. L. (2010). *Research-based reading strategies in the library for adolescent
    learners.* Denver, CO: Linworth.

Collins, S. (2010). *The hunger games.* New York: Scholastic Press.

Fisher, D., & Frey, N. (2009). *Background knowledge: The missing piece of the comprehension puzzle.* Portsmouth, NH: Heinemann.

Johnson, D. D., & Johnson, B. (2011). *Words: The foundation of literacy.* Philadelphia, PA: Westview.

Keane, N. J. (2005). *Using literature in the middle school classroom.* Worthington, OH: Linworth.

Keene, E. O. (2008). *To understand: New horizons in reading comprehension.* Portsmouth, NH: Heinemann.

Keene, E. O., & Zimmermann, S. (1997). *Mosaic of thought: Teaching comprehension in a reader's workshop.* Portsmouth, NH: Heinemann.

Rea, D. M., & Mercuri, S. P. (2006). *Research-based strategies for English language learners: How to reach goals and meet standards, K-8.* Portsmouth, NH: Heinemann.

Riddle, J. (2008). *Engaging the eye generation: Visual literacy strategies for the K-5 classroom.* Portland, ME: Stenhouse.

Tate, M. L. (2008). *Graphic organizers and other visual strategies.* Thousand Oaks, CA: Corwin Press.

Tompkins, G. E., & Blanchfield, C. (2004). *Teaching vocabulary: 50 creative strategies, Grades K-12.* Upper Saddle River, NJ: Pearson.

Zwiers, J. (2008). *Building academic language: Essential practices for content classrooms, grades 5–12.* San Francisco, CA: Wiley.

9

Understanding the Literary Techniques and Complexities of a Work

To deepen understanding of a work requires delving into the complexities of the techniques used by the author or the illustrator. In Analyze 3.2.1, ideas for integrating library instructional activities for understanding an author's or illustrator's style will be presented. In Analyze 3.2.2, literary elements will be discussed, with ideas for incorporating those into the library program.

AUTHOR STUDIES

R. L. Stine was quoted as saying that "if you read a lot of different authors, you pick up their styles, tricks, and skills even [without] realizing it. You learn how to phrase things. You learn how to build a story" (Anonymous, 2010, p. 23).

In fiction writing, the author is challenged to create a world in which the characters interact, solve problems, and are, in some way, transformed through these events. Each writer will approach this challenge differently by creatively combining language and literary elements. Thompkins (2003) states that an author "must create a vivid and believable world that the reader will enter willingly and leave with reluctance" (p. 297). Understanding an author's decisions and style will deepen the student's understanding of their works. It is hoped that expanding students' understanding of a broad range of authors and their works, in the long term, will lead to a lifelong aesthetic appreciation of literature.

Author studies are one way that school librarians can help students connect to authors and their work. Author studies offer an opportunity for students to delve deeper into the author's background and style. Calkins (2001) uses this strategy in both classroom work and learning centers. She states "that in an author study we need to revisit texts, look closely and think hard about how the author writes" (p. 325).

Author studies can be limited in scope or more extensive, depending on the instructional purpose and time available, as well as the reading and grade levels of the students. In general, author studies focus on aspects of the author and their literary style such as the following:

READS Component	READS Indicator	AASL *Standards for the 21st-Century Learner**	Common Core State Standards—English Language Arts**
Analyze structure and aesthetic features of creative works			
The student will:			
3.2 Understand the literary techniques and complexities of a work.	3.2.1 Identify an author's or illustrator's style (e.g., word choice, use of figurative language, medium).	• 4.1.3 Respond to literature and creative expressions of ideas in various formats and genres. • 4.2.3 Maintain openness to new ideas . . .	• Language—4a Determine or clarify the meaning of unknown and multiple-meaning words and phrases: Use context . . . • Language—5 Demonstrate understanding of figurative language, word relationships, and nuances in word meanings. • Reading: Literature—4 Determine the meaning of words and phrases . . . • Reading: Literature—5 Analyze how an author's choices . . . contribute to its overall structure and meaning as well as its aesthetic impact. • Reading: Literature—9 Demonstrate knowledge of foundational works of American literature . . .

*Excerpted from *Standards for the 21st-Century Learner* by the American Association of School Librarians, a division of the American Library Association, copyright © 2007 American Library Association. Available for download at www.ala.org/aasl/standards. Used with permission.
**Excerpted from *Common Core State Standards for English Language Arts*. National Governors Association Center for Best Practices and Council of Chief State School Officers Commercial License. Copyright © 2010. Used with permission of NGA Center/CCSSO.

- researching an author's background and how it influences their writing and choice of topics;
- analyzing the literary elements used (e.g., characters, setting, plot); and/or
- identifying vocabulary choices, figurative language, and other literary devices used and their impact on the work.

Brisson (2002) offers some general advice on conducting author studies, suggesting the following tips: read a selected author's books, discuss genres, review copyright dates, explore style, review jacket blurbs and dedications, check reference tools (pp. 48–49).

As students progress through the language arts curriculum, they are exposed to more complex writing by authors that require more in-depth study. The school library instructional program can collaboratively supplement author studies that originate in the classroom by using a variety of approaches and production techniques. If working with assigned classes, then the school librarian can initiate this type of activity.

Working with Authors

- Author's bio: Have students locate an author's website to read the biographical information. Then, have students locate two interviews of or speeches by the author (either in print or digital). (Some authors are available on Scholastic's *Audio Video Index* site at http://www.scholastic.com/teachers/lesson-plan/author-video-index or Reading Rockets video interviews of top *Children's Book Authors and Illustrators* at http://www.readingrockets.org/books/interviews/.)

- Compare/contrast: Work with the Gifted Education teacher on an author study in which the students will research two contemporary young adult authors, representing one genre. Contemporary adult writers or selected authors from the classics may also be used. Have the students research the backgrounds of the authors, noting differences and similarities. Instruct the students to complete a compare or contrast chart or Venn diagram, working either individually or in a group. Extend the activity by instructing the students to reflect on how the authors' backgrounds may have influenced their writing.

- Personal connections: Work with language arts students to discuss the connection that is established between writer and reader. Read the following passage from Katherine Paterson's essay entitled *Heart in Hiding* that was quoted by Kate DiCamillo (2010): "So what happens is a reciprocal gift between writer and reader: one heart in hiding reaching out to another. We are trying to communicate that which lies in our deepest heart, which has no words, which can only be hinted at through the means of a story" (p. 15). Discuss the passage with the students and ask if they feel a personal connection to authors that they have read. Choose one familiar or recently studied author and title to expand the discussion. Ask the students if their reactions to the story were shaped by the "literary tools (diction, foreshadowing, imagery, voice, plot structures) the author used" (Keene, 2008, p. 24). This activity could be paired with The Learning Network lesson entitled *Deep Impact: Considering Personal Connections to Writers and Artists* at http://learning.blogs.nytimes.com/2010/05/20/deep-impact-considering-personal-connections-to-writers-and-artists/.

- Online author scrapbook: Plan an author study with language arts teachers, using the online application *Glogster.* Introduce the students to *Glogster* and share examples of student work. Explain to students that they will be working with a partner to create an online scrapbook that features a favorite or assigned author. Have students research the author and plan their *Glogster* presentation. Author information can include a short biography, timeline or listing of works, short video interview, photograph(s), student comments, or review of titles.

- Author timeline: Working collaboratively with English teachers, have students construct a timeline of an author's works. Discuss with students the scope of the author's body of work and its impact on the literary world. Does the work reflect the time period in which it was written? If so, how is this manifested? If not, why not? After working with several classes, display a collection of the timelines in the library, accompanied by a book display and bookmarks listing the works.

- Author interview: After working with several classes, arrange an author visit, either face-to-face or virtually through Skype or other videoconferencing software. Prepare the students for the visit by having them read one or more books by the author, prepare questions in advance, read articles and websites about the author, and conduct discussions about the author's works (Messner, 2010, p. 42). For further information, visit the *Skype an Author Network* at http://skypeanauthor.wetpaint.com.

- Blogging for connections: Introduce teachers and students to the instructional benefits of blogging. Explain that some authors maintain blogs so that they can easily communicate with their readers. Johnson (2010) states that "children's and young adult authors are very aware of the emotional connections they create with their young readers through their books. Rather than remaining at a distance, many of these authors desire to create a stronger connection with their readers, which blogging allows them to do" (p. 172). Prepare the students for blogging with authors by having them read several of their books. After further discussions and author research, have the students follow the blog for several days. Instruct the students to prepare their messages, noting that their blog posts will be read by a real audience.

- Why did the author . . . ? Collaboratively work with language arts teachers to conduct an author study that focuses on a book's literary elements and the impact of these choices on the overall work. Explain to students that the author study will culminate in a written analysis. Hayden (2008) suggests posing to students a number of questions to guide their work, focusing on genre choice, character relationships, plot intricacies, and setting descriptions or interactions.

Word Choice and Figurative Language

Salwak (2011) commented that "when Mozart was three years old, he first sat at his sister's clavier . . . 'to find notes that like one another'. That became his life's work. . . . I hear in it a metaphor for the writer, who strives to find words that like one another" (p. 44). Words, of course, bring stories to life. The unique combinations of words give the story its flavor and reflect the author's writing style. For instance, does the author use simple, direct, commonly used language or more complex, flowery choices? Does the writer use similes, metaphors, or symbols to describe characters, setting, or actions? Does the author use more dialogue or narrative to move the story forward? Do the characters use formal English, slang, or a dialect?

In READS Chapter 8, the importance of vocabulary development is discussed. In this section, the focus is on identifying an author's wording choices and how these influence the overall feel of the story. The school librarian can work collaboratively with teachers to expand the students' understanding of language usage in independently read or classroom assigned literature.

- Comparisons: Review with students language usage in a classic novel (e.g., Cooper's *Last of the Mohicans*) with a contemporary adult or young adult novel (e.g., Paulsen's *Woods Runner*), representing the same genre. Project a descriptive paragraph from each novel and have the students discuss the differences, noting sentence structure (e.g., simple, complex, compound), length of paragraph, word choices, and figurative language. Discuss with students how the time and culture in which the novel was written may influence the writer's style. Have students complete a graphic organizer to record their observations.

- Sample of "What I like": After students have successfully completed a book trailer on a favorite book, have each student choose a representative paragraph from their novel. Encourage students to discuss their justifications for choosing that selection. The following questions can be posed to guide their thinking: (1) Does the dialogue reflect a favorite character? (2) Do the word choices clearly depict a particularly memorable point in the plot? Why? Or, (3) Do the word choices and figurative language used paint a visual picture in the mind that is memorable?

- Sophisticated word choices: Work with an English teacher's classes to write short narratives of no more than 350 words. Explain to the students that their work may be posted on the library web page, read during morning announcements, and/or displayed in the library. Encourage students to expand their use of more creative word choices through various vocabulary development activities. Beck, McKeown, and Kucan (2008) also suggest asking the students the following questions:

- "What words can you use to *show* your reader instead of *telling* your reader?
- What picture are you trying to create?
- What do you want your reader to know?
- What do you want your reader to think about all this?" (p. 35)

- A book is like a . . .—Work with middle school social studies classes and historical fiction selections. Present a booktalk featuring the selected titles. Review with students the use of figurative language (e.g., similes, metaphors, idioms) and present various examples. Have the students choose one of the featured books and instruct the students to read for pleasure, but to also note figurative language examples on a worksheet like the following one. Students may place a check under the appropriate type or include the sentence. (Refer to the Sunshine State Young Readers Award site at http://myssyra.org/ for middle school book lists and examples of figurative language usage in the *Curriculum Connections* sections.) After the students have read a book and completed the worksheet, follow up this activity with a discussion on how the figurative language impacted their understanding of the story and an appreciation for the author's craft, having them give specific examples.

- Creating mental images: Collaboratively work with the art teacher to reinforce the importance of visualization in reading. According to Wilhelm (2008), "visual imaging encourages students to access and apply their prior knowledge as they read, increases comprehension, and improves the ability to predict, infer, and remember what has been read" (p. 158). Begin the activity by sharing several picture books with the students and discussing how the illustrator has captured the action and characters in the story. Then, read a descriptive passage from a novel and have the students draw the scene from their mental image. Ask for volunteers to share their drawings.

ILLUSTRATOR STUDIES

The elementary school curriculum integrates the skills needed to interpret and create visuals. These skills are also integrated into the secondary curriculum in a variety of creative ways including analyzing political cartoons and primary source documents, combining original poems and drawings, creating digital stories, and producing photo or visual essays. The importance of integrating visual literacy skills into the curriculum is reinforced by Olshansky (2008) who states that "pictures are a powerful tool for thinking and recording ideas" (p. 25). For our visually connected students, the world is filled with rapidly

Book Title:			
Student's Name:			
Page	Metaphor	Simile	Idiom or Expression
My favorite metaphor was:			
My favorite simile is:			
My favorite idiom or expression is:			

changing visual information; consequently, correctly reading visual messages is a survival skill. Riddle (2009) reinforces the importance of visually presented information in the following comment: "Today's students are often manipulators and creators of their own information and entertainment. Bombarded by visual cues, they seem to translate images and information effortlessly" (p. 1).

School librarians can take advantage of students' affinity for visually presented information by conducting lessons that feature illustrators and their artwork. From an early age, students are introduced to picture books by school librarians, teachers, and parents. In the primary grades, picture books are used to tell stories, as well as to learn about story elements. Although picture books are an important part of the elementary school library collection, they can also be successfully incorporated into the secondary curriculum.

When one of your book authors opened three new high schools, she included an Easy section in the collection for two reasons. First, the books were used by the preschool children that were housed in each of the schools. Second, the books were used by teachers and the librarian to reinforce concepts covered in their curriculum. For instance, the television production teacher, as well as the librarian, used the books to reinforce visual literacy skills. The art teacher used picture books to highlight a particular medium used by the illustrator. The ELL and world language teachers used them to reinforce vocabulary development and cultural understandings. Language arts teachers used picture books to reinforce prediction and inference skills.

The use of picture books has advantages "because picture books are so succinct, they can be easily read, reread, and analyzed during a class period" (Van Horn, 2008, p. 50). Picture books also offer quality examples of how text and pictures are woven together to tell a story. Van Horn (2008) emphasizes that it is the way "in which text and image are combined [that] provides the reader with a new challenge" (p. 127). However, Olshansky (2008) emphasizes the need "to analyze how authors and illustrators separately establish these key literary elements using their own distinct languages to convey meaning" (p. 26).

Caldecott medal winners are excellent examples to use with classes to spark a discussion on illustrators and their artwork, placing emphasis on how the illustrations tell a story as well as the text. To begin planning for these activities, visit the *Caldecott Medal & Honor Books, 1938-Present on the* Association for Library Service to Children (ALSC) website at http://www.ala.org/alsc/awardsgrants/bookmedia/caldecottmedal/caldecotthonors/caldecottmedal, which provides brief descriptions of the illustrator's techniques. For example, David Diaz's illustrations in *Smokey Night* are described as "thickly textured, expressionistic acrylic paintings set against mixed-media collages." These descriptions can be shared with classes or used to launch a discussion of the medium featured. A few lesson ideas for the school librarian are listed as follows:

- Medium: Work collaboratively with the art teacher to present Caldecott winning books to the students, emphasizing the medium used by the illustrator. Ask the teacher to demonstrate the art medium used in each title. As a follow-up, have the students use one of the art techniques to create an illustration. Feature the student work on Voicethread (http://voicethread.com/), giving a brief description of the medium used. A sampling of the books and the medium used include:
  - *Golem*—paper-cuts
  - *Joseph Had a Little Overcoat*—watercolor, gouache, pencil, ink, and collage
  - *Kittens First Full Moon*—gouache and colored pencil
  - *The Lion & the Mouse*—textured watercolors

- *The Man Who Walked between the Towers*—ink and oil paintings
- *Snowflake Bentley*—woodcuts
- Online illustrator scrapbook: Plan a research project on book illustrators that culminates in using the online application *Glogster*. Introduce the students to *Glogster* and share examples of student work. Explain to students that they will be working with a partner to create an online scrapbook that features a favorite or assigned illustrator. Have students research the illustrator and plan their *Glogster* presentation. Illustrator information can include a short biography, timeline or listing of works, short video interview (if available) photograph(s), student comments on the illustrator's style, and a student work sample that features the same medium used by the illustrator.
- Let the pictures tell the story: Use a Caldecott winner such as *The Invention of Hugo Cabret* showing only the illustrations to the students or use a wordless selection such as *Flotsam*. Ask the students to retell the story as they perceive it by using only the pictures. Van Horn (2008) suggests "isolating the pictures from text [which] makes it easier to consider the job of the pictures" (p. 47). Follow up this activity by sharing the description of the book from the ALSC website, which states that "neither words nor pictures alone tell this story, which is filled with cinematic intrigue. Black & white pencil illustrations evoke the flickering images of the silent films to which the book pays homage." Have the students write their description of this book or another picture book of their choosing.

In summary, presenting activities to secondary students that focus on the illustrations and illustrators of Caldecott award winners or other picture books provides an opportunity to widen the dialogue concerning visual literacy skills. This is one more step toward producing students who are more sophisticated consumers of images and their messages.

LITERARY ELEMENTS

At the elementary level, school librarians conduct storytimes, reading a variety of children's books that introduce the students to literary elements such as characters, plot, and setting. In follow-up activities, the literary elements are compared and discussed in the classroom as well as in the library, to build a strong foundation for literary appreciation. At the middle and senior high levels, literary elements remain in the instructional program but with a more complex approach. In this section of Analyze, four story elements are discussed, including plot, characters, setting, and point of view. Theme was covered in the Explore chapter 5. For the purposes of this discussion, the story elements will be discussed separately; however, depending on the instructional situation, several literary elements may be reinforced during one lesson.

Plot

Plot is often described as the plan or outline of a story. According to Thompkins (2003), "Plot is the sequence of events involving characters in conflict situations" (p. 284). Conflicts may involve an internal conflict of the main character or a tension between a character and nature, society, or another character (p. 284). The conflict drives the plot and moves the story forward from the beginning, through the middle, to the end. In other words, the plot is the itch that needs to be scratched. At the beginning of the story, the author introduces the setting, characters, and the problem. For instance, on the first page of *Roll of Thunder, Hear My Cry*, Taylor (2004) introduces readers to the siblings Cassie, Stacey, Christopher John, and Little Man as they are walking to school on a dusty Mississippi road. As the story

READS Component	READS Indicator	AASL *Standards for the 21st-Century Learner**	Common Core State Standards—English Language Arts**
colspan4 **Analyze structure and aesthetic features of creative works**
colspan4 The student will:
3.2 Understand the literary techniques and complexities of a work.	3.2.2 Compare and contrast literary elements (e.g., characters, setting, or plot) in multiple works.	• 4.1.3 Respond to literature and creative expressions of ideas in various formats and genres.	• Language—4a Determine or clarify the meaning of unknown and multiple-meaning words and phrases: Use context . . . • Language—5 Demonstrate understanding of figurative language, word relationships, and nuances in word meanings. • Reading: Informational Text—6 Determine an author's point of view or purpose . . . • Reading: Literature—3 Analyze the impact of the author's choices . . .

*Excerpted from *Standards for the 21st-Century Learner* by the American Association of School Librarians, a division of the American Library Association, copyright © 2007 American Library Association. Available for download at www.ala.org/aasl/standards. Used with permission.

**Excerpted from *Common Core State Standards for English Language Arts*. National Governors Association Center for Best Practices and Council of Chief State School Officers Commercial License. Copyright © 2010. Used with permission of NGA Center/CCSSO.

continues to unfold, readers learn that this African American family must face the challenges of segregation and bigotry in the southern United States during the 1930s. Events continue to escalate during the middle of the story until the end brings a resolution to the current challenges.

Thompkins (2003) further explains that "plot development involves four components" (p. 285): a problem, road blocks, a high point or climax, and a solution. For instance, within the first few pages of Myers's *Kick* (2011), Sergeant Brown is called into the judge's chambers and asked to help a young boy whose policeman father had been killed in the line of duty. The young 13-year-old is charged with stealing a car, "kidnapping, driving without a license, damaging city property—the light pole—plus traffic violations" (p. 5). This scene introduces the reader to the problem and how the main characters are involved with one another. It also engages the reader into questioning how this problem will be resolved.

The importance of plot and a credible story line that has a beginning, middle, and end can be reinforced through the library instructional program. The following ideas are offered to begin thinking about ways for the school librarian to work with teachers or assigned classes to reinforce this literary element.

- Plot the action: Work with small groups of students and assign the same book (e.g., print or e-book) to at least two groups. Have the students read and analyze the plot, noting the significant events in the story. Introduce the students to the *Prezi* online application and have them document the main story events to present to the class. Have the two groups that analyzed the same book present at the same time and have the groups compare their findings. If or when differences emerge, have the groups reflect on their choices.

- Teach plots: During the end of a semester, collaboratively work with a social studies teacher to correlate the events in historical fiction books with the periods of history studied. First, teach the students to insert shapes onto a PowerPoint slide that will represent the main plot events with lines connecting them. Next, show students how to use the action settings to link the shape (e.g., plot event) to another slide that contains a brief plot event summary and its correlation to an historical event.

- Picture that: Collaboratively work with gifted students to create picture or pop-up books that will be sent to a feeder pattern elementary school. Review plot guidelines, noting the need for escalating conflict to engage the reader. Use at least one picture book as an example (e.g., *Alexander and the Terrible, Horrible, No Good, Very Bad Day)* and review the conflicts presented and the plot events that drive the story. Work with students as they create their plot lines and, finally, their picture books.

- Reading art: Work with the art teacher to reinforce visual literacy skills by having students analyze a famous painting. Explain that paintings depict a moment in time that is dependent on actions that preceded it. Use paintings (e.g., *The Gulf Stream* or *Boys in a Dory* by Winslow Homer or *The Hatch Family* by Eastman Johnson) to illustrate this point; lead a discussion on details in the paintings and what they tell about the story of the painting. Choose another painting, divide the class into small groups or triads, and have them construct a plot line for the painting. Have each group present their interpretation to the class.

- Television sitcoms: Work with a television production class and review the components of plot. For homework, have the students watch a favorite television situation comedy and create a story map, indicating the problem, critical events, and resolution.

- Reader's theater: Work with the drama teacher to locate reader's theater pieces that the students will perform either for the class or for feeder pattern schools. Remind students that "reader's theatre is a staged reading of literature that emphasizes the importance of text" (Poe, 2010, p. 28). Also, according to Fredericks (2011), "It is an oral interpretation of a piece of literature" (p. 42). Invite several students to rehearse and perform a reader's theater selection for the class. Afterwards, discuss with the class the events that propelled the story forward. As a follow-up, have the students write a reader's theater selection based on a short story of their choosing.

Characters

From the time that most are very young, they hear and experience stories that are based on lively characters that face and conquer conflicts and problems. For instance, fairy tales such as Cinderella pit the beautiful young maid against the wicked stepmother and her selfish daughters. A spell sends Sleeping Beauty into a deep100-year sleep from which she only awakens after the handsome prince kisses her. These are characters that we learn to love and who have transcended time.

Consequently, stories are based on characters that may be "people or personified animals who are involved in the story" (Thompkins, 2003, p. 288). Well-crafted characters engage the reader in the story and keep them reading to see what will happen to them. Will they succeed in their quest to overcome evil? Will the young maiden meet and marry the handsome prince? In other words, the characters provide the cement that holds the story together as they react to the problem and events presented in the plot.

Haven (2007) explains "that what characters do and what they say—how they act—are the result of, and a reflection of, the characters' intent" (p. 36). He further clarifies that intent is made up of goals and motives that are, in turn, based on the character's beliefs and values (p. 36). Specific character traits become evident as the characters meet each twist of the plot. For example, we learn that Doon and Lina are courageous 12-year-olds in *The City of Ember.* After they locate a map that informs the Ember citizens of a way to exit their dying underground city, Doon and Lina explore the passages and lead the way to the outside world. It is through their actions that the reader forms an understanding of each character's flaws, strengths, beliefs, and values.

Authors also assist the reader in understanding their characters by describing their physical attributes. Mikaelsen (1998) gives the reader the first glimpse of Petey with the following description: "The baby's expressionless face looked like a caricature placed on top of the tiny, twisted body. His eyes were little brown orbs, frozen in a hollow gaze. His lips squeezed tightly askew under some hidden tension" (p. 3). Readers can quickly picture Angus's physical attributes from Crutcher's (1991) descriptions, "I mean, my mom had to go to the husky section of Safeway to buy me Pampers" (p. 6). However, "I am *incredibly* quick for a fat kid, and I have world-class reflexes. It is nearly impossible for the defensive lineman across from me to shake me, such are my anticipatory skills" (p. 8). In the first example, the narrator describes the baby, and in the second example, the author uses the character's words to describe himself.

Consequently, another way that authors develop three-dimensional characters is through dialogue, not only what they say but also how they say it. Characters in Hurston's *Their Eyes Were Watching God* (1998) use the early 20th-century dialect spoken by blacks in the southern United States who were of African and Caribbean descent, for instance, "Where all dat money her husband took and died and left her?" (p. 2). Although Hurston received some criticism for the use of the dialect, it does immediately help the reader understand the location and culture portrayed. Crutcher (2009) offers quick paced, sometimes humorous, dialogue, to flesh out his characters in *Angry Management*, as well as to advance the story line. Readers also learn what characters are thinking through the author's use of point of view, which is explained in the following text. A main character may speak directly to the reader or the author may narrate the story, describing the thoughts and actions of multiple characters.

As students move through the grades, they are exposed to more complex, demanding characters that require more intense study. The school library program can supplement classroom character studies using a variety of approaches and production techniques.

- Characters build the story: Create a group of characters from which students will create a short story. The characters' descriptions can be as complete or limited as needed. Ideas for characters could include:
  - One tall, young girl who plays soccer
  - One very loud dog
  - One handsome boy who likes to read
  - One jewelry thief who escapes from prison

After completing the stories, students can post them on a library display, produce picture books, record podcasts of either the entire narrative or a story trailer, or video record a skit based on the story and post it to a website.

- Character swap: Review with students some of the unique characters from classic or contemporary fiction, discussing the flaws and strengths of each. Divide the class into small groups or triads and have them create a list of four to five original characters. Then, have the groups swap their lists and write short stories based on the new list.

- Genre characteristics: Work collaboratively with the language arts teacher to choose a genre on which to conduct a character study. For example, the horror genre is a favorite among many teens. Have students identify the characteristics of the main protagonists in these novels, referring to Saricks (2009, p. 118) for additional clarification. Instruct the students to list adjectives that describe characters featured in the horror genre.

- Stereotypes or originals?: Work with an arts teacher to discuss the characteristics of stereotypical characters in stories. To illustrate the discussion, review characters in a few of the students' favorite contemporary books, fairy tales, or familiar picture books. Additionally, excerpts from movies based on young adult novels could also be used. To conclude the discussion, have students work with a partner to draft a story character that exhibits unique personality characteristics. Collaborate with the students' language arts teachers to have the students write short stories that feature their character.

- Friending a character: Work with the computer science teacher and have students choose a favorite character (or assign one, if necessary). Students will create a website or Facebook page that provides a profile, pictures, and friends of the character. Supplement this activity with a short narrative in which the students provide justifications for their choices. Refer to the ReadWriteThink.org *Story Character Homepage* for a scoring rubric.

- Compare and contrast: Work with the reading teacher to discuss with students the transformations that characters undergo during a well-crafted story. Review the *Eight Levels of Character Transformation* as delineated by Ohler (2008, p. 109). Have the students choose one of the eight transformation types (e.g., physical or kinesthetic, inner strength, emotional, moral, psychological, social, intellectual or creative, spiritual) and apply it to characters with which they are familiar.

- Character analysis: Collaboratively work with an English teacher whose classes are currently studying a Shakespeare play. Have the students identify the supporting characters in the play. Have students construct a character analysis chart in which they will list the supporting characters, their actions, and their impact on the main protagonist and the play's outcome. Organize the class into small groups and have students discuss their findings, providing justifications for their decisions.

- Blog talk: Work with a language arts teacher or an assigned class and set up a blog that will be used by two groups of students. Assign a book that features two strong protagonists (e.g., *Kick* or *The Pigman*) and assign one of the characters to each group. Explain to the students that they will be communicating with the other group as though they were that character. Have the students review the traits and perspective of each character, as well as word choices and sentence structure.

- Character trailers: Work with language arts classes that are completing author studies on young adult novelists. Review with students the components of a typical book trailer that is plot-driven (e.g., short, visually appealing) and the purpose (e.g., entice people to read the book). Share school-generated examples or those available online. (Many examples are available on YouTube at http://youtube.com/education and on Authors and Trailer's *Meet Authors and Their Books* at http://authorsandtrailers.weebly.com/index.html.) Then, explain to students that they will be creating character trailers designed to inform, but also entice students to read more about the character. Students may focus on the following aspects of the character: age, interests, friends, family, and/or conflicts.

In summary, character studies provide opportunities for students to develop their critical reading skills. By working collaboratively with teachers across the content areas, students can experience character development from multiple viewpoints.

Setting

Setting is the where and when of the story. According to Thompkins (2003), the four dimensions of setting are "location, weather, time period, and time" (p. 290). Location is particularly important in genres such as fantasy, adventure, and historical fiction. For example, the *Harry Potter* series exists in a parallel world in which much of the action takes place in the Hogwarts School of Witchcraft and Wizardry. The protagonist in an adventure story, such as *Hatchet* by Gary Paulsen, places the central character in a conflict with nature and is set in the Canadian wilderness. Ann Rinaldi's characters in *The Fifth of March: A Story of the Boston Massacre* must deal with the social and political conflicts in colonial Boston. In each of these examples, the setting is an important element that significantly contributes to the telling of the story.

Another dimension of setting is weather. Scary stories and mysteries may take place at night during stormy, dark conditions to heighten the drama. Weather may also play a significant role in adventure stories or realistic fiction. For instance, Peg Kehret's young characters must deal with a tsunami in *Escaping the Giant Wave*.

The third dimension of setting is the time period. For example, science fiction stories may be set in the future in which futuristic technological devices may be used. Historical fiction titles are set in a time period that predates the author's lifetime or experiences and require an accurate depiction of the social, political, and/or cultural aspects of the time. For example, in Laurie Halse Anderson's *Fever 1793*, Mattie Cook and her family are faced with the rapid spread of a deadly fever while living in Philadelphia during a time when medical knowledge and care was in its infancy.

The fourth dimension of setting is time that, according to Thompkins (2003), "involves both time of day and the passage of time" (p. 290). In many novels, the action takes place in the daytime with occasional scenes set during the night to add to the tension in the story. For instance, in Carl Hiaasen's *Scat*, Libby's dad, Jason Marshall, is awakened at 2:20 A.M. by their barking dog. He and the dog venture outside to investigate. Finding nothing out of the ordinary, Jason decides the dog must have heard a raccoon. However, when they re-enter the house, he discovers that the dog has retrieved his daughter's asthma inhaler that had been lost in the Black Vine Swamp during the day's school field trip. So who dropped the inhaler on the porch in the middle of the night? An example of the passage of time is Charlotte Bronte's classic *Jane Eyre* that takes the heroine from a 10-year-old orphan to a mature young woman who is self-reliant and morally responsible.

A variety of activities that focus on setting can be included in the school library instructional program. Beyond using photographs or other visuals and websites to expand students' background knowledge on geographical places or historical time periods, the school librarian can work with teachers in multiple subject areas to reinforce this literary element.

- Impact of setting: Work with a guidance counselor and a small group of students. First, read aloud *Touching Spirit Bear* by Ben Mickaelsen, discussing the settings described in the novel. Ask students why they think it was important for 15-year-old Cole Matthews to be sent to an isolated island, Ketchikan, off the coast of Alaska. What were the advantages and disadvantages for Cole during his stay on the island? How did the location influence Cole? Would the outcome of the story have been different if Cole remained in his home? Why? In a follow-up activity, have students use a line drawing of the United States on which to trace Cole's journey from Minnesota to Alaska.

- Similarities and differences: Collaboratively work with social studies teachers to review with students two historical fiction novels that are set during the same time period. Have students complete a Venn diagram, noting the differences and similarities in the settings. Additionally, a timeline of the period could be developed and compared to the events in the stories.
- Alternative setting: Work with language arts teachers to choose several novels on which to base an alternative setting activity. Organize the students into small groups or triads and assign a familiar or recently studied novel to each group. Have the students review the setting of the novel and then suggest an alternative setting, providing a justification for why this setting would work for the existing characters' actions and story line.
- Setting vocabulary: Have students work with a partner to locate the descriptive words, phrases, and sentences used by the author that help the reader visualize the setting. Review examples with the students. For instance, Diane Mott Davidson (2007) describes a catering hall in *Sweet Revenge* with the following statement: "Artificial trees and thousands of tiny colored lights had transformed the place into the proverbial winter wonderland" (p. 7). In *Roll of Thunder, Hear My Cry*, Taylor (2004) describes "the second crossroads, where deep gullies lined both sides of the road and the dense forest crept to the very edges of high, jagged, clay-walled banks" (p. 12). As a follow-up activity, have the students use the words and phrases located to construct their own sentences.

Point of View

Regardless of the genre, writing is always approached from a point of view. This perspective provides the lens through which the reader views the events or conflicts and other characters in the story. Smith and Wilhelm (2010) state that "the way a story is told—its point of view—is crucially important" (p.111). Frey, Fisher, and Berkin (2009) describe the three points of view: "In the first person, the story is told from the perspective of the narrator," (p. 65) using the first-person pronoun "I." When an author uses the first-person viewpoint, one character, usually the main protagonist, tells the story. Paul Zindel expanded on this approach in *The Pigman*, in which the story is told in alternating chapters from the point of view of either John or Lorraine, both high school students who feel alienated from society. This approach is also used by Myers and Workman in *Kick*. To add depth to the story and to present an adult's as well as a young person's point of view, the story is told in the first-person viewpoint, alternating chapters between Sergeant Brown and young Kevin.

"In the second person, the narrator speaks directly to the reader," explains Frey et al. (2009, p. 65). This point of view is the least commonly used in fiction, but may be found in the *Choose Your Own Adventure* series, video games, and other informational texts that use the pronoun "you" (*The Writer's Craft* at http://www.the-writers-craft.com/second-person-point-of-view.html). According to Dorfman and Cappelli (2009), "The use of the second-person voice creates an immediate rapport with an audience. The friendly tone invites the reader in to learn more" (p. 215).

When an author uses the third-person point of view, "the narrator is omniscient (all-knowing) and can convey different perspectives at different times" (Frey et al., 2009, p. 65). This is the most commonly used point of view. It offers more flexibility for the author and uses the pronouns of "he," "she," and "they." The reader can be exposed to the thoughts and feelings of various characters in the story or by using the limited omniscient viewpoint, the author can focus on one character (Thompkins, 2003, p. 292).

Exploring different points of view can lead to a deeper understanding of and appreciation for well-crafted stories. Reflective, critical thinking activities such as the ones that follow can encourage readers to delve into varying perspectives and prepare them for assessing the validity of a character's actions:

- Assessing the first-person perspective: Work with a small group of students and a book written from the first-person perspective that was read aloud or previously studied. Lead a discussion on what the students perceive as the limitations of the first-person viewpoint. Using the novel as a guide, ask the students which of the characters' voices or points of view are missing or discounted in the story? Why?

- Varying points of view: Collaboratively work with an English teacher to review how the author's choice of viewpoint impacts the story. Discuss various fairy tales and use a site such as http://academic.brooklyn.cuny.edu/english/melani/pv.html that presents a fairy tale from different characters' points of view. Discuss how the basic actions in the story remain the same, but the reader's reactions to the story may differ depending on which character is narrating the story. As a follow-up, have the students complete a similar writing exercise, choosing another fairy tale.

- Believability: Collaboratively work with a language arts teacher to critique the characters points of view in Myers and Workman's *Kick*. Read the novel to the class or use an audiobook. Using multiple copies of the book, have small groups of students analyze the account of events as told by either Sergeant Brown or Kevin to determine which character is the most credible. Have the students note justifications for their decision and be prepared to defend it during a class discussion.

- Newspaper critiques: Work with the journalism teacher to review point of view using newspaper articles. Project two editorials or letters to the editor that represent differing points of view for the students to read. Ask the students which of the editorials or letters is more persuasive and why? Do the students think that the viewpoint skews their reaction to the editorials or letters, particularly if it agrees or disagrees with the students' opinion on the topic?

- Differing poetry perspectives: Work with social studies students to analyze differing perspectives on America as described in three poems. Use the readwritethink.org lesson plan "Varying Views of America" and the interactive Venn diagram provided for the students to record their comparisons of the three poems.

As students advance through the grades, school librarians can continue to reinforce the importance of story elements, using a variety of texts, visuals, and media. In this way, students learn to appreciate the complexities of well-crafted literature, increasing their reading comprehension and pleasure.

READS LESSONS AND ACTIVITIES

Analyze Structure and Aesthetic features of Creative Works

Understand the Literary Techniques and Complexities of a Work

Author's and Illustrator's Styles

Are you a fish out of water? Learning English idioms. By Dinah Mack and Holly Epstein Ojalvo. The Learning Network: *The New York Times*. (Gr. 9–12)

Analyzing style and intertextuality in *Twilight*. By K. B. Bull. (2009). *English Journal, 98* (3), 113–116.

Deep impact: Considering personal connections to writers and artists. By Amanda Christy Brown and Holly Epstein Ojalvo. The Learning Network: *The New York Times.* (Gr. 6–12)

Figurative language awards ceremony. By Lisa Storm Fink. Includes Books Containing Figurative Language list and Figurative Language Awards Bookmark. ReadWriteThink. (Gr. 5 up)

Figuratively speaking: Exploring how metaphors make meaning. By Amanda Christy Brown and Holly Epstein Ojalvo. The Learning Network: *The New York Times.* (Gr. 6–12) http://learning.blogs.nytimes.com/2011/04/14/figuratively-speaking-exploring-how-metaphors-make-meaning/

Getting figurative with poetry. By Melissa Nelson. (2011). *School Library Monthly, 27* (6), 19–20. (Gr. 6–8)

Introducing metaphors through poetry. By Jennifer Foley. EDSITEment. (Gr. 9–12) http://edsitement.neh.gov/view_lesson_plan.asp?id=605#ACTIVITY01

Irony in "The Gift of the Magi." By Mariama Sesay-St. Paul. Scholastic. (Gr. 9–12) http://www2.scholastic.com/browse/lessonplan.jsp?id=622&FullBreadCrumb=%3Ca+href%3D%22http%3A%2F%2Fwww2.scholastic.com%2Fbrowse%2Fsearch%2F%3FNtx%3Dmode%2Bmatchallpartial%26_N%3Dfff%26Ntk%3DSCHL30_SI%26query%3Dirony%2520in%2520the%2520gift%2520of%2520the%2520magi%26N%3D0%26Ntt%3Dirony%2Bin%2Bthe%2Bgift%2Bof%2Bthe%2Bmagi%22+class%3D%22endecaAll%22%3EAll+Results%3C%2Fa%3E

King Arthur: Man or legend? Includes Symbolism in the Legend of King Arthur. ArtsEdge. (Gr. 5–8 up)

Literary pilgrimages: Exploring the role of place in writers' lives and work. By Holly Epstein Ojalvo. The Learning Network: *The New York Times.* (Gr. 6–12) http://learning.blogs.nytimes.com/2010/01/21/literary-pilgrimages-exploring-the-role-of-place-in-writers-lives-and-work/

Reading symbols. Scholastic. (Gr. 8–12) http://www2.scholastic.com/browse/lessonplan.jsp?id=805&FullBreadCrumb=%3Ca+href%3D%22http%3A%2F%2Fwww2.scholastic.com%2Fbrowse%2Fsearch%2F%3FNtx%3Dmode%2Bmatchallpartial%26_N%3Dfff%26Ntk%3DSCHL30_SI%26query%3Dreading%2520symbols%26N%3D0%26Ntt%3Dreading%2Bsymbols%22+class%3D%22endecaAll%22%3EAll+Results%3C%2Fa%3E

So what do you think? Writing a review. By Susanne Rubenstein. Includes Components of a Review and Review Guidelines for composing an author review. ReadWriteThink. (Gr. 9–12) http://www.readwritethink.org/classroom-resources/lesson-plans/what-think-writing-review-876.html

Stairway to heaven: Examining metaphor in popular music. By Sue Carmichael. Includes Songs with Metaphor and Literary Graffiti Tool. ReadWriteThink. (Gr. 9–12) http://www.readwritethink.org/classroom-resources/lesson-plans/stairway-heaven-examining-metaphor-975.html

Style: Defining and exploring an author's stylistic choices. By Traci Gardner. Includes Checklist: Elements of Literary Style. ReadWriteThink. (Gr. 9–12) http://www.readwritethink.org/classroom-resources/lesson-plans/style-defining-exploring-author-209.html

Style: Translating stylistic choices from Hawthorne to Hemingway and back again. By Traci Gardner. ReadWriteThink. (Gr. 9–12)

Using technology to analyze and illustrate symbolism in Night. By Catherine Thomason. Includes Literary Graffiti tool. ReadWriteThink. (Gr. 6–8) http://www.readwritethink.org/classroom-resources/lesson-plans/using-technology-analyze-illustrate-903.html

Young adults connecting with authors. By Alison Timm. *School Library Monthly, 27* (6), 17–19. (Gr. 6–8)

Complexities of a Work

Action is character: Exploring character traits with adjectives. By Traci Gardner. ReadWriteThink. (Gr. 6–8) http://www.readwritethink.org/classroom-resources/lesson-plans/action-character-exploring-character-175.html

Analyzing character development in three short stories about women. By Patricia Alejandra. ReadWrite-Think. (Gr. 9–12)

The big bad wolf: Analyzing point of view in texts. By Laurie A. Henry. ReadWriteThink. (Gr. 6–8) http://www.readwritethink.org/classroom-resources/lesson-plans/wolf-analyzing-point-view-23.html

Book report alternative: Creating careers for characters. By Traci Gardner. Includes Writing Resumes for Fictional Characters. ReadWriteThink. (Gr. 6–8) http://www.readwritethink.org/classroom-resources/lesson-plans/book-report-alternative-creating-245.html

Charting characters for a more complete understanding of the story. By Cammie Singleton. Includes Character Perspective Chart. ReadWriteThink. (Gr. 5 up) http://www.readwritethink.org/classroom-resources/lesson-plans/charting-characters-more-complete-267.html

Critical reading: Two stories, two authors, same plot? By Patricia Alejandra Lastiri. Includes Interactive Literary Elements Map. ReadWriteThink. (Gr. 9–12)

Developing characterization in Raymond Carver's "A small good thing." By Patsy Hamby. Includes Interactive: Literary Elements Map. ReadWriteThink. (Gr. 9–12) http://www.readwritethink.org/classroom-resources/lesson-plans/developing-characterization-raymond-carver-1050.html

Developing story structure with paper-bag skits. By Nancy J. Kolodziej. ReadWriteThink. (Gr. 6–8)

Elements of a novel and *Photo Story.* By Elena Johnson. (2000). *School Library Monthly, 26* (4), 11–12. (Gr. 10 up)

Exploring setting: Constructing character, point of view, atmosphere, and theme. By Scott Filkins. ReadWriteThink. (Gr. 9–12)

Heroes are made of this: Studying the character of heroes. By John Paul Walter. ReadWriteThink. Includes Interactive: Literary Elements Map. (Gr. 9–12)

Id, ego, and superego in Dr. Seuss's The Cat in the Hat. By Junius Wright. Includes An Introduction to Psychoanalytic Criticism and Defining Characterization. ReadWriteThink. (Gr. 9–12) http://www.readwritethink.org/classroom-resources/lesson-plans/superego-seuss-800.html

It's the same old story. By Holly Epstein Ojalvo. The Learning Network: *The New York Times.* (Gr. 8 up) http://learning.blogs.nytimes.com/2008/11/20/its-the-same-old-story/

Lights, camera, action: Interviewing a book character. By Kristina McLaughlin. ReadWriteThink. (Gr. 6–8) http://www.readwritethink.org/classroom-resources/lesson-plans/lights-camera-action-interviewing-140.html?tab=4#tabs

Literary criticism. (Resource) Includes pathfinder and criticism of authors. Internet Public Library. http://www.ipl.org/div/litcrit/

Literary elements mapping: Character map. (Resource) ReadWriteThink. (Gr. 6–12) http://www.readwritethink.org/files/resources/lesson_images/lesson390/character.pdf

Male and female courageous protagonist project. By Michael Stencil Sr. (2009). *School Library Media Activities Monthly,* 25 (6), 13–15. (Gr. 6–8).

The New York Times used the slogan "All the News That's Fit to Print." (Calendar resource) ReadWrite Think. (Gr. 7–12) http://www.readwritethink.org/classroom-resources/calendar-activities/york-times-used-slogan-20412.html

Novel news: Broadcast coverage of character, conflict, resolution, and setting. By Traci Gardner. Includes Interactive Literary Elements Map. ReadWriteThink (Gr. 9–12) http://www.readwritethink.org/classroom-resources/lesson-plans/novel-news-broadcast-coverage-199.html

Plot structure: A literary elements mini-lesson. By Traci Gardner. Includes Plot PowerPoint Presentation and Plot Diagram interactive. ReadWriteThink. (Gr. 6–8) http://www.readwritethink.org/classroom-resources/lesson-plans/plot-structure-literary-elements-904.html

Political cartoons: Finding point of view. Library of Congress. (Gr. 6–12) http://www.loc.gov/teachers/classroommaterials/lessons/political-cartoons/procedure.html

'Retale' value. By Michelle Sale and Yasmin Chin Eisenhauer. Includes application of seven basic plot lines. The Learning Network: *The New York Times.* (Gr. 6–12) http://learning.blogs.nytimes.com/2005/04/15/retale-value/

Rules of notice for character. (Resource) Scholastic. http://www2.scholastic.com/content/collateral_
resources/pdf/r/reading_bestpractices_comprehension_rulesofnoticechart.pdf

Story character homepage. By Patricia Schulze. Includes Interactive Literary Elements Map. Read-
WriteThink. (Gr. 6–12) http://www.readwritethink.org/classroom-resources/lesson-plans/
story-character-homepage-50.html

Student crossword: Famous literary characters. By Frank Longo. The Learning Network: *The New
York Times*. (Gr. 6–12) http://learning.blogs.nytimes.com/2010/01/14/student-crossword-
famous-literary-characters/

Teaching plot structure through short stories. By Patricia Schulze. ReadWriteThink. (Gr. 9–10) http://
www.readwritethink.org/search/?sort_order=relevance&q=teaching+plot+structure+throug
h+short+stories&old_q=&srchgo.x=15&srchgo.y=8

Teaching point of view with Two Bad Ants. By Sharon Morris. Include Point of View chart. Read-
WriteThink. (Gr. 5 up) http://www.readwritethink.org/classroom-resources/lesson-plans/
teaching-point-view-with-789.html

Varying views of America. By Sharon Webster. Includes comparison of poems. ReadWriteThink.
(Gr. 9–12) http://www.readwritethink.org/classroom-resources/lesson-plans/varying-
views-america-194.html

What a character! Comparing literary adaptations. By Amanda Christy Brown and Holly Epstein
Ojalvo. The Learning Network: *The New York Times*. (Gr. 9–12) http://learning.blogs.nytimes.
com/2010/01/14/what-a-character-comparing-literary-adaptations/

Visual Literacy

Analyzing the purpose and meaning of political cartoons. By Victoria Mayers, Lynn Stone, and Beth
O'Connor. Includes Editorial Cartoon Analysis. ReadWriteThink, (Gr. 9–12) http://www.
readwritethink.org/classroom-resources/lesson-plans/analyzing-purpose-meaning-politi
cal-794.html?tab=4#tabs

Analyzing the stylistic choices of political cartoonists. By Traci Gardner. Includes Comic Vocabulary Definitions and Examples: Text Containers. ReadWriteThink. (Gr. 9–12) http://www.readwrite-
think.org/classroom-resources/lesson-plans/analyzing-stylistic-choices-political-923.html

Blogging with Photovoice: Sharing pictures in an integrated classroom. By Krista Sherman. Includes Photovoice Project Instructions and Picture Description Sheet. ReadWriteThink. (Gr. 9–12) http://
www.readwritethink.org/classroom-resources/lesson-plans/blogging-with-photovoice-
sharing-1064.html?tab=1#tabs

Critical lenses. By Amanda Christy Brown, Kristin McGinn Mahoney, and Holly Epstein Ojalvo.
The Learning Network: *The New York Times*. (Gr. 6–12) http://learning.blogs.nytimes.
com/2009/05/22/critical-lenses/

Every image tells a story. By Susannah Tamarkin. *From the creative minds of 21st century librarians*:
e-book. pp. 208–210. (Gr. 9) http://digital-literacy.syr.edu/page/view/221

How to read (a photograph). By Debbie Abilock. http://www.noodletools.com/debbie/literacies/
visual/diglitnews.pdf

Music and me: Visual representations of lyrics to popular music. By Deborah Kozdras and Denise Haun-
stetter. Includes Music and Me Idea Map and Using Movie Maker to Create Photomontage
Movies. ReadWriteThink. (Gr. 9–12)

TV 411: Reading photographs. Includes photo analysis worksheets. PBS Teachers. (Gr. 9–12) http://
www.pbs.org/teachers/connect/resources/5209/preview/

Visual literacy. (Resource) By Debbie Abilock. NoodleTools. (Gr. 9–12) http://www.noodletools.
com/debbie/literacies/visual/diglitnews.pdf

Visual literacy. (Resource) By Frank W. Baker. http://www.frankwbaker.com/vis_lit.htm

Visual literacy resources on the web: A look at what is available. (Resource) Association of College &
Research Libraries. http://www.ala.org/ala/mgrps/divs/acrl/publications/crlnews/2007/
sep/Visual_literacy_resources_on_the_Web1.cfm

READS INTERNET RESOURCES

Analyze Structure and Aesthetic features of Creative Works

Understand the Literary Techniques and Complexities of a Work

Aaron Shepard's reader's theater page. http://www.aaronshep.com/rt/index.html

Association for Library Service to Children: *Caldecott Medal & Honor Books, 1938-Present.* http://www.ala.org/alsc/awardsgrants/bookmedia/caldecottmedal/caldecotthonors/caldecott medal

Authors and Trailers: Meet authors and their books. http://authorsandtrailers.weebly.com/index.html

Authors4teens.com. http://www.authors4teens.com/links.asp

Barnes & Noble Studio: Meet the authors. Includes YA authors. http://www.barnesandnoble.com/bn-studio/videos-podcasts/index.asp?

Conversing with the author check sheet. Scholastic/Teachers. http://www2.scholastic.com/content/collateral_resources/pdf/r/reading_bestpractices_comprehension_authorchecksheet.pdf

James Patterson's READKIDDOREAD.COM. http://readkiddoread.ning.com/page/page/show?id=2244625%3APage%3A64

Literary History.com: Literary criticism. http://www.literaryhistory.com/

Margie Palatini reader's theater guides. http://www.margiepalatini.com/whats-l3–2/readers-theater

Multnomah County Public Library Homework Center: High school literature. http://www.multcolib.org/homework/hslit.html

Multnomah County Public Library Homework Center: Literature & authors. http://www.multcolib.org/homework/lithc.html

Reading Rockets video interviews of top children's book authors and illustrators. http://www.readingrockets.org/books/interviews/

Scholastic's audio video index. http://www.scholastic.com/teachers/lesson-plan/author-video-index

Scholastic's Teaching Caldecott Winners. http://www.scholastic.com/teachers/article/teaching-caldecott-winners

Skype an author network. http://skypeanauthor.wetpaint.com

TeachingBooks.net. Subscription-based service. teachingbooks.net

VirtualLit: Elements of fiction. http://bcs.bedfordstmartins.com/virtualit/fiction/elements.asp

The writer's craft. Web English Teacher. http://www.webenglishteacher.com/index.html http://www.the-writers-craft.com/second-person-point-of-view.html

YA author blogs. http://bookleads.wikispaces.com/YA+author+blogs

Young adult literature. Web English Teacher. http://www.webenglishteacher.com/ya.html

YouTube.com/education. http://youtube.com/education

WORKS CITED

Anonymous. (2010). The write stuff. *Scholastic News, 66* (5), 23–24.

Beck, I, L., McKeown, M. G., & Kucan, L. (2008). *Creating robust vocabulary: Frequently asked questions & extended examples.* New York: Guildford Press.

Brisson, P. (2002). An author's tips for doing author studies. *Teaching PreK-8, 32* (8), 48–49.

Calkins, L. M. (2001). *The art of teaching reading.* New York: Longman.

Crutcher, C. (1991). *Athletic shorts: Six short stories.* New York: Greenwillow.

Crutcher, C. (2009). *Angry management: Three novellas.* New York: Greenwillow.

Davidson, D. M. (2007). *Sweet revenge.* New York: Avon.

DiCamillo, K. (2010). The story you told me. *The Horn Book, 86* (2), 15.

Dorfman, L. R., & Cappelli, R. (2009). *Nonfiction mentor texts: Teaching informational writing through children's literature, k-8.* Portland, ME: Stenhouse.

Fredericks, A. D. (2011). Building literacy bridges with reader's theater. *School Library Monthly, 27* (4), 42–44.

Frey, N., Fisher, D., & Berkin, A. (2009). *Good habits, great readers: Building the literacy community.* Boston, MA: Pearson.

Haven, K. (2007). *Story proof: The science behind the startling power of story.* Westport, CT: Libraries Unlimited.

Hayden, K. (2008). *Author's style or influence lesson.* Retrieved from http://kellie-hayden.suite101.com/author-style-or-influence-lesson-a44436#ixzz1h0tyxVNL.

Hurston, Z. N. (1998). *Their eyes were watching God.* New York: Perennial Classics.

Johnson, D. (2010). Teaching with authors' blogs: Connections, collaboration, creativity. *Journal of Adolescent & Adult Literacy, 54* (3), 172–180.

Keene, E. O. (2008). *To understand: New horizons in reading comprehension.* Portsmouth, NH: Heinemann.

Messner, K. (2010). An author in every classroom. *School Library Journal, 56* (9), 42.

Mikaelsen, B. (1998). *Petey.* New York: Hyperion.

Ohler, J. (2008). *Digital storytelling in the classroom: New Media pathways to literacy, learning, and creativity.* Thousand Oaks, CA: Corwin.

Olshansky, B. (2008). *The power of pictures: Creating pathways to literacy through art.* San Francisco, CA: Jossey-Bass.

Poe, E. A. (2010). From children's literature to reader's theatres. *American Libraries, 41* (5), 28–31.

Riddle, J. (2009). *Engaging the eye generation: Visual literacy strategies for the K-5 classroom.* Portland, ME: Stenhouse.

Salwak, D. (2011). Listen to your sentences. *The Times Higher Education Supplement* (1993), 44.

Saricks, J. G. (2009). *The readers' advisory guide to genre fiction* (2nd ed.). Chicago, IL: American Library Association.

Smith, M., & Wilhelm, J. D. (2010). *Fresh takes on teaching literary elements: How to teach what really matters about character, setting, point of view, and theme.* New York: Scholastic Teaching Resources.

Taylor, M. D. (2004). *Roll of thunder, hear my cry.* New York: Puffin.

Thompkins, G. E. (2003). *Literary for the 21st century* (3rd ed.). Upper Saddle River, NJ: Merrill Prentice Hall.

Van Horn, L. (2008). *Reading photographs to write with meaning and purpose, grades 4–12.* Newark, DE: International Reading Association.

Wilhelm, J. D. (2008). *"You gotta be the book:" Teaching engaged and reflective reading with adolescents.* New York: Teachers College Press.

FURTHER READING

Bentheim, C. (2010). From book museum to learning commons: Riding the transformation train. *Teacher Librarian, 37* (4), 37–39.

Blachowicz, C., & Ogle, D. (2001). *Reading comprehension: Strategies for independent learners.* New York: Guilford Press.

Black, A., & Stave, A. M. (2007). *A comprehensive guide to readers theatre: Enhancing fluency and comprehension in middle school and beyond.* Newark, DE: International Reading Association.

Booth, D. (2008). *It's critical!: Exploring strategies for promoting critical and creative comprehension.* Portland, ME: Pembroke.

Donham, J. (2005). *Enhancing teaching and learning* (2nd ed.). New York: Neal-Schuman.

Elkins, J. (Ed.) (2008). *Visual literacy.* New York: Routledge.

Follos, A.M.G. (2006). *Reviving reading: School library programming, author visits and books that rock!* Westport, CT: Libraries Unlimited.

Fontichiaro, K. (2008). *Podcasting at school.* Westport, CT: Libraries Unlimited.

Frazel, M. (2010). *Digital storytelling guide for educators.* Washington, DC: International Society for Technology in Education.

Gorman, R., & Eastman, G. S. (2010). "I see what you mean": Using visuals to teach metaphoric thinking in reading and writing. *English Journal, 100* (1), 92–99.

Graves, M. F., Van Den Broek, P., & Taylor, B. M. (1996). *The first R: Every child's right to read.* New York: Teachers College, Columbia University.

Hyerle, D. (2009). *Visual tools for transforming information into knowledge* (2nd ed.). Thousand Oaks, CA: Corwin Press.

Moreillon, J. (2007). *Collaborative strategies for teaching reading comprehension: Maximizing your impact.* Chicago, IL: American Library Association.

Small, R. V., & Arnone, M. P. (2011). Creative reading: The antidote to Readicide. *Knowledge Quest, 39* (4), 12–15.

Tate, M. L. (2008). *Graphic organizers and other visual strategies.* Thousand Oaks, CA: Corwin Press.

Wood, K. D., Lapp, D., Flood, J., & Taylor, D. B. (2008). *Guiding readers through text: Strategy guides for new times.* Newark, DE: International Reading Association.

Part 5

Develop a Literary-Based Product

10

Creating and Producing a Product

According to AASL's *Standards for the 21st-Century Learner*, students should be able to "use technology and other information tools to organize and display knowledge and understandings in ways that others can view, use, and assess" (Standard 3: Skill Indicator 3.1.4). To accomplish this goal and to create more complex projects, students need to be able to do more than read and write text. Today's students must possess a wide range of literacy skills, including the broad spectrum covered in transliteracy skills. According to Jaeger (2011), "transliteracy is the ability to read, listen to, view, understand, synthesize, and apply what we gather across differing platforms" (p. 1). For instance, for some of the production methods listed in this chapter, students are required to know how to effectively use technology tools to seamlessly integrate sound, visuals, and text into a coherent project, as well as to effectively use presentation tools to share the product.

By creating products, students have the opportunity to aggregate their learning and to construct new understandings and knowledge. In particular, hands-on projects engage and motivate students to be creative and to practice decision-making and problem-solving skills. Student products also promote reading comprehension and language development skills as they research, read, organize, write, and construct their products; consequently, hands-on products in all formats engage students in the learning process. Multiple examples are also offered throughout the other READS chapters.

This concept is substantiated by Dale's Cone of Experience created by Edgar Dale in the 1950s (Lalley & Miller, 2007). Dale was an Ohio State University professor and a noted scholar on media applications for instructional purposes. His Cone of Experience has undergone several modifications over the years, but it is still referenced today in instructional design education. In one example reprinted by Lalley and Miller (2007), Dale's Cone is represented by the level of engagement and correlated to the percentage of learning retention. Specifically, "people generally remember:

- 10% of what they read;
- 20% of what they hear;
- 30% of what they see;
- 50% of what they hear and see;
- 70% of what they say or write; and
- 90% of what they say as they do an activity" (Lalley & Miller, 2007, p. 68).

CHOOSING A PRESENTATION METHOD

Assessing Resources

Over the past decades, school librarians have been actively engaged in collaboratively planning and facilitating student production projects using a broad range of ever-changing formats. School librarians and teachers recognize that these production projects can be fun, but challenging, experiences. One of this book's authors recalls working with a high school advanced placement American history teacher and 148 excited, creative students to produce visual essays on topics ranging from the Holocaust to contemporary sexual mores. In an exit survey, students mentioned that the visual essay project was one of the most stressful, but also one of the most meaningful, projects in which they had ever participated!

In order for the visual essay project to be successful, students needed access to cameras, microphones, editing machines, playback equipment, and televisions, as well as computers and printers for script writing and storyboarding. Moreover, all of the equipment had to be available from the school, because the students did not personally own any of the equipment. Consequently, before beginning production projects, the school librarian may need to inventory the types of technologies, network capabilities, application software, and supplies available as an initial step in the collaboration and production process. A starting point could be completing the following chart that lists types of equipment, supplies needed, and accessibility issues. With this background information readily available, the school librarian can make informed decisions and suggestions when collaboratively working with teachers and students.

Based on the limitations and strengths of the equipment, network bandwidth, software, and supplies available, a more informed decision can be made for the types and frequency of student productions that can be facilitated through the school library. Projects such as the visual essays usually serve as a culminating experience for a thematic unit, but

READS Component	READS Indicator	AASL *Standards for the 21st-Century Learner**	Common Core State Standards—English Language Arts**
Develop a literary-based product			
The student will:			
4.1 Develop an original work or a response to creative works, working in groups or individually.	4.1.1 Choose a method to present an original work or a response to a creative work based on appropriateness and personal preference.	• 2.1.4 Use technology and other information tools to analyze and organize information.	• Speaking and Listening—5 Make strategic use of digital media in presentations . . .

*Excerpted from *Standards for the 21st-Century Learner* by the American Association of School Librarians, a division of the American Library Association, copyright © 2007 American Library Association. Available for download at www.ala.org/aasl/standards. Used with permission.

**Excerpted from *Common Core State Standards for English Language* Arts. National Governors Association Center for Best Practices and Council of Chief State School Officers Commercial License. Copyright © 2010. Used with permission of NGA Center/CCSSO.

Equipment Checklist			
Equipment Type	Accessibility (Number of Devices)	Accessibility (Scheduling Issues)	Supplies (Required/Available)
Desktop computers: – Monitors – Drive types – Audio capabilities – Network access			
Laptop computers: – Drive types – Audio capabilities – Network access			
Printers: – Laser – Color			
Scanners			
Digital cameras			
Microphones			
Headphones/buds			
Televisions			
DVD players			
Projectors			
Visualizers			
Whiteboards			
Screens			
Poster printer			
Die cut machine			
Copy machine			
E-readers			
Assistive technology devices required			

shorter, less intensive projects also offer experiences that engage and motivate students to creatively respond to literary works. Consequently, based on the instructional need, the teacher may present ideas for student projects or, alternately, the teacher may ask the school librarian for suggestions. Students may be required to produce one type of project or offered a variety of options. If students are given presentation options, they will usually gravitate to choices that make the best use of their strengths. For instance, artistic students will choose a visual medium while writers will select text-based projects. However, if working in groups, a broader range of skill sets can be merged into a more complex project. In any case, the projects chosen should be doable and appropriate for the instructional purpose, equipment available, students' abilities, and time allotted.

Project Suggestions

Today, possibilities for literature-based projects are varied and ever-changing, ranging from journaling or multimedia presentations to Internet-based projects. Although most projects today are digitally-based or contain digitally-produced elements, traditional pens or pencils and craft supplies may be used to engage students in literary-based projects when access to computers is limited. For instance, in Godin's *Amazing Hands-On Literature Projects for Secondary Students,* creative literary-based projects can be produced using minimal technology support. The following table (Suggestions for Production Methods) lists both traditional and contemporary options offering a wide variety of presentation possibilities for student products.

Today's software applications provide a broad spectrum of production choices ranging from easy-to-use site-based products to Internet-based cloud computing offerings. For

Suggestions for Production Methods		
Advertisements	Diagrams	Pantomimes
Animations	Dioramas	Photoessays
Audio recordings	Diaries	Photographs
Banners	Documentaries	Plays
Bibliographies—annotated	Drawings	Podcasts
Book or magazine covers	Editorials	Poems
Book trailers	Essays	Posters
Bookmarks	Experiments	Public service announcements
Books:	Facebook pages	Puppets—puppet plays
Accordion	Family trees	QR codes
Fold-up	Flannel board stories	Quotations
Pop-up	Flash cards—authors/characters	Radio programs—simulated
Upside-down	Games	Reader response journals
Book talks	Graffiti boards	Reader's theater
Brochures	Graphs	Reports
Bulletin board displays	Illustrated opinion column	Research papers
Bumper stickers	Interviews—authors/experts	Résumés
Cartoons	Internet sites	Reviews—books/movies

(Continued)

Suggestions for Production Methods		
Character trading cards	Journals	Role playing scenarios
Charts	Lectures—student delivered	Round table discussion
Character sketches	Lessons—student taught	Scrapbooks
Collages	Literature exhibits	Short stories
Comic strips	Maps	Skits
Commentaries	Mediated oral reports	Songs—lyrics
Commercials	Mobiles	Story map/web
Correspondence:	Models	Surveys and analysis
Blogs	Multimedia presentations	Table-top displays
E-mails	Murals	Virtual fieldtrips
Letters	Music—compositions	Visual or video essays
Tweets	News articles/stories	Vocabulary banks
Critical literary analysis	Newsletters	Wiki pages
Crossword puzzles	Newspapers—student designed	Word clouds
Debates	Oral histories or stories	Word searches
Demonstrations	Paintings	Worksheets—student designed
Dialogues	Panel discussions	

example, word processing software provides the foundation for many student products (e.g., reports, articles, essays). Student-friendly desktop publishing software may be used for creating brochures, newsletters, and scripts. Clip art and photographs can easily be added to these types of products to make them more engaging and colorful; free, educationally appropriate websites offer a wealth of selections. Data-driven graphs and charts may be produced using a spreadsheet program and printed for inclusion in a display, report, brochure, or newsletter. Paint, drawing and photography altering programs expand the possibilities for students to create photoessays, picture books, bookmarks, or banners.

Internet-Based Computing Tools

Program	Description	Project Ideas
Animoto: http://animoto.com	Facilitates production of videos from user-selected photographs, music, and video segments	Oral interviews, book discussions, book trailers
Glogster: http://www.glogster.com/	Provides an interactive online scrapbooking tool for adding sound, video, and text	Author studies, book or movie reviews, graffiti boards
Google.docs: http://www.google.com	Provides online site for creating/sharing documents, spreadsheets, presentations, and forms	Collaborative author studies, critical literary analysis, charts
Makebeliefscomix.com: http://www.makebeliefscomix.com	Provides characters, objects, and scenes to facilitate creating a comic strip	Comic strip book promotion, comment on theme or plot of a book or movie
Prezi: http://prezi.com/	Provides an online interactive presentation tool in which original presentations can be created or PowerPoint/Keynote slides can be "prezified"	Mediated oral reports, author studies, story map, resumes
QR Stuff.com: http://www.qrstuff.com/	Generates a QR code by encoding URL, telephone, or text information	Links to book trailers or author websites, literary phrases
Tagxedo: http://www.tagxedo.com/	Creates word-based visual images that can represent a person, place, or thing	Word clouds, book jacket covers, book report illustrations
Voicethread: (http://voicethread.com/)	Provides a forum for digital conversations accompanied by digital media presentations (e.g., slides containing images, text, and/or video)	Book trailers, critical responses to literary works, illustrated poems, picture book
Voki: http://www.voki.com	Creates talking characters or avatars using student's own voice that can be imported into blogs or websites to customize greetings	Book reviews, commercials, public service announcements
Wordle: http://www.wordle.net/	Creates a word cloud	Word clouds, book jacket covers, book report illustrations

Beyond site-based software programs, Internet-based cloud computing tools offer access to unique, engaging applications (see table Suggestions for Production Methods). Siegle (2010) explains that "cloud computing is a computing technology that uses the Internet and central remote servers to maintain data and applications" (p. 41). Siegle (2010) further explains that, "this technology involves much more efficient computing by centralizing storage, memory, processing, and bandwidth" (p. 41). The advantage is that educators and students can use these applications without purchasing or downloading the software onto personal or school computers, effectively conserving technology funds for other applications. Additionally, Johnson (2011) states that "cloud computing can be done with less powerful computers, such as netbooks" (p. 50), reducing hardware costs for schools. Another advantage is that student products are accessible from any computer either at home or at school, in the library or classroom. For several of these applications (e.g., Google Docs), multiple students can work on the same project, but from different computers and locations, enabling collaborative virtual projects within the school or with multiple schools. A representative group of these tools is listed in the following table (Internet-Based Computing Tools) and matches them with student products from the previous table (Suggestions for Production Methods).

GENERATING AND ORGANIZING IDEAS

Organizing Ideas

After the decision on the presentation method(s) has been made, the school librarian can collaboratively work with the classroom teacher to suggest ways for students to organize their ideas while working in groups or individually. Brainstorming sessions are an excellent method for activating the creative juices. Individually, a student can brainstorm ways to refine and present their topic using techniques such as freewriting, listing, or cubing. (See University of North Carolina at Chapel Hill Writing Center at http://www.unc.edu/depts/wcweb/handouts/brainstorming.html.)

In small production groups, students can conduct informal brainstorming sessions by selecting a team leader who will ask open-ended questions and a scribe who will document the ideas using a whiteboard, flip chart, or software tool (e.g., Inspiration or Webspiration, bubbl.us diagram, or word processing program). Initially, establishing rules of conduct during these timed sessions will help ensure a more productive and successful session. One basic principle underlies brainstorming rules of conduct—respect other people's suggestions and ideas.

ORGANIZING BRAINSTORMING SESSIONS

1. Prepare supplies (e.g., computers, software, projectors or flip charts, sticky notes, and markers).
2. Focus students on the purpose of the session and relate it to the goals of the project.
3. Explain the rules of conduct during the session, stressing respectful and courteous behavior.
4. Organize students into small production groups and move them to brainstorming centers.
5. Have groups choose a leader and a scribe or recorder.
6. Give leader ideas for open-ended questions (e.g., How can/will we . . ? or In what ways will we . . ?)
7. Give students a time limit and continue with incremental reminders throughout the session.
8. Reconvene groups and have groups recap session results.

READS Component	READS Indicator	AASL *Standards for the 21st-Century Learner**	Common Core State Standards— English Language Arts**
Develop a literary-based product			
The student will:			
4.1 Develop an original work or a response to creative works, working in groups or individually.	4.1.2 Generate and organize ideas for an original work or a response to a creative work read, heard or viewed (e.g., graphic organizer, group discussion, or brainstorming).	• 1.2.1 Display initiative and engagement by posing questions . . . • 1.2.4 Maintain a critical stance . . . • 2.1.2 Organize knowledge so that it is useful. • 2.1.3 Use strategies to draw conclusions from information and apply knowledge . . . • 2.1.5 Collaborate with others to exchange ideas, develop new understandings, make decisions, and solve problems. • 2.2.2 Use both divergent and convergent thinking to formulate alternative conclusions and test them against the evidence. • 2.2.3 Employ critical stance in drawing conclusions . . . • 3.1.4 Use technology and other information tools to organize and display knowledge and understanding in ways that others can view, use, and assess. • 3.2.2 Show social responsibility by participating actively with others in learning situations and by contributing questions and ideas during group discussions. • 3.3.1 Solicit and respect diverse perspectives while searching for information, collaborating with others, and participating as a member of the community. • 4.1.3 Respond to literature and creative expressions of ideas in various formats and genres. • 4.1.8 Use creative and artistic formats to express personal learning. • 4.2.3 Maintain openness to new ideas . . .	• Speaking and Listening—1a Initiate and participate effectively in a range of collaborative discussions: Come to discussions prepared, having read and researched material . . . • Speaking and Listening—1b Initiate and participate effectively in a range of collaborative discussions: Work with peers to promote civil, democratic discussions . . . • Speaking and Listening—1c Initiate and participate effectively in a range of collaborative discussions: Propel conversations by posing and responding to questions . . . • Speaking and Listening—1d Initiate and participate effectively in a range of collaborative discussions: Respond thoughtfully to diverse perspectives . . . • Speaking and Listening—2 Integrate multiple sources of information presented in diverse formats and media . . . • Speaking and Listening—5 Make strategic use of digital media in presentations . . . • Writing—1b Write arguments to support claims: Introduce precise, knowledgeable claim(s) . . . • Writing—2a Write informative/explanatory texts: Introduce a topic; organize complex ideas, concepts, and information . . . • Writing—2b Write informative/explanatory texts: Develop the topic thoroughly . . . • Writing—8 Gather relevant information from multiple authoritative print and digital sources, using advanced searches effectively . . .

READS Component	READS Indicator	AASL *Standards for the 21st-Century Learner**	Common Core State Standards—English Language Arts**
		• 4.3.1 Participate in the social exchange of ideas, both electronically and in person.	• Writing—9 Draw evidence from literary or informational texts to support analysis . . .

*Excerpted from *Standards for the 21st-Century Learner* by the American Association of School Librarians, a division of the American Library Association, copyright © 2007 American Library Association. Available for download at www.ala.org/aasl/standards. Used with permission.

**Excerpted from *Common Core State Standards for English Language Arts*. National Governors Association Center for Best Practices and Council of Chief State School Officers Commercial License. Copyright © 2010. Used with permission of NGA Center/CCSSO.

Sampling of Graphic Organizers on the Web

- Freeology.com: http://freeology.com/graphicorgs/
- edhelper.com: http://edhelper.com/teachers/graphic_organizers.htm
- Education Place by Houghton Mifflin Harcourt: http://www.eduplace.com/graphicorganizer/
- Eduscapes.com: http://eduscapes.com/tap/topic73.htm
- Holt Interactive Graphic Organizers: http://my.hrw.com/nsmedia/intgos/html/igo.htm
- pppst.com: http://themes.pppst.com/graphic-organizers.html
- ReadWriteThink.com: http://www.readwritethink.org/classroom-resources/student-interactives/
- Super Teacher Worksheets: http://www.superteacherworksheets.com/graphic-organizers.html
- TeacherFiles.com: http://www.teacherfiles.com/resources_organizers.htm
- TeacherVision.com: http://www.teachervision.fen.com/graphic-organizers/printable/6293.html
- Thinkport: http://www.thinkport.org/technology/template.tp
- WriteDesign Online: http://www.writedesignonline.com/organizers/index.html

Once the ideas are generated, graphic organizers can assist students with arranging their ideas. Traditional methods include outlining, mindmapping, clustering, concept mapping, webbing, flowcharting, storyboarding, or compare or contrast charting (Hyerle, 1996). Refer to the following table (Sampling of Graphic Organizers on the Web) for prepared downloadable or interactive graphic organizers such as those offered at the ReadWriteThink site. Additional lessons that include graphic organizers to aide students in their project development are located in this chapter's Lessons and Activities section.

Designing the Product

The school librarian's role during the preparation and production of the project will depend on several factors, including the type of project, technology tools required, time allocated, and skill sets of the students; consequently, the school librarian's involvement can range from a passive role of scheduling the center for equipment access and work space, to actively teaching and assisting students throughout the process.

Topics for teaching include foundational computer skills, software program applications, visual literacy techniques, and sound or video editing. The depth and breadth of instruction needed for a successful project depends on the time allocated, the complexity 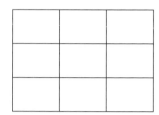 of the project, and the students' background knowledge. For instance, if students are working on a project that involves images, the school librarian and/or teacher may need to introduce or reinforce basic composition and design concepts. Strategies for teaching these concepts include the following:

- Rule of thirds introduction: Illustrate for students the rule of thirds by projecting an image of a photograph or painting on the screen and overlaying it with the rule of thirds grid. Ask the students what areas of the image are located in each quadrant and why? How does the placement or composition of the image(s) strengthen or weaken the message? Continue this discussion using other images from magazines, newspapers, books, websites, or captured television advertisements.

- Rule of thirds follow-up: Organize students into their production groups and distribute worksheets with the rule of thirds quadrants defined. Have students sketch their illustration ideas on the worksheets, paying particular attention to image placement and overall composition.

- Power of color: Choose an image that is available in both black and white and color. Project the black and white image on the screen and ask students to explain the message presented. Then, project the color image and ask students if their reactions (e.g., emotional, intellectual) are different, based on the use of color. Does the use of color add to or detract from the message?

- Layout tips: Create a composition checklist handout and distribute to students before they begin their projects. Include the following concepts:
  - Balance: Place text, white space, and images in a balanced composition, using either a symmetrical or asymmetrical layout.
  - Proportion: Create elements that are proportionate in relation to each other.
  - Focus: Guide the audience's attention first to the most important aspects of the message, using text size, color, and placement.
  - Unity: Create a product that represents a cohesive whole.

Additionally, during the introductory stages of the project, the school librarian and/or teacher may share design tips such as KISS (keep it simple stupid).

KISS Tips

- Choose images carefully, reducing the number and increasing the size to enhance the impact.
- Keep dialogue and text focused and purposeful, using language appropriate for the audience.
- Highlight areas of the screen, page, or project with judicial use of color.
- Use composition principles (e.g., balance, proportion, focus, and unity) to develop a cohesive project.

READS Component	READS Indicator	AASL *Standards for the 21st-Century Learner**	Common Core State Standards—English Language Arts**
Develop a literary-based product			
The student will:			
4.1 Develop an original work or a response to creative works, working in groups or individually.	4.1.3 Create an original work or a response to creative work, reflecting on progress and editing as needed.	• 1.2.3 Demonstrate creativity by using multiple resources and formats. • 1.4.3 Monitor gathered information, and assess for gaps or weaknesses. • 1.4.4 Seek appropriate help when it is needed. • 2.1.2 Organize knowledge so that it is useful. • 2.1.4 Use technology and other information tools to analyze and organize information. • 2.1.5 Collaborate with others to exchange ideas, develop new understandings, make decisions, and solve problems. • 2.1.6 Use the writing process, media and visual literacy, and technology skills to create products that express new understandings. • 2.2.1 Demonstrate flexibility in the use of resources . . . • 2.2.4 Demonstrate personal productivity by completing products to express learning. • 2.4.1 Determine how to act on information . . . • 2.4.2 Reflect on systematic process, and assess for completeness of investigation. • 2.4.3 Recognize new knowledge and understanding.	• Language—1 Demonstrate command of the conventions of standard English grammar and usage when writing or speaking . . . • Language—2 Demonstrate command of the conventions of standard English capitalization, punctuation, and spelling when writing . . . • Speaking and Listening—1a Initiate and participate effectively in a range of collaborative discussions: Come to discussions prepared, having read and researched material . . . • Speaking and Listening—1c Initiate and participate effectively in a range of collaborative discussions: Propel conversations by posing and responding to questions . . . • Speaking and Listening—1d Initiate and participate effectively in a range of collaborative discussions: Respond thoughtfully to diverse perspectives . . . • Speaking and Listening—4 Present information, findings, and supporting evidence, conveying a clear and distinct perspective . . . • Speaking and Listening—5 Make strategic use of digital media in presentations . . . • Writing—1c Write arguments to support claims: Use words, phrases, and clauses . . . • Writing—1d Write arguments to support claims: Establish and maintain formal style . . . • Writing—1e Write arguments to support claims: Provide a concluding statement or section . . .

(Continued)

READS Component	READS Indicator	AASL *Standards for the 21st-Century Learner**	Common Core State Standards— English Language Arts**
		• 3.1.4 Use technology and other information tools to organize and display knowledge and understanding in ways that others can view, use, and assess. • 4.1.3 Respond to literature and creative expressions of ideas in various formats and genres. • 4.1.8 Use creative and artistic formats to express personal learning. • 4.3.1 Participate in the social exchange of ideas, both electronically and in person.	• Writing—2a Write informative/explanatory texts: Introduce a topic; organize complex ideas . . . • Writing—2b Write informative/explanatory texts: Develop topic thoroughly . . . • Writing—2c Write informative/explanatory texts: Use appropriate and varied transitions and syntax . . . • Writing—2d Write informative/explanatory texts: Use precise language, domain-specific vocabulary, and techniques . . . • Writing—2f Write informative/explanatory texts: Provide a concluding statement or section . . . • Writing—3a Write narratives to develop real or imagined experiences or events: Engage and orient the reader by setting out a problem, situation, or observation . . . • Writing—3b Write narratives to develop real or imagined experiences or events: Use narrative techniques . . . • Writing—3c Write narratives to develop real or imagined experiences or events: Use a variety of techniques to sequence events . . . • Writing—3d Write narratives to develop real or imagined experiences or events: Use precise words and phrases, telling details . . . • Writing—3e Write narratives to develop real or imagined experiences or events: Provide a conclusion . . . • Writing—4 Produce clear and coherent writing . . . • Writing—5 Develop and strengthen writing as needed . . . • Writing—10 Write routinely over extended time frames and shorter time frames . . .

* Excerpted from *Standards for the 21st-Century Learner* by the American Association of School Librarians, a division of the American Library Association, copyright © 2007 American Library Association. Available for download at www.ala.org/aasl/standards. Used with permission.

** Excerpted from *Common Core State Standards for English Language Arts.* National Governors Association Center for Best Practices and Council of Chief State School Officers Commercial License. Copyright © 2010. Used with permission of NGA Center/CCSSO.

CREATING THE PRODUCT

Importance of Writing

In the preceding chart, the correlation of the READS Develop component is closely aligned to the Common Core production methods, particularly writing skills, as well as speaking and listening. The ability to speak and write well, to articulate a clear and cohesive message, is a foundational skill that impacts educational success and, in the future for our students, workplace achievement. Consequently, integrating opportunities for students to practice their communication skills across an ever-broadening range of formats is essential to the success of school library programs and, ultimately, to the improvement of student achievement.

The importance of offering multiple opportunities for students to practice their writing skills is reinforced in the National Council of Teachers of English position statement entitled *NCTE Beliefs about the Teaching of Writing*, which states, "As is the case with many other things people do, getting better at writing requires doing it—a lot. This means actual writing." The position statement further states that "writing is a tool for thinking" (http://www.ncte.org/positions/statements/writingbeliefs). Offering writing experiences through student responses to literary and informational materials is the basis for the Develop component. In addition to methods previously mentioned, there are alternative types of writing experiences now available with the inclusion of social media tools. For instance, organizing a student blog can be facilitated through edublogs.org or blogger.com. Facebook pages and Twitter accounts can also be facilitated by the school librarian for specific class projects. By using various communication tools, students will understand that the writing process will vary based on the purpose and audience. Whatever the method chosen, the school librarian can play a central role in facilitating the learning experience through the use of contemporary technologies.

Working Individually or in a Group

In Develop, students have the opportunity to respond to literary works by either working independently or in a group. Guiding students while they are working on projects is an active role of the school librarian. The instructional situation will dictate the length of the project, as well as the group or team configuration. A teacher may give students the choice to either work by themselves or in a team. A ninth grade gifted teacher working on a pop-up books project left the decision up to the students, which meant that some of the students formed working teams while others opted to work alone, depending on their learning styles and interests.

If appropriate for the instructional need, group work lends itself to addressing the social nature of today's tweens and teens, as well as preparing them for tomorrow's socially interactive workforce. Crane (2009) reinforces this idea by stating that "Through collaboration children acquire social skills, experience different viewpoints, and learn how to work together with people who are the same and with those different from themselves" (p. 7). Additionally, Wilhelm (2007) discusses the advantage of learning interactively by stating that "There is a need to learn relationally from characters, authors, and experts through our transactions with various texts. And learning is always more engaging and powerful when we learn through dialogue and joint productive activity with others" (p. 37).

Vaca, Lapp, and Fisher (2011) explain that group work is a time "for students to engage in productive and accountable collaboration around a task or problem that causes them to rely on one another's part or participation to ensure successful completion" (p. 372).

In collaborative learning situations, the assignment or task must be carefully crafted to ensure that accountability rests with both the individual and the group. Johnson and Johnson (2000) further clarify these responsibilities by explaining that a "cooperative learning group is one that has positive interdependence, where shared goals link group members; individual accountability, where each group member needs to know the material; and cooperative skills, where students support one another rather than put one another down" (p. 39).

Consequently, for a group production project, it is important to delineate both the individual's responsibilities and the overall outcome expected of the group. Before students start on specific tasks, the librarian and teacher must organize the students into their working teams, either allowing the students to choose their team members or assigning them to teams. Next, team member roles need to be assigned or chosen by the group and will, of course, change with the project requirements. Ideas for role responsibilities include:

- Leader, organizer, manager, producer, or director
- Recorder or scribe or writer or vocabulary or word smith editor
- Researcher, fact finder, statistician, or problem-solver
- Artist, graphic designer, illustrator, image collector, image editor
- Sound collector, sound engineer or editor
- Summarizer, final writing editor, final video or graphics editor

After the roles and responsibilities are established, specific tasks can be distributed that fairly distribute accountability among the individuals and the group. Vaca et al. (2011) achieve this balance by defining five tasks that focus on either the individual or the group. They explain that "when planning group work, it is important to design tasks that promote conversation and also allow measurement of each student's individual and group participation" (p. 375). A generic modification of this approach aligns with the collaborative teacher and librarian group work scenario and offers a starting point from which to design projects. A generic framework for the five tasks includes:

Task 1: Individual work: Have students individually complete a task related to the group project (e.g., research facts; gather informational text or literary resources; write brief response to a movie segment, blog entry, TeacherTube video, or poem).

Task 2: Group work: Have students share their findings or observations (e.g., compare or contrast observations on an author, illustrator, or actor). Then, have team members relate findings or observations to the group project (e.g., determine which facts or responses should be included in the Glog and why?).

Task 3: Individual work: Have each student complete a component of the project, stressing the need to consistently confer with other team members to ensure cohesiveness, unity for the completed project. Have students complete a rubric evaluating their component.

Task 4: Group work: Have students present their group project and critique their work with either a written response and/or evaluation rubric (e.g., Does the finished product effectively address the topic? Does the project include perspectives and input from all members of the group?).

Task 5: Individual work: Have students individually write or record a response to a follow-up question (e.g., Would you read more books by this author, and why? What other methods could you use to promote this author's works to other students?).

Encouraging Good Work Habits

Time management is a critical component of the production process. For students with limited experience or control issues, the school librarian and teacher may choose to impose time limits and frequent incremental deadlines throughout this process. As an added

---

Topic

- Have I clearly defined the topic?
- Have I gathered enough background information on the topic? If not, what other resources can I use?
- Is the topic coverage appropriate for the intended audience and medium? If not, what changes do I need to make (e.g., vocabulary, medium)?

Process

- If working on a team or with a partner, did I actively participate in the planning sessions?
- Did I help organize the information into a workable format for the intended audience and product?
- Did I assist in locating additional information, if needed?
- In what role did I contribute to the production process (e.g., recorder, writer, artist, producer)?
- Did I fulfill my responsibilities during the production process? If not, what should I have done differently?
- Did I successfully use all the technology tools to produce the product? If not, what other skills or information do I need?

Final Product and Presentation

- Am I satisfied with the final product? If not, given more time, what would I improve?
- Does my product meet the highest quality level on the evaluation rubric?
- Did I use appropriate presentation techniques (e.g., voice level, eye contact with audience)?
- Was I a good listener when my other teammates or classmates presented?
- Did I use the technology presentation tools appropriately and knowledgeably? (If not, what other skills or information do I need?

Self-Reflection

- Did I fulfill my responsibilities in a timely manner?
- Was I a successful team member who worked well with others? If not, do I need to change my attitude or conduct?
- In what ways could I improve my behavior to make the production process more successful?

incentive, depending on the teacher's intent and assignment structure, students may earn interim grades for completing phases of the production process (e.g., brainstorming sessions, initial storyboards or scripts, or graphic organizers).

The production process offers a valuable opportunity for teaching students strategies for self-reflection and self-monitoring that they can use throughout their lives. One strategy is to provide students with a production checklist that the students can refer to throughout the process. Production checklists can take various forms such as to-do lists that help students monitor their progress and assist students in meeting interim deadlines. Production checklists can also be designed to pose questions arranged into categories that prompt students to practice self-reflection and self-monitoring techniques throughout the process.

Throughout the production process, students should be guided or taught how to reflect on the development and final evaluation of the product. One method for guiding students through this process is to provide an evaluation rubric that lists the criteria, preferably distributing it during the initial introduction to the assignment. By clarifying the final assessment rubric before beginning to work, students will have a clearer target in mind based on the quality criteria presented in the rubric. The school librarian or the teacher may collaboratively create an original assessment rubric that reflects unique aspects of the assignment and product. Additional information on rubrics is at the end of this chapter.

READS Component	READS Indicator	AASL *Standards for the 21st-Century Learner**	Common Core State Standards—English Language Arts**
Develop a literary-based product			
The student will:			
4.1 Develop an original work or a response to creative works, working in groups or individually.	4.1.4 Demonstrate understanding of and respect for copyright laws and intellectual property rights (e.g., use standard bibliographic format to credit sources).	• 1.3.1 Respect copyright/ intellectual property rights of creators and producers. • 1.3.3 Follow ethical and legal guidelines in gathering and using information. • 2.1.3 Use strategies to draw conclusions from information and apply knowledge . . . • 3.1.6 Use information and technology ethically and responsibly.	• Writing—8 Gather relevant information from multiple authoritative print and digital sources . . . avoiding plagiarism and overreliance on any one source and following a standard format for citation.

*Excerpted from *Standards for the 21st-Century Learner* by the American Association of School Librarians, a division of the American Library Association, copyright © 2007 American Library Association. Available for download at www.ala.org/aasl/standards. Used with permission.

**Excerpted from *Common Core State Standards for English Language Arts*. National Governors Association Center for Best Practices and Council of Chief State School Officers Commercial License. Copyright © 2010. Used with permission of NGA Center/CCSSO.

RESPECTING COPYRIGHT LAWS AND INTELLECTUAL PROPERTY RIGHTS

Today's students grow up in world surrounded by digital technologies. According to Prensky (2001), "They have spent their entire lives surrounded by and using computers, videogames, digital music players, video cams, cell phones, and all the other toys and tools of the digital age" (p. 1). Prensky refers to the creation of this environment as a "singularity" or "an event which changes things so fundamentally that there is absolutely no going back. This so-called 'singularity' is the arrival and rapid dissemination of digital technology in the last decades of the 20th century" (p. 1). Digital natives are accustomed to rapidly locating information and, perhaps, to synthesizing and using it in new ways. But although today's students comfortably use technology tools, they may not always use them ethically or legally.

Ribble and Bailey (2007) further define these actions as "digital rights and responsibilities" that include "using online material ethically, including citing sources and requesting permissions" (p. 30). Integrated throughout the document, the AASL's *Standards for the 21st-Century Learner* reinforce the importance of ethical behaviors. Two examples are in Standard 1: 1.3.1: *Respect copyright/intellectual property rights of creators and producers* and 1.3.3: *Follow ethical and legal guidelines in gathering and using information.* Recognizing the ongoing need to address these behaviors in today's social context, the READS Develop section includes teaching students to respect copyright laws and intellectual property rights. Prime teaching moments for addressing these issues are interwoven throughout the production process.

First, to discourage students from plagiarizing, the project prompt should be phrased in such a way that students will have to synthesize what they have read, heard, or viewed in order to construct the product. As Christenbury (2009) states "teachers have a responsibility to create assignments where blatant plagiarism is less likely" (p. 22). For example, "why" assignment prompts require thoughtful responses as opposed to simply retelling facts.

Second, if necessary, skills such as summarizing and paraphrasing, which are covered in READS—Analyze, should be taught or reviewed before beginning production activities. Graphic organizers, as previously mentioned, also provide tools for extrapolating bits of information from what was read, heard, or viewed and provide constructs for reconfiguring the information into an original product.

Third, production projects at all complexity levels should require a bibliography of works cited either within the product or in an ancillary submission (e.g., poster with written works cited list on the back or submitted separately). If possible, it is advisable for secondary schools to choose one bibliographic format for assignments in all subject content areas. This enables students to develop a deeper understanding of the format and to consistently practice it from course to course and grade to grade.

The most commonly used citation formats include the following: American Psychological Association (APA) (http://www.apastyle.org/), Modern Language Association (MLA) (http://www.mla.org/), and Turabian (Chicago) (http://www.uwp.edu/departments/library/guides/turabian.htm). Various university sites such as the Purdue Online Writing Lab (OWL) (http://owl.english.purdue.edu/owl/resource/560/01/) provide examples of citations using various formats. Online bibliography makers provide students with interactive tools that are either free or inexpensive. For example, NoodleTools' NoodleBib offers an inexpensive bibliography maker at http://www.noodletools.com/; Landmark Projects' Son of a Citation Machine is available at http://citationmachine.net/; Bibme hosted by GreenRiver.org is accessed at http://www.bibme.org/; and EasyBib is located at http://www.easybib.com/.

Fourth, as much as possible, students should use non-copyrighted images, music, and videos in their products or, if not, then students should seek permission from the copyright holder, particularly if the student products will be uploaded to the Internet or submitted in a media production contest. The copyright licensing tools offered through Creative Commons (http://creativecommons.org/) (e.g., photographs from Flickr site) should be reviewed with the students for their potential use of these resources or for submitting their own original work. Copyrighted materials may be used in student productions as long as the use falls within the Fair Use guidelines. According to Valenza (2011), the "Code of Best Practices in Fair Use for Media Literacy Education" (http://www.centerforsocial-media.org/fair-use/related-materials/codes/code-best-practices-fair-use-media-literacy-education) "outlines how students and teachers may legally and ethically use copyrighted materials in an academic setting without asking permission or paying for it" (p. 30).

COMMUNICATE AND EVALUATE WORK

As indicated earlier in the Common Core State Standards—English Language Arts correlation chart, standards that are included in students sharing their completed projects involve language, writing, speaking, and listening skills. A few examples include the scriptwriting and audio narrations needed for *iMovies*, radio plays, book trailers, or podcasts. Research reported on a wiki or other website requires carefully crafted prose for a potentially wider audience than classmates. Pop-up, shape, or mini storybooks hinge on creating, visually and textually, a cohesive story line running through the beginning, middle, and end of the narrative. Beyond the sharing of their work, students must also learn respectful behaviors for face-to-face presentations, as well as for reading and evaluating online peer work.

Many assessment tools are available to be used by the school librarian and the classroom teacher to assess student work and behaviors. For instance, rubrics are an excellent method for assisting students with self-assessing the development, communication, and evaluation of their work and behaviors. Carol Brown (2008) observes that by using rubrics, "students are able to self-assess their own work habits, evaluate the quality of their projects, and reflect on what has been learned during the process" (p. 16). She suggests working collaboratively with teachers and students to design rubrics that will clarify the project and behavioral expectations, using a four-step method that focuses on the standards to be addressed, process and product expectations, evaluation depth, and rating scale (Brown, 2008, pp. 16–17).

Yoshina and Harada (2007) reinforce the efficacy of using rubrics to identify "criteria for a successful performance" and product (p. 11). They further agree with Brown that involving the students leads to their having a "better understanding of what must be done to reach expectations" (p. 11). Their guidelines for constructing rubrics include examining models, listing criteria, and differentiating performance levels (p. 11).

Whether creating an original rubric, modifying an existing one, or using as-is a ready-made version, rubrics can be a powerful assessment tool. Preconstructed assessment rubrics are available from school districts and student production books. Student production books such as those by Crane (2009), Harada, Kirio, and Yamamoto (2008), and Conover (2007, 2009) offer multiple variations on student product assessment rubrics. Additional rubrics for specific lessons are included in the professional journals as well as sites such as readwritethink.org. There are also a wealth of preconstructed rubrics, templates, and rubric generator tools online including the following:

READS Component	READS Indicator	AASL *Standards for the 21st-Century Learner**	Common Core State Standards—English Language Arts**
Develop a literary-based product			
The student will:			
4.2 Communicate and evaluate an original work or response to creative works, working in a group or individually.	4.2.1 Use appropriate methods to share and evaluate product.	• 2.2.4 Demonstrate personal productivity by completing products to express learning. • 3.1.2 Participate and collaborate as members of a social and intellectual network of learners. • 3.1.3 Use writing and speaking skills to communicate new understandings effectively. • 3.1.4 Use technology and other information tools to organize and display knowledge and understanding in ways that others can view, use, and assess. • 3.2.1 Demonstrate leadership and confidence . . . • 3.3.5 Contribute to the exchange of ideas within and beyond the learning community. • 3.4.2 Assess the quality and effectiveness of the learning product. • 4.1.8 Use creative and artistic formats to express personal learning. • 4.4.5 Develop personal criteria for gauging how effectively own ideas are expressed.	• Language—1 Demonstrate command of the conventions of standard English grammar and usage when writing or speaking . . . • Language—3 Apply knowledge of language to understand how language functions in different contexts . . . • Speaking and Listening—6 Adapt speech to a variety of contexts and tasks . . . • Writing—6 Use technology, including the Internet, to produce, publish, and update individual or shared writing products . . .

- *Kathy Schrock's Guide for Educators* (http://school.discoveryeducation.com/schrock-guide/assess.html) includes a compilation of assessment rubrics that cover a wide range of curriculum topics.
- *RubiStar* (http://rubistar.4teachers.org/) is a free tool that has a number of templates (e.g., oral, writing, multimedia, and music projects, etc.) from which to choose. Rubrics can be saved and retrieved for editing.
- *teAchnology* (http://www.teach-nology.com/web_tools/rubrics/) includes a "Learn All about Rubrics" section that features "5 Features of a Highly Effective Rubric," "How to Make a Rubric in Less Than 5 Minutes," and "How to Tell If Your Rubric Works." Rubric-making tools include a "Behavior Rubric Generator."

In summary, by actively generating projects, students are given the opportunity to express themselves and hone multiple literacy skills. If asked, students will usually respond, as the advanced placement Social Studies students did, that although production projects can be stressful at times, they can also be the most meaningful and memorable of educational experiences.

READS LESSONS AND ACTIVITIES

Develop a Literary-Based Product

Select a Presentation Format, Organize Information, and Generate Product, Working in Groups or Individually

Book report alternative: Character and author business cards. By Traci Gardner. Includes Planning Sheet for Business Card Book Reports. ReadWriteThink. (Gr. 6–8) http://www.readwritethink.org/classroom-resources/lesson-plans/book-report-alternative-character-143.html?tab=4#tabs

Book report alternative: Characters for hire! Studying character in drama. By Haley Fishburn Moore. Includes Writing Resumes for Fictional Characters and link to The OWL at Purdue Resume Workshop. ReadWriteThink. (Gr. 9–12)

Book reviews, annotation, and web technology. By Patricia Schultze. Includes rubric. ReadWriteThink. (Gr. 6–8)

Campaigning for fair use: Public service announcements on copyright awareness. By Traci Gardner. Includes Fair Use Survey and Interactive Fair Use Travelogue. ReadWriteThink. (Gr. 6–8) http://www.readwritethink.org/classroom-resources/lesson-plans/campaigning-fair-public-service-939.html

Cite your sites! By Rachel McClain. The Learning Network: *The New York Times.* (Gr. 6–12) http://learning.blogs.nytimes.com/2001/06/29/cite-your-sites/

Compiling an annotated bibliography (into the curriculum). By Dana St. John. Includes guide and rubric. *School Library Media Activities Monthly, 24* (8), 14–16. (Gr. 11 up)

Creating better presentation slides through glance media and billboard design. By Drew Schrader. Includes Learning Slide Design from Billboards Teachers Guide. ReadWriteThink. (Gr. 9–12) http://www.readwritethink.org/classroom-resources/lesson-plans/creating-better-presentation-slides-1167.html

Crossword puzzles: Student interactives. (Resource) ReadWriteThink. (K-12) http://www.readwritethink.org/parent-afterschool-resources/games-tools/crossword-puzzles-a-30183.html

Defining literacy in a digital world. Includes activity identifying various formats for expressing ideas. By Traci Gardner. ReadWriteThink. (Gr. 9–12) http://www.readwritethink.org/classroom-resources/lesson-plans/defining-literacy-digital-world-915.html?tab=4#tabs

NPR's this I believe. By Claudine Dixon. *From the creative minds of 21st century librarians*: e-book. pp. 198–201. (Gr. 12) http://digital-literacy.syr.edu/page/view/221

Short story fair: Responding to short stories in multiple media and genres. Includes Literary Elements Map and The Elements of Fiction tutorial. ReadWriteThink. (Gr. 9–12) http://www.readwrite think.org/classroom-resources/lesson-plans/short-story-fair-responding-418.html

Students as creators: Exploring copyright. By Cassandra Love. Includes "Can I Use It" Checklist for Copyright Clearance. ReadWriteThink. (Gr. 6–8) http://www.readwritethink.org/classroom-resources/lesson-plans/students-creators-exploring-copyright-1085.html

Students as creators: Exploring multimedia. By Cassandra Love. Includes Multimedia Project Planning Sheet, Image and Sound Organizer, and Multimedia Tools and Tutorials list. ReadWriteThink. (Gr. 6–8 up) http://www.readwritethink.org/classroom-resources/lesson-plans/students-creators-exploring-multimedia-1088.html

What are the qualities of an effective blog post? By Buffy Hamilton. *From the creative minds of 21st century librarians*: e-book. pp. 142–147. (Gr. 9–12) http://digital-literacy.syr.edu/page/view/221

Where credit is due. By Ana Canino-Fluit. *From the creative minds of 21st century librarians*: e-book. pp. 59–61. (Gr. 7) http://digital-literacy.syr.edu/page/view/221

Communicate and Evaluate an Original Work or a Response to Creative Works

Group processing evaluation form. (Resource) Center for Teaching Excellence. (Gr. 9–12) http://openedpractices.org/files/group%20process%20eval%20St%20Edwards.pdf

Group work rubrics and checklists. (Resource) National Adult Literacy Databases (Canada). (Gr. 6–12) http://www.nald.ca/library/learning/btg/ed/evaluation/groupwork.htm

Self-reflection: Taking part in a group (Resource). ReadWriteThink. (Gr. 6–8 up) http://www.read writethink.org/files/resources/lesson_images/lesson877/FilmSelfReflection.pdf

READS INTERNET RESOURCES

Select a Presentation Format, Organize Information, and Generate Product, Working in Groups or Individually

About.com: Inventors: Understanding intellectual property. http://inventors.about.com/od/patenttrademarkcopyright/u/Intellectual_Property.htm

Book trailers for all. http:bicktrailers4all.4shared.com

Clipart ETC: An online service of Florida's educational technology clearing house. University of South Florida. http://etc.usf.edu/clipart/index.htm

Copyright friendly and copyleft images and sound (mostly!) for use in media projects and web pages, blogs, wikis, etc. By Joyce Valenza. Springfield Township High School Virtual Library. http://copyrightfriendly.wikispaces.com/

Creative Commons. http://creativecommons.org/

Digital storytelling. AASL Smackdown. http://aaslsmackdown.wikispaces.com/Digital+Storytelling

The ethical researcher. By Debbie Abilock. http://www.noodletools.com/debbie/ethical/

Grammar and style guide. Rochester Institute of Technology. http://www.rit.edu/upub/grammar-proofreader_marks.html

The graphic organizer. http://www.graphic.org/goindex.html

Images for projects. St. Mary's Library. http://sites.google.com/site/smsresearchresources/home/imagesforprojects

Middle school/high school collaboration rubric. University of Wisconsin—Stout. http://www.uwstout.edu/static/profdev/rubrics/secondaryteamworkrubric.html

New York Public Library's digital gallery. New York Public Library. http://digitalgallery.nypl.org

OWL Purdue online writing lab. APA (American Psychological Association). http://owl.english.purdue.edu/owl/resource/560/01/

OWL Purdue online writing lab. MLA (Modern Language Association). https://owl.english.purdue.edu/owl/resource/747/01/

Pre-laureate MLA style 6-point rubric. Gulf Coast High School. http://collier.k12.fl.us/gch/media/ccpsresearch/6%20%20Evaluate%20the%20Process/Pre-Laureate%206%20point%20rubric.pdf

Research & writing links. IPL2 (Internet Public Library2). http://www.ipl.org/div/aplus/linkswritingstyle.htm

Research report: MLA format rubric. http://tcas.dreamteamtech.com/media/EDocs/MLA_format_rubric.doc

Sound for projects. St. Mary's Library. http://sites.google.com/site/smsresearchresources/home/sound-for-projects

Taking audience into account. University of Richmond Writing Center. http://writing2.richmond.edu/writing/wweb/audience.html

TRAILS: Tools for real-time assessment of information literacy skills. Institute for Library and Information Literacy Education. Kent State University. http://www.trails-9.org/

What is plagiarism? Rutgers University. http://library.camden.rutgers.edu/EducationalModule/Plagiarism/whatisplagiarism.html

Writing book reviews. Literacy education online. St. Cloud State University. http://leo.stcloudstate.edu/acadwrite/bookrev.html

Zippy scenarios for teaching Internet ethics. University of Illinois. http://www.uni.illinois.edu/library/computerlit/scenarios.php

Communicate and Evaluate an Original Work or a Response to Creative Works

10 tips for public speaking. Toastmasters International. http://www.toastmasters.org/tips.asp

Speaking behaviors checklist. http://www.beaconlearningcenter.com/documents/1219_01.pdf

WORKS CITED

Brainstorming. The Writing Center at University of North Carolina at Chapel Hill. Retrieved from http://www.unc.edu/depts/wcweb/handouts/brainstorming.html .

Brown, C. A. (2008). Building rubrics: A step-by-step process. *Library Media Connection, 26* (4), 16–18.

Christenbury, L. (2009). It's not as simple as it seems: Doing honest academic work in an age of point and click. *Knowledge Quest, 37* (3), 16–23.

Conover, P. R. (2007). *Technology projects for library media specialists and teachers.* Worthington, OH: Linworth Books.

Conover, P. R. (2009). *Technology projects for library media specialists and teachers, volume II.* Columbus, OH: Linworth Books.

Crane, B. E. (2009). *Using web 2.0 tools in the K-12 classroom.* New York: Neal-Schuman.

Godin, D. (2010). *Amazing hands-on literature projects for secondary students.* Gainesville, FL: Maupin House.

Harada, V. H., Kirio, C. H., & Yamamoto, S. H. (2008). *Collaborating for project-based learning in grades 9–12.* Columbus, OH: Linworth Books.

Hyerle, D. (1996). *Visual tools for constructing knowledge.* Alexandria, VA: Association for Supervision and Curriculum Development.

Jaeger, P. (2011). Transliteracy—new library lingo and what it means for instruction. *Library Media Connection, 30* (2), 44–47.

Johnson, D. (2011). Libraries in the cloud. *Library Media Connection, 29* (6), 50–51.

Johnson, D. W., & Johnson, R. T. (2000). How can we put cooperative learning into practice? *Science Teacher, 67* (1), 39.

Lalley, J. P., & Miller, R. H. (2007). The learning pyramid: Does it point teachers in the right direction? *Education, 12* (1), 64–79.

National Council of Teachers of English. *NCTE beliefs about the teaching of writing.* Retrieved from http://www.ncte.org/positions/statements/writingbeliefs

Prensky, M. (2001). Digital natives, digital immigrants. *On the Horizon, 9* (5), 1.

Ribble, M., & Bailey, G. (2007). *Digital citizenship in schools.* Eugene, OR: International Society for Technology in Education.

Siegle, D. (2010). Cloud computing: A free technology option to promote collaborative learning. *Gifted Child Today, 33* (4), 41–45.

Vaca, J., Lapp, D., & Fisher, D. (2011). Real-time teaching. *Journal of Adolescent & Adult Literacy, 54* (5), 372–375.

Valenza, J. K. (2011). Opening gates: On celebrating Creative Commons and flexing the Fair Use muscle. *Library Media Connection, 29* (4), 30–32.

Wilhelm, J. D. (2007). *"You gotta BE the book": Teaching engaged and reflective reading with adolescents* (2nd ed.) New York: Teachers College Press.

Yoshina, J. M., & Harada, V. H. (2007). Involving students in learning through rubrics. *Library Media Connections, 25* (5), 10–14.

FURTHER READING

Achterman, D. (2006). Beyond Wikipedia. *Teacher Librarian, 34* (2), 19–22.

Barron, A. E., Ivers, K. S., Lilavois, N., & Wells, J. A. (2006). *Technologies for education: a practical guide* (5th ed.). Westport, CT: Libraries Unlimited.

Berger, P. (2010). Student inquiry and Web 2.0. *School Library Monthly, 26* (5), 14–17. [Includes Inquiry Model & Web 2.0 tools integration chart.]

De Abreu, B. S. (2007). *Teaching media literacy: A how-to-do-it manual and CD-ROM.* New York: Neal-Schuman.

Fontichiaro, K. (2008). *Podcasting at school.* Westport, CT: Libraries Unlimited.

Frazel, M. (2010). *Digital storytelling guide for educators.* Washington, DC: International Society for Technology in Education.

Hamalainen, M. (2007). Useful tips on avoiding plagiarism. *Library Media Connection, 25* (6), 40–41.

Keane, J. (2007). Choosing the right medium: Reference guide. *Library Media Connection, 26* (6), 46.

Keane, N. J., & Cavanaugh, T. W. (2008). *The tech-savvy booktalker: A guide for 21st-century educators.* Westport, CT: Libraries Unlimited.

Lehman, K. (2009). Teaching information ethics to high school students. *Library Media Connection, 27* (6), 28–30.

Lehman, K. (2010). Stemming the tide of plagiarism: One educator's view. *Library Media Connection, 29* (2), 44–46.

Lowell, P. (2010). Five easy steps to making a great book trailer that your students and even technophobes (like me) can master. *Voice of Youth Advocates, 32* (6), 464–465.

Ohler, J. (2008). *Digital storytelling in the classroom: New media pathways to literacy, learning, and creativity.* Thousand Oaks, CA: Corwin Press.

Riddle, J. (2009). *Engaging the eye generation: Visual literacy strategies for the K-5 classroom.* Portland, ME: Stenhouse.

Roberts, J., & Stiles, R. (2010). Flip your way to easy video production. *Knowledge Quest, 38* (4), 34–39.

Rosenblatt, L. M. (1978). *The reader, the text, the poem: The transactional theory of the literary work.* Carbondale, IL: Southern Illinois University Press.

St. John, D. (2008). Compiling an annotated bibliography. *School Library Media Activities Monthly, 24* (8), 14–15.

Vosen, M. A. (2008). Using Bloom's Taxonomy to teach students about plagiarism. *English Journal, 97* (6), 43–46.

Part 6

Score Reading Progress

11

Participating in and Reflecting on the Reading Experience

In essence, this book is about motivating and enabling students to read for personal fulfillment and academic success. In the Read chapters, students are connected to reading, listening, and viewing resources using a variety of methods. In Explore, a closer look is taken at the genres and themes of creative works, as well as award-winning titles. In Analyze, the focus is on supporting teachers and students by reinforcing and expanding the skills necessary for understanding and appreciating informational and fictional resources. In Develop, students are encouraged to create thoughtful and creative projects in response to creative works. In Score, the emphasis is on nurturing the student's ability to monitor and reflect on one's reading and learning progress by participating in individual and group activities. To implement this goal of motivating and enabling students to read, the resources, skills, and motivational strategies introduced in the earlier READS sections must be used.

LITERACY COMMITTEE

In many schools, responsibility for investigating the literacy needs of the community and planning reading motivational activities is entrusted to a literacy committee. Members are typically administrators, usually teachers from every grade, literacy coaches, and the school librarian. In some areas, representative students, perhaps from a student library advisory group, and parents are members of the literacy committee. A foremost objective of a librarian new to the school should be to volunteer as a member of the literacy committee, if not automatically placed on the group. The mission of the group, according to Leslie B. Preddy (2009), is "to support and develop the building literacy initiative, implement schoolwide reading promotion projects, increase reading awareness, and promote lifelong literacy habits in students, staff, and parents" (p. 43). She points out that staff training and gathering resources, materials, and grants to support the projects are major aspects of the work of the committee.

Taking the mission of improving the many aspects of literacy in the school a step further, Loertscher, Koechlin, and Zwann (2008) propose that the entire effort should be centered in the library, referring to it as a learning commons or "literacy central" (p. 33). Their term for the organizing group is "learning literacies leadership team," which they define

READS Component	READS Indicator	AASL *Standards for the 21st-Century Learner**	Common Core State Standards—English Language Arts**
Score reading progress			
The student will:			
5.1 Engage in literacy-based motivational programs and activities.	5.1.1 Participate in school library activities and reading celebrations (e.g., Banned Book Week activities).	• 3.1.2 Participate and collaborate as members of a social and intellectual network of learners. • 3.2.1 Demonstrate leadership and confidence . . . • 3.2.2 Show social responsibility by participating actively with others in learning situations and by contributing questions and ideas during group discussions. • 3.2.3 Demonstrate teamwork by working productively with others. • 3.3.1 Solicit and respect diverse perspectives while searching for information, collaborating with others, and participating as a member of the community. • 4.1.1 Read, view, and listen for pleasure and personal growth. • 4.1.7 Use social networks and information tools to gather and share information. • 4.2.1 Display curiosity by pursuing interests through multiple resources. • 4.2.2 Demonstrate motivation by seeking information to answer personal questions and interests . . .	• Speaking and Listening—1a Initiate and participate effectively in a range of collaborative discussions: Come to discussions prepared, having read and researched material . . . • Speaking and Listening—1b Initiate and participate effectively in a range of collaborative discussions: Work with peers to promote civil, democratic discussions . . . • Speaking and Listening—1c Initiate and participate effectively in a range of collaborative discussions: Propel conversations by posing and responding to questions . . . • Speaking and Listening—5 Make strategic use of digital media in presentations . . . • Writing—6 Use technology, including the Internet, to produce, publish, and update individual or shared writing products . . .

(Continued)

READS Component	READS Indicator	AASL *Standards for the 21st-Century Learner**	Common Core State Standards—English Language Arts**
		• 4.3.3 Seek opportunities for pursuing personal and aesthetic growth. • 4.4.1 Identify own areas of interest.	

*Excerpted from *Standards for the 21st-Century Learner* by the American Association of School Librarians, a division of the American Library Association, copyright © 2007 American Library Association. Available for download at www.ala.org/aasl/standards. Used with permission.
**Excerpted from *Common Core State Standards for English Language Arts*. National Governors Association Center for Best Practices and Council of Chief State School Officers Commercial License. Copyright © 2010. Used with permission of NGA Center/CCSSO.

as "the group of adults and learner representatives working together to create conditions to improve the skill levels of all learners and across all literacies" (p. 124).

Through the implementation of a variety of motivational activities, a literacy committee expects to involve each student in the school in one or multiple programs during the year. Activities that can be viewed as a singular event (no more than a week or month), sustained silent reading, summer reading programs, the mentoring role of the school librarian, and book clubs will be discussed in Score 5.1.1. Ongoing independent reading programs will be covered in Score 5.1.2. Finally, reading motivational programs with management components will be described in 5.1.3.

SCHOOLWIDE READING CELEBRATIONS

One Book/One School

Uniting the students and staff of a school through reading one book has become a popular reading motivation practice. Reading the same title through all classes opens the door to book discussions from multiple points of view and perspectives. Selection of a book that appeals to a wide audience is key to success with a one school, one book project. It is also important that the title is not used in any classes in the school. Other criteria for selection of a title include reading level, a plot with various discussion points and values, inexpensive-to-purchase mass copies, a possible tie-in to the local community, and availability in audio format and Spanish or other languages, as well as English (Hunter, 2009; Jewett, Wilson, & Vanderburg, 2011; Van Dyke, 2005). In some situations, an existing faculty committee planned the literacy event while in other cases, a special group, for example, a steering committee, was organized (Van Dyke, 2005). It can be advantageous to include faculty members from different departments on the committee to ensure staff support and to provide expertise in production of promotional materials and leaders' guides. Providing time for students to read the book is another issue. In one school, 10 minutes of reading time in each class was arranged for the duration of the project (Van Dyke, 2005). Students read the book as required summer reading in at least one school (Hunter, 2009). Funding of the books is sometimes provided through the school budget, with grants and community sponsorships as other options.

Students gain from participating in a fun community reading event, viewing teachers and administrators in a new light as readers. In various departments, discussions and projects about the theme of the book provided extended learning opportunities. Benefits to the school include a renewed sense of educational purpose, with enjoyment of one literature selection as a focus in all departments. According to Hunter (2009), "Educators themselves saw literacy as a social entity that unites diverse individuals—regardless of their age, socioeconomic statues, and culture—into a club of like experiences and understandings" (p. 39). This high school in New Jersey chose this time to provide staff training on reading across the curriculum techniques, which allowed for immediate application of the strategies recommended in the class (Hunter, 2009).

Variations on the one school, one book model include involving parents and, perhaps, the public library in the community read. Further discussions of these activities are included in Chapter 4.

Battle of the Books

Capitalizing on the social nature of adolescents, battle of the books programs engage students in reading selected titles independently before competing with peers to answer questions on the details of the books. Many students enjoy the challenge of outwitting their classmates on the details of the characters, plots, and settings of the books. Usually staged annually, these contests require sufficient copies of the chosen books, questions for each book, publicity, and the scheduling of the final tournament. The competition may involve two classes, a grade level, multiple grade levels, two schools, or multiple schools within the district.

The best scenario for the building level librarian is for the district to coordinate plans for the program. For example, the Palm Beach County (Florida) School District's Library Media Services and Educational Technology departments sponsor the Battle of the Books annually, using books from the current year's state student choice programs, Sunshine State Young Readers' Award and Florida Teens Read. The rules of the contest are posted on the district website (http://pbspaces.com/botb/) including contest rules, titles, dates, trophies to be awarded, areas for student comments and rating of books, and video recordings of the previous year's competition. Background information on the origin of the term "battle of the books" is also posted. According to this school district site, "The term 'Battle of the Books' first appeared in a satire written by Jonathan Swift at the end of the seventeenth century in France. Swift wrote in response to an ongoing argument over the question of whether contemporary learning . . . had surpassed that of learning during the Classical Age in Greece and Rome." The Chicago Public Library sponsored a radio program in the 1940s with the same title, leading to the adaptation of the program to schools, the history section of the web page reveals.

Instructions on how to organize such events are available in journals and books, from LM_NET and professional organizations, and finally, from a volunteer group for a fee. Details of how the competition was organized by two private schools are provided by Penny Bower (2008) in an article in *School Library Media Activities Monthly*. The purpose of these programs is to offer a pleasurable competitive activity centered around books and reading. Several states combine a battle of the books contest with their state student choice reading programs, which will be covered in the next section of this chapter. A volunteer staff of educators, America's Battle of the Books: A Voluntary Reading Incentive Program, provides book lists, questions, training, and contact list of possible sponsors for a fee. All questions provided by this organization begin with "In which book . . ." To contact this organization, go to their website, http://www.battleofthebooks.org/. Finally, Joan Collins (2008) offers details on how to organize these contests as well as questions for numerous titles in her book, *Motivating Readers in the Middle School.*

National Reading Promotion Programs

Many school calendars include several national reading events. Usually, the first celebration of the year is Banned Books Week in late September. Several ideas for this event are in the discussion of intellectual freedom in Chapter 7. October brings Teen Read Week, sponsored by the Young Adult Library Services Association (YALSA) and International School Library Day on the fourth Monday of the month. November is associated with Children's Book Week, a project of the Children's Book Council, which is targeted at the elementary level but also observed in K-8 schools. For the first time in 2012, Digital Learning Day was celebrated on February 1. Sponsored by the Alliance for Excellent Education, The American Association of School Librarians (AASL) is a core educational partner for this event, which aims to increase opportunities for students to learn with digital resources and prepare for college and the workplace. Read across America falls on March 2, the birthday of Dr. Seuss, sponsored by the National Educational Association. Another March event is Teen Tech Week, which is sponsored by YALSA and emphasizes the competent and ethical use of technologies. Several library organizations claim April as their time for celebration including AASL's School Library Month, American Library Association's (ALA) National Library Week, and The Association for Library Association to Children's (ALSC) El Dia de los Ninos/El Dia de los Libros on April 30. For an expanded list of reading and library programs sponsored by library professional organizations, go to the ALA website, http://www.ala.org/ala/conferencesevents/celebrationweeks/index.cfm.

Another recurring event sponsored by national organizations is The Big Read, supported by the Institute of Museum and Library Services, the National Endowment for the Arts, and Arts Midwest (Institute of Museum and Library Services, 2010). These organizations offer grants and online resources to local institutions, which schedule their own celebrations. Often, multiple community organizations apply for grants together, involving readers of different ages. A single book is selected from the more than 30 selections from the United States and world literature featured in this program. The database of support materials for the books is open to all and offers many resources including readers' and teachers' guides, graphics related to the book, author information, audio guides, Spanish translations for selected program materials, and guidelines for running a community reading event. On the website for The Big Read, you can search for an event scheduled near your location, http://www.neabigread.org/.

The choices of national reading and technology events are plentiful, so that school librarians can choose which to celebrate, depending on local schedules and grade level configurations. In many areas, these programs are jointly sponsored by several local and national library organizations, providing rich opportunities for community involvement. These joint celebrations offer glimpses into the literary lives of adults, documenting the possibilities of lifelong learning.

Family Literacy Events

Though family reading nights are more commonly found in elementary schools, the many schools with K-8 populations ensure that librarians plan evening reading activities for families. In addition, secondary administrators want to provide opportunities for students and parents to focus on the value of reading in an enjoyable atmosphere, according to an article titled "Older Students Need Reading Support, Too" in *Reading Today* (2005). Mainstay activities for such events are storytellers, guest readers, author visits, book swaps, and/or book fairs. Consider adding some literacy presentations by students, such as reading raps, readers' theater activities, book trailers, among others. This would be an opportune time to discuss the changing options for reading formats with families, perhaps with a demonstration of tablet computers, if available in the school. If in a K-8 school, older students could read to young children during a portion of the program. Other good choices are bringing in public and academic librarians from the community, in addition to museum educators. Author visits are frequently scheduled as part of reading events and are a great way to combine classroom and library agendas (Auguste & Fesko, 2010; Harvey, 2005). Adults and youth also appreciate the talents of storytellers, whose performances add a rich dimension to literacy events.

Reading coaches or other literacy educators from the school or district may also welcome the opportunity to discuss the school's reading program with parents and students. Another option is bringing in community leaders to discuss a literacy topic (e.g., reading requirements for a particular career or the role reading plays in their adult lives). Both parents and students will appreciate refreshments and door prizes. For more ideas on community programs, turn to Chapter 4.

Another activity sometimes scheduled in combination with general family events is the book fair. Other times, a book fair may be planned as part of an event with a more targeted purpose, such as a parent's night for teacher conferences. While middle school book fairs are usually successful, book fairs are not planned as often in senior high schools. This topic is frequently discussed in LM_NET, including issues with the selection of books for high schools offered by the large book fair companies.

Specialized Programs and Groups

Other events supported by the library program are centered around specific programs or groups, (e.g., science or history fairs, poetry celebrations, art exhibits, and an ESE or ELL Open House). Often, the school librarian will work with other staff members in staging these events. Perhaps, an art fair could also exhibit the technology projects of library aides, in addition to the work of the students of the art teacher. A display of art resources from the library's collection would be of interest to students, parents, and teachers. Sharing the workload of organizing these events is a benefit to all educators involved.

A poetry week celebration could feature the works written and spoken by students and teachers (Figel, 2011) or could be the culminating event of a Poetry Out Loud contest. An informative conference session with a school librarian, who had implemented the national poetry program, demonstrated how a librarian without a talent for writing poetry could implement this contest using the resources provided by the national organization Poetry Out Loud (http://www.poetryoutloud.org/). Participation in the event provides valuable public speaking experiences for students, preparing them for life after high school.

School librarians share a concern for respecting and honoring the potential and accomplishments of all individuals with teachers and parents of students with special learning needs. Through partnering with teachers in reading guidance, instruction, mentoring, and celebrating the accomplishments of these students, librarians can make a difference in their lives (Canter, Voytecki, Zambone, & Jones, 2011). By volunteering to host or cospon-sor celebratory events in the library for ESE or ELL students in the library, we can play a part in delivering full-service education to these students and their families.

In some schools, a grand event celebrates accomplishments in various curricular areas. An interdisciplinary fair titled History Rocks for a middle school is described by Carrie Sanders (2007) in *School Library Media Activities Monthly*, including a detailed lesson plan and instructions for organizing the event. Combining events may be a viable solution to the issues of reduced staff and resources common in schools today.

Contests created around literary themes or games provide a lively element in some school library programs, especially at the middle school level. To learn more about vari-ous contests that have been successful in promoting literacy, read the article by Rebecca C. Moore (2006) in *Voice of Youth Advocates* (*VOYA*) and check the archives of LM_NET.

Promoting civic literacy is another goal of schools and school library programs. It is listed as a 21st-century theme in AASL's *Empowering Learners* (2009). Librarians frequently arrange schoolwide events promoting civic responsibilities such as mock elections sched-uled around state or national elections or supporting U.S. military troops, often in collabo-ration with social studies teachers and community organizations such as military veterans' groups or other civic organizations. In Port St. Lucie, Florida, Lynn Gruszka, middle school librarian, has arranged programs in the library for Veteran's Day, bringing in veterans to speak to groups of students. Displays of patriotic symbols and learning resources engage students' interest, setting the stage for lively discussions with returning soldiers. These activities provide an opportunity for students to explore the disposition of social responsi-bility as described in Indicator 3.2.2 (*Standards for the 21st-Century Learner*, 2007, p. 9) and enables implementation of the responsibilities of engaging in public conversation on com-mon concerns (3.3.3), discussing ideas beyond the school community (3.3.5), and applying information on democratic values (3.3.6). In addition, this event connected academic learn-ing in social studies to relevant community issues, encouraging students to think about community participation and lifelong learning.

Increased interest in civics education has been stimulated by the disappointing perfor-mance of secondary students on the *Nation's Report Card: Civics 2010*. In a report released in 2011 by the National Assessment of Educational Progress (NAEP), students in fourth grade made progress from the 2006 test, but students in grade 8 did not show significant prog-ress and grades of students in grade 12 were lower than in 1998 or 2006. An organization founded by former Supreme Court Justice Sandra Day O'Conner, iCivics, offers web-based resources including lesson plans as well as interactive games and activities. To access these resources, go to http://www.icivics.org/. For additional information on organizing mock national elections, check the site of the National Student/Parent Mock Election, http://www.nationalmockelection.org/.

The library program benefits in several ways from hosting these special events. In many of the situations featuring student projects, the librarian may have been involved in the research process leading to the development of the final products. Participation in the culminating activity provides a showcase for students' work, encourages creativity and productive work habits by students, highlights collaborative efforts by teachers and the librarian, builds community awareness of the library program, and supports the school's and library's missions.

For more ideas and instructions on how to plan and implement schoolwide read-ing promotional programs, we recommend Lesley B. Preddy's book *Social Readers: Promot-ing Reading in the 21st Century* (2010). She provides many examples of activities, specific instructions for organizing events including book fairs, and templates for promotional materials.

A key part of planning and implementing schoolwide events is getting the word out to students, staff, parents, and the broader community. The daily news show is a convenient forum within the school for announcements of upcoming events. Promotional segments and visuals created by students promoting events will capture the attention of young people and provide an authentic audience for student projects. School or library websites can reach parents and the broader community, in additional to traditional media outlets of the local newspaper and radio and television stations.

Sustained Silent Reading (SSR)

Across the country, many secondary school improvement groups have been seeking solutions to poor academic performance by students and low high school graduation rates. Concern is widespread that schools are not producing high school graduates with the literacy skills required by the workforce, essential for success in college, and also needed for productive adult life. Educators agreed that a primary cause for lack of academic success by secondary students is poor performance in reading. Wise writes in 2009, "Most students in middle and high schools read below grade level and are unable to comprehend their increasingly complex texts and course materials. Thus, they fall behind and struggle to advance through the grades" (p. 373). The causes of reading difficulties in secondary students are complex and the subject of numerous books and articles. Kelly Gallagher (2009) provides an overview of this complicated issue: "As teachers consider the decline of reading, most point to the usual suspects—poverty, lack of parental education, print-poor environments at home, second language issues, the era of the hurried child, and other (and easier) entertainment options that lure students away from reading" (p. 4). Before discussing the instructional practices of teachers as possible contributors to the national reading dilemma, Gallagher introduces two other potential causes: "Schools value the development of test-takers more than they value the development of readers [and] schools are limiting authentic reading experiences" (p. 5). Braunger and Lewis (2006) also discuss the difficulties of increasing literacy levels for all students, "Children who are poor or who are members of ethnic and cultural minorities do not by definition experience difficulty in learning to read. However, these are the groups with whom public schools have had the least success overall in achieving high levels of literacy" (pp. 5–6).

Stephen Krashen (2009) attributes reading difficulties to insufficient time spend in free voluntary reading. He asserts, "Those who read more read better. They also write better, spell better, have larger vocabularies, and have better control of complex grammatical constructions" (p. 18). Proposed solutions include sustained silent reading (SSR) or similar programs. Many educators, especially in schools with large populations of lower socioeconomic students (SES), implement SSR because it addresses the differences in home reading experiences of middle class and SES students (Krashen, 2006). Among the primary characteristics of SSR programs are providing time within the school day to read self-selected materials for the purpose of deriving pleasure from the reading.

Diane Ravitch (2007), educational researcher, provides a definition of SSR. It is "A time set aside in the school day for uninterrupted, independent reading. Homework and conversation are not allowed during SSR periods. Variations on SSR include Free Voluntary Reading (FVR); Daily Individual Reading Time (DIRT); Sustained Quiet Uninterrupted

Reading Time (SQUIRT); and Drop Everything and Read (DEAR)" (p. 208). Various versions of this activity have been used in schools since the 1960s (Jensen & Jensen, 2002). Major advocates for this program include Stephen Krashen (2004, 2006, 2009), Jim Trelease (2006), Robert J. Marzano (2004), and Douglas Fisher (2004). Krashen specifies that educators may expect an increase in students' performances in reading when this innovation is implemented over a period of time.

Though SSR has been used in schools for decades, some have observed a reduction in implementation of this intervention recently (Gallagher, 2009; Gordon, 2010). Gallagher (2009) observes: "Sustained silent reading time is being abandoned because it is often seen as 'soft' or 'nonacademic'" (p. 4). In an interview titled "Linguist, Educational Researcher, and Activist: Steven Krashen," this ardent supporter of SSR and libraries explains the origin of this view of SSR, which was based on the 2000 report of the National Reading Panel:

This report . . . concluded that they have "serious concerns" about the effectiveness of SSR. . . . I argued that there is a very strong support for SSR, but the point . . . is that the National Reading Panel did not say that SSR didn't work. . . . Their cautious position . . . was somehow transformed into "reading doesn't work," which resulted in fewer SSR programs and less funding for libraries. (pp. 79–80)

Garan and DeVoogd (2009) reinforce Krashen's view of the role of the National Reading Panel's influence on the value of SSR. They explain:

First, as consumers of research, teachers must understand that the NRP did not find that SSR is ineffective. Nowhere did the report state that having children read in school is a bad idea. What it claimed was that there were not enough studies meeting the panel's methodological requirements to draw any conclusions. (p. 337)

Various models for SSR are found both in the educational literature and in schools around the country. It is beneficial for school librarians to be familiar with the features of this reading intervention so they may provide appropriate input to staff discussions and serve as advocates for students in their schools. Garan and DeVoogd (2009) comment on the variations to this program:

Like other instructional methods, it can and does operate along a continuum. At one end of the continuum is pure SSR as a time devoted to free reading during which students read books of their own choice, without assessment, skills work, monitoring, or instruction from the teacher. In fact, often the teacher reads a book along with the students, thus providing a model of literacy for the class. Other teachers implement SSR by monitoring the type and the number of books students read; they may also administer assessments, keep reading checklists, and ask questions or encourage student discussion about books. (p. 337)

Fisher and Frey (2009) discuss the distinctions between SSR and independent reading, pointing out that the goal of SSR is reading for pleasure and the aim of independent reading is reading for knowledge acquisition. Text choice also varies in the two reading approaches, with students selecting from a wide range of materials in SSR and teachers providing a limited list in independent reading. Fisher and Frey (2009) also specify that no reports or assigned reading logs are part of SSR, whereas reading logs, written summaries, and discussion groups are part of independent reading (p. 101).

Marzano (2004) presents a similar version of SSR, describing eight essential elements of SSR, which he attributes to Pilgreen: access to reading materials; appeal (referring to reading materials that students think are highly interesting and are at appropriate reading levels); conducive environment; encouragement; staff training; nonaccountability; follow-up activities (encouraging, but not requiring, students to interact with peers about reading); and distributed time to read, both frequent and systematic (pp. 42–44). These elements are helpful to leaders in schools planning interventions and to those who are reevaluating and modifying existing SSR programs. However, it is interesting to note that Marzano's eight elements, or factors, go beyond the basic definition by Ravitch of uninterrupted reading by suggesting follow-up activities encouraging student discussion about books and reading.

Marzano (2004), widely respected by administrators, curriculum experts, and other educators, maintains that a school staff needs to understand the characteristics and intent of SSR before committing to the program. The program outlined by Marzano in *Building Background Knowledge for Academic Achievement: Research on What Works in Schools* (2004) expands the basic SSR program to create learning conditions conducive to gaining background knowledge from the reading experience. Marzano comments, "Key to the success of this approach is to systematically engage students in sustained reading, reflection, and interaction with other students" (p. 118). He goes on to suggest five steps to be discussed by administrators and teachers who are considering implementing an SSR program. The first step, according to Marzano, is: "Students identify topics of interest to them" (p. 46). He describes the importance of recognizing personal interests that are the result of both common needs of all people and the specific interests of an individual. He moves on to the second step: "Students identify reading materials" (p. 50). Self-selection of reading material from a broad range of choices is a key element of motivating students to read. Marzano's examples include books, magazines, newspapers, DVDs, and websites on the topic selected (p. 50). In a middle school scenario, Marzano refers to a teacher taking a class to the library "where the librarian has identified sources based on the list of topics generated the day before" (p. 51).

The third step of SSR in Marzano's book is: "Students are provided uninterrupted time to read" (p. 52). He acknowledges the challenges in finding regular time periods for SSR in secondary schools and concludes that it is helpful to implement SSR in a specific course such as language arts. He also recommends a conducive environment, including comfortable furniture. The fourth step is: "Students write about or represent the information in their notebooks" (p. 54). Marzano calls for students to respond to their reading in an academic notebook. The purpose of this activity is to enable the building of background knowledge by processing the information gained from reading. He returns to the key SSR concept of nonaccountability and specifies that the written responses take place after the reading period.

The fifth and final step of SSR as described by Marzano (2004) is "Students interact with the information" (p. 59). Marzano explains that this step continues the processing of the information read so that it is stored in permanent memory. He emphasizes that discussion of the information read with peers in a social environment "not only increases the amount of exposure students have to information, but also dramatically expands their base of language experience" (p. 59).

Because these programs are frequently recommended by state departments of education and the professional literature in the reading, language arts, and curriculum fields, they are often included in school improvement plans. School librarians are not always included in the planning phases of such programs. This was the case when one of the book's authors went to a high school library position in 2006 and found the SSR program firmly in place as established by the school's administrators. In this model of SSR, the librarian worked in a reading advisory role and facilitated circulation of books to students and classes. In this school, students were not allowed to read magazines, newspapers, or information from the Internet during SSR. While she initially observed that this implementation of SSR was more limited than the descriptions in the educational literature, the decision was made to support this current schoolwide effort and continue to learn about the school climate. Because of prior research on collaboration among administrators, teachers, and school librarians, she knew that a librarian needs to prove to other staff members that you are a team player before the group will allow you to become a leader. Anyone can become a leader only with the consent of the group, especially the school administrators. Fortunately, other school librarians (Gardiner, 2007; Preddy, 2007, 2009; Roberts, 2006) are on the planning committees organizing and revitalizing SSR programs, providing responsive and lively activities that engage and motivate students to read.

When a school staff is considering the implementation of SSR, the challenge is for members to agree on a schedule for the reading sessions. Examples of scheduling from various schools include the following:

- SSR is often implemented in English/language arts classrooms for 10 to 20 minutes at least twice per week.
- The school schedule builds an extra 15 to 20 minutes into one period for SSR (e.g., before classes begin or after lunch).
- Each school day includes a homeroom period and SSR is part of that time block.
- On a certain day of the week in language arts or communications classes, all students practice SSR.
- Each of the major departments in the school implement a 20-minute SSR period on a certain day (e.g., Monday—language arts; Tuesday—math; Wednesday—social studies—Thursday—science; Friday—special areas). An advantage of this system is the frequency of SSR and the participation of all staff members. Limitations could be inconsistency in reading conditions in classrooms and lack of time for discussion of books after the SSR period.
- On a certain day of the week, the entire student body and staff reads for 30 minutes.

Summer Reading Programs

Summer reading and school librarians, what is the connection? In the past, many school libraries in Title I schools were open for six weeks during traditional vacation time as part of the summer school program. Title I programs, funded by the federal government, are present in many schools with certain percentages of low-socioeconomic students, providing additional services to low-achieving students. For low-socioeconomic and low-achieving students in Title I schools, a summer school program with structured reading instruction and lots of independent reading in school was considered to be a solution to summer reading loss. Both book authors have worked in Title I schools in a large urban school district in the southeastern part of the United States. In these schools, both federal and state funds supported the summer school programs. However, in recent years, summer school programs have been significantly reduced because of shrinking budgets (Kim & White, 2011) while concerns over students' scores on standardized tests have grown.

One of the issues identified as contributing to low student achievement in American schools is the summer reading slump. Richard Allington, reading researcher at the University of Tennessee—Knoxville, has been writing about this phenomenon for years and conducted research studies on it. He and McGill-Franzen (2008) assert that "Summer reading setback is a primary source of the reading achievement gap" (p. 20). They cite research studies reporting that reading setback accounts for "approximately 80 percent of the reading achievement gap between poor and nonpoor students at age 14" (p. 20).

Allington and McGill-Franzen (2008) describe a study in 17 high-poverty schools in Florida that they led in 2001–2004, with a large sample of students and a longitudinal design. The two hypotheses tested in the randomized field study were: "(1) providing low-income students with easy access to appropriate books would increase the amount of summer reading and (2) increasing the amount of reading would ameliorate summer reading setback" (p. 21). The primary grade students in the study were invited to a book fair organized by the researchers and allowed to select 12 paperback books to read over the summer. Students were provided with a book log to complete, though Allington and McGill-Franzen report that few returned it at the beginning of school. The students received the books for three consecutive summers.

The results of the three year study were encouraging. Scores from the Florida Comprehensive Assessment Test required throughout the state were used to compare the study group of 842 students to a control group of 428 students with similar characteristics from the same schools. Allington and McGill-Franzen reveal: "We found that the reading achievement of the students who received the summer books for three years was significantly higher than the control group" (p. 21).

The details that Allington and McGill-Franzen provide on the books selected by the students, a mainly African American group, is of interest to school personnel, especially librarians:

> They generally chose books that reflected everyday popular culture rather than books related to African American issues. The top choices of both boys and girls were related to the media—Hangin' with Hilary Duff, Hangin' with Lil' Romeo, and so on. The Captain Underpants series was also popular. When students did select literature representing the experiences of African Americans, they reported doing so because their teachers had earlier introduced the book to them. (p. 21)

These researchers emphasize the crucial importance of students choosing their own titles for maximum benefit from such reading interventions. Allington and McGill-Franzen (2008) explain: "Sean, a 3rd grader, told us, 'I think the book fair was great. I like it when we pick our own books to read. 'Cause some books other people pick, when you start reading, it's stupid'" (p. 22).

Allington and McGill-Frazen (2008) suggest actions that schools could implement to increase reading by students and that provide direction for the efforts of school librarians to improve learning opportunities for students in their schools:

- Rethink access to school book collections. School libraries are typically the largest and nearest supply of age-appropriate books for low-income students, but in too many cases there is no access to school and classroom libraries during summer vacation.
- Revisit the school budget to create programs similar to our experimental intervention, routinely sending students home for the summer with a collection of self-selected books.
- Acknowledge the role of popular culture in students' lives. Rather than denigrating series books or books that derive from movies or video games, build on this prior knowledge to create communities of readers who share, discuss, and swap favorite books.
- Identify local knowledge. Children and families in particular communities know a lot about some animals or habitats. For example, our informational books in Florida focused on alligators and swamps in one community and sharks and oceans in another, building on students' interests and background knowledge (p. 23).

In June 2010, writer Greg Toppo published an article in *USA Today* titled "Books Block 'Summer Slide' in Kids." He includes the results of the study of Allington and McGill-Franzen in his article and makes the point that providing free books to students is much more cost-effective than paying for a summer school program. Toppo interviewed Rebecca Constantino, a researcher and instructor at the University of California, Irvine, in this article. She points to the cause and effect relationship of book ownership for students: "When kids own books, they get this sense, 'I'm a reader,'" she says. "It's very powerful when you go to a kid's home and ask him, 'Where is your library?'" (p. 7D).

Other researchers are continuing to study the impact of providing high-interest books on appropriate reading levels to at-risk students for summer reading. Kim and White (2011) report on a study they conducted in 2008 in which the free distribution of books to students was combined with teacher support in comprehension and fluency activities in the weeks before school ended. In this study, parents were also enlisted to interact with their children with summer reading activities. Kim and White (2011) are also currently involved in a similar study in North Carolina, which includes teacher scaffolding in a voluntary summer reading program. In an article published earlier in *The Reading Teacher* in 2008, White and Kim provided examples of a reading postcard sent to at-risk students receiving books in a summer project. This postcard reviewed reading strategies emphasized by teachers in the weeks before school ended and called for self-evaluation of reading progress by the student, to be signed by a parent. In this chapter, strategies are suggested for school librarians to implement in support of summer reading programs.

Summer Reading for All

Kelly Gallagher addresses the topic of summer reading loss in *Readicide: How Schools Are Killing Reading and What We Can Do about It* (2009), commenting, "If we are serious about preventing summer reading loss, then we have to get serious about discussing how to motivate our students to read over the summer" (p. 55). After citing studies of reading loss, he questions current practices:

> *Isn't it interesting that many school systems require students in the honors track to read over the summer, but often do not have any summer reading expectations for students in the nonhonors track? The irony . . . is that the nonhonors students are the students who most need summer reading. Why should we have high expectations only for advanced students, while less-proficient readers fall farther behind each summer? (p. 55)*

Gallagher, a middle school teacher, maintains that all students should be required to read in the summer. He suggests that a creative solution to the summer reading problem is to assign students to the same language arts or English teacher for two years, so that students could be assigned summer reading to be discussed at the beginning of school. In his classes, he requires one specific title and a second recreational reading title is selected by each student. He clarifies his purpose for summer reading, to develop recreational reading habits. He declares, "We should be putting high-interest, accessible books into their hands: *The Kite Runner*, not *Heart of Darkness*. Our goal should be to nurture young readers, not to kill them" (p. 56).

Returning to the question of how school librarians are connected to summer reading programs, a range of possibilities exist. On the first rung of a ladder of options is collaborating with secondary classroom teachers on the selection of titles for summer reading lists. Many high schools require a classic novel that will be studied in English or language arts classes during the school year. In addition, students may be required to select one or more from a list of titles for each grade. Frequently, librarians may be consulted on the choice of titles. A variety of criteria may be used to select books for these lists. Nonfiction titles should be among the choices on this list. Many students prefer nonfiction and all students accrue benefits from reading nonfiction including expanding background knowledge and preparation for standardized testing. Graphic novels should be considered because of student interest in the format and the benefits of combining visual clues with text for at-risk readers. If English and language arts teachers are concerned about the quality of the literature selected, librarians could consult the awards lists generated by professional journals in all fields and professional organizations. At least one high school's summer reading list required a classic title to be used in classrooms and offered a selection of fiction and nonfiction from the state readers' choice titles for the next school year. This solution offers considerable choice of titles and reading levels as well as supporting a library and school initiative.

Established schools, especially high schools, may have an entrenched tradition of summer reading requirements in place. A school librarian who is a newcomer to the school would be well-advised to listen and learn about existing patterns of practice and then determine the best way to contribute to improving learning opportunities for students.

An activity that ranks on the lower level of support for summer reading is selling summer reading books to students in the school library. In one library position in an established high school, one of the book's authors found that an expectation of the library staff was ordering copies of books from the summer reading list and selling them in the library during an open house for incoming freshmen and their parents in the spring. The sale of the books to students continued before and during the school day through the end of the school year and during opening weeks of the new school year. In this school, students in Advanced Placement, International Baccalaureate, and honors language arts classes were expected to complete assigned summer reading. The books were sold at a reduced price to students and no profit was made by the library.

Another way that school librarians can easily contribute to summer reading activities is by partnering with the local public librarian in informing students about options for checking out books and participating in summer activities at the public library (Gorman, 2010). The school librarian's role may be distributing flyers and other promotional materials provided by the public library to students or by arranging for the public librarian to come to the school and speak to students about the summer programs in person or through a televised appearance. Providing a list of the school's reading lists, as early as possible, is another important aspect of school librarian and public librarian collaboration. Read more about school librarian and public librarian interactions in Chapter 4 of this book.

At a higher level of involvement in promoting summer reading, school librarians can lead or participate in a conversation with colleagues in the school about the purposes of a summer reading program. A literacy committee or similar group would be an appropriate venue for such a discussion. Depending on the local circumstances, a school librarian may want to confer with the principal about expectations or restrictions on activities sponsored by the school before meeting with other staff members. When meeting with the principal, the librarian may want to present a brief summary of research findings from the professional literature on the summer reading slump and recommend the distribution of the information to staff members on the literacy committee before the discussion of school goals on the topic. This research will likely be appropriate for most schools, depending on school demographics, but may not apply to private schools or public schools in affluent areas.

This preliminary meeting with the school's principal is the time to explore the possibility of providing access to the school library collection during the summer months. First, circulation of the collection to all interested students can be recommended. If this is not acceptable to the administrator, limited circulation to target populations could be proposed. For example, in one high school, International Baccalaureate students checked out books for the summer. Since the extended essay required of these students is due when school opens, it makes sense to allow these students to use books over the summer months. Some titles had been purchased for student's research topics, after meeting with students and advisors. Other target populations could be students identified as low socioeconomic groups with low reading levels. This group is most likely to be impacted by summer reading loss.

Though possibility of losing books checked out in the summer is a concern of many, the potential benefit to student achievement is of paramount importance. If approval of the principal is not forthcoming for the limited checkout, a final position could be the circulation of paperback books only to minimize the financial loss to the library collection and school. If necessary, parents could be required to sign a form accepting responsibility for the books checked out. A printout of titles checked out could easily be provided.

When the literacy committee meeting date is set, it may be advantageous to invite any faculty member to participate in the discussion. A first action could be the identification of purposes for a summer reading program. After members have compiled their initial list of purposes and expectations for a summer reading program, the school librarian may want to share the findings of a research project by a public librarian conducted in North Carolina.

Gorman (2010), writing from the perspective of a public librarian involved with planning summer reading programs, identifies eight purposes for summer reading lists identified in a survey she conducted with educators. She implemented the survey in interviews with school librarians, teachers, and an administrator in public high schools, private schools, and a public school system that requires summer reading by all students. These reasons are summarized in a List in a Box format. Though Gorman (2010) addresses the topic of summer reading loss in her article in *Teacher Librarian*, it was not prioritized by the school personnel in her interviews in the Chapel Hill—Durham area. She reports that "this was one of the least-cited reasons given for creating reading lists" (p. 54).

This perspective provided by Gorman (2010) from other educators may bring up additional points to be considered by the committee. Once the purposes of the school's summer reading program have been finalized, the details for implementation can be addressed. At this point, areas of responsibility for school staff members will emerge. At this time, school librarians may want to suggest new approaches, depending on the local needs of students. Among the possibilities gathered from the literature and our experiences are these suggestions:

Purposes of Summer Reading Lists

Research by Libby Gorman

1. Encouraging leisure reading
2. Fulfilling academic goals
3. Meeting parental expectations
4. Encouraging lifelong or independent reading
5. Maintaining school community during summer
6. Identifying quality books
7. Encouraging new types of reading
8. Protecting the institution of reading

From: Gorman, L. (2010). Purposes behind summer reading lists. *Teacher Librarian, 37*(5), 54.

- Provide a range of options for summer reading selections. Propose that students, especially in middle school, check out fiction, nonfiction, graphic novels, or audiobooks. Share the list of titles for the next year of the students' choice awards and suggest consideration of the titles for summer reading lists.

- If documentation is required of summer reading by a school, offer to contribute to the development of a reading log format. The primary issue here is to advocate for a choice of types of reading, listening, and viewing. Students like to read magazines, e-books, and websites (Lu & Gordon, 2007), as well as listen to audiobooks and podcasts. These literary experiences should count for summer reading credit. It may be easier to open up the range of reading materials at the middle school level than at high school.

- Display online pages from The Learning Network of *The New York Times* to show the possibilities of students participating in the summer online reading activities. See the READS Internet Resources for the web address of this site. Demonstrate the reading comprehension tools that are available for use with the latest news stories from the *New York Times*. Students are also invited to respond to surveys and questions posed online (Schulten, 2011).

- Propose that options are developed to encourage students to share reading experiences during the summer months. Offer to work with technology teachers to create wikis and other online means for pairs and small groups of students to share responses to a book all have read. If requested by the literacy committee, questions could be developed to encourage thoughtful responses to books. The literature offers multiple examples of students sharing thoughts about books online (Corrigan, 2010; Moreillon, 2010). This option acknowledges the social nature of tweens and teens and capitalizes on it to promote reading. Even though one reading partner may be out of town on vacation, thoughts on books can continue to be shared online. If required, this format for reader responses offers the potential for monitoring student exchanges.

- Offer to support teacher instruction for reading strategies to be used in summer reading activities. Suggest a session in the library for at-risk middle school students to motivate them to participate in summer reading activities. Provide committee members with a lively preview of a potential read-aloud, *My Life as a Book* by Janet Tashjian. The first chapter of this book captures the dismayed reaction of a struggling reader to mention of the summer reading requirement by his mother (Wilson, Dunbar, & Lovley, 2010). To capture the attention of teachers, use an iPad to show the pages and illustrations of the first chapter of this book. If the school librarian has scheduled classes in the library, this entire short book could be read aloud. Short stories on the theme of reading and books offer another possibility for reading aloud to a class and stimulating conversation among students on the values of reading.

- Suggest that science, social studies, and other content area teachers contribute to the summer reading lists to create buy-in for the inclusion of nonfiction. Show the web pages of annual reading lists of the National Science Teachers' Association (Metz, 2009) and the National Council for Social Studies.

- Propose seeking input from students on current views on the existing summer reading program and suggestions of titles and changes to the program (Gordon, 2008). The school librarian may offer to develop a survey with others to gather opinions from students.

- Create a plan to inform parents, the public library, and community about the new summer reading program using the library or school website, school and community newspaper, fliers, and parent–student orientation sessions (Moore, 2008).

- Consider asking the literacy committee to support a request to the principal and school board to fund opening the library several times during the summer for exchange of books (Heaser, 2011).

Reading Log				
Date	Title of Text	Type of Text (Book; magazine or newspaper article; online news [Yahoo, ESPN]; audiobook)	Discussion Partner (Mother; father; sister; friend; group)	Discussion Format (Personal; e-mail; wiki)

At the highest level of involvement on summer reading programs by school librarians is writing grants to provide free books for at-risk students. Consider collaborating with others on the literacy council or a parent group to write grants for books to give to students for summer reading. Apply to local organizations or national foundations to implement a program in the school similar to the successful projects described earlier by researchers. This action can impact students' achievement levels now and help to instill the lifelong reading habits that are the focus of the READS Curriculum.

Mentoring

Because school librarians work with individuals as well as groups of students, school librarians are in a good position to serve as mentors to students. School libraries have always been a favorite spot in the school for certain students, usually students who love to read. When many authors speak to audiences of school librarians, they tell stories of their treasured days in their school libraries and how much the attention of the librarian meant in their lives.

Marzano (2003) defines mentoring as a "one-on-one relationship between a caring adult and a youth who needs support" (p. 136). In schools, such relationships may emerge naturally as a result of contact between with students and teachers and may be described as informal mentoring. In structured or planned mentoring programs, students, or selected groups of students, may be matched with faculty members (Marzano, 2003). These planned mentoring programs may be part of school efforts to improve achievement on tests or as part of drop-out prevention initiatives.

Educators often look closely at successful school programs to identify elements that contribute to positive outcomes. In *Best Schools: How Human Development Research Should Inform Educational Practice*, Thomas Armstrong (2006) looks first at middle school programs. He points to positive adult relationships as a practice that meets the primary developmental need of students in this age group to form a personal identity. In many schools, all students are assigned to homeroom teachers who serve as mentors or advisors. Armstrong considers the preparation of students to live independently in the real world to be the primary purpose of high schools. He suggests that high school teachers should serve as mentors to encourage students, model "mature adult thinking and behavior" (p. 143), and assist them in planning for their future.

In Armstrong's vision (2006), these mentoring services would be systematically provided to all students. However, in other situations, these planned mentoring programs may be provided for targeted groups of students for the purposes of increasing test scores and graduation rates. A teacher may be assigned to work with individuals at risk of failing. Marzano (2003) describes the teacher's role in working with struggling students and suggests appropriate practices:

- Serve as an on-campus advocate for the student.
- Provide a steady presence for the student.
- Communicate with the mentee about how time together will be used, respecting the student's opinion.
- Accept responsibility for initiating meetings.
- Include pleasant or fun elements in the relationship (p. 136).

If assigned to work with individual struggling students in a structured mentoring situation, teachers or school librarians may need to explain the program to the student in the first session. It may also be appropriate to ask students for their personal assessment of the situation and potential solutions. In the example of assigned mentoring first provided in Chapter 3, one student with low reading scores on the state required examination responded quickly to the question about possible causes of his problems. He declared that he had been placed in the wrong classes when he recently moved to the school and could not keep up with the work. In subsequent discussions with counselors, it was learned that the student's academic records from the previous county had not been received by the school. Further investigation by the guidance department revealed that the student had been tested and placed in special education classes in the previous school district. Subsequently, the student was reassigned to appropriate classes, improving his attitude about school. For school librarians, an informal mentoring relationship may start as part of a reading advisory or instructional session, or a teacher or school counselor may contact the librarian about a student who needs special attention.

Many school librarians have embraced the role of mentor at various levels over the years. Dr. Jami Jones, faculty member in the Department of Library Science at East Carolina University in Greenville, North Carolina, first focused on this aspect of librarianship when working as a school librarian at a high school in Florida. After reflecting on the tragic death of a friend of her son, she became more interested in influences on the lives of young people. After further observing the difficult social, academic, and personal situations experienced by many students in her school, she began to investigate the concept of resiliency. Jones was seeking to learn why some individuals overcome difficult obstacles while others are profoundly impacted by the stress of similar events. Resiliency is defined by the *Ameri-*

*can Heritage Dictionary of the English Languag*e (1992) as "the ability to recover quickly from illness, change, or misfortune; buoyancy" (p. 1535). As part of her search to understand the factors permitting some people to cope with difficulties and still lead productive lives, she found the Kauai Longitudinal Study conducted in Hawaii and published in 1992, which focused on the events and quality of life of all children born on the island in 1955. Jones (2004) explains:

> *All children . . . were followed over a period of thirty years to assess their responses to such high-risk conditions as poverty, parental separation and divorce, and school failure. In addition to such facts as intelligence, an easy temperament, and socioeconomic advantages that protect children from adversity, positive relationships were key; resilient children had at least one nonparent adult who provided consistent emotional support, nurturance, and guidance. (p. 44)*

The researchers involved with the Kauai Longitudinal Study identified significant protective factors separating the resilient from the less successful individuals. Jones (2007) reports on one these conditions: "Being able to rely on supportive organizations such as churches, youth groups, or schools. Resilient children often remember a supportive and encouraging teacher" (p. 495). Another key finding of the research study is the value of competence in reading to protect students from difficulties in life. In an interview with one of the original researchers in the Kauai Longitudinal Study, Dr. Emmy E. Werner, Jones (2007) asked the expert about the role of reading in empowering youth to survive difficulties. Werner replied: "What we found in the research is that the children who succeed later in life do more reading. Those who like to read have the ability to grow and become autonomous and feel in control of their lives. These are important resiliency buffers" (p. 497).

Working from her belief that librarians can provide several of the valuable protective factors including compassionate attention needed by many students, Jones (2007) developed a Library Ladder of Resiliency featuring five levels: "making connections; reading; problem-solving skills; social skills; and hobbies and interests" (p. 496). In various articles, Jones has described how librarians can address the various levels of this ladder to improve the lives of students. The elements of Jones's ladder also reflect the objectives of this book:

1. Making connections: School librarians can recognize the value of the mentoring role and display an approachable and friendly attitude toward all students. This role is discussed in Chapter 3 of this book, as part of the Read as a personal activity component of the READS curriculum. In these difficult days of reduced staffing, many school librarians are constantly rushing to meet the needs and demands of administrators and teachers and may need to be reminded to stay tuned to the needs of students. Jones (2007; 2009b) also writes about the role of public librarians in providing safe and nurturing spaces for young people to reach their potential. In Chapter 4, the many ways school librarians can improve learning opportunities for students have been explored. These include collaborating with public and academic librarians and other educators to increase awareness of community resources.

2. Reading: The potential for competency in reading to impact the future of young people is a primary reason for the development of the READS Curriculum and strategies that school librarians can employ to increase opportunities for students to learn to read are discussed throughout the pages of this book. Jones (2005) comments: "Library media specialists who understand that reading promotes resiliency are more likely to collaborate with reading specialists to develop book clubs and other reading events" (p. 26).

3. Problem-solving skills: Jones (2005; 2009a) maintains that school librarians support students in developing problem-solving skills when they teach a systematic approach to information literacy skills, including finding information appropriate to a real-life or academic need. While information literacy instruction is not the primary focus of this book, aspects of it have been addressed in the chapters on using nonfiction materials and developing a product as a response to literature.

4. Social skills: Youths with the skills to interact well with other students and the adults in their lives are more capable of dealing with adversity. In this book, many scenarios call for students to serve on teams and to develop cooperative learning skills. In addition, we have discussed the social nature of today's tweens and teens as they spend much of their free time communicating with each other through social media technologies. Many examples have been shared of how school librarians have helped facilitate the development of social skills by arranging for students to work together on assignments, to attend reading promotional events, and to participate in club activities.

5. Hobbies and interests: This fifth protective factor focuses on how young people develop self-esteem and competence by pursuing personal interests and hobbies. School librarians should provide and promote library collections that are responsive to the interests and needs of students in their schools. It is suggested that facilitating and sponsoring club activities is an appropriate way for school librarians to contribute to student growth, encourage pleasure reading, and support the mission of the school.

During her career as a Florida high school librarian, Jami Jones worked with her state professional organization at the time, the Florida Association for Media in Education (FAME), to promote mentoring by school librarians by creating a recognition program, the Amanda Award. This award is presented annually to one or more librarians in the state who make a difference in the lives of students in a secondary school through activities designed to strengthen students (Jones, 2004). Since the award was first presented to a Florida middle school librarian and high school librarian in 2002, the award has gone to librarians creating a variety of programs including a library lunch bunch (Nellie Martin in 2002); a one book, one community program (Dana Thompson in 2004); a schoolwide reader recognition program (Janice Saulsby in 2004); an activity combining laughter and literacy (Bunnie McCormack in 2005); a reading group lunch bunch tutoring program for football players (Deb Svec in 2006); and a poetry visibility program (Jodie Delgado in 2010) (Jones, 2004, 2009; Terelli, 2011).

Deb Svec from Palm Beach, Florida, an Amanda Award winner in 2006, is continuing her literacy project with football players (Svec, 2006) and has now added another reading promotion project, Cranium CoRE (Community of Reading Engagement). Svec is using the appeal of technology to entice reluctant readers and students in mainstream classes to read and improve their comprehension scores. Cranium CoRE is a web-based video game application that engages students in the essential work of reading books, one chapter at a time, then answering textually complex questions. The first step in a typical sequence of use for the program is for individuals, as part of a small group or class, to hear a chapter of a book read aloud while reading along in their own text. The next step is to answer comprehension questions competitively in a team format using radio frequency receivers (clickers), one per team. Students are encouraged to use the book to find answers to questions, which are phrased in a format similar to standardized state test items. After the questions are answered, the teacher leads the group in a discussion of how answers were determined, reinforcing recommended comprehension procedures. The winners for the session are acknowledged after all questions for the chapter are answered. Svec is using Cranium CoRE in a variety of collaborative ways, including a struggling readers lunch bunch, intensive reading classes (for students not passing the state standardized reading test), as well as mainstream science and language arts classes.

In Palm Beach County Schools, competitions using the Cranium CoRE program are growing among various groups, classes, and schools. In 2010, a competition was held between groups in two school districts hundreds of miles apart, creating great excitement, team spirit, and enthusiasm for reading. This subscription-based resource has received great reviews from students, librarians, teachers, and library educators, which are posted on the Cranium Core website, http://www.craniumcore.com/s/default/index.cfm.

Cranium CoRE is a valuable tool for use in the library setting, as part of special projects and with scheduled library classes. It is a great way to entice students to improve their reading skills using appealing books and gaming strategies. Most importantly, students practice the essential reading skills that will help them to prepare for the workplace and future academic success. When working with this program, school librarians serve as mentors, tutors, reading coaches, literature experts, and student advocates.

Book Clubs

The term book club is used widely in the language arts and library literature. The constants in this concept are books of some form, discussions, students, and facilitators. Among the common variations in book clubs are purpose, location, and timing. Other variables may be book format or type of reading response, if a formal response is required. The term learning clubs is used by Heather K. Casey (2009) in *Journal of Adolescent & Adult Literacy* for a group formed based on a common interest in a classroom setting. Casey continues to explain the concepts for reading groups in classrooms, "The terms literature circles and book clubs are often used interchangeably and share similar grouping procedures, though literature circles traditionally include more prescriptive roles than book clubs" (p. 285). Many teachers create several book clubs within a classroom to allow students to choose book titles and engage in small group discussions with the teacher as facilitator or with student leaders supervised by the teacher. Similar groups may be called literature discussion groups (Appleman, 2006). From the library perspective, activities such as these are called book clubs or groups, both in school and public libraries.

School librarians need to be knowledgeable about all aspects of the school's instructional program, but are especially interested in reading activities. As part of literacy groups within the school, librarians need to be aware of existing strategies employed to provide appropriate support for teachers and students and to avoid duplication of titles used in various activities with them. In order to plan appealing independent reading activities, librarians consider the characteristics and interests of all students in the school. Especially in senior high schools, many options for activities may already exist for academically successful students. Carol Littlejohn (2011) suggests that librarians may want to offer book club options for reluctant readers including ELL students and individuals from low-income families who may not adequate reading materials at home. Littlejohn describes a wide range of approaches to reading clubs in her book, *Book Clubbing! Successful Book Clubs for Young People.*

To illustrate the potential of such literary groups, Book Club Profiles were created demonstrating several models with various purposes, settings, and schedules. The first example, the Classroom Model, represents the learning experiences implemented by many

	Book Club Profile: Classroom Model
Purpose/Goal	To systematically discuss books and other texts; to facilitate development of reader identity and self-awareness; to develop range of reading skills and disciplinary habits of mind; to access and seek background knowledge; to gain knowledge of text structures
Description	Flexible format; variety of response methods; includes writing activities; students read text independently or during silent reading time in class
Participants	4–6 students, grades 6–12
Timing	Weekly meeting
Location	Classroom
Selection Process	Student choice from teacher selection; teacher book talks 5 to 6 texts at various reading levels on a theme, genre, or author study
Discussion Pattern	Dependent on student needs, teacher's objectives, and educational standards; teacher-directed questions
Sample Titles	*Hatchet, Milkweed; Holes; The Haunting; Hoot; The River Between Us; Speak; Slam; The First Part Last; In the Time of the Butterflies; Beloved; On the Road; The Chosen; 1984*
Distinctive Aspect	Students complete visual reading logs before class meeting; complete reading inventory
Does Not Include	Reading aloud by students or teacher during session
Librarian's Role	Optionally recommending titles to teacher and/or providing book talks
Example	O'Donnell-Allen, C. (2006). *The book club companion.*

teachers during instructional time. The role for school librarians in this model may be recommending titles and providing copies of titles selected by students and teachers (Kasten & Wilfong, 2005; O'Donnell-Allen, 2006).

The second profile, Typical School Librarian Model, distills the experiences of many librarians as described in journal articles and LM_NET. Dozens of variations on this model create positive reading experiences for students and offer a comfortable place to go on club days in secondary schools.

The third model is based on the experiences of Deb Svec, the Florida school librarian whose library projects were discussed in the previous section on mentoring. In the Book Club Profile: Motivational & Remedial using Cranium CoRE, the inclusion of technological devices adds appeal for the struggling readers targeted in this intervention, which was designed to increase academic achievement in an enjoyable, social learning environment.

The Transition to Life-Long Reading model based on Deborah Appleman's book published in 2006 describes a collaborative project in which the school librarian and teachers work together to plan, organize, and implement the reading club. Students signed up for this literary club on a voluntary basis, which is scheduled outside school hours. Sharing the responsibilities of sponsoring a club is beneficial for the educators involved, allowing

	Book Club Profile: Typical School Librarian Model
Purpose/Goal	Celebration of pleasure reading in social club environment
Description	Usually voluntary outside of classroom time; emphasis on reading enjoyment and sharing book titles; could use audiobooks or reading tablets (Kindles, iPads, etc.); may include literary (vocabulary or language) discussions
Participants	Students in grades 6–12; could target boys, ESE, or ESL students; librarian; possibly teacher or public librarian
Timing	Weekly meeting for designated period; timing may vary
Location	Library
Title Selection Process	Student or librarian choice; genre
Discussion Pattern	Librarian- or student-driven talk
Sample Titles	*Hope Was Here; My Sister's Keeper; Maze Runner; The Lovely Bones; Twilight; Adoration of Jenna Fox; Beastly; Dragon Flight* (LM_NET Archives)
Distinctive Aspect	Usually voluntary before or after school or lunchtime; social club atmosphere with food
Does Not Include	Focus on basic reading skills or standardized test-type questions
Librarian's Role	Publicizing event; selecting and procuring books; providing snacks; perhaps obtaining parent permission for out of school event; seeking teacher or public librarian as cosponsor; writing grant for funding; selecting questions for discussion
Example	Preddy, L. B. (2010). *Social readers*; Harlan, P. (2010), The high school book club—now with Kindles; Stevenson, S. (2009). My *Bluford High* boys.

for one professional to miss a session without cancelling the event for students. This model will be discussed further later in this chapter, as it addresses the goal of developing habits for lifelong learning.

The final model, a Library Online Book Club, combines pleasure reading, face-to-face sessions in the library, and online exchanges among students and the librarian to discuss the group topic. This is a flexible model, allowing for multiple reading, listening, and viewing formats, use of a single book or multiple titles, in the same or different genres. The focus of the group could be avid readers, reluctant readers, those interested in a special hobby, among others. For variations on the online model, sometimes referred to as virtual literature circles, read about the projects described by Shantz-Keresztes (2005), Peowski (2010), Scharber (2009), Stewart (2009), and Bowers-Campbell (2011).

Now that five models for book clubs in school libraries are described, variations that provide appeal to special interests and needs of students include:

- Create a club for avid readers to be the first to read and write reviews for new titles in the library. Call the group "Book Critics Club," "Out-of-the-Box Readers," or any other

	Book Club Profile: Online Book Club
Purpose/Goal	Promotion of pleasure reading in social networking environment
Participants	Students in grades 6–12 (mixed or targeted groups); librarian; possibly teacher or library assistant
Timing	Group meetings (biweekly or monthly) and online interactions
Location	Library and online environment: wiki, educator blog, or other online discussion forum
Selection Process	Librarian or students propose titles; final choice by student group
Discussion Pattern	Librarian and students pose questions.
Sample Books	Print or e-books; middle school or high school reader choice program titles; current or classic fiction and nonfiction
Distinctive Aspect	Discussions about books in online social setting
Does Not Include	Use of standardized test-type questions; emphasis on basic reading skills
Librarian's Role	Organizer; participant; arrange funding through grants, etc.
Example	Scharber, C. (2009). Online book clubs; Shantz-Keresztes, L. (2005). Avid readership: "Wired for words" online youth book club.

clever name you can conjure up. Put the students of the school television news show to deliver their descriptions or feature their reviews in bulletin boards and displays. This idea came from Cindy Dobrez and Lynn Rutan on the Bookends Blog on the *Booklist Online* (2011).

- Partner with an ELL teacher (one who is fluent in the target language) to create a club for second language learners. If you do not read and speak the language fluently, then select a book available in English and the appropriate second language. Conduct discussions in both languages, as appropriate for the group. Students will be more likely to use the library after you have reached out and established the library as a comfort zone. Learn more about working with second language learners in the excellent article by Blair, Bradfield, Crenshaw, and Mosedale (2011) in *School Library Monthly*.

- Gather up reading selections in alternative formats to reach wider groups of students. Mary Burkey describes audiobook clubs in two articles from 2010. Appeal to the gamers and techie kids with a "Transmedia Book Club," Find a recent transmedia title and explore the various ways of experiencing a story with the students. Harland (2010) provides details of her experience with a book club using Kindles.

- Combine fitness and listening using audiobooks in MP3 players, Playaway format, or on iPods for an after school club. Invite a physical education teacher or other exercise buff teacher to join the group. Since likely each participant may be listening to a different title, focus discussions on common features (e.g., characters, setting, problems, themes, etc.). Encourage students to promote the book they read to others in the group. Betsy Long (2008) came up with a clever name for her listening group, "W.A.L.K. (We Are Literate Kids) Club" (p. 18), described in an article in *School Library Media Activities Monthly*. She arranged for the walking to take place during the school day.

	Book Club Profile: Motivational and Remedial Using Cranium CoRE
Purpose/Goal	To provide fun, motivating reading experience using gaming strategy and technology tools; to improve student achievement on standardized tests; to generate interest in reading
Participants	Struggling readers; librarian and/or teacher
Timing	Weekly or more frequently, for fixed period (month, quarter)
Location	Library or classroom
Selection Process	Titles with quizzes available; student choice from educator's list
Discussion Pattern	Students answer standardized questions in competitive format and teacher leads discussion of appropriate responses, reteaching as needed.
Sample Books	*Runner; We Beat the Street; The Maze Runner; Flush; Black and White; Thirteen Reasons Why; The Bully*
Distinctive Aspect	Students or teacher reads aloud chapter and students use radio frequency devices to answer questions and discuss chapter; continue through book; students or educator can create questions and publish to the Cranium CoRE website.
Does Not Include	Emphasis on authors' writing styles
Librarian's Role	Organizer; secures books, program, and hardware; reinforces reading skills; motivates students; collaborates with teachers
Example	Deb Svec: Interview.

- Lunch Bunch reading groups are implemented throughout the country in a variety of ways. In some situations, the principal pays for the books and other expenses. Read about how it worked in one middle school in Patricia P. Drogowski's 2006 article in *School Library Media Activities Monthly*. She recommends surveying students during the final meeting about their opinions and suggestions for future sessions.
- Consider a club on reading about specific interests (e.g., fishing, surfing, photography, and needlework) and bring in all sorts of reading and learning resources on the topic: magazines, novels, nonfiction, biographies, online sites including blogs, or guest speakers.
- Go traditional and implement the Great Books Program. These familiar discussion groups will appeal to parents of many secondary students.
- Join forces with the local community and public librarians and begin planning for a joint book club targeting at-risk youth. Likely some of the students impacted will be from your school. Apply for a Great Stories Club grant from ALA. Check out the details at http://www.programminglibrarian.org.
- Demonstrate techniques for sharing stories with peers and younger students for book club members including reading aloud, creating reader's theatre productions, buddy reading, and so on. Share the news of your students' skills with other library colleagues in your district and accept invitations for your book club members to present programs in other schools.
- How about an iPad club? That is the suggestion of Dr. David Loertscher (2010). Somehow, librarians may learn more from students in such an environment! Have participants

	Book Club Profile: Transition to Lifelong Reading
Purpose/Goal	Enrichment; introduction to adult books; invitation to lifelong reading; create community of readers
Participants	Junior or senior students (ages 18–60); teachers; librarian; academic researcher
Description	Breakfast Book Club; outside of class; elective
Timing	Before school; biweekly; monthly; quarterly
Location	Classroom
Selection Process	Educators provide choices of titles; students in group select one title or one of two used for session.
Discussion Pattern	Student driven; limited adult input
Sample Books	*The Kite Runner; Peace Like a River; Life of Pi; Persepolis; A Step from Heaven; It's Not about the Bike; The Lovely Bones; Crow Lake; Fast Food Nation; The Tao of Pooh*
Distinctive Aspect	Participation in discussion is optional; lively complex exchanges between students
Does Not Include	Literary history; interpretive agenda; reading aloud by teacher or student
Librarian's Role	Collaboratively organizes books and materials with teachers; secures funding for project
Example	Appleman, D. (2006). *Reading for themselves: How to transform adolescents into lifelong readers through out-of-class book clubs.*

recommend and demonstrate resources in various areas (e.g., news sources, sports events, other entertainment, free books, learning sites, production tools, connecting with other devices, etc.). Publish the group's recommendations for iPad or iPhone and other platform applications in school and staff newsletters.

Useful resources for planning book clubs are available in Leslie B. Preddy's book, *Social Readers: Promoting Reading in the 21st Century*. From invitations and permission letters to step-by-step directions, you will find practical ideas for getting started with book clubs in this professional source.

Leading and facilitating discussions in book clubs may be a concern for school librarians without reading and language arts backgrounds. Teaming up with classroom teachers or experienced public librarians is a good way to ease into this aspect of literacy activities. The value of adding a social component to reading experiences to involve students in the traditional and current literary worlds is well-documented in both language arts (Allen, 2009; Ferriter, 2010; Wilhelm, 2008) and the library world (Preddy, 2010). The chapter on the role of discussion in classrooms in *Teaching Literature to Adolescents* by Beach, Appleman, Hynds, and Wilhelm (2011) can be very helpful in collaborating with teachers and when planning for activities involving discussions in the library.

Gathering ideas for generic questions about books is another approach to developing comfort with guiding literary discussions. While it is often the goal for students in volun-

READS Component	READS Indicator	AASL Standards for the 21st-Century Learner*	Common Core State Standards— English Language Arts**
Score reading progress			
The student will:			
5.1 Engage in literacy-based motivational programs and activities.	5.1.2 Participate in structured independent reading programs (e.g., Florida Teens Read).	• 3.1.2 Participate and collaborate as members of a social and intellectual network of learners. • 4.1.7 Use social networks and information tools to gather and share information. • 4.2.1 Display curiosity by pursuing interests through multiple resources. • 4.3.3 Seek opportunities for pursuing personal and aesthetic growth. • 4.4.1 Identify own areas of interest. • 4.4.6 Evaluate own ability to select resources that are engaging and appropriate for personal interests and needs.	• Reading: Informational Text—10 Read and comprehend literary nonfiction in the grade text complexity band . . . • Reading: Literature—10 Read and comprehend literature in the grade text complexity band . . . • Speaking and Listening—1a Initiate and participate effectively in a range of collaborative discussions: Come to discussions prepared, having read and researched material . . . • Speaking and Listening—1b Initiate and participate effectively in a range of collaborative discussions: Work with peers to promote civil, democratic discussions . . . • Speaking and Listening—1c Initiate and participate effectively in a range of collaborative discussions: Propel conversations by posing and responding to questions . . . • Speaking and Listening—5 Make strategic use of digital media in presentations . . .

* Excerpted from *Standards for the 21st-Century Learner* by the American Association of School Librarians, a division of the American Library Association, copyright © 2007 American Library Association. Available for download at www.ala.org/aasl/standards. Used with permission.

** Excerpted from *Common Core State Standards for English Language Arts*. National Governors Association Center for Best Practices and Council of Chief State School Officers Commercial License. Copyright © 2010. Used with permission of NGA Center/CCSSO.

tary reading groups to generate their own questions, many librarians prefer to be prepared to guide the conversation if needed. Consider these questions from experienced discussion leaders:

• "What is the attitude you feel from this book? Optimistic? Goofy? Good-naturedly obnoxious? What kind of attitude do you like in books? What do you not like?" "Did the book live up to its opening line? Authors work hard on the first pages of their books. . . .

Did the author keep up the good work throughout the book?" (Kunzel & Hardesty, 2006, p. 204).

- "How is the main character different from you?" "What is one thing in this story that has happened to you?" (Lesesne, 2003, p. 138) "If you were to film this story, what characters would you eliminate if you couldn't use them all?" (Lesesne, 2003, p. 137).

- "What do you know that is helping you understand the story? What might you need to know more about to understand more of the story?" (Wilhelm, 2008, p. 209) "What impressions are you forming in your mind of people and places in the story? What pictures do you have in your mind's eye?" (Wilhelm, 2008, p. 211).

- "Why do you think the author wrote this? What are some themes that emerged in . . .?" "So how can we apply this idea to our lives? What can we learn from this character/ part/story?" (Zwiers & Crawford, 2009, p. 71).

- Generic questions for nonfiction: "Do the issues affect your life? How so—directly on a daily basis, or more generally? Now or sometime in the future?" "Talk about specific passages that struck you as significant—or interesting, profound, amusing, illuminating, disturbing, sad . . .? What was memorable?" (Lit Lovers: A Well Read Online Community. Retrieved from http://litlovers.com/run-a-book-club/questions-for-nonfiction).

State Readers' Choice Programs

Students in many schools have been empowered to cast their own votes for authors of favorite books for over 70 years. Librarians have observed for years that the books with the gold and silver medals on the covers from the traditional awards were not necessarily popular in their schools and public libraries. While a few students gravitate to the traditional award-winning titles selected by professionals, others are not impressed by the choices of adults. In an article by Rogers, Szymanski, Cavanaugh, and Dunphy (2010) on the establishment of the Massachusetts Teen Choice Book Award, a student is quoted after returning a book, "Why did that win an award? I had such a hard time getting into it! It seems that all these books that are award-winning are not ones that I would pick up to read!" (p. 27).

The reasons for the effectiveness of readers' choice programs begin with the enthusiastic approach to reading and the positive interactions with other students and adults who are reading the same books. These factors alone contribute to students' psychological need of relatedness, which contributes to intrinsic motivation (Crow, 2010). The other significant factor is the choice of which book to read or whether to participate at all. Crow (2010) encourages librarians and teachers never to require students to read the books on the list or to read only the books on the list. She emphasizes, "When participation is voluntary, when children can choose which books to read, and when there are plenty of copies available, the autonomy support aspects of the program are enhanced and [students] are more likely to participate" (p. 13).

Since 1940, students in states around the country have been participating in readers' choice awards. The oldest contest is the Pacific Northwest Library Association's Young Reader's Choice Award, in which students from five states, Alaska, Idaho, Montana, Oregon, and Washington, and two Canadian provinces participate (Hilbun & Claes, 2007). According to Hilbun and Claes (2007), this award was established by a Seattle bookseller, Harry Hartman, and remains the only program to serve multiple states.

All states now have some form of student readers' choice program, though one, Mississippi, currently involves only students in grades 3–5. Plans to expand the program to higher grades have been announced on the website. Kansas was the first individual state to involve students in choosing favorite books, establishing the William Allen White Children's Book Award in 1952 (Hilbun & Claes, 2007). The sponsoring organization for this award is Emporia State University.

Sponsoring organizations for the various programs include school library professional organizations, state libraries, public libraries, state affiliates of IRA, as well as universities. Many awards are sponsored by multiple organizations. Students in some states have the option of voting in public libraries or school libraries.

Another variable in the state programs is the nominating process for selecting books for inclusion on the annual list. The titles for some lists are chosen exclusively by librarians and teachers, school, university, or public, while students have partial or complete input into the lists in other states.

Logos, bookmarks, brochures, ballots, and annotated lists are commonly provided by states for use in implementing the programs. Online voting procedures simplify the work of the committees and speed up the process of determining winners in some states. Several states offer curriculum activities to encourage the integration of the reading programs into classroom routines. Creating these materials facilitates the use of the multiple copies of books in classrooms in subsequent years, in literature circles, or other activities.

The following chart compiles details of the programs implemented in all 50 states and regions. Many states offer multiple programs, often from different organizations. At least four online sites include data on the student choice awards and have been helpful in collecting information: Cynthia Leitich Smith's Childrens' and YA Literature Resources; *The Horn Book*: State and Regional Awards; McBookwords: State and Regional Book Awards; and TeachingBooks.net, a subscription service. Web addresses for these sites are included at the end of the chart. Perhaps the details from the various state awards will provide you with fresh ideas for your own programs!

Reading Motivation Programs

Many schools across the country use a reading motivation program with computerized management components such as Accelerated Reader (AR) or Reading Counts (RC), for the purposes of improving reading comprehension and encouraging students to read. Each program offers a computerized test to establish a student's reading level, the Star Reading Assessment for AR and the Scholastic Reading Inventory (SRI) for RC. Text reading levels are set by the ATOS reading formula for AR (Cregar, 2011) and the Lexile Framework for Reading for RC (Harvey, 2011). Though school library leaders and practitioners have sharply divided opinions on this topic, many school librarians find themselves in situations in which support of the local reading initiative is a job requirement. An ebb and flow of the popularity and implementation of these programs continues from district to district, but they are still widely used. The topic continues to be debated in professional journals.

These reading motivation programs are described in a variety of ways in the educational literature. Descriptions include "recreational reading management" (Balajthy, 2007); "elaborate commercial programs" (Kohn, 2010); "leveled reading program" (Cregar, 2011); "reward programs" (Fisher, 2008); "'forced' reading incentive" (Small, 2009); and "text leveling system" (Harvey, 2011). Essentially, AR and RC are reading improvement programs based on establishing an individual reading level score for a student through a computerized reading comprehension test; prescribing books to be read by matching books with

State Readers' Choice Programs Table

State	Title	Levels	Sponsor	Resources
Alabama	Camellia Children's Choice Book Award: http://alex.state.al.us/librarymedia/Emphasi sonReading.html	Grades 4–6	Alabama Library Media Online	Activity Guide
Alaska	Pacific Northwest Library Association's Young Reader's Choice Award: http://www.pnla.org/yrca/index.htm	Junior Division: Grades 4–6; Intermediate Division: Grades 7–9; Senior Division: Grades 10–12	The Pacific Northwest Library Association	Discussion Guides
Arizona	Grand Canyon Young Reader Award: http://www.grandcanyonreaderaward.org/	Tween Books; Teen Books	Arizona Library Association	
Arkansas	Charlie Mae Simon Children's Book Award Arkansas Teen Book Award: http://www.library.arkansas.gov/Childrens BookAwards/Pages/default.aspx	Grades 4–6. Level 1 Grades 7–9 Level 2 Grades 10–12	Arkansas State Library Public Librarians; School Library Media Specialists	
California	Young Reader Medal Young Adult Picture Books for Older Readers: http://www.californiayoungreadermedal.org/	Middle School/Junior High Grades 4 up	California Association of Teachers of English; California Library Association; California Reading Association; California School Library Association	Resource Book Includes Readers' Theatre Scripts
Colorado	Blue Spruce Young Adult Book Award: http://cal-webs.org/bluespruce/		Colorado Association of Libraries; Colorado Council for International Reading Association; Colorado Language Arts Society	

Connecticut	Connecticut's Nutmeg Book Award: http://www.nutmegaward.org/	Intermediate List; Teen List	Connecticut Library Association; Connecticut Association of School Librarians	
Delaware	Blue Hen Award: Teen Books: http://wilmlib.org/bluehenteen.html	Ages 12 up	Children's Services Division of the Delaware Library Association; Public Library	
Florida	Sunshine State Young Readers Award: http://myssyra.org/ Florida Teens Read: http://www.floridamedia.org/?page=Flo_Teen_Gen_Info	Grades 6–8 Grades 9–12	Florida Association for Media in Education	Activity & Resource Guide
Georgia	Georgia Children's Book Award: Middle Grade Novels: http://gcbac.com/ Georgia Peach Award for Teen Readers: http://www.glma-inc.org/peachaward.htm	Grades 4–8 Grades 9–12	Department of Language and Literacy Education. University of Georgia; Georgia Department of Education Georgia Library Media Association; Georgia Library Association; Georgia Public Library Service; Georgia Association of Educators	
Hawai'i	Nene Award: http://hla.chaminade.edu/programs/nene.html	Grades 4–6	Hawai'i Association of School Libraries, Hawai'i Library Association, Hawai'i State Teachers Association	
Idaho	Pacific Northwest Library Association's Young Reader's Choice Award: http://www.pnla.org/yrca/index.htm	Junior Division: Grades 4–6; Intermediate Division: Grades 7–9; Senior Division: Grades 10–12	The Pacific Northwest Library Association	Discussion Guides

(Continued)

State Readers' Choice Programs Table

State	Title	Levels	Sponsor	Resources
Illinois	Rebecca Caudill Young Readers Award: http://www.rcyrba.org/ Abraham Lincoln Award: Illinois High School Readers' Choice Award: http://www.islma.org/lincoln.htm	Grades 4–8 Grades 9–12	Illinois Association of Teachers of English; Illinois Reading Council; Illinois School Library Media Association Illinois School Library Media Association	Activities Guide Battle of the Books Wiki
Indiana	Young Hoosier Book Award: http://www.ilfonline.org/yhba/about-yhba/ Eliot Rosewater (Rosie) High School Book Award: http://www.ilfonline.org/programs-awards/eliot-rosewater-indiana-high-school-book-award/	Middle School High School	Association of Indiana School Library Educators Indiana Library Federation	
Iowa	Iowa Teen Award: http://awards.iasl.io-wapages.org/id2.html Iowa High School Book Award: http://awards.iasl.iowapages.org/id3.html	Grades 6–9 Grades 9–12	Iowa Association of School Librarians	
Kansas	William Allen White Children's Book Awards Kansas: http://www.emporia.edu/libsv/wawbookaward/	Grades 6–8	Kansas Emporia State College	Curriculum Guides
Kentucky	Kentucky Bluegrass Award: http://kba.nku.edu/	Grades 6–8 Grades 9–12	Kentucky Reading Association Kentucky School Media Association	Book Summary PowerPoints
Louisiana	Young Readers' Choice Award: http://www.state.lib.la.us/literacy-and-reading/louisiana-young-readers-choice Teen Readers' Choice Award: http://www.state.lib.la.us/ltrc2012/	Grades 6–8 Grades 9–12	State Library of Louisiana	Study Guides Book talks

			Websites of Interest
Maine	Maine Student Book Award: http://efolio. umeedu.maine.edu/~masl/msba/	Grades 4–8	Maine Library Association; Maine Association of School Librarians
Maryland	Black-Eyed Susan Book Award: http://www. maslmd.org/	Grades 6–9 High School	Maryland Association of School Librarians
Massachu- setts	Massachusetts Children's Book Award: http://www.salemstate.edu/academics/ schools/3698.php	Grades 4–6	Salem State University
Michigan	Great Lakes Book Award: http://www.michi ganreading.org/index.php?option=com_con tent&view=article&id=93&Itemid=43 Thumbs Up! Award: http://www.mla.lib. mi.us/awards	Grades 6–8; Grades 9–12 Ages 12–18	Michigan Reading Associa- tion Michigan Library Associa- tion
Minnesota	Maud Hart Lovelace Award: http://www. maudhartlovelace.org/	Division II Grades 4–8	Minnesota Youth Reading Awards
Mississippi	Magnolia Award: Mississippi Children's Choice Award: http://www.usm.edu/bookfest/ MagInfo.htm	Currently Grades 3–5, with plans for expan- sion	Mississippi Department of Education; Mississippi Library Commission; Mississippi Reading As- sociation; University of Southern Mississippi
Missouri	Mark Twain Readers Award: http://www. maslonline.org/?page=marktwain_readers Truman Readers Award: http://www.maslon line.org/?page=truman_award Gateway Readers Award: http://www.maslon line.org/?page=gateway_readers	Grades 4–6 Grades 6–8 Grades 9–12	Missouri Association of School Librarians

(Continued)

	State Readers' Choice Programs Table			
State	**Title**	**Levels**	**Sponsor**	**Resources**
Montana	Pacific Northwest Library Association's Young Reader's Choice Award: http://www.pnla.org/yrca/index.htm	Junior Division: Grades 4–6 Intermediate Division: Grades 7–9 Senior Division: Grades 10–12	The Pacific Northwest Library Association	Discussion Guides
Nebraska	Golden Sower Award: http://www.nebraskalibraries.org/goldensower/	Grades 3–6; Intermediate Grades 4–6; Young Adult Grades 6–9	Nebraska Library Association/School Children's and Young People's Section	
Nevada	Nevada Young Readers' Award: http://www.nevadalibraries.org/Divisions/NYRA/	Intermediate Grades 6–8 Young Adult Grades 9–12	Nevada Library Association	
New Hampshire	The Flume Teen Reader's Choice: http://www.nashua.lib.nh.us/YALS/Flume.htm	Grades 9–12	New Hampshire Young Adult Librarians New Hampshire Library Association	
New Jersey	Garden State Teen Book Awards: http://www.njla.org/honorsawards/book/teen.html	Fiction Grades 6–8 Fiction 9–12; Nonfiction 6–12	New Jersey Library Association	
New Mexico	Land of Enchantment Award: http://www.loebookaward.com/	Young Adult. Grades 6–9	New Mexico Library Association New Mexico Council of International Reading Association	
New York	3 Apples Book Award: http://www.3applesbookaward.org/childrens/index.cfm Teen 3 Apples Book Award: http://www.3applesbookaward.org/teens/index.cfm Charlotte Award: http://www.nysreading.org/Awards/charlotte/	Grades 3–6 Grades 7–12 Middle School/High School	New York Library Association New York Library Association New York State Reading Association	

			Interesting Links
North Carolina	Young Adult Book Award: http://www.ncslma.org/bookcompetitions/yaaward/ncslmayaaward.htm	Grades 7–12	North Carolina School Library Media Association
North Dakota	Flicker Tale Children's Book Award: http://www.ndla.info/ftaward.htm	Juvenile—Grades 5–8 Nonfiction—PK–Grades 8	North Dakota Library Association—School Library and Youth Services
Ohio	Buckeye Children's Book Award: http://www.bcbookaward.info/index.htm The Teen Buckeye Book Award: http://www.bcbookaward.info/teens/index.html	Grades 6–8 Grades 9–12	Ohio Educational Library Media Association; Ohio Council of the International Reading Association; Ohio Council of Teachers of English and Language Arts; Ohio Library Council, and State Library of Ohio
Oregon	Oregon Reader's Choice Award (ORCA): http://www.olaweb.org/mc/page.do?sitePageId=109508	Intermediate Division: Middle School Senior Division: High School	Oregon Library Association; Oregon Association of School Libraries; Oregon Reading Association; Pacific Northwest Booksellers Association
Pennsylvania	Keystone to Reading Book Award: http://www.ksra.org/keystoneToReading.cfm Young Adult Book Award: http://www.ksra.org/resources.cfm	Intermediate Grades 4–6 Middle School Grades 6–8 High School Grades 9–12	Keystone State Reading Association

(Continued)

State Readers' Choice Programs Table

State	Title	Levels	Sponsor	Resources
Rhode Island	Children's Book Award: http://www.ri.net/RIEMA/bookaward.html Teen Book Award: http://www.yourlibrary.ws/ya_webpage/ritba/ritbaindex.htm	Grades 3–6 Age 12–18	Rhode Island State Council of International Reading Association; Rhode Island Library Association; Rhode Island Educational Media Association Rhode Island Library Association; Rhode Island Educational Media Association	
South Carolina	Children's Book Award: http://scasl.net/bookawards/cba.htm Junior Book Award: http://scasl.net/bookawards/jba.htm Young Adult Book Award: http://scasl.net/bookawards/yaba.htm	Grades 3–6 Grades 6–8 Grades 9–12	South Carolina Association of School Librarians	Activity Guides Podcasts PowerPoints
South Dakota	Young Adult Reading Program: http://library.sd.gov/LIB/YAS/yarp/index.aspx	Middle School High School	South Dakota Library Association	
Tennessee	Volunteer State Book Award: http://www.discoveret.org/tasl/vsba.htm	Intermediate Grades 4–6 YA Grades 7 up	Tennessee Library Association; Tennessee Association of School Librarians	
Utah	Beehive Book Awards. Utah Children's Book Award: http://www.clau.org/ Utah Children's Informational Book Award Young Adult's Book Award Poetry Book Award	Grades 3–6 Grades 3–6 Grades 7–12 Grades 7–9	Children's Literature Association of Utah	

			Discussion Questions
Vermont	Dorothy Canfield Children's Book Award: http://www.dcfaward.org/ Green Mountain Book Award: http://libraries.vermont.gov/libraries/gmba	Grades 4–8 Grades 9–12	Vermont State PTA; Vermont Department of Libraries Vermont School Library Association; Vermont Library Association; Vermont Department of Libraries	
Virginia	Virginia Readers Choice: http://www.vsra.org/VRCindex.html	Middle High	Virginia State Reading Association	
Washington	Sasquatch Award: http://old.wlma.org/book awards# Evergreen Young Adult Book Award 2012: http://www.kcls.org/evergreen/ Pacific Northwest Library Association's Young Reader's Choice Award: http://www.pnla.org/yrca/index.htm	Grades 4–8 Grades 7-12 Junior Division: Grades 4–6; Intermediate Division: Grades 7–9; Senior Division: Grades 10–12	Washington Library Media Association Washington State Young Adult Review Group Pacific Northwest Library Association	Discussion Guides
Wisconsin	Golden Archer Award: http://www.wemta.org/programs/golden_archer_awards.cfm	Middle School/Junior High	Wisconsin Educational Media and Technology Association	Battle of the Books with Golden Archer Award titles and others
Wyoming	Indian Paint Brush Award: http://www.wyla.org/paintbrush Soaring Eagle Award: http://www.wyla.org/soaringeagle/index.php	Grades 4–6 Grades 7–12	Wyoming Library Association; Wyoming State Reading Council	

273

READS Component	READS Indicator	AASL Standards for the 21st-Century Learner*	Common Core State Standards—English Language Arts**
Score reading progress			
The student will:			
5.1 Engage in literacy-based motivational programs and activities.	5.1.3 Participate in reading motivation programs with management components (e.g., *Accelerated Reader* or *Reading Counts*) (optional).	• 4.1.2 Read widely and fluently to make connections with self, the world, and previous reading. • 4.1.7 Use social networks and information tools to gather and share information. • 4.3.3 Seek opportunities for pursuing personal and aesthetic growth. • 4.4.1 Identify own areas of interest. • 4.4.6 Evaluate own ability to select resources that are engaging and appropriate for personal interests and needs.	• Reading: Informational Text—10 Read and comprehend literary nonfiction in the grade text complexity band . . . • Reading: Literature—10 Read and comprehend literature in the grade text complexity band . . . • Speaking and Listening—5 Make strategic use of digital media in presentations . . .

*Excerpted from *Standards for the 21st-Century Learner* by the American Association of School Librarians, a division of the American Library Association, copyright © 2007 American Library Association. Available for download at www.ala.org/aasl/standards. Used with permission.

** Excerpted from *Common Core State Standards for English Language Arts*. National Governors Association Center for Best Practices and Council of Chief State School Officers Commercial License. Copyright © 2010. Used with permission of NGA Center/CCSSO.

approximately the same reading level (based on ATOS levels or Lexile levels) as the student's score; and testing the student with low-level comprehension questions from the book. When students are successful on the tests for books, their reading levels are increased. Students may be rewarded for reading points accumulated individually with tangible prizes and/or grades. Team competitions may also be used to select the highest achieving class at the grade level for prizes or grades.

Text reading levels generated by the Lexile Framework for Reading are also used by schools, districts, and other educational groups to establish grade level expectations for reading. It is used by the Common Core State Standards to measure text complexity (Harvey, 2011). For example, in Appendix A of the Common Core State Standards, the Text Complexity Grade Band for Gr. 9–10 is 1080–1305, reflecting the increased college and career readiness expectations (Appendix A, p. 8).

While a comprehensive discussion of reading motivation systems is beyond the scope of this book, issues are considered from the perspective of the school librarian. The positive aspects of implementing these programs are, typically, an increase in the number of books read by students; additional time allowed for free reading; and, in many instances, improved reading scores during implementation periods. Also, students benefit from understanding what their reading level is, as calculated by the reading software, compared to grade level and testing requirements. Library circulation rates may go up when teachers are more willing to send students to the library to check out books. Also, parents may appreciate the increased accountability for reading.

Reports of negative consequences of these reading motivation systems include limitations on student choice of reading materials; some teachers insist all books checked out by students must have quizzes available and have a certain reading level. A second negative point is pressure from teachers and/or administrators to facilitate easy location of appropriate books in the library by (1) labeling books on the outside with reading level and point value, and (2) arrangement of the library collection by reading level. Many teachers and librarians report that students who enjoyed reading in the past now resent the pressure to read certain books and no longer enjoy reading for pleasure.

The lack of enthusiasm for these reading programs centers around a lack of research evidence of the success in improving reading long term and the impact on motivation to read. Leading the considerable list of educators challenging the value of Accelerated Reader is Dr. Stephen Krashen (2007). While he acknowledges the strong points of AR as surrounding students with books and providing time for independent reading, he questions the use of testing on low level facts about the books and the use of prizes for reading (Krashen, 2007). He emphasizes that proper research studies have not provided evidence of the value of these programs. He concludes: "There is still no clear data supporting the test and prize aspects of Accelerated Reader" (2007).

Dr. Ruth V. Small (2009) is most concerned about the impact of these programs on students' motivation to read. She details the results of exposing students to extrinsic rewards, or tangible items, for reading, which she believes "often undermines students' intrinsic motivation" (p. 31). She encourages school librarians to provide multiple opportunities for students to develop internal motivation to read, which support long-term reading habits. For a detailed discussion of types of reading motivation, read Dr. Small's article in the May 2009 issue of *School Library Monthly*.

The reality is that implementation of a reading motivation program requires the investment of significant financial resources. Annual charges apply for each student enrolled in the program. Book quizzes are expensive, though school districts sometimes cover these costs. In many schools, the number of computers required for determining students' reading levels and taking quizzes on books is problematic. Librarians may be pressured to use library funds for books with quizzes available, rather than purchasing the best quality titles.

The level of involvement of a librarian in the implementation of AR or Reading Counts ranges from minimal to serving as implementation leader and staff trainer, depending to some degree on the librarian's inclination and the administrator's wishes. Most librarians in schools with these programs will be involved with purchasing books and quizzes, providing guidance to students and teachers in locating titles at appropriate reading levels, modifying library catalog records to include reading program information, instruction in using the catalog to locate books by reading level, and, perhaps, applying reading program labels on books. Many librarians, by choice or assignment by an administrator, also find themselves involved in implementing rewards programs for AR or Reading Counts.

When a librarian accepted a position in a brand new elementary school in 2001, it quickly became apparent that AR would be a major component of the instructional program. The first teacher hired by the principal was a national AR trainer who was active in providing training in the school district. Fortunately, the implementation plan did not emphasize specific individual rewards for points achieved on reading test tests. In fact, the librarian was not involved in the rewards aspect of the program at all. Early in the planning of the library program, the librarian proposed that books with reading quizzes available would have an AR label on the spine with the information on reading level and points included inside the book, which was the recommendation of the district library supervisor's office. All books were shelved in the traditional easy, fiction, or nonfiction areas, not by reading level. Plans for the library program included implementation of two state reading programs for different age groups, a proactive, collaborative information literacy program integrating skills into content area units, and support of the AR program that was implemented in classrooms. Though aware of the criticism of AR by many educators, she found it possible to implement an active library agenda that provided literature and research skill activities for each grade while supporting and coexisting with an AR program implemented primarily by teachers.

After moving to a high school in another school district, this librarian found that RC was the reading program selected by the district. However, after consulting with the assistant principal in charge of curriculum, the school decision was to implement Reading Counts only when requested by a teacher. The program was used in special education and a few intensive reading classrooms. Another concern was that the school district required that all freshmen, sophomores, and juniors be tested on SRI program four times per year. The 30 computers in the library were scheduled for class use with SRI testing during many weeks of the year, significantly limiting information literacy instruction. Library orientation for freshmen could not be implemented early in the year because of the required SRI testing.

Additional issues arising at the secondary level were misunderstandings by students and teachers of the meaning of reading levels. For example, a high school junior scored 550 on an SRI test, but did not understand that this score was at a second or third grade level (Common Core State Standards, Appendix A, p. 8). Similarly, some teachers expected that high scoring students should check out only books within their SRI test reading range (e.g., Lexile 1300–1350). In fact, the library had relatively few books on that reading level. Restricting high school students to reading such books as *A Clockwork Orange* (Lexile: 1310) or *The Last of the Mohicans* (Lexile: 1350) is not recommended. If teachers placed such restrictions on students, it would mean that they might not be able to read the books on their state reader's choice programs. The Lexile ranges of typical books from recent lists are significantly below 1300 (e.g., *The Book Thief*: Lexile 730; *Thirteen Reasons Why*: 550; *The Hunger Games*: 810; *Shiver*: 740). Librarians in schools using AR, RC, SRI or Lexile levels have a responsibility to collaborate with reading coaches or language arts department heads to provide friendly, accessible explanations to students and teachers about the meaning of the reading system numbers and a broad view of the value of various types of reading.

From another perspective, a former school library supervisor in a large urban school district and state program director for library media services felt that differences of opinion between administrators, reading leaders, and librarians sometimes cause conflict within a school. Teachers, sometimes backed by administrators, wanted the library arranged so that students could quickly find books on their reading level. In one situation, the administration in a high school backed a reading specialist who wanted the entire library collection arranged by AR levels. This plan for arranging the library was implemented but later reversed as the result of a regional accrediting organization review. In such situations in secondary schools, the middle ground is to put students' long-term needs first, arranging the collection so that it is usable for research as well as recreational fiction and nonfiction reading.

Most library catalogs currently provide access to resources by reading levels and can be used to locate materials quickly. By providing instruction as needed in locating materials using call numbers in the local library, students can be also be prepared to use other libraries. Temporary displays of materials can also be used to meet immediate and specialized needs of students. For students with specialized needs, the librarian can collaborate with the teacher to create instructional sessions on locating materials, provide individualized reading guidance, and create personalized lists. A primary goal in such situations is to assist students in finding books without causing embarrassment about lack of reading skills. One partial solution that was used at the high school level was to create categories within the Destiny Library Catalog system for books within the lower reading levels (200–300 Lexile, 300–400 Lexile, etc.). Lists were printed out for teacher use and instructions provided for teachers in locating the constantly updated lists online. An additional advantage of this approach was recognizing the need for more books to match students' levels. These lists were also used with vendors to request publication of sufficient materials at an appropriate interest and developmental level for secondary students.

In summary, the school librarian's role is to consider how the library program can support schoolwide initiatives such as AR and RC and also serve the ongoing reading and learning needs of students. In an article titled "Managing Your Computerized Reading Program—Before It Manages You!" published in *School Library Media Activities Monthly* in 2006, Franklin and Stephens advise, "The library media center should support the AR or RC program as much as possible without compromising the overall development of a solid library collection and program for the entire school community" (p. 49). These programs are best used with specific populations of students at the secondary level, especially high schools. Competent and advanced readers in high school have no patience with such management systems and will be turned off reading if forced to participate in them. However, librarians need to find ways to offer amenable solutions to their colleagues seeking to improve reading skills of low-achieving students.

LIFELONG LEARNING

The intent of the READS curriculum is to create both practical and aesthetic readers. Therefore, we embrace two complementary but not identical phrases, lifelong learning and lifetime reading. We thank one of our respected professional colleagues, Teri Lesesne (2010), for reminding us of the term "lifetime reading" in *Reading Ladders: Leading Students from Where They Are to Where We'd Like Them to Be*. Our national library guidelines have switched focus from the goal of creating lifelong readers to lifelong learners (AASL. *Empowering Learners*, 2009). Our vision for young people includes the integration of both concepts into their lives to promote success in the workplace as versatile learners and in the personal aspects of reading for enjoyment and to gain wisdom from literature.

READS Component	READS Indicator	AASL *Standards for the 21st-Century Learner**	Common Core State Standards— English Language Arts**
Score reading progress			
The student will:			
5.2 Develop habits for lifelong learning	5.2.1 Maintain lifelong literacy skills by relating reading, listening, and viewing to real world situations (e.g., career and technical journals, online newscasts) and choosing a literate lifestyle (e.g., reading for pleasure and personal fulfillment).	• 2.1.3 Use strategies to draw conclusions from information and apply knowledge . . . • 3.1.2 Participate and collaborate as members of a social and intellectual network of learners. • 3.1.5 Connect learning to community issues. • 3.4.1 Assess the processes by which learning was achieved in order to revise strategies and learn more effectively in the future. • 4.1.2 Read widely and fluently to make connections with self, the world, and previous reading. • 4.4.1 Identify own areas of interest.	• Reading: Informational Text—10 Read and comprehend literary nonfiction in the grade text complexity band . . . • Reading: Literature—10 Read and comprehend literature in the grade text complexity band . . . • Speaking and Listening—1a Initiate and participate effectively in a range of collaborative discussions: Come to discussions prepared, having read and researched material . . . • Speaking and Listening—1b Initiate and participate effectively in a range of collaborative discussions: Work with peers to promote civil, democratic discussions . . . • Speaking and Listening—5 Make strategic use of digital media in presentations . . . • Writing—6 Use technology, including the Internet, to produce, publish, and update individual or shared writing products . . .

*Excerpted from *Standards for the 21st-Century Learner* by the American Association of School Librarians, a division of the American Library Association, copyright © 2007 American Library Association. Available for download at www.ala.org/aasl/standards. Used with permission.
** Excerpted from *Common Core State Standards for English Language Arts*. National Governors Association Center for Best Practices and Council of Chief State School Officers Commercial License. Copyright © 2010. Used with permission of NGA Center/CCSSO.

If implemented throughout the K-12 experience, the READS scope and sequence provides a systematic, scaffolded framework that supports the development of a wide range of literacy skills, increasing the relevancy of the library instructional and programmatic activities. The ultimate goal is to nurture and empower today's students to grow into lifelong learners.

Lifelong learning is a self-directed, purposeful process through which individuals acquire and adapt information to meet workplace challenges and personal needs; consequently, lifelong learners will consistently reevaluate their skills, beliefs, and behaviors within an ever-changing global context. The practice of lifelong learning is enabled by dispositions that include flexibility, adaptability, curiosity, and persistence (*Standards for the 21st-Century Learner*, 2007). In addition, lifelong learners will need to command a broad range of literacy skills, including reading, writing, listening, and viewing skills. These traditional literacy skills now form the basis for the broader, overarching transliteracy skills that enable students to function successfully across a wide range of literacy platforms. According to Bobbi Newman in a *School Library Journal* article titled "Innovators" (2011), the concept of transliteracy is "the ability to understand and create content on a broad range of communication media."

To understand the impact of the digital environment on reading and comprehension skills, Alan Liu from the Department of English at the University of California at Santa Barbara established the Tranliteracies Research Project. He introduced the term "transliteracies" and is continuing to focus on the evolving definition of online reading. To date, this group has established the working definition of online reading as "the experience of 'text-plus'" media by individuals and groups in digital, networked information environments. The "plus" indicates the zone of negotiation—of mutation, adaptation, cooptation, hybridization, and so forth—by which the older dialogue among print, writing, orality, and audiovisual media commonly called "text" enters into new relations with digital media and with networked communication technologies (online file). In the future, the project will be developing recommendations for best practices relating to the integration of digital media with social and reading skills.

For the school librarian, this broader concept of literacy offers many exciting opportunities to engage students in reading across platforms (both digital and print) and in creating original responses to the world—both fictional and informational. By correlating a range of digital communication methods to educational needs through in-services and collaborative teaching, the school librarian can relate literacy skills to real-world situations for students, making learning relevant to a current assignment and to lifelong learning.

Additionally, in this era of flipped classrooms (e.g., students view/listen to lectures as homework and apply skills during class time) and virtual courses, school librarians are in an excellent position to offer physical and intellectual access to resources that will enrich the in-class learning experience.

Habits for Lifelong Learning and Lifetime Reading

In a sense, most of the best practices in school librarianship that we have presented in this book are targeted at encouraging students to be lifelong learners and readers. While many professional organizations, journal articles, and books address the goals of lifelong reading and learning, most offer only general prescriptions for educators: offer rich collections of reading materials; provide choice of reading materials to students; offer personal reading advisory services to students; focus on a student's individual interests when making recommendations; make time available during the school day for reading; model reading constantly and consistently; and encourage parents and caregivers to create a multimodal, literate environment at home with many types of learning and reading resources. These recommendations typically are part of the reading motivation topic. However, few sources provide specific activities for teachers and librarians to use in engaging students in the development of these valuable habits. In this chapter, we offer specific approaches and lessons to address the development of lifelong learning and lifetime reading habits. We also integrate a focus on understanding and forming good attitudes and habits now that will be the stepping stones to a lifetime of learning, achievement, and fulfillment through reading, listening, and viewing activities.

The 2007 AASL Standards promote the value of metacognitive strategies, which offer one of the promising avenues for creating learning scenarios for young people. Most of the library literature resources on the use of metacognitive strategies with students are connected to the inquiry process and encourage reflection on the evaluation of sources, products, and research processes. This type of reflection is discussed in Chapter 10 as students develop their own creative projects and respond to the literary works of others.

In this final component of the READS Curriculum, Score, the first priority is creating conditions that enable assessment of oneself as a learner in a broad sense, reflecting on personal patterns and habits that may facilitate or limit academic and personal success. For example, students who can read at an appropriate level but choose not to read may fall behind academically and ultimately limit their options for further education.

The second priority is to call attention to the values that reading can provide over a lifetime. AASL's *Standards for the 21st-Century Learner* (2007) call for students to "show an appreciation for literature by electing to read for pleasure and expressing an interest in various literary genres" (indicator 4.2.4). Through the ongoing application of literary and artistic responses to literature developed in schools, young people will be able "to continually seek a meaningful life of loving wisdom" (p. 126, Wilhelm & Novak, 2011). We are including activities in this chapter which provide a glimpse into how reading needs and interests will change and evolve over the years of adulthood.

In the preface to the 2007 report by the National Endowment to the Arts, *To Read or Not to Read: A Question of National Consequence*, rewards for adult readers go beyond the traditional documented academic and workforce benefits. The research conducted by this organization found correlations between higher levels of adult reading and attending concerts and theatre, participating in exercise and sports, and activity in civic and community life, including voting and volunteerism (pp. 5–6).

Jane Fenn (2005), a high school principal, emphasizes the importance of school librarians taking action to promote literacy:

> The habit of reading for pleasure and information is one of the most valuable markers for future success in school and out. The habit of exploring libraries, books, and reading is the cornerstone of many life rewards. If students leave school knowing they can always find interesting reading and needed information in a library, then the goals of lifelong literacy and information literacy are well on the way to being met. (p. 51)

Reflection

The key term from the metacognitive research is reflection. Diane Ravitch (2007) defines reflection as "the process of thinking about what one is doing or what one has just finished doing. For example, students may be encouraged to reflect on their writing . . . . Reflection on one's behavior and efforts should involve self-critique, self-analysis, and self-evaluation" (p. 81). In the activities we have developed for this chapter, we are also encouraging students to consider the future consequences of the decisions they make today, in terms of completing homework, reading widely and often, and responding to classroom and standardized test scores. As part of this process, students will be evaluating their strengths and weaknesses, leading to the setting of goals to move toward independence as learners. Further, we ask students to reflect on their future lives as readers, learners, and citizens, considering how community resources can contribute to their own well-being and that of their families.

In an article intended to create a "portrait of literate readers" (p. 28) in *English Journal*, VanDeWeghe (2011) promotes the use of habits of mind. In a time when young people are constantly distracted, moving from one activity to another, VanDeWeghe observes, "Mindfulness slows learners down, forces focus, makes them notice and appreciate, in natural ways" (p. 30). The habits of mind promoted by VanDeWeghe are also often described as traits or dispositions.

A distinguishing characteristic of the *Standards for the 21st-Century Learner* is the inclusion of the strand Dispositions in Action (AASL, 2007). The definition of dispositions frequently cited by school library educators (Arnone, 2010; Jones & Dotson, 2010; Lamb, 2011) comes from Lillian G. Katz (1993): "A disposition is a tendency to exhibit frequently, consciously, and voluntarily a pattern of behavior that is directed to a broad goal" (p. 1). While all of the dispositions included in the library standards are related to lifelong learning, specific ones are displayed by lifetime readers more directly: curiosity; motivation; choice; openness to new ideas; diverse perspectives; critical stance; self-direction; social responsibility; divergent thinking; and appreciation for literature (Stripling, 2008). It is helpful to weave these personal traits into discussions with students about lifelong learning and lifetime reading, to add focus and food for thought into their reflections.

Essential Questions

The use of questioning in the work of school librarians has been primarily centered in the areas of inquiry projects and literary understanding. Recently, Judi Moreillon and Maria Cahill have provided guiding questions for multicultural books which are broad, thought-provoking, and open-ended (Moreillon & Cahill, 2010). The *Common Core Curriculum Mapping: English Language Arts* (2010) project also connects questions, which are essential questions, to literature units of study (e.g., How can we learn to appreciate our similarities and differences through literature?).

Essential questions are considered by many to be the gold standard of curriculum writing and delivery. Grant Wiggins and the Coalition of Essential Questions have been associated with essential questions for more than 30 years (McKenzie, 2005). Wiggins and McTighe (2005) define an essential question: "A question that lies at the heart of a subject or a curriculum (as opposed to being either trivial or leading), and promotes inquiry and uncoverage of a subject" (p. 342). These authors discuss the use of essential questions written by teachers or curriculum directors which are intended to focus the design of a unit of study, including goals, performance tasks, and assessments.

The development of students' questioning skills as part of the research process has been evolving over recent decades. Leaders in the school library world for development of instructional materials on the creation of essential questions by students are Jamie McKenzie and Joyce Valenza. McKenzie provides both print, *Learning to Question to Wonder to Learn* (2005), and online resources (The Question Mark: Essential Questions: http://questioning. org/index.html) for teaching students to write essential questions. Joyce Valenza (2003) also provides online (http://sdst.libguides.com/content.php?pid=184760&sid=1552990) and print materials on composing essential questions with instructions for students as well as examples.

Characteristics of Essential Questions

Broad and worthy of consideration
Concise and focused, encouraging deep thought
Express the central issues of a topic
Open-ended, arguable
Deny a simplistic answer
Relevant to students' lives
Stimulate curiosity
Evoke emotional, intellectual response
Lead to subsidiary questions that are related to and explore meaning of the essential question
Provide connections between current practices and future expectations

The use of essential questions with secondary students to stimulate thinking about literacy issues has great potential. Because essential questions encourage deep thinking on broad issues relevant to students' lives, igniting both emotional and intellectual responses to the issues, they are appropriate for use in encouraging reflective thinking on reading and learning. The writings of Wiggins and McTighe (2005) emphasize perspective and self-knowledge as "facets of understanding" (p. 120), which are promoted through the use of essential questions, supporting the use of the strategy in this context.

Middle school students can respond to essential questions designed by librarians and teachers to direct their thinking about their reading progress, to examine their reading and learning habits, and to recognize the connection between their current actions and future opportunities in high school and beyond. High school students can frame their own essential questions to examine their current performance and its impact on their future educational possibilities; to consider how their roles as readers and learners will evolve as they continue their academic journey and/or enter the workforce; and to project how reading and learning can add great dimension and richness to their adult lives.

Lesson Approaches

We have developed a variety of lesson approaches for use in libraries and/or classrooms to assist students in reflecting on and understanding the value and potential of reading and learning to make a difference in their lives. A primary intention of these activities is to increase personal accountability and capacity for independent learning in order to encourage the development of habits and dispositions that will prepare students for achievement in all areas of their lives. As we brainstormed strategies to implement these goals, we considered the following tenets about literacy development:

1. All reading and writing, both in and out of school, contributes to the development of literacy.
2. Reading in all formats, online and printed materials, contributes to the development of all types of literacy.
3. Assignments involving reading, writing, and production activities in all classes contribute to the development of literacy.
4. Assessment data collected by the school provide one indication of an individual's literacy level status but may be impacted by other factors (e.g., test anxiety, health issues, etc.).
5. Metacognitive awareness of one's literacy status can increase student motivation to learn, complete homework, and engage willingly in assessments (e.g., Star testing for AR, testing for Lexile levels, state and national reading and writing tests, local tests, etc.). To encourage students to expend maximum effort in academic endeavors, they may benefit from discussions with educators in a positive environment.

DEVELOP HABITS FOR LIFELONG LEARNING AND LIFETIME READING

Gr. 6–7   Lesson Approach: Reading Selection Options
Gr. 6–7   Lesson Approach: Thinking about Learning
Gr. 6–8   Lesson Approach: Discovering the Perfect Gift
Gr. 6–10   Lesson Approach: How Can Reading Connect You with Your Interests?
Gr. 8–10   Lesson Approach: Does Curiosity Contribute to a Rich & Fulfilling Life?
Gr. 11   Lesson Approach: Lifelong Learning & Lifetime Reading Seminar
Gr. 10–12   Lesson Approach: Thinking Ahead about Reading in a Career
Gr. 12   Lesson Approach: Envision Your Future

---

6. Linking current assessment data, effort expended in school work, and future learning and career opportunities in a positive manner may assist in focusing students on school performance and its impact on their lives.

7. The amount of fiction and informational texts read will fluctuate from time to time. This is natural for everyone. Individuals read at differing paces for multiple reasons. Quantity of text read or production of writing is not the only measure of literacy achievement.

8. A high level of literacy is typically achieved as a combination of access to multiple sources, appropriate instruction, productive habits, and encouragement from educators and others significant in a young person's life (e.g., families, peers, coaches, mentors, etc.).

LESSON APPROACH: READING SELECTION OPTIONS

Grade Levels: 6–7 grades

Overview

This activity is intended for English and Language Arts classes coming to the library every week or biweekly to check out books. The teacher will work with the librarian to provide reading guidance for students. The activity could also be adapted for classes assigned to the librarian.

Planning

1. Design and prepare simple exit passes with methods for locating books (e.g., use of catalog, browsing, displays, peer recommendation, teacher or librarian recommendation) for the session. Students will check off the method used or add other method.

2. After the session, the librarian will sort the slips by selection method to form groups of four or six with a variety of methods.

3. For the second session, prepare an exit pass with future selection strategies (online public or academic library catalog, browsing in library, library displays, peer recommendation, family recommendation, book reviews in newspapers or online, librarian recommendation), options for locating books (libraries, borrowing from friends or family, purchasing from book stores or online—Amazon, etc.), and genres of reading materials.

4. Preview online reading advisory sites from the Read Online Resources; suggest that teachers continue the discussion of reading in the future in the classroom after session 2.

5. Arrange for a local public librarian to speak to the class about adult reading choices or arrange for a Skype session with the public librarian.
6. For session 3, summarize the results of student data gathered for future reading in graphics or orally for presentation to the class.

Direct Instruction

Session 1

1. Describe several methods for locating books on the desired topic: use of catalog, browsing, displays, peer recommendation, teacher or librarian recommendation.
2. Provide time for students to select books using preferred method and check them out.
3. Have students complete an exit pass on book selection method used.
4. Collect the exit passes.

Session 2

1. Review methods for locating books and return exit slips to students.
2. Explain the jigsaw activity to students and give directions for forming groups. Within the groups, each student will describe and discuss preferred method of book selection and answer questions from group members. Each group will determine which method is used by the majority of members currently.
3. Have one member of each group report preferred methods to the class.
4. Ask students to think ahead 20 years and imagine how and where they will locate reading materials. Discuss public libraries, Oprah's book club, adult book groups, formats for reading books, and how reading interests may change in the future. Introduce and demonstrate online sites for reading selection.
5. Have students return to groups to discuss future selection strategies, expanded options for locating books, and the genres of books they expect to read as adults. Have each student complete a Future Reading Exit Pass. Encourage students to continue thinking about reading patterns 20 years in the future and to talk with their teacher, parents, and family members about adult reading habits. Collect the exit passes.
6. Encourage students to select and check out books.

Session 3

1. Present summaries of responses from students in the class during the previous session on future selection strategies, choices for locating books, and genres identified for future reading. Invite students to share their responses from the exit passes and information gathered on adult reading habits with the class.
2. Discuss and summarize the project by reflecting on future reading patterns.
3. Encourage students to select and check out books.

LESSON APPROACH: THINKING ABOUT LEARNING

Grade Level: 6–7

Overview

This lesson will encourage students to reflect on their progress as readers and writers and to link their efforts to success in high school and postsecondary education. The lesson

Literacy Log

Name: _____   Language Arts Teacher & Room: _____

Quarter: _____   Librarian: _____

Books Checked Out & Read from Library	

Books Read from Classroom Library	

Books Read in Class	

Books Read Outside of School	

Magazines Read	

Movies & Television Shows Viewed	

Websites Visited on Regular Basis	

Social Media Regularly Used	

Major Writing/Production Assignments Completed for All Classes	
Writing Outside of School	
Library Reading Program Participation	
State Student Choice Award	
Book Club	
Other Activities	
Assessment Data	
AR/Lexile Level	
State Reading Test This Year	
State Reading Test Previous Year	
Local Reading Tests	
State Writing Test Score	
Local Writing Tests	

could be used with all language arts or reading classes or could be implemented with students needing improvement in reading and writing.

Planning

The librarian and teacher will plan and implement this lesson, modifying as needed to meet the needs of students. Decide on a definition of literacy (e.g., reading, writing, listening, viewing, and other communicating skills).

Direct Instruction

1. (Project images of graduating students; high school students studying, in science labs, debating, etc.) Open lesson with "Today we will discuss your future as a student. How are you preparing now to be successful in high school? What learning habits are you using to be successful now and in life after high school?"
2. Ask students to define literacy. Add to the definition as appropriate.
3. Ask students to think about their own level of literacy. How can you judge your progress as a reader and writer? (Possible responses: grades in language arts and other classes, AR or Lexile levels, state test scores, numbers of books checked out and read).

4. Present scenarios of two students at varied achievement levels and ask students to suggest numbers for a Literacy Progress Log for each, with students supplying typical scores and numbers. Demonstrate, filling in a sample Literacy Log form for Student A (low achieving) and Student B (high achieving).

5. Question class about how Student A could improve her or his level of literacy. (e.g., complete all assignments; participate in class discussions; increase independent reading; checking out library books on personal reading level in addition to books on personal interests; meeting with reading or language arts teacher to discuss progress; joining a tutoring group; participating in literacy programs such as state readers' choice programs; joining a reading club; talking with parents about need to improve reading and writing skills).

6. Discuss the role of the library program in supporting student learning.

7. Inform students that their teacher will provide a Literacy Log form in class to be used to track progress as a learner. Invite students to bring their form to the library to complete the section on number of books checked out so far this school year. From this point on, students will fill out the log with library books and other books read.

8. Advise students as they select books to check out.

LESSON APPROACH: DISCOVERING THE PERFECT GIFT

Grade Level: 6–8

Overview

This lesson is intended to stimulate students to think about the interests and needs of others and to make appropriate reading choices for friends, relatives, and other adults in their lives. Participation in this activity will create an opportunity for students to reflect on the value of lifelong reading and learning. The final part of the assignment requires students to reflect on their own interests and characteristics and to project reading gifts they would like to receive at the age of 30, 40, or 50.

Planning

1. Schedule this activity for several weeks or a month before the winter holidays. The activity could be adapted for birthdays and used at another time of the year.

2. Prepare the Selecting a Perfect Gift assignment on a wiki, website, or in paper format. If on paper, provide three copies of the Family & Friends Profile Form.

Direct Instruction

Session 1

1. Introduce the holiday giving season with musical selections, scenes from shopping malls, or family holiday gatherings with gifts. Ask students how they are preparing for the holidays. Invite them to join you in an activity to plan ahead for the holidays.

2. Provide examples of people on your shopping list. Describe interests and traits or dispositions of each person. Ask students to help you think of perfect gifts for this person. Specify that each person will receive a book, magazine, song, and website suggestion. Discuss the tradition of giving no-cost gifts, such as a poem or especially selected website, that will have special meaning to the recipient.

3. Offer these or your own examples: Uncle Harry likes sports and fishing; he takes vacations every summer in his RV, traveling to different locations in North America. Uncle

Harry is outgoing and confident, making new friends wherever he travels. Erica, your daughter, loves fashions and makeup. She is in college and planning a career in acting or fashion merchandising. Erica is creative and curious as well as determined to persevere in getting a job in one of her preferred career fields. Record recommendations for gifts (e.g., a book, magazine, song, and website) for each person from students, prompting their thinking as needed.

4. Project assignment on a screen or monitor and discuss the various elements of the project. Instruct students to complete the project in class with their teacher or at home.

Session 2

1. Express your curiosity in what students selected as gifts for family, friends, and themselves. Add that you are hoping to gather some ideas for people on your own shopping list.

2. Assign students to work in groups of four or six to share their ideas for gift giving and receiving. Each group will select the three best gifts for friends, for family members, and the two best gift request ideas. A representative from each group will be selected to announce the choices to the class.

3. Ask students to reflect on what they have learned about making choices about reading throughout a lifetime. If appropriate for the class, use a writing model (e.g., I have learned _____; The reason for this opinion is _____.). Conclude the session by wishing the students a pleasant and thoughtful shopping experience and happy holidays!

DISCOVERING THE PERFECT GIFT ASSIGNMENT

Create your holiday shopping list by analyzing the interests and needs of the people on your list. Select three people from different age groups for your hypothetical shopping list; only one person can be under 20 years of age. Complete the Family & Friends Profile for each of the three people and select two possible gift items related to reading. Finally, make out a gift request list for yourself at some point in the future, using the Personal Profile Form. Select a topic for the website suggestion. All gifts selected and requested must be under $50.00 in today's market!

Family & Friends Profile Form

1. Name of gift recipient:
2. Personal interests:
3. Needs and life situation including age:
4. Personal traits/dispositions:
5. Gift item choices (book, magazine, song, website):
6. Rationale for gift choices:

Personal Profile Form

1. Your name:
2. Age for project (30, 40, 50):
3. Personal interests:
4. Needs and life situation:

5. Personal traits/dispositions
6. Gift item choices (book, magazine, song, website topic):
7. Rationale for requesting the gifts:

LESSON APPROACH: HOW CAN READING CONNECT YOU WITH YOUR INTERESTS?

Grade Level: 6–10

Overview

This activity encourages students to think about personal interests that can provide life-long reading pleasure.

Planning

Duplicate the worksheet, modifying it as appropriate. Plan an example relating metacognitive concepts. For example: Gardening.

1. Consider how your interest in the topic evolved. (Activate prior knowledge and experience.) My grandmother had a wonderful garden and shared her knowledge of plants.
2. Maintain interest through practice and learning. (Read widely and consult experts.) Create pleasing landscapes with favorite plants and visit gardens when traveling. Before visiting a formal garden, read about it, so that a mental framework is created, enabling a higher level of comprehension of descriptions by the guide.
3. Plan an extended tour of gardens, led by an expert in horticulture, garden history, and landscape design. (Monitor, evaluate, and adjust learning processes.) Complete recommended reading and viewing before the trip to increase background knowledge of types and design of gardens and plants used in the region.

Source consulted: Dunlap, J. C. (2005).

Direct Instruction

1. Open lesson by displaying books on the hobbies and interests of a popular teacher in school or a celebrity. Introduce topic of learning about hobbies by reading. Describe your own hobbies and how reading about them provides knowledge and pleasure.
2. Relate metacognitive concepts to reading for personal interests, using an example of one of your interests.
3. Encourage students to think about their own interests and how they could find reading materials on those topics. Project the topics from the worksheet and ask students to add any other broad topic areas. Suggest that students think about their own family members and the interests that bring them pleasure throughout their lives.
4. Inform students that each will locate three books, three websites, one magazine, and one other item (song, craft, etc.) on the interest or hobby.
5. Review as needed how to use the school library and public library catalogs and the use of appropriate subject headings in the catalogs, databases, and search engines.
6. Provide time for use of computers and other electronic devices to locate resources, assisting as needed.
7. Have students exchange papers with table mates to gain other ideas for information sources.

HOW CAN READING CONNECT YOU WITH YOUR INTERESTS?

Locate three books, three websites, one magazine, and at least one other resource on your interest or hobby.

Areas of Interest or Hobby: Sports, the Arts (specific areas), Nature, Literature (specific areas), Culture (specific country), Geography, History

Personal Interest Selected: _____

Books (3)

Websites (3)

Magazine (1) Suggested source: http://www.thepaperboy.com/

Other (1) (e.g., song, craft, etc.)

LESSON APPROACH: DOES CURIOSITY CONTRIBUTE TO A RICH AND FULFILLING LIFE?

Grade Level: 9–10

Overview

Students will interview the elders in their lives (or others) to discover their interests and the sources used to learn about their interests. Students will research the interests of the elders to recommend additional learning sources.

Planning

1. Prepare a Personal Curiosity Log for students to use to record responses to questions asked during the class, altering the form provided as appropriate.
2. Gather images showing elders involved in hobbies to engage students in the topic and to stimulate their thinking about the typical activities of adults beyond the workplace and during the retirement years.

Direct Instruction

Session 1

1. Open the lesson by sharing an anecdote from your life about investigating one of your ongoing interests and the pleasure it brings to you. Share how you became curious about this interest and why you have maintained interest in the topic over the years. Briefly describe curiosity as a desirable disposition or habit that can be a positive force in one's life.

	Personal Curiosity Log	
1.	What are you curious about? List three different ongoing interests.	
2.	Select one of the topics you listed above. _____ Why are you curious about this topic?	
3.	Which learning formats do you use now to follow your interest?	
4.	Which learning formats do you expect to use to follow your interest in the future?	
5.	Reflect on your choice of an interest and learning format after your discussion with an elder. Would you change any of your responses now?	

2. Ask students to list on the Personal Curiosity Log at least three topics about which they are curious and lead a discussion on how they learn about their interests.
3. Direct students to choose one of their interests that they expect to continue to follow as an adult. Have students write several sentences about why they are curious about this topic.
4. Query students about which learning modes they expect to use in the future to keep up with their interests. Have them record this information on the Personal Curiosity Log.
5. Ask students "What are the elders in your life curious about? What do they want to learn?" Show images of elders involved in hobbies.
6. Provide an example of an elderly person who has passionate interests and continues to learn about the topics. Describe some of the ways that the elder continues to learn about the hobby or interest. Invite students to suggest additional ways that the elder could learn about the topic.
7. Ask students to consider any limitations elders may have in pursuing their interests. Suggest that students may possess technology and communication skills that elders do not have.

8. Explain project of interviewing elders about their interests and methods used to continue learning about the interests.
9. Encourage students to contact you with questions about the assignment. Inform students that the group will meet again to share information gathered during their interviews.

Session 2

1. Open a dialogue about students' interview project, asking volunteers to share their findings.
2. Direct one student to record on the board the interests of elders discovered by classmates.
3. Continue the dialogue by asking students to identify the methods used to continue learning about their interests. Have another student record the methods used for learning.
4. Ask students if they detected any limitations experienced by elders in continuing to learn about their interests. Have a different student serve as a scribe to record the limitations.
5. Query students about responses to the question on whether the person felt that following the interest contributed to a rich and fulfilling life.
6. Inquire if any elders were not comfortable with use of the Internet (if this point did not emerge as a limitation in the earlier discussion).
7. Challenge students to continue working with the elder person to suggest additional ways of learning about their interests, such as websites on the Internet.

LESSON APPROACH: LIFELONG READING AND LEARNING SEMINAR

Grade Level: 11

Overview

This small group activity is designed to stimulate students to reflect on their current status and future as readers and learners. To be most productive, it should be collaboratively planned and implemented by a teacher and the school librarian. It could be implemented in a learning center approach, with other students in the class checking out books, researching other topics, and so forth, in the library or classroom. It is important for the teacher and the school librarian to participate in the discussion.

Planning

Working with a teacher, edit, modify, or add questions to fit the learning profile of the group of students.

Direct Instruction

1. Introduce the practice of reflective thinking about reading and learning now and after high school.
2. Distribute the Reflection on Reading & Learning survey to students to complete individually. Inform them that the questions will be discussed in a small group on a voluntary basis.
3. Facilitate the discussion, asking probing questions as appropriate.

4. Conclude discussion with these questions: Did you expand your thinking about the role of reading in your future? How?

5. Encourage students to participate in library activities and to consult with the school librarian and teacher for reading and learning guidance.

Reflection on Reading and Learning

1. I have the reading skills I need to handle research challenges effectively and efficiently.

   Strongly agree ___ Agree ___ Disagree ___ Strongly disagree ___

2. I have the information finding skills I need to handle research challenges effectively and efficiently.

   Strongly agree ___ Agree ___ Disagree ___ Strongly disagree ___

3. I have the writing skills I need to handle research challenges effectively and efficiently.

   Strongly agree ___ Agree ___ Disagree ___ Strongly disagree ___

4. I explore important questions and issues arising out of the content of this class.

   Strongly agree ___ Agree ___ Disagree ___ Strongly disagree ___

5. The work we do in class and the tasks we must perform are going to prepare me for my life as an adult—both as a worker and as a community member.

   Strongly agree ___ Agree ___ Disagree ___ Strongly disagree ___

6. I currently read fiction in a variety of formats for pleasure.

   Strongly agree ___ Agree ___ Disagree ___ Strongly disagree ___

7. I currently read informational text in a variety of formats for pleasure.

   Strongly agree ___ Agree ___ Disagree ___ Strongly disagree ___

8. I expect to continue reading as an adult for pleasure.

   Strongly agree ___ Agree ___ Disagree ___ Strongly disagree ___

9. I expect to continue reading as an adult to learn about my career field, interests, and hobbies.

   Strongly agree ___ Agree ___ Disagree ___ Strongly disagree ___

10. I expect to continue reading as an adult to gain perspective on my life and to learn about others.

    Strongly agree ___ Agree ___ Disagree ___ Strongly disagree ___

Note: The first five questions on this survey appear in Appendix A of *Learning to Question to Wonder to Learn* by Jamie McKenzie (2005) and are used with his permission.

LESSON APPROACH: THINKING AHEAD ABOUT READING IN A CAREER

Grade Level: 10–12

Previous Instruction

Previous lessons on use of community resources (e.g., public library catalog, databases provided by state, other community libraries online resources, real-world genres, services of government agencies).

	Job Info	Housing	Education or Training	Recreation Hobbies/ Travel	Health & Fitness	Schooling for Children	Consumer Data
Public Library							
Academic Library							
State or Federal Websites							
Social Networks							
Newspapers & Magazines							
Online Sources							

REAL-WORLD REFLECTION

1. Select the three most crucial information needs from the seven listed on the matrix.
2. Justify your choices of information sources for the three most important information needs.
3. How can your teachers and the library staff assist you in preparing for your literacy needs of the future?

Planning

Create life scenarios 10 years in the future: professional athlete, local government worker and part-time sports coach, park ranger, small business owner, clerk in a clothing store, teacher, scientist, actor/actress, musician, construction worker, job seeker, waiter/waitress, child care worker, writer, commercial fisherman.

Create matrix for reading/information need and reading/information sources.
Devise rubric for assessment.

Direct Instruction

1. Introduce project of planning ahead for reading and learning needs in future career and life situations.
2. Demonstrate various sources for practical, personal, and career information.
3. Explain project. Direct students to work individually or in pairs to select a scenario or to develop their own career path, subject to teacher approval.
4. Provide directions on researching and completing matrix.
5. Have students complete the Real-World Reflection Form.

LESSON APPROACH: ENVISION YOUR FUTURE

Grade Level: 12

Overview

This lesson targets lifelong reading and learning, including the evolving formats of reading resources. Students will be stimulated to think about their future and how they will read and learn. Students will be required to write an essential question and to select a habit or mind or disposition that will most useful in creating a satisfying adult life.

Planning

1. Collaborate with the teacher to determine the need for teaching students to write essential questions. If students are experienced with this task, you may not need to use this section of the lesson.
2. Select an essential question to deconstruct to teach the process of creating thoughtful questions. For example: How do excellent literacy skills prepare you for a good life? Possible responses from students include: underlying or subsidiary questions: What is a good life and what are excellent reading skills? Possible qualities of a good life include: education that you want, meaningful job, financial security, satisfying family life, rewarding interests and hobbies, participation in community, and contribution to society. Excellent reading skills include the ability to read to meet the requirements of a desired lifestyle.

Direct Instruction

Session 1

1. Open the lesson with this statement or a variation: "Today we are focusing on your future. How are you going to read and learn in the future?" Ask students to identify the assumptions in this question. (Typical responses: We will read and learn in the future. We will have a choice of reading formats.) Use probing questions if needed to explore the topics.
2. Ask students to list the advantages of continuing to read in post-secondary life, recording responses. Follow up with a question and discussion about various types of reading (e.g., light reading to pass the time; reading to learn a practical skill or how to use a product; reading to learn content for a test; reading to experience current and classic literature; reading to learn about one's community, country, world; reading to prepare for active role as a citizen (e.g., voting, reading to prepare for travel, deep reading to ponder human issues, relationships, etc.)
3. Propose the use of essential questions to encourage deep thinking about issues of major concern. Ask students how they have used essential questions in other classes. Describe essential questions as broad, overview questions without simple answers and which encourage thinking on important issues. Essential questions lead to more direct and specific questions related to the broad issue called subsidiary questions.
4. Deconstruct an essential question, identifying the underlying issues: How do excellent reading skills prepare you for a good life? Describe the subsidiary questions (e.g., what is a good life and what are excellent reading skills?). Question students on the qualities of a good life and excellent reading skills, supplementing responses as needed.

Structuring Essential Questions

Essential questions address the big questions in life, fields of knowledge, and society, focusing on broad concepts without simple "yes" or "no" answers. These questions may never be answered, but stimulate curiosity, analysis, and reflection on the issues. They often begin with what, how, or why, seek to answer "so what?", and are open to debate. Subsidiary questions address an aspect of the essential question.

Essential Questions to Stimulate Reflection		
Question Stems	**Question Example**	**Subsidiary Questions**
What? (Identifies a broad question and leads search for answers)	What is a friend? What is my role in creating a literate community?	What are the characteristics of a friend? What can I do to become a friend? What are the elements of literacy? What can I do to improve educational opportunities in my community? What is needed in my community to improve educational opportunities for all?
How? (Examines conditions and problems, identifying facts, possibilities, and solutions)	How will my actions today impact my health in the future? How does literature provide guidance for our lives?	What are healthy habits? What habits do I have that could cause harm to my body in the future? How can I learn to conduct my life from reading biographies? How can the decisions made by another person influence my actions?
What if? (Presents a hypothetical scenario to examine issues and options)	What if I could start over in middle school?	What if I had changed/improved my attitudes toward school and reading in 6th grade? How can I help other family members or students understand the importance of reading, engaging in lessons, and school attendance in 6th grade? What can I do now to improve my chances of succeeding in college? What can I do now to learn more about the world?
Should? (Requires a practical or moral position based on examining evidence)	Should all high school students take a life management course? Should the government provide technological resources for families without them to equalize learning opportunities for all?	What topics would be included in a life management course? Would the skills taught in a life management class help students make good decisions about finances, time management, healthy eating, and caring for a dorm room or apartment? How many families do not have technological resources in their homes? How do technological resources contribute to equalizing learning opportunities? What institutions in the community provide technological resources for public use?
Why? (Focus on cause and effect, analysis of issues, understanding of world and others)	Why is the United States falling behind many other countries in education? Why is curiosity essential to a good life?	How is educational accomplishment measured? What is the position of the United States in various measurements of educational accomplishment? What is the length of the school day and school year in various countries? How does curiosity lead to learning?
Adapted in part from Valenza, J. Asking Good Questions.		

5. Provide guidelines for writing essential questions, using the Structuring Essential Questions resource page. Suggest that students begin questions with what, how, what if, should, or why.
6. Inform students that each will construct an essential question. Organize students into groups to share ideas on various aspects of reading formats and lifelong reading and learning before writing their own question. Students will bring completed essential and subsidiary questions to the next session.

Session 2

1. Review the topic of reading and learning in the future. Ask students to share their questions on a volunteer basis. Collect questions.
2. Challenge students to think about reading throughout their lives and to consider which habits of mind or dispositions will be required to read for a productive career and for pleasure. Display these words: initiative, curiosity, confidence, questioning, self-direction, productivity, persistence, motivation, critical stance, perseverance. Direct students to select one word and write a short essay describing how this disposition or characteristic will be helpful in establishing lifelong reading habits.
3. Encourage students to continue reflecting on the role of reading in their lives with a bibliography of books and articles on the topic.

Mini-Lesson Ideas for Lifetime Reading and Lifelong Learning

These ideas could be shared with teachers or used in combination with other activities (e.g., circulation sessions, orientations, etc.).

- Thoughtful questions: Which fiction book that you read this year prepares you for life? Which nonfiction book that you read prepares you for life?
- Brainstorm a list of careers with students. Pair careers with similar reading demands (e.g., attorney and journalist, farmer and fisherman). Pairs of students will prepare and debate which career will require more reading and learning, (e.g., as a park ranger, I will use reading skills more than . . . because . . .).
- Request students to keep a reading log for a week of materials read outside of school, including the format of the reading. Next, have students envision themselves in 10 years and project what they would be reading outside of the workplace, including format. Discuss ideas generated by various students.
- Provide a variety of quotations on the value of reading. Have students select one of the quotations and respond to it. Alternatively, have students find websites for quotations on reading, select their quote, and respond to it. (See Gallagher, 2003, pp. 46–47.)
- Edge, a website for technology and advanced thinking, proposes an annual question. The query for 2010 was "How is the Internet changing the way you think?" More than 170 responses to the question are posted on the site. Working in pairs, have students go to the website (http://edge.org/responses/how-is-the-internet-changing-the-way-you-think), select a response to the question, and support it to the class or have students write an original response to the question.

- Challenge a book club or other group to create reading motivation posters or signs for younger students. Feature their products in morning announcements, in displays in the library, as part of reading events, or in the cafeteria. Highlight the contribution of students to the development of a literate community.

- Have students work in groups to identify life challenges after high school in various situations and stages of life. Create a list with information sources in multiple formats. Jeffrey Wilhelm (2008) refers to similar lists as "Life's Little Instruction Calendar of Ideas or Suggestions for Better Living" (p. 214).

- Compile a diverse collection of excerpts from resources (e.g., biographies, memoirs, interviews, podcasts, etc.) in which individuals comment on the value of reading in their lives (adapted from Browne, Hirsh, & Koehler, 2011). Working in groups, direct students to read a comprehensive list of reasons to read, then share these with the class.

CODA: OPEN QUESTIONS AND FINAL THOUGHTS

Having explored hundreds of topics in this book and provided considerable background information on many of them with the intention of preparing librarians to earn the professional respect of their faculty and administrators with their knowledge of literacy concepts, one may still be curious about many of the big issues confronting our profession today. This disposition or theme of curiosity is key to the future of school librarianship and to our own lives. Several recent articles have focused on dispositions displayed by school librarians (Bush & Jones, 2011; Fontichiaro, 2008; Levitov, 2011). The most vital of the AASL dispositions for the continuation of a strong role of the librarian in a school is, first and foremost, curiosity. Many questions have bubbled to the surface while exploring the READS themes through conference sessions and the literature of librarianship, reading, and language arts and sometimes social studies:

- How can a single librarian make a difference in one school? That question intensifies for the many librarians now assigned to multiple schools. Many possibilities have been identified for impacting students' lives and teachers' professional lives, but the final choice of activities is up to the local librarian and administration based on local conditions and priorities.

- How will the implementation of the Common Core Curriculum impact the work of school librarians? The correlation charts from the Common Core Curriculum to the READS Curriculum start the process, but much more thought needs to be directed to this question. A corollary issue is the changing role of nonfiction in library activities, which is a key point in the Common Core Curriculum. You may wish to follow Marc Aronson's blog, Nonfiction Matters (http://blog.schoollibraryjournal.com/nonfiction matters/author/marcaronson/), as he thoughtfully, expertly, and eloquently addresses this question.

- How can the READS Curriculum be implemented in elementary schools? It will be easier to envision and plan the balanced approach to reading activities at the elementary level because of easier access to students and teachers and increased participation by parents. Because some states (e.g., Florida) are already phasing in the implementation of the Common Core Standards beginning in kindergarten, the need for elementary curricula and examples is crucial.

LITERACY-FOCUSED BLOGS

AASL Blog. http://www.aasl.ala.org/aaslblog/
ALSC Blog. Association for Library Services to Children. http://www.alsc.ala.org/blog/
Audiobooker. Mary Burkey. http://audiobooker.booklistonline.com/
The Blue Skunk Blog. Doug Johnson. http://doug-johnson.squarespace.com/
Bookends. Cindy Dobrez and Lynn Rutan. http://bookends.booklistonline.com/
e-Literate Librarian. Tamara Cox. http://www.e-literatelibrarian.blogspot.com/
The Goddess of YA Literature. Teri Lesesne. http://professornana.livejournal.com/
The Hub: Your Connection to Teen Reads. YALSA. http://www.yalsa.ala.org/thehub/
I.N.K. Interesting Nonfiction for Kids. http://inkrethink.blogspot.com/
Kathy Schrock's Kaffeeklatsch. Kathy Schrock. http://blog.kathyschrock.net/
Neverending Search. Joyce Valenza. http://blog.schoollibraryjournal.com/neverendingsearch
Nonfiction Matters. Marc Aronson. http://blog.schoollibraryjournal.com/nonfictionmatters/author/
    marcaronson/
The Unquiet Librarian. Buffy Hamilton. http://theunquietlibrarian.wordpress.com/
YA Books and More. Naomi Bates. http://naomibates.blogspot.com/
YALSABlog. Young Adult Library Services. http://yalsa.ala.org/blog/

- How can the delivery of a reading program such as described in this book contribute to the development of a librarian into a building level leader? While this has occasionally been commented on, the leadership characteristics emerging from implementation of the READS program, would take more space and time to pursue this theme.
- How will implementation of activities with students targeting the development of dispositions impact their attitudes toward their daily work, lifetime reading, and lifelong learning? The use of a survey to measure student attitudes before and after implementation of activities could provide helpful data.
- How can student-created essential questions be used as a tool for increasing self-awareness of the value and impact of reading, good work habits, and attention to other dispositions? This book starts the process and dialogue, but this is a rich area for further development. The book's authors would like to hear your thoughts and referrals to other resources on applying the essential question format to motivation for reading and lifelong learning.
- How will virtual learning programs change the high school landscape? What will be the role of school librarians in virtual learning programs?

In order to develop viable and productive library programs to meet the challenges of the evolving educational environment, school librarians must continue to learn about today's youth, new reading formats, literature for 6–12 students, and professional developments in librarianship, reading, and language arts, as well as other content areas. Following and contributing to the implementation of the Common Core Curriculum in local educational communities is especially important. Attendance at professional conferences, personally or virtually, and networking with local and national colleagues are critical to keep up with current thinking and developments in the field. Reading the professional literature in your preferred format is also essential. Newer sources for current thinking and opinions on professional issues are the blogs that are freely available on the web. This section concludes with a top 15 list of valuable blogs for school librarians and other literacy educators.

READS LESSONS AND ACTIVITIES

Score Reading Progress

Engage in Literacy-based motivational Programs and Activities

Accountable book clubs: Focused discussion. By Darla Salay. Includes Critical Thinking Map and Rubric for Paired Book Club Discussions. ReadWriteThink. (Gr. 7–8 up) http://www.readwrite think. org/classroom-resources/lesson-plans/accountable-book-clubs-focused-1163.html

Announcing the Learning Network Reading Club. (Resource) By Katherine Schulten and Holly Epstein Ojalvo. The Learning Network: *The New York Times*. http://learning.blogs.nytimes. com/2011/09/16/announcing-the-learning-network-reading-club/

Beyond the story: A Dickens of a party. By Patricia E. Carbone. Includes Party Planner and Stage Two: Rubric for Individual Characterization. ReadWriteThink. (Gr. 6–8 up)

Celebrate international literacy day! (Calendar activity) ReadWriteThink. (Gr. K-12)

A daily DEAR program: Drop everything and read!. By Traci Gardner. ReadWriteThink. (Gr. 3–5)

Give them a hand: Promoting positive interaction in literature circles. By Lane Clarke. ReadWriteThink. (Gr. 6–8) http://www.readwritethink.org/classroom-resources/lesson-plans/give-them-hand-promoting-1078.html?tab=1#tabs

Learning clubs: Motivating middle school readers and writers. By Heather Casey and Suzanne Gespass. ReadWriteThink. (Gr. 6–8) http://www.readwritethink.org/classroom-resources/lesson-plans/learning-clubs-motivating-middle-1168.html

Questions to use in book chats. (Resource). Provides questions to use in book clubs. ReadWrite-Think. (Gr. 3 up) http://www.readwritethink.org/files/resources/lesson_images/lesson55/RWT061–1.PDF

Read a book! The third week of October is Teen Read Week. (Calendar activity) ReadWriteThink. (Grades 6–12)

SSR extension activities. (Resource) ReadWriteThink. (Gr. 6–8) http://www.readwritethink.org/files/resources/lesson_images/lesson141/ssr.pdf

Student contracting. By Laurie A. Henry. Useful with individuals and groups. ReadWriteThink. (Gr. 6–8) http://www.readwritethink.org/classroom-resources/lesson-plans/student-contracting-141.html?tab=1#tabs

Thoughtful threads: Sparking rich online discussions. By Lotta C. Larson. Includes Creating Prompts. ReadWriteThink. (Gr. 5–12) http://www.readwritethink.org/classroom-resources/lesson-plans/thoughtful-threads-sparking-rich-1165.html

Develop Habits for Lifelong Learning and Lifetime Reading

Considering the future of reading: Lessons, links and thought experiences. (Resource) By Katherine Schulten and Shannon Doyle. Includes discussion of the future of reading and books. The Learning Network: *The New York Times*.

Every waking minute? Examining personal media habits. By Shannon Doyle and Holly Epstein Ojalvo. The Learning Network: *The New York Times*. (Gr. 6–12)

Explore your reading self: (Activity) ReadWriteThink. (Gr. 9–12) http://www.readwritethink.org/parent-afterschool-resources/activities-projects/explore-your-reading-self-30156.html?maintab=3#tabs

Exploring literacy in cyberspace. By Valerie A. Stokes. ReadWriteThink. (Gr. 9–12) http://www.readwritethink.org/classroom-resources/lesson-plans/exploring-literacy-cyberspace-212.html

Get down and book-ie! By Michelle Sale and Yasmin Chin Eisenhauer. The Learning Network: *The New York Times*. (Gr. 6–8) http://learning.blogs.nytimes.com/2006/08/04/get-down-and-book-ie/

I remember that book: Rereading as a critical investigation. By Tom Lynch. Involves reflection on memories of self as a reader and encourages rereading books. ReadWriteThink. (Gr. 9–12) http://www.readwritethink.org/classroom-resources/lesson-plans/remember-that-book-rereading-1150.html

Independence day: Developing self-directed learning projects. (Resource) By Dinah Mack and Holly Epstein Ojalvo. Includes link to "The Independent Project" YouTube video. The Learning Network: *The New York Times.* http://learning.blogs.nytimes.com/2011/03/21/independence-day-developing-self-directed-learning-projects/

Join the club! Supporting independent reading with book groups. Uses blog post "Where does a love of reading come from?" By Amanda Christy Brown and Holly Epstein Ojalvo. The Learning Network: *The New York Times.* (Gr. 6–12) http://learning.blogs.nytimes.com/2010/01/28/join-the-club-supporting-independent-reading-with-book-groups/

Online safety. (Strategy guide). By Traci Gardner. ReadWriteThink. (Gr. 6–12) http://www.readwritethink.org/professional-development/strategy-guides/online-safety-30107.html

Read on. By Katherine Schulten. Includes article Literature's greatest hits: Instructions for users. The Learning Network: *The New York Times.* (Gr. 6–12) http://learning.blogs.nytimes.com/2000/06/02/read-on/?pagemode=print

Reading online. (Strategy guide) By Suzanne Linder. ReadWriteThink. (Gr. 6–12) http://www.readwritethink.org/professional-development/strategy-guides/reading-online-30096.html

We have the Internet, so who needs books? By Terri Jeffrey. *School Library Media Activities Monthly, 21* (3), 13–16. (Gr. 6–8) (You may want to update the topics by adding Steve Jobs to the list of possible people. Consider iPad and Kindle for the list of things.)

What's your reading history? Reflecting on the self as reader. By Amanda Christy Brown and Holly Epstein Ojalvo. Includes My History as a Reader. The Learning Network: *The New York Times.* (Gr. 6–12) http://learning.blogs.nytimes.com/2010/03/04/whats-your-reading-history-reflecting-on-the-self-as-reader/

Would you like to take a class online? (Resource) By Shannon Doyle and Holly Epstein Ojalvo. Includes student opinions on the topic. The Learning Network: *The New York Times.* (Gr. 8–12) http://learning.blogs.nytimes.com/2011/10/05/would-you-like-to-take-a-class-online/

READS PROFESSIONAL RESOURCES

Score Reading Progress

Engage in Literacy-Based Motivational Programs and Activities

Reading Programs

Battle of the books 2012. Presented by Library Media Services with Educational Technology. Palm Beach County Public Schools. http://pbspaces.com/botb/

The big read: Our books. National Endowment for the Arts. http://www.neabigread.org/books.php

Celebrate Children's Book Week with classroom activities. http://www.educationworld.com/a_special/book_week.shtml

Children's Book Council. http://www.cbcbooks.org/

El dia de los ninos/El dia de los libros. http://dia.ala.org/

Florida Teen Book Map Project for adolescent literature. http://www.flreads.org/adolescent_lit/FL_book_map/index.htm

Great Books Foundation. http://www.greatbooks.org/

iCivics. (Lessons on civics education, online games and activities) http://www.icivics.org/

International Literacy Day. http://www.un.org/Depts/dhl/literacy/

Library promotional events. http://www.ala.org/ala/mgrps/divs/aasl/conferencesandevents/
librarypromoevents/librarypromotional.cfm

Literature Circles Resource Center. http://www.litcircles.org/

National student/parent mock election. http://www.nationalmockelection.org/

Planet Book Club. http://www.planetbookclub.com/home.html

School Library Media Month. http://www.ala.org/ala/mgrps/divs/aasl/aaslissues/slm/school
library.cfm

State Awards for Children's and Young Adult Books. http://www.cynthialeitichsmith.com/lit_
resources/awards/stateawards.html

Sunshine State Young Readers' Award. http://myssyra.org/

"Sustained silent reading" helps develop independent readers (and writers). http://www.educationworld.
com/a_curr/curr038.shtml

Teen Read Week. YALSA. http://www.ala.org/ala/mgrps/divs/yalsa/teenreading/trw/trw2010/
home.cfm

Teenreads.com. The Book Report Network. http://www.teenreads.com/

Readers' Theater

Literacy connections: Readers' theater. http://www.literacyconnections.com/ReadersTheater.php

RT tips: A guide to reader's theater. http://www.aaronshep.com/rt/Tips.html

Develop Habits for Lifelong Learning and Lifetime Reading

Edge. http://edge.org/responses/how-is-the-internet-changing-the-way-you-think

Exit slips. All about adolescent literature. http://www.adlit.org/strategies/19805

Googlereader. (Manages personal learning networks.) http://www.google.com/reader/

LibraryThing. http://www.librarything.com/

The question mark. Essential questions. Jamie McKenzie. http://questioning.org/index.html

Quotation collection: Quotes on reading. http://www.quotationcollection.com/tag/reading/quotes

Quotation garden: Quotes about learning. http://www.quotegarden.com/learning.html

Reading for understanding: Using this book in school libraries. http://inls745-readingforunderstanding.
wikispaces.com/Introduction

Spartan guides. Asking good questions. Joyce Valenza. http://sdst.libguides.com/content.php?pid=
184760&sid=1552990

Technology for learning. Using essential questions to focus teaching and learning. http://www.techfor
learning.org/essquest.html

Themes and essential questions. Greece Central School District. http://www.greece.k12.ny.us/aca
demics.cfm?subpage=923

WORKS CITED: SCHOOLWIDE EVENTS

American Association of School Librarians. (2007). *Standards for the 21st-century learner.* Chicago, IL:
American Library Association.

American Association of School Librarians. (2009). *Empowering learners: Guidelines for school library
media programs.* Chicago, IL: American Library Association.

Auguste, M., & Fesko. (2010). It takes a village: Author visits as community events. *Voice of Youth
Advocates, 33* (1), 43–44.

Bower, P. (2008). Battle of the books! *School Library Media Activities Monthly, 25* (3), 21–22.

Canter, L.L.S., Voytecki, K., Zambone, A., & Jones, J. (2011). School librarians: The forgotten partners.
Teaching Exceptional Children, 43 (3), 14–20.

Collins, J. (2008). *Motivating readers in the middle grades*. Columbus, OH: Linworth.

Figel, N. C. (2011). Bringing poetry week to high school. *School Library Monthly, 27* (6), 23–24.

Harvey, C. A. (2005). Bringing authors to students. *School Library Media Activities Monthly, 22* (4), 28–30.

Hunter, A. (2009). Join the literacy club. *Principal Leadership, 9* (9), 36–39.

Institute of Museum and Library Services. (2010). *IMLS joins the NEA in celebrating the fifth year of The Big Read with $1 million in grants*. Retrieved from http://imls.gov/news/2010/070810.shtm

Jewett, P. S., Wilson, J. L., & Vanderburg, M. A. (2011). The unifying power of a whole-school read. *Journal of Adolescent & Adult Literacy, 54* (6), 415–424.

Loertscher, D., Koechlin, C., & Zwann, S. (2008). *The new learning commons: Where learners win!* Salt Lake City, UT: Hi Willow.

Moore, R. C. (2006). From library jeopardy to microfiction Mprovs: Contest and activities for the school library. *Voice of Youth Advocates, 29* (3), 219–223.

National Center for Educational Statistics. (2011). *The nation's report card: Civics: 2010*. Retrieved from http://nces.ed.gov/pubsearch/pubsinfo.asp?pubid=2011466

Older students need reading support, too: Two award-winning schools highlight reading at upper levels. (2005). *Reading Today, 22* (4), 11.

Palm Beach County Public Schools. *Battle of the books 2012*. Retrieved from http://pbspaces.com/botb/

Preddy, L. B. (2009). Literacy committee: Creating a community of readers. *School Library Monthly, 26* (1), 43–47.

Preddy, L. B. (2010). *Social readers: Promoting reading in the 21st century*. Santa Barbara, CA: Libraries Unlimited.

Sanders, C. (2007). Making history rock with an interdisciplinary fair. *School Library Media Activities Monthly, 23* (5), 29–30.

Van Dyke, D. (2005). "Building a community of readers": A one book program. *Library Media Connection, 23* (5), 20–22.

WORKS CITED: SUSTAINED SILENT READING (SSR)

Braunger, J., & Lewis, J. P. (2006). *Building a knowledge base in reading* (2nd ed.). Newark, DE: International Reading Association/The National Council of Teachers of English.

Fisher, D. (2004). Setting the "opportunity to read" standard: Resuscitating the SSR program in an urban high school. *Journal of Adolescent & Adult Literacy, 48* (2), 138–150.

Fisher, D., & Frey, N. (2009). *Background knowledge: The missing piece of comprehension*. Portsmouth, NH: Heinemann.

Gallagher, K. (2009). *Readicide: How schools are killing reading and what you can do about it*. Portland, ME: Stenhouse.

Garan, E. M., & DeVoogd, G. (2009). The benefits of sustained silent reading: Scientific research and common sense. *The Reading Teacher, 62* (4), 336–344.

Gardiner, S. (2007). Librarians provide strongest support for sustained silent reading. *Library Media Connection, 25* (5), 16–18.

Gordon, C. (2010). Meeting readers where they are. *School Library Journal, 56* (11), 32–37.

Jensen, T. L., & Jensen, V. S. (2002). Sustained silent reading and young adult short stories for high school classes. The *ALAN Review, 30* (1), 58–60.

Krashen, S. (2004). *The power of reading: Insights from the research* (2nd ed.). Westport, CT: Libraries Unlimited.

Krashen, S. (2006). Free reading. *School Library Journal, 52* (9), 42–45.

Krashen, S. (2009). Anything but reading. *Knowledge Quest, 37* (5), 18–25.

Linguist, educational researcher, and activist: Stephen Krashen. (2010). *Teacher Librarian, 37* (3), 79–80.

Marzano, R. J. (2004). *Building background knowledge for academic achievement: Research on what works in schools*. Alexandria, VA: Association for Supervision and Curriculum Development.

Preddy, L. B. (2007). *SSR with intervention. A school library action research project*. Westport, CT: Libraries Unlimited.

Preddy, L. B. (2009). Literacy committee: Creating a community of readers. *School Library Monthly, 26* (1), 43–47.

Ravitch, D. (2007). *EdSpeak: A glossary of educational terms, phrases, buzzwords, and jargon*. Alexandria, VA: Association for Supervision and Curriculum Development.

Roberts, J. (2006). Building a community of high school readers. *Knowledge Quest, 35* (1), 24–29.

Small, R. V. (2009). Reading incentives that work: No-cost strategies to motivate kids to read and love it! *School Library Media Activities Monthly, 25* (9), 27–31.

Trelease, J. (2006). SSR—sustained silent reading, reading aloud's silent partner. [Chapter 5] *The read-aloud handbook* (6th ed.). New York: Penguin. Retrieved from http://www.trelease-on-reading.com/rah-ch5.html

Wilson, S. L., Dunbar, L., & Lovley, B. S. (2010). Response to literature: Perspectives, voices, discovery, and identity. *New England Reading Association Journal, 46* (1), 85–96.

Wise, B. (2009). Adolescent literacy: The cornerstone of student success. *Journal of Adolescent & Adult Literacy, 52* (5), 369–75.

FURTHER READING: SUSTAINED SILENT READING

Clark, R. C. (2011). Reversing readicide. *Knowledge Quest, 39* (4), 10–11.

Every adult advocates, every student graduates: Columbus Unified High School. *Principal Leadership, 11* (9), 34–39.

Fisher, D., & Ivey, G. (2006). Evaluating the interventions for struggling adolescent readers. *Journal of Adolescent & Adult Literacy, 50* (3), 180–189.

Gardiner, S. (2005). A skill for life. *Educational Leadership, 62* (2), 67–70.

Humphrey, J., & Preddy, L. (2008). Keys to successfully sustaining an SSR program. *School Library Media Connection, 26* (6), 30–21.

Irvin, J. L., Meltzer, J., & Dukes, M. (2007). *Taking action on adolescent literacy: An implementation guide for school leaders*. Alexandria, VA: Association for Supervision and Curriculum Development.

Moser, A. M. (2006). Sustained silent reading. *School Library Media Activities Monthly, 23* (2), 43–45.

Nichols, B. W. (2009). What does the research tell us about sustained silent reading? *Library Media Connection, 27* (6), 47.

Parr, J. M., & Maguiness, C. (2005). Removing the silent from SSR: Voluntary reading as social practice. *Journal of Adolescent & Adult Literacy, 49* (2), 98–107.

Siah, P., & Kwok, W. (2010). The value of reading and the effectiveness of sustained silent reading. *The Clearing House, 83* (5), 168–174.

WORKS CITED: SUMMER READING ACTIVITIES

Allington, R., & McGill-Franzen, A. (2008). Got books? *Educational Leadership, 65* (7), 20–23.

Corrigan, J. (2010). Improving writing with wiki discussion forums. *Principal Leadership, 11* (3), 44–47.

Gallagher, K. (2009). *Readicide: How schools are killing reading and what you can do about it*. Portland, ME: Stenhouse.

Gordon, C. A. (2008). A never-ending story: Action research meets summer reading. *Knowledge Quest, 37* (2), 34–41.

Gorman, L. (2010). Purposes behind summer reading lists. *Teacher Librarian, 37* (5), 52–56.

Heaser, C. (2011). Bridging the summer reading gap: Collaborative ideas to keep your students reading. *Library Media Connection, 29* (6), 24–26.

Kim, J. S., & White, T. B. (2011). Solving the problem of summer reading loss. *Kappan, 92* (7), 64–67.

Lu, Y., & Gordon, C. (2007). Reading takes you places: Study of a web-based summer reading program. *School Library Media Research* 10. Retrieved from http://www.ala.org/ala/mgrps/divs/aasl/aaslpubsandjournals/slmrb/slmrcontents/volume10/lu_reading.cfm

Metz, S. (2009). Closing the gap with summer reading. *The Science Teacher, 76* (5), 8.

Moore, A. (2008). From summer to four seasons: Growth of a high school reading program. *Library Media Connection, 26* (6), 26–27.

Moreillon, J. (2010). Multicultural conversations: Online literature circles focused on social issues. *WOW Stories, 3* (1). Retrieved from http://wowlit.org/on-line-publications/stories/storiesiii1/3/

Schulten, K. (2011). Summer 2011 on The Learning Network. *The New York Times.* Retrieved from http://learning.blogs.nytimes.com/2011/05/27/summer-2011-on-the-learning-network/

Toppo, G. (2010). Books block "summer slide" in kids: Study: Reading improves in low-income students. *USA Today, 7* (June 1).

White, T. G., & Kim, J. S. (2008). Teacher and parent scaffolding of voluntary summer reading. *The Reading Teacher, 62* (2), 116–125.

Wilson, S. L., Dunbar, L., & Lovley, B. S. (2010). Response to literature: Perspectives, voices, discovery, and identity. *New England Reading Association Journal, 46* (1), 85–96.

FURTHER READING: SUMMER READING ACTIVITIES

Byerly, G. (2010). School's out—some summer vacation web sites. *School Library Monthly, 26* (10), 29–31.

Constantino, R. (2005). Print environments between high and low socioeconomic status (SES) communities. *Teacher Librarian, 32* (3), 22–25.

Fiore, C., & Roman, S. (2010). Proof positive. *School Library Journal, 56* (11), 26–28.

Gordon, C. (2006). A study of a three-dimensional action research training model for school library programs. *School Library Media Research* 9. Retrieved from http://www.ala.org/ala/mgrps/divs/aasl/aaslpubsandjournals/slmrb/slmrcontents/volume09/gordon_study3daction.cfm

Gordon, C. (2010). Meeting readers where they are: Mapping the intersection of research and practice. *School Library Journal, 56* (11), 32–37.

Lin, S., Shin, F., & Krashen, S. (2007). Sophia's choice: Summer reading. *Knowledge Quest, 35* (3), 52–55.

McGill-Franzen, A., & Allington, R. (2001). Summer reading: Importance of giving children access to books throughout summer months. *Reading Today, 18* (6), 10.

Shin, F. H., and Krashen, S. D. (2008). *Summer reading: Program and evidence.* Englewood, CO: Libraries Unlimited.

Stopping summer slide. (2010). *Reading Today, 27* (6), 1–2.

WORKS CITED: MENTORING

Armstrong, T. (2006). *The best schools: How human development research should inform educational practice.* Alexandria, VA: Association for Supervision and Curriculum Development.

Jones, J. (2009). What is the Amanda Award? Building resilience through the Amanda Award. *Florida Media Quarterly, 35* (1), 10–12.

Jones, J. L. (2004). Whether fact or fiction, mentoring counts. *Knowledge Quest, 32* (3), 44–45.

Jones, J. L. (2005). Promoting resilience: Ways library media specialists strengthen children. *School Library Media Activities Monthly, 22* (3), 25–27.

Jones, J. L. (2007). "Somewhere to walk and someone to walk with": Resiliency experts discuss how libraries and librarians strengthen youth. *VOYA, 29* (6), 495–498.

Jones, J. L. (2009a). Dropout prevention through the school library: Dispositions, relationships, and instructional practices. *School Libraries Worldwide, 15* (2), 77–90.

Jones, J. L. (2009b). "Shelters from the storm" teens, stress, and libraries. *Young Adult Library Services, 7* (2), 16–20.

Marzano, R. J. (2003). *What works in schools: Translating research into action.* Alexandria, VA: Association for Supervision and Curriculum Development.

Svec, D. (2006). How to promote your media program: Let's all get out of the box! *Florida Media Quarterly, 32* (1), 10–11.

Terelli, K. B. (2011). FAME 2010 award winners. *Florida Media Quarterly, 36* (2), 9.

WORKS CITED: BOOK CLUBS

Allen, P. A. (2009). *Conferring: The keystone of reader's workshop.* Portland, ME: Stenhouse.

Appleman, D. (2006). *Reading for themselves: How to transform adolescents into lifelong readers through out-of-class book clubs.* Portsmouth, NH: Heinemann.

Beach, R., Appleman, D., Hynds, S., & Wilhelm, J. (2011). *Teaching literature to adolescents* (2nd ed.). New York: Routledge.

Blair, C., Bradfield, A., Crenshaw, K., & Mosedale, A. (2011). School librarians: Bridging the language gap for English language learners. *School Library Monthly, 27* (6), 34–37.

Bowers-Campbell, J. (2011). Take it out of class: Exploring virtual literature circles. *Journal of Adolescent & Adult Literacy, 54* (8), 557–567.

Burkey, M. (2010). Audiobooks & book clubs: Perfect partners. *Booklist Online.* Retrieved from http://audiobooker.booklistonline.com/2010/01/08/audiobooks-book-clubs-perfect-partners/

Burkey, M. (2010). Voices in my head: Audiobook book clubs. *The Booklist, 106* (9/10), 109.

Casey, H. K. (2009). Engaging the disengaged: Using learning clubs to motivate struggling adolescent readers and writers. *Journal of Adolescent & Adult Literacy, 52* (4), 284–294.

Dobrez, C., & Rutan, L. (2011). Death cloud by Andrew Lane. *Bookends.* Retrieved from http://bookends.booklistonline.com/

Drogowski, P. P. (2006). Between pages, personalities and pizza—a middle school book club. *School Library Media Activities Monthly, 23 (4),* 32–34.

Ferriter, W. M. (2010). Can't get kids to read? Make it social. *Educational Leadership, 67* (6), 87–88.

Harland, P. (2010). The high school book club—now with Kindles! *Teacher Librarian, 37* (5), 57–59.

Kasten, W. C., & Wilfong, L. G. (2005). Encouraging independent reading with ambiance: The book bistro in middle and secondary school classes. *Journal of Adolescent & Adult Literacy, 48* (8), 656–664.

Kunzel, B., & Hardesty, C. (2006). *The teen-centered book club: Readers into leaders.* Westport, CT: Libraries Unlimited.

Lesesne, T. S. (2003). *Making the match: The right book for the right reader at the right time, grades 4–12.* Portland, ME: Stenhouse.

Lit Lovers: A well read online community. Retrieved from http://litlovers.com/run-a-book-club/questions-for-nonfiction

Littlejohn, C. (2011). *Book clubbing! Successful book clubs for young people.* Santa Barbara, CA: Linworth.

Loertscher, D. (2010). Learning to read and reading to learn: Meeting the international challenge. *Teacher Librarian, 37* (5), 48–50.

Long, B. (2008). W.A.L.K. (we are literate kids) club: A walking and listening program for the library media center. *School Library Media Activities Monthly, 24* (5), 18–19.

O'Donnell-Allen, C. (2006). *The book club companion: Fostering strategic readers in the secondary classroom.* Portsmouth, NH: Heinemann.

Peowski, L. (2010). Where are all the teens? Engaging and empowering them online. *Young Adult Library Services, 9* (2), 26–28.

Preddy, L. B. (2010). *Social readers: Promoting reading in the 21st century.* Santa Barbara, CA: Libraries Unlimited.

Scharber. C. (2009). Online book clubs: Bridges between old and new literacies practices. *Journal of Adolescent & Adult Literacy, 52* (5), 433–437.

Shantz-Keresztes, L. (2005). Avid readership: "Wired for words" on-line youth book club. *School Libraries in Canada, 25* (1), 48–54.

Stevenson, S. (2009). My *Bluford High* boys. *School Library Journal, 55* (5), 34–36.

Stewart, P. (2009). Facebook and virtual literature circle partnership in building a community of readers. *Knowledge Quest, 37* (4), 28–33.

Wilhelm, J. D. (2008). *"You gotta BE the book": Teaching engaged and reflective reading with adolescents.* New York: Teachers' College Press.

Zwiers, J., & Crawford, M. (2009). How to start academic conversations. *Educational Leadership, 66* (7), 70–73.

WORKS CITED: STATE READERS' CHOICE PROGRAMS

Crow, S. R. (2010). Children's Choice Book Award Programs: Effective weapons in the battle to get and keep kids reading. *School Library Monthly, 26* (9), 12–13.

Hilbun, J., & Claes, J. (2007). Coast to coast: Exploring state book awards. *Book Links, 16* (6), 18–20.

Rogers, M. A., Szymanski, S., Cavanaugh, L., & Dunphy, M. (2010). Massachusetts teen choice book award: Our partnership for Massachusetts teens. *Young Adult Library Services, 9* (1), 26–27.

WORKS CITED: READING MOTIVATION PROGRAMS

American Association of School Librarians. (2011). *Position statement on labeling books with reading levels.* Retrieved from http://www.ala.org/ala/mgrps/divs/aasl/aaslissues/position-statements/labeling.cfm

Balajthy, E. (2007). Technology and current reading. Literacy assessment strategies. *The Reading Teacher, 61* (3), 240–247.

Cregar, E. (2011). Browsing by numbers and reading for points. *Knowledge Quest, 39* (4), 40–45.

Fisher, D. (2008). Struggling adolescent readers. *Teacher Librarian, 35* (3), 36–37.

Franklin, P., & Stephens, C. G. (2006). Manage your computerized reading program—before it manages you! *School Library Media Activities Monthly, 23* (4), 47–49.

Gallagher, K. (2009). *Readicide: How schools are killing reading and what you can do about it.* Portland, ME: Stenhouse.

Harvey, C. A. (2011). An inside view of Lexile measures: An interview with Malbert Smith III. *Knowledge Quest, 39* (4), 56–59.

Kohn, A. (2010). How to create nonreaders: Reflections on motivation, learning, and sharing power. *English Journal, 100* (1), 16–22.

Krashen, S. (2007). Accelerated Reader: Once again, evidence lacking. *Knowledge Quest Web Edition, 36* (1). Retrieved from http://www.ala.org/ala/mgrps/divs/aasl/aaslpubsandjournals/knowledgequest/kqwebarchives/v36/361/ALA_print_layout_1_444829_444829.cfm

Small, R. V. (2009). Reading incentives that work: No-cost strategies to motivate kids to read and love it! *School Library Monthly, 25* (9), 27–31.

FURTHER READING: READING MOTIVATION PROGRAMS

Everhart, N. (2011). Reversing readicide. *Knowledge Quest, 39* (4), 4–5.

Gallagher, K. (2009). *Readicide: How schools are killing reading and what you can do about it*. Portland, ME: Stenhouse.

Hedrick, W. (2006). Reading incentives don't necessarily grow readers. *Voices from the Middle, 14* (2), 77–78.

Krashen, S. (2005). Accelerated Reader: Evidence still lacking. *Knowledge Quest, 33* (3), 48–49.

McKee, S., & Torp, K. (2011). Leaving levels and moving to real reading. *School Library Monthly, 27* (8), 31–33.

Moyer, M. (2006). Accelerated Reader sparks high school reading excitement. *Knowledge Quest, 35* (1), 34–39.

Pfeiffer, C. (2011). Achieving a standard of reading excellence in Kansas. *Knowledge Quest, 39* (4), 60–67.

Scales, P. (2010). The blame game. *School Library Journal, 56* (1), 16.

Scales, P. (2010). Success stories. *School Library Journal, 56* (3), 19.

Solley, K. (2011). Accelerated Reader can be an effective tool to encourage and bolster student reading. *Knowledge Quest, 39* (4), 46–49.

Thompson, G., Madhuri, M., & Taylor, D. (2008). How the Accelerated Reader program can become counterproductive for high school students. *Journal of Adolescent & Adult Literacy, 51* (7), 550–560.

WORKS CITED: LIFELONG LEARNING AND LIFETIME READING

American Association of School Librarians. (2007). *Standards for the 21st-century learner*. Chicago, IL: American Library Association.

American Association of School Librarians. (2009). *Empowering learners: Guidelines for school library media programs*. Chicago, IL: American Library Association.

Arnone, M. (2010). How do school librarians perceive dispositions for learning and social responsibility? *School Library Monthly, 26* (7), 40–43.

Browne, K., Hirsh, K., & Koehler, E. (2011). Resolving the quiet crisis: Reading apprenticeships in middle and high school. *School Library Monthly, 27* (4), 34–36.

Bush, G., & Jones, J. L. (2011). Forecasting dispositions of school librarians. *School Library Monthly, 27* (4), 54–56.

Common Core Curriculum Mapping Project: English language arts. (2010). Common Core. Retrieved from http://commoncore.org/free/

Dunlap, J. C. (2005). Changes in students' use of lifelong learning skills during a problem-based learning project. *Performance Improvement Quarterly, 18* (1), 5–33.

Fenn, J. (2005). 8 ways your librarian can help promote literacy. *Principal Leadership, 5* (6), 49–51.

Fontichiaro, K., (2008). Dancing down the rabbit hole: Habits of mind for embracing change. *School Library Monthly, 23* (3), 56–58.

Gallagher, K. (2003). *Reading reasons: Motivational mini-lessons for middle and high school*. Portland, ME: Stenhouse.

Innovators. (2011). *Library Journal, 136* (5), 26–31.

Jones, J. L., & Dotson, K. B. (2010). Building the disposition of reflection through the inquiry-focused school library program. *School Libraries Worldwide, 16* (1), 33–46.

Katz, L. G. (1993). Dispositions as educational goals. ERIC Digest. Retrieved from http://www.ericdigests.org/1994/goals.htm

Lamb, A. (2011). Bursting with potential: Mixing a media specialist's palette. *TechTrends, 55* (4), 27–36.

Lesesne, T. S. (2010). *Reading ladders: Leading students from where they are to where we'd like them to be.* Portsmouth, NH: Heinemann.

Levitov, D. D. (2011). School librarians are super heroes. *School Library Monthly, 28* (1), 4.

McKenzie, J. (2005). *Learning to question to wonder to learn.* Bellingham, WA: FNO Press.

McKenzie, J. *The question mark. Essential questions.* Retrieved from http://questioning.org/index.html

Moreillon, J., & Cahill, M. (2010). When cultures meet. *School Library Monthly, 27* (2), 27–29.

National Endowment for the Arts. (2007). *To read or not to read: A question of national consequence.* Office of Research & Analysis. Retrieved from http://www.nea.gov/research/toread.pdf

Ravitch, D. (2007). *EdSpeak: A glossary of educational terms, phrases, buzzwords, and jargon.* Alexandria, VA: Association for Supervision & Curriculum Development.

Stripling, B. (2008). Dispositions: Getting beyond "whatever." *School Library Media Activities Monthly, 25* (2), 47–50.

Transliteracies Project. (2007). Working definition of online reading. *Research in the technological, social, and cultural practices of online reading.* Retrieved from http://transliteracies.english.ucsb.edu/category/research-project/definition-of-online-reading

Valenza, J. *Asking good questions.* Spartan guides. Retrieved from http://sdst.libguides.com/content.php?pid=184760&sid=1552990

Valenza, J. K. (2003). *Power research tools: Learning activities and posters.* Chicago, IL: American Library Association.

VanDeWeghe, R. (2011). A literacy education for our time. *English Journal, 100* (6), 28–33.

Wiggins, G., & McTighe, J. (2005). *Understanding by design.* Alexandria, VA: Association for Curriculum and Development.

Wilhelm, J. D., & Novak, B. (2011). *Teaching literacy for love and wisdom: Being the book and being the change.* New York: Teachers College Press.

FURTHER READING: LIFELONG LEARNING AND LIFETIME READING

Brown, K. (2009). Questions for the 21st-century learner. *Knowledge Quest, 38* (1), 24–29.

Donham, J. (2007). Graduating students who are not only learned but also learners. *Teacher Librarian, 35* (1), 8–12.

Donham, J. (2010). Creating personal learning through self-assessment. *Teacher Librarian, 37* (3), 14–21.

Duncan, S. P. (2010). *The use of motivational reading practices in middle schools in Mississippi.* Doctoral dissertation. Retrieved from http://search.proquest.com.ezproxylocal.library.nova.edu/dissertations/docview/858213584/13216C75D1B23880C1E/1?accountid=6579

Moreillon, J., Luhtala, M., & Russo, C. T. (2011). Learning that sticks: Engaged educators + engaged learners. *School Library Monthly, 28* (1), 17–20.

Warlick, D. F. (2009). *Redefining literacy 2.0* (2nd ed.). Columbus, OH: Linworth.

Wilhelm, J. D. (2008). *"You gotta be the book": Teaching engaged and reflective reading with adolescents* (2nd ed.). New York: Teacher's College Press.

Part 7

Appendices

Appendix A

READS Annual Calendar— Ninth and Tenth Grades

READS Topic	August/ September	October
R E A D	910.1.1.1/2 Update Internet sites focused on teen reading lists on library media website as needed	910.1.1.1/2 Update Internet sites focused on teen reading lists on library media website, as needed
	910.1.1.1/2 Distribute interest reading survey	910.1.1.1/2 Calculate results of interest reading survey and share with students/teachers via website posting, emails, and/or television announcements
	910.1.2.1 Host lunch bunch activities highlighting preselected students performing readings or music	910.1.2.1 Host lunch bunch activities highlighting preselected students performing readings or music
	910.1.3.1 Collaborate with teachers to bring students in for checkout	910.1.3.1 Collaborate with teachers to bring students in for checkout

READS Topic	September	October
E X P L O R E	910.2.1.1 Create display, bibliography, and/or bulletin board for highlighted monthly author and genre—contemporary fiction-Banned Books Week/ Chris Crutcher	910.2.1.1 Create display, bibliography, and/or bulletin board for highlighted monthly author and genre—vampires and supernatural/Stephanie Meyer
	910.2.2.2 Celebrate Hispanic Heritage month by collaborating with ESOL and foreign language teachers on projects (e.g., biography reports in various formats, magazine article reviews, book trailers on authors such as Rita Williams-Garcia and Pam Muñoz Ryan)	
		910.2.3.1 Celebrate Hispanic Heritage month by collaborating with ESOL and foreign language teachers on projects focusing on Pura Belpré Award winners
		910.2.3.2 Collaborate with business education teacher on week-long activities on intellectual freedom

READS Topic	September	October
A N A L Y Z E		910.3.1.1 Collaborate with ESE teachers on literature-based lesson(s) using film adaptations of short stories and working with students to make inferences and predictions on content
	910.3.2.1 Collaborate with ESOL teachers to reinforce author's use of figurative language or illustrator's style	910.3.2.1 Collaborate with Language Arts teachers to reinforce author's use of figurative language or illustrator's style

READS Topic	September	October
D E V E L O P	910.4.1.1/2 Review with ESOL students technologies and methods for creating literature-based presentations for Hispanic Heritage Month	
		910.4.2.1 Work with ESOL and foreign language students' to produce projects focusing on Pura Belpré Award winners
		910.4.1 Work with business education students on Banned Books Week production activities

READS Topic	September	October
S C O R E		910.5.1.1 Work with business education students on Banned Books Week activities
	910.5.1.2 Work school-wide to promote Florida Teens Read program	910.5.1.2 Work school-wide to promote Florida Teens Read program
	910.5.2.1 Provide selection of career-related magazines and promote usage	910.5.2.1 Provide selection of career-related magazines and promote usage

Appendix B.1

READS Grade Summaries
Grade Six

Read as a personal activity	Explore characteristics, history, and awards of creative works	Analyze structure and aesthetic features of creative works	Develop a literary-based product	Score reading progress
Sixth Grade	The student will:	READS		
Read as a personal activity				
6.1.1 Select and read literary and informational texts at an appropriate reading level.	6.1.1.1 Choose age and ability appropriate literature to read based on interest or curriculum need.			
	6.1.1.2 Choose age and ability appropriate informational texts to read based on interest or curriculum need.			
6.1.2 Select listening and viewing resources for enjoyment and information.	6.1.2.1 Participate in listening and viewing activities (e.g., audiobooks, podcasts).			
6.1.3 Use community resources for recreational and informational needs.	6.1.3.1 Visit the school or other libraries virtually or in person to access resources.			
	6.1.3.2 Visit museums, galleries, science centers, and parks virtually or in person (e.g., Library of Congress Memory Project).			
Explore characteristics, history, and awards of creative works				
6.2.1 Identify and critically analyze literary and media genres and themes.	6.2.1.1 Compare and contrast literary and media genres (e.g., historical fiction, fantasy, short stories).			
	6.2.1.2 Explain and compare literary themes in text, visual, and digital resources ((e.g., good v. evil, man v. nature).			
6.2.2 Recognize that social, cultural, political and historical events influence ideas and information.	6.2.2.1 Identify and compare historically and culturally significant works in various formats (e.g., Greek or Roman mythology).			
	6.2.2.2 Recognize cultural and ethnic diversity through creative and literary works.			
6.2.3 Appreciate literary and artistic excellence.	6.2.3.1 Identify award-winning authors, illustrators, and producers of literary and creative works (e.g., Sunshine State Young Reader's Award winners).			
	6.2.3.2 Identify the concept of intellectual freedom.			

Analyze structure and aesthetic features of creative works	
6.3.1 Identify and analyze key ideas and details of a work.	6.3.1.1 Connect prior and background knowledge to textual or visual clues to understand a literary work (e.g., inferring, predicting).
	6.3.1.2 Determine central ideas and supporting details of a work (e.g., paraphrasing, summarizing).
6.3.2 Understand the literary techniques and complexities of a work.	6.3.2.1 Identify an author's or illustrator's style (e.g., word choice, use of figurative language, medium).
	6.3.2.2 Compare and contrast story elements (e.g., characters, setting, or plot) in multiple works.
Develop a literary-based product	
6.4.1 Develop an original work or a response to a creative work, working in groups or individually.	6.4.1.1 Choose a method to present an original work or a response to a creative work based on appropriateness and personal preference.
	6.4.1.2 Generate and organize ideas for an original work or a response to a creative work read, heard, or viewed (e.g., graphic organizer, group discussion, or brainstorming).
	6.4.1.3 Create an original work or a response to a creative work, reflecting on progress and editing as needed (e.g., rubric, peer review, checklist).
	6.4.1.4 Practice respect for copyright laws and intellectual property rights (e.g., use standard bibliographic format to credit sources).
6.4.2 Communicate and evaluate an original work or response to creative works, working in a group or individually.	6.4.2.1 Use appropriate methods to share and evaluate product.
Score reading progress	
6.5.1 Engage in literacy-based motivational program and activities.	6.5.1.1 Participate in library media activities and reading celebrations (e.g., School Library Media Month celebrations).
	6.5.1.2 Participate in structured independent reading programs (e.g., Sunshine State Young Reader's Award).
	6.5.1.3 Participate in reading motivation programs with management components (e.g., *Accelerated Reader* or *Reading Counts*). (optional)
6.5.2 Develop habits for lifelong learning.	6.5.2.1 Practice lifelong literacy skills by relating reading, listening, and viewing to real world situations (e.g., hobby magazines, online newscasts) and choosing a literate lifestyle (e.g., reading for pleasure and personal fulfillment).

Appendix B.2

READS
Grade Seven

Read as a personal activity	Explore characteristics, history, and awards of creative works	Analyze structure and aesthetic features of creative works	Develop a literary-based product	Score reading progress
	READS			
Seventh Grade	The student will:			
Read as a personal activity				
7.1.1 Select and read literary and informational texts at an appropriate reading level.	7.1.1.1 Choose age and ability appropriate literature to read based on interest or curriculum need.			
	7.1.1.2 Choose age and ability appropriate informational texts to read based on interest or curriculum need.			
7.1.2 Select listening and viewing resources for enjoyment and information.	7.1.2.1 Participate in listening and viewing activities (e.g., audiobooks, podcasts).			
7.1.3 Use community resources for recreational and informational needs.	7.1.3.1 Visit the school or other libraries virtually or in person to access resources.			
	7.1.3.2 Visit museums, galleries, science centers, and parks virtually or in person (e.g., Louvre, National Gallery of Art).			
Explore characteristics, history, and awards of creative works				
7.2.1 Identify and critically analyze literary and media genres and themes.	7.2.1.1 Compare and contrast literary and media genres (e.g., adventure, mystery, documentary).			
	7.2.1.2 Explain and compare literary themes in text, visual, and digital resources (e.g., good v. evil, man v. nature).			
7.2.2 Recognize that social, cultural, political and historical events influence ideas and information.	7.2.2.1 Identify and compare historically and culturally significant works in various formats (e.g., political cartoons, African American handmade quilts).			
	7.2.2.2 Recognize cultural and ethnic diversity through creative and literary works.			
7.2.3 Appreciate literary and artistic excellence.	7.2.3.1 Identify award-winning authors, illustrators, and producers of literary and creative works (e.g., Edgar Allen Poe Award winners).			
	7.2.3.2 Acknowledge the importance of intellectual freedom.			

(Continued)

Analyze structure and aesthetic features of creative works		
7.3.1 Identify and analyze key ideas and details of a work.	7.3.1.1 Connect prior and background knowledge to textual or visual clues to understand a literary work (e.g., inferring, predicting).	
	7.3.1.2 Determine central ideas and supporting details of a work (e.g., paraphrasing, summarizing).	
7.3.2 Understand the literary techniques and complexities of a work.	7.3.2.1 Identify an author's or illustrator's style (e.g., word choice, use of figurative language, medium).	
	7.3.2.2 Compare and contrast story elements (e.g., characters, setting, or plot) in multiple works.	
Develop a literary-based product		
7.4.1 Develop an original work or a response to a creative work, working in groups or individually.	7.4.1.1 Choose a method to present an original work or a response to a creative work based on appropriateness and personal preference.	
	7.4.1.2 Generate and organize ideas for an original work or a response to a creative work read, heard, or viewed (e.g., graphic organizer, group discussion, or brainstorming).	
	7.4.1.3 Create an original work or a response to a creative work, reflecting on progress and editing as needed (e.g., rubric, peer review, checklist).	
	7.4.1.4 Demonstrate understanding of and respect for copyright laws and intellectual property rights (e.g., use standard bibliographic format to credit sources).	
7.4.2 Communicate and evaluate an original work or response to creative works, working in a group or individually.	7.4.2.1 Use appropriate methods to share and evaluate product.	
Score reading progress		
7.5.1 Engage in literacy-based motivational program and activities.	7.5.1.1 Participate in library media activities and reading celebrations (e.g., School Library Media Month celebrations).	
	7.5.1.2 Participate in structured independent reading programs (e.g., Sunshine State Young Reader's Award).	
	7.5.1.3 Participate in reading motivation programs with management components (e.g., *Accelerated Reader* or *Reading Counts*). (optional)	
7.5.2 Develop habits for lifelong learning.	7.5.2.1 Practice lifelong literacy skills by relating reading, listening, and viewing to real world situations (e.g., career magazines, online newscasts) and choosing a literate lifestyle (e.g., reading for pleasure and personal fulfillment).	

Appendix B.3

READS
Grade Eight

Read as a personal activity	Explore characteristics, history, and awards of creative works	Analyze structure and aesthetic features of creative works	Develop a literary-based product	Score reading progress
Eighth Grade		READS		
		The student will:		
Read as a personal activity				
8.1.1 Select and read literary and informational texts at an appropriate reading level.	8.1.1.1 Choose age and ability appropriate literature to read based on interest or curriculum need.			
	8.1.1.2 Choose age and ability appropriate informational texts to read based on interest or curriculum need.			
8.1.2 Select listening and viewing resources for enjoyment and information.	8.1.2.1 Participate in listening and viewing activities (e.g., audiobooks, podcasts).			
8.1.3 Use community resources for recreational and informational needs.	8.1.3.1 Visit the school or other libraries virtually or in person to access resources.			
	8.1.3.2 Visit museums, galleries, science centers, and parks virtually or in person (e.g., Louvre, National Gallery of Art).			
Explore characteristics, history, and awards of creative works				
8.2.1 Identify and critically analyze literary and media genres and themes.	8.2.1.1 Analyze literary and media genres (e.g., poetry, drama, biography, documentary).			
	8.2.1.2 Explain and compare literary themes in text, visual, and digital resources (e.g., ability of human spirit to rise above grief and loss).			
8.2.2 Recognize that social, cultural, political and historical events influence ideas and information.	8.2.2.1 Identify and compare historically and culturally significant works in various formats (e.g., Hispanic poetry and situational comedies).			
	8.2.2.2 Recognize cultural and ethnic diversity through creative and literary works.			
8.2.3 Appreciate literary and artistic excellence.	8.2.3.1 Identify award-winning authors, illustrators, and producers of literary and creative works (e.g., Laura Ingalls Wilder Award winners).			
	8.2.3.2 Acknowledge the importance of intellectual freedom.			

Analyze structure and aesthetic features of creative works	
8.3.1 Identify and analyze key ideas and details of a work.	8.3.1.1 Connect prior and background knowledge to textual or visual clues to understand a literary work (e.g., inferring, predicting).
	8.3.1.2 Determine central ideas and supporting details of a work (e.g., paraphrasing, summarizing).
8.3.2 Understand the literary techniques and complexities of a work.	8.3.2.1 Identify an author's or illustrator's style (e.g., word choice, use of figurative language, medium).
	8.3.2.2 Compare and contrast story elements (e.g., characters, setting, or plot) in multiple works.
Develop a literary-based product	
8.4.1 Develop an original work or a response to a creative work, working in groups or individually.	8.4.1.1 Choose a method to present an original work or a response to a creative work based on appropriateness and personal preference.
	8.4.1.2 Generate and organize ideas for an original work or a response to a creative work read, heard, or viewed (e.g., graphic organizer, group discussion, or brainstorming).
	8.4.1.3 Create an original work or a response to a creative work, reflecting on progress and editing as needed (e.g., rubric, peer review, checklist).
	8.4.1.4 Demonstrate understanding of and respect for copyright laws and intellectual property rights (e.g., use standard bibliographic format to credit sources).
8.4.2 Communicate and evaluate an original work or response to creative works, working in a group or individually.	8.4.2.1 Use appropriate methods to share and evaluate product.
Score reading progress	
8.5.1 Engage in literacy-based motivational program and activities.	8.5.1.1 Participate in library media activities and reading celebrations (e.g., televised book talks or reviews).
	8.5.1.2 Participate in structured independent reading programs (e.g., Sunshine State Young Reader's Award).
	8.5.1.3 Participate in reading motivation programs with management components (e.g., *Accelerated Reader* or *Reading Counts*). (optional)
8.5.2 Develop habits for lifelong learning.	8.5.2.1 Maintain lifelong literacy skills by relating reading, listening, and viewing to real world situations (e.g., career magazines, online newscasts) and choosing a literate lifestyle (e.g., reading for pleasure and personal fulfillment).

Appendix B.4

READS
Grades Nine and Ten

Ninth and Tenth Grades	Explore characteristics, history, and awards of creative works	Analyze structure and aesthetic features of creative works	Develop a literary-based product	Score reading progress
	The student will:			
Read as a personal activity				
9.10.1.1 Select and read literary and informational texts at an appropriate reading level.	9.10.1.1.1 Choose age and ability appropriate literature to read based on interest or curriculum need.			
	9.10.1.1.2 Choose age and ability appropriate informational texts to read based on interest or curriculum need.			
9.10.1.2 Select listening and viewing resources for enjoyment and information.	9.10.1.2.1 Participate in listening and viewing activities (e.g., audiobooks, podcasts).			
9.10.1.3 Use community resources for recreational and informational needs.	9.10.1.3.1 Visit the school or other libraries virtually or in person to access resources.			
	9.10.1.3.2 Visit museums, galleries, science centers, and parks virtually or in person (e.g., National Portrait Gallery, Museum of Modern Art).			
Explore characteristics, history, and awards of creative works				
9.10.2.1 Identify and critically analyze literary and media genres and themes.	9.10.2.1.1 Demonstrate knowledge of the distinguishing characteristics of literary and media genres (e.g., historical fiction, biography, documentary).			
	9.10.2.1.2 Analyze universal themes in text, visual, and digital resources (e.g., transforming quality of culture).			
9.10.2.2 Recognize that social, cultural, political and historical events influence ideas and information.	9.10.2.2.1 Analyze and compare a variety of historically and culturally significant works in various formats (e.g., Impressionist paintings, Shakespeare's plays and sonnets).			
	9.10.2.2.2 Demonstrate an appreciation for cultural and ethnic diversity by selecting appropriate creative and literary works.			
9.10.2.3 Appreciate literary and artistic excellence.	9.10.2.3.1 Identify award-winning authors, illustrators, and producers of literary and creative works (e.g., Pura Belpré Award winners).			
	9.10.2.3.2 Demonstrate a knowledge of and respect for the concept of intellectual freedom.			

(Continued)

Analyze structure and aesthetic features of creative works	
9.10.3.1 Identify and analyze key ideas and details of a work.	9.10.3.1.1 Connect prior and background knowledge to textual or visual clues to understand a literary work (e.g., inferring, predicting).
	9.10.3.1.2 Determine central ideas and supporting details of a work (e.g., paraphrasing, summarizing).
9.10.3.2 Understand the literary techniques and complexities of a work.	9.10.3.2.1 Identify an author's or illustrator's style (e.g., word choice, use of figurative language, medium).
	9.10.3.2.2 Compare and contrast story elements (e.g., characters, setting, or plot in multiple works.
Develop a literary-based product	
9.10.4.1 Develop an original work or a response to a creative work, working in groups or individually.	9.10.4.1.1 Choose a method to present an original work or a response to a creative work based on appropriateness and personal preference.
	9.10.4.1.2 Generate and organize ideas for an original work or a response to a creative work read, heard, or viewed (e.g., graphic organizer, group discussion, or brainstorming).
	9.10.4.1.3 Create an original work or a response to a creative work, reflecting on progress and editing as needed (e.g., rubric, peer review, checklist).
	9.10.4.1.4 Demonstrate understanding of and respect for copyright laws and intellectual property rights (e.g., use standard bibliographic format to credit sources).
9.10.4.2 Communicate and evaluate an original work or response to creative works, working in a group or individually.	9.10.4.2.1 Use appropriate methods to share and evaluate product.
Score reading progress	
9.10.5.1 Engage in literacy-based motivational program and activities.	9.10.5.1.1 Participate in library media activities and reading celebrations (e.g., Banned Book Week activities).
	9.10.5.1.2 Participate in structured independent reading programs (e.g., Florida Teens Read).
	9.10.5.1.3 Participate in reading motivation programs with management components (e.g., *Accelerated Reader or Reading Counts*). (optional)
9.10.5.2 Develop habits for life-long learning.	9.10.5.2.1 Maintain lifelong literacy skills by relating reading, listening, and viewing to real world situations (e.g., career and technical journals, online newscasts) and choosing a literate lifestyle (e.g., reading for pleasure and personal fulfillment).

Appendix B.5

READS
Grades Eleven and Twelve

	Read as a personal activity	Explore characteristics, history, and awards of creative works	Analyze structure and aesthetic features of creative works	Develop a literary-based product	Score reading progress

Eleventh and Twelfth Grades

READS

The student will:

Read as a personal activity

Standard	Benchmark
11.12.1.1 Select and read literary and informational resources at an appropriate reading level.	11.12.1.1.1 Choose age and ability appropriate literature to read based on interest or curriculum need.
	11.12.1.1.2 Choose age and ability appropriate informational texts to read based on interest or curriculum need.
11.12.1.2 Select listening and viewing resources for enjoyment and information.	11.12.1.2.1 Choose age and ability appropriate resources for listening and viewing activities (e.g., podcasts, music).
11.12.1.3 Use community resources for recreational and informational needs.	11.12.1.3.1 Visit the school or other libraries virtually or in person to access resources.
	11.12.1.3.2 Visit museums, galleries, science centers, and parks virtually or in person (e.g., Smithsonian museums, Museum of Science and Industry).

Explore characteristics, history, and awards of creative works

Standard	Benchmark
11.12.2.1 Identify and critically analyze literary and media genres and themes.	11.12.2.1.1 Demonstrate knowledge of the distinguishing characteristics of literary and media genres (e.g., historical fiction, biography, documentary).
	11.12.2.1.2 Analyze universal themes in text, visual, and digital resources (e.g., modern alienation from the natural world).
11.12.2.2 Recognize that social, cultural, political and historical events influence ideas and information.	11.12.2.2.1 Analyze and compare a variety of historically and culturally significant works in various formats (e.g., film noir, Greek plays).
	11.12.2.2.2 Demonstrate an appreciation for cultural and ethnic diversity by selecting appropriate creative and literary works.
11.12.2.3 Appreciate literary and artistic excellence.	11.12.2.3.1 Identify award-winning authors, illustrators, and producers of literary and creative works (e.g., Pulitzer Prize winners).
	11.12.2.3.2 Demonstrate a knowledge of and respect for the concept of intellectual freedom.

Analyze structure and aesthetic features of creative works	
11.12.3.1 Identify and analyze key ideas and details of a work.	11.12.3.1.1 Connect prior and background knowledge to textual or visual clues to understand a literary work (e.g., inferring and predicting).
	11.12.3.1.2 Determine central ideas and supporting details of a work (e.g., paraphrase, summarize).
11.12.3.2 Understand the literary techniques and complexities of a work.	11.12.3.2.1 Identify an author's or illustrator's style (e.g., word choice, use of figurative language, medium).
	11.12.3.2.2 Compare and contrast literary elements (e.g., characters, setting, or plot) in multiple works.
Develop a literary-based product	
11.12.4.1 Develop an original work or a response to a creative work, working in groups or individually.	11.12.4.1.1 Choose a method to present an original work or a response to a creative work based on appropriateness and personal preference.
	11.12.4.1.2 Generate and organize ideas for an original work or a response to a creative work read, heard or viewed (e.g., graphic organizer, group discussion, or brainstorming)
	11.12.4.1.3 Create an original work or a response to creative work, reflecting on progress and editing as needed.
	11.12.4.1.4 Demonstrate understanding of and respect for copyright laws and intellectual property rights (e.g., use standard bibliographic format to credit sources).
11.12.4.2 Communicate and evaluate an original work or response to creative works, working in a group or individually.	11.12.4.2.1 Use appropriate methods to share and evaluate product.
Score reading progress	
11.12.5.1 Engage in literacy-based motivational program and activities.	11.12.5.1.1 Participate in library media activities and reading celebrations (e.g., Banned Book Week activities).
	11.12.5.1.2 Participate in structured independent reading programs (e.g., Florida Teens Read).
	11.12.5.1.3 Participate in reading motivation programs with management components (e.g., *Accelerated Reader* or *Reading Counts*). (optional)
11.12.5.2 Develop habits for lifelong learning.	11.12.5.2.1 Maintain lifelong literacy skills by relating reading, listening, and viewing to real world situations (e.g., career and technical journals, online newscasts) and choosing a literate lifestyle (e.g., reading for pleasure and personal fulfillment).

Appendix C.1

READS K-12 Chart—Read as a Personal Activity

Read	Kindergarten	First	Second	Third	Fourth	Fifth	Sixth	Seventh	Eighth	Ninth/Tenth	Eleventh/Twelfth
1.1 Select and read literary and informational texts at an appropriate reading level.											
The student will:											
	K.1.1.1 Choose easy literature to read.	1.1.1.1 Choose easy literature to read based on interest or curriculum need.	2.1.1.1 Choose age and ability appropriate literature to read based on interest or curriculum need.	3.1.1.1 Choose age and ability appropriate literature to read based on interest or curriculum need.	4.1.1.1 Choose age and ability appropriate literature to read based on interest or curriculum need.	5.1.1.1 Choose age and ability appropriate literature to read based on interest or curriculum need.	6.1.1.1 Choose age and ability appropriate literature to read based on interest or curriculum need.	7.1.1.1 Choose age and ability appropriate literature to read based on interest or curriculum need.	8.1.1.1 Choose age and ability appropriate literature to read based on interest or curriculum need.	910.1.1.1 Choose age and ability appropriate literature to read based on interest or curriculum need.	1112.1.1.1 Choose age and ability appropriate literature to read based on interest or curriculum need.
	K.1.1.2 Choose easy informational texts to read.	1.1.1.2 Choose easy informational texts to read based on interest or curriculum need.	2.1.1.2 Choose age and ability appropriate informational texts to read based on interest or curriculum need.	3.1.1.2 Choose age and ability appropriate informational texts to read based on interest or curriculum need.	4.1.1.2 Choose age and ability appropriate informational texts to read based on interest or curriculum need.	5.1.1.2 Choose age and ability appropriate informational texts to read based on interest or curriculum need.	6.1.1.2 Choose age and ability appropriate informational texts to read based on interest or curriculum need.	7.1.1.2 Choose age and ability appropriate informational texts to read based on interest or curriculum need.	8.1.1.2 Choose age and ability appropriate informational texts to read based on interest or curriculum need.	910.1.1.2 Choose age and ability appropriate informational texts to read based on interest or curriculum need.	1112.1.1.2 Choose age and ability appropriate informational texts to read based on interest or curriculum need.
1.2 Select listening and viewing resources for enjoyment and information.											
	K.1.2.1 Participate in listening and viewing activities (e.g., story times, songs).	1.1.2.1 Participate in listening and viewing activities (e.g., story times, songs).	2.1.2.1 Participate in listening and viewing activities (e.g., story times, read alouds, songs).	3.1.2.1 Participate in listening and viewing activities (e.g., read alouds, podcasts).	4.1.2.1 Participate in listening and viewing activities (e.g., read alouds, podcasts).	5.1.2.1 Participate in listening and viewing activities (e.g., audiobooks, podcasts).	6.1.2.1 Participate in listening and viewing activities (e.g., audiobooks, podcasts).	7.1.2.1 Participate in listening and viewing activities (e.g., audiobooks, podcasts).	8.1.2.1 Participate in listening and viewing activities (e.g., audiobooks, podcasts).	910.1.2.1 Participate in listening and viewing activities (e.g., audiobooks, podcasts).	1112.1.2.1 Choose age and ability appropriate resources for listening and viewing activities (*e.g., audiobooks, podcasts*).

(Continued)

1.3 Use community resources for recreational and informational needs.

K	1	2	3	4	5	6	7	8	910	1112
K.1.3.1 Visit the school or other libraries virtually or in person o access resources.	1.1.3.1 Visit the school or other libraries virtually or in person to access resources.	2.1.3.1 Visit the school or other libraries virtually or in person to access resources.	3.1.3.1 Visit the school or other libraries virtually or in person to access resources.	4.1.3.1 Visit the school or other libraries virtually or in person to access resources.	5.1.3.1 Visit the school or other libraries virtually or in person to access resources.	6.1.3.1 Visit the school or other libraries virtually or in person to access resources.	7.1.3.1 Visit the school or other libraries virtually or in person to access resources.	8.1.3.1 Visit the school or other libraries virtually or in person to access resources.	910.1.3.1 Visit the school or other libraries virtually or in person to access resources.	1112.1.3.1 Visit the school or other libraries virtually or in person to access resources.
K.1.3.2 Visit museums, galleries, science centers, and parks virtually or in person (*e.g.,* Exploratorium After School).	1.1.3.2 Visit museums, galleries, science centers, and parks virtually or in person (*e.g.,* local county park).	2.1.3.2 Visit museums, galleries, science centers, and parks virtually or in person (*e.g.,* local county park)	3.1.3.2 Visit museums, galleries, science centers, and parks virtually or in person (*e.g.,* Florida Department of Environmental Protection – Kids' Page).	4.1.3.2 Visit museums, galleries, science centers, and parks virtually or in person (*e.g.,* Florida Memory Project).	5.1.3.2 Visit museums, galleries, science centers, and parks virtually or in person (*e.g.,* National Museum of Natural History, Challenger Center).	6.1.3.2 Visit museums, galleries, science centers, and parks virtually or in person (*e.g.,* Library of Congress Memory Project).	7.1.3.2 Visit museums, galleries, science centers, and parks virtually or in person (*e.g.,* National Museum of African Art, National Zoological Park).	8.1.3.2 Visit museums, galleries, science centers, and parks virtually or in person (*e.g.,* Louvre, National Gallery of Art).	910.1.3.2 Visit museums, galleries, science centers, and parks virtually or in person (*e.g.,* National Portrait Gallery, Museum of Modern Art).	1112.1.3.2 Visit museums, galleries, science centers, and parks virtually or in person (*e.g.,* Smithsonian museums, Museum of Science and Industry).

Appendix C.2

READS K-12 Chart—Explore Characteristics, History, and Awards of Creative Works

2.1 Identify and critically analyze literary and media genres and themes.

The student will:

Explore	Kindergarten	First	Second	Third	Fourth	Fifth	Sixth	Seventh	Eighth	Ninth/Tenth	Eleventh/Twelfth
	K.2.1.1 Identify basic characteristics of literary and media genres (e.g., nursery rhymes, fairy tales).	1.2.1.1 Identify basic characteristics of literary and media genres (e.g., nursery rhymes, fairy tales).	2.2.1.1 Identify basic characteristics of literary and media genres (e.g., folktales, *pourquoi* stories, fables).	3.2.1.1 Identify basic characteristics of literary and media genres (e.g., folktales, fables, poetry).	4.2.1.1 Identify distinguishing characteristics of literary and media genres (e.g., historical fiction, adventure).	5.2.1.1 Compare and contrast literary and media genres (e.g., historical fiction, fantasy, short stories).	6.2.1.1 Compare and contrast literary and media genres (e.g., historical fiction, fantasy, short stories).	7.2.1.1 Compare and contrast literary and media genres (e.g., adventure, mystery, documentary).	8.2.1.1 Analyze literary and media genres (e.g., poetry, drama, biography, documentary).	910.2.1.1 Demonstrate knowledge of the distinguishing characteristics of literary and media genres (e.g., historical fiction, biography, documentary).	1112.2.1.1 Demonstrate knowledge of the distinguishing characteristics of literary and media genres (e.g., historical fiction, biography, documentary).
	K.2.1.2 Identify literary themes in text, visual, and digital resources (e.g., happiness, friendship).	1.2.1.2 Identify literary themes in text, visual, and digital resources (e.g., happiness, friendship).	2.2.1.2 Identify literary themes in text, visual, and digital resources (e.g., honesty, love).	3.2.1.2 Identify literary themes in text, visual, and digital resources (e.g., beauty, truth).	4.2.1.2 Identify literary themes in text, visual, and digital resources (e.g., friendship, courage, loyalty).	5.2.1.2 Identify and explain literary themes in text, visual, and digital resources (e.g., friendship, courage, loyalty).	6.2.1.2 Explain and compare literary themes in text, visual, and digital resources (e.g., good v. evil, man v. nature).	7.2.1.2 Explain and compare literary themes in text, visual, and digital resources (e.g., good v. evil, man v. nature).	8.2.1.2 Explain and compare literary themes in text, visual, and digital resources (e.g., ability of human spirit to rise above grief and loss).	910.2.1.2 Analyze universal themes in text, visual, and digital resources (e.g., transforming quality of culture).	1112.2.1.2 Analyze universal themes in text, visual, and digital resources (e.g., alienation from society).

2.2 Recognize that social, cultural, political, and historical events influence ideas and information.

K	1	2	3	4	5	6	7	8	910	1112
K.2.2.3 Identify historically and culturally significant works in various formats (e.g., Mother Goose rhymes, cumulative tales).	1.2.2.3 Identify and select historically and culturally significant works in various formats (e.g., Mother Goose rhymes, talking animal tales).	2.2.2.3 Identify and select historically and culturally significant works in various formats (e.g., trickster stories, African American tales).	3.2.2.3 Identify historically and culturally significant works in various formats (e.g., Haiku poetry, Aesop's fables, Andersen's fairy tales).	4.2.2.3 Identify historically and culturally significant works in various formats (e.g., Haiku poetry, American tall tales).	5.2.2.3 Identify historically and culturally significant works in various formats (e.g., limericks, Native American tales).	6.2.2.3 Identify and compare historically and culturally significant works in various formats (e.g, Greek or Roman mythology).	7.2.2.3 Identify and compare historically and culturally significant works in various formats (e.g., political cartoons, African American handmade quilts).	8.2.2.3 Identify and compare historically and culturally significant works in various formats (e.g., Hispanic poetry, situation comedies).	910.2.2.3 Analyze and compare a variety of historically and culturally significant works in various formats (e.g., Impressionistic paintings, Shakespeare's plays and sonnets).	1112.2.2.3 Analyze and compare a variety of historically and culturally significant works in various formats (e.g, film noir, Greek plays).
K.2.2.2 Explore cultures through literature and other creative works.	1.2.2.2 Explore cultures through literature and other creative works.	2.2.2.2 Explore cultures through literature and other creative works.	3.2.2.2 Expand knowledge of other cultures through creative and literary works.	4.2.2.2 Recognize cultural and ethnic diversity through creative and literary works.	5.2.2.2 Recognize cultural and ethnic diversity through creative and literary works.	6.2.2.2 Recognize cultural and ethnic diversity through creative and literary works.	7.2.2.2 Recognize cultural and ethnic diversity through creative and literary works.	8.2.2.2 Recognize cultural and ethnic diversity through creative and literary works.	910.2.2.2 Demonstrate an appreciation for cultural and ethnic diversity by selecting appropriate creative and literary works.	1112.2.2.2 Demonstrate an appreciation for cultural and ethnic diversity by selecting appropriate creative and literary works.

(Continued)

2.3 Appreciate literary and artistic excellence.

K	1	2	3	4	5	6	7	8	9-10	11-12
K.2.3.1 Identify award-winning authors, illustrators, and producers of literary and creative works (e.g., Caldecott Medal winners).	1.2.3.1 Identify award-winning authors, illustrators, and producers of literary and creative works (e.g., Caldecott Medal winners).	2.2.3.1 Identify award-winning authors, illustrators, and producers of literary and creative works (e.g., Florida Reading Association Awards).	3.2.3.1 Identify award-winning authors, illustrators, and producers of literary and creative works (e.g., Jane Addams Book Award winners).	4.2.3.1 Identify award-winning authors, illustrators, and producers of literary and creative works (e.g., Hans Christian Andersen Award winners).	5.2.3.1 Identify award-winning authors, illustrators, and producers of literary and creative works (e.g., Newbery Medal winners).	6.2.3.1 Identify award-winning authors, illustrators, and producers of literary and creative works (e.g., Sunshine State Young Reader's Award winners).	7.2.3.1 Identify award-winning authors, illustrators, and producers of literary and creative works (e.g., Edgar Allen Poe Award winners).	8.2.3.1 Identify award-winning authors, illustrators, and producers of literary and creative works (e.g., Laura Ingalls Wilder Award winners).	910.2.3.1 Identify award-winning authors, illustrators, and producers of literary and creative works (e.g., Pura Belpré Award winners).	1112.2.3.1 Identify award-winning authors, illustrators, and producers of literary and creative works (e.g., Pulitzer Prize winners).
		2.2.3.2 Begin to identify the concept of intellectual freedom.	3.2.3.2 Begin to identify the concept of intellectual freedom.	4.2.3.2 Begin to identify the concept of intellectual freedom.	5.2.3.2 Identify the concept of intellectual freedom.	6.2.3.2 Identify the concept of intellectual freedom.	7.2.3.2 Acknowledge the importance of intellectual freedom.	8.2.3.2 Acknowledge the importance of intellectual freedom.	910.2.3.2 Demonstrate a knowledge of and respect for the concept of intellectual freedom.	1112.2.3.2 Demonstrate a knowledge of and respect for the concept of intellectual freedom.

Appendix C.3

READS K-12 Chart—Analyze Structure and Aesthetic Features of Creative Works

Analyze

3.1 Identify and analyze key ideas and details of a work.

The student will:

Kindergarten	First	Second	Third	Fourth	Fifth	Sixth	Seventh	Eighth	Ninth/Tenth	Eleventh/Twelfth
K.3.1.1 Use prior and background knowledge to interpret textual and visual clues to understand a literary work.	1.3.1.1 Use prior and background knowledge to interpret textual and visual clues to understand a literary work.	2.3.1.1 Use prior and background knowledge to interpret textual and visual clues to understand a literary work.	3.3.1.1 Use prior and background knowledge to interpret textual and visual clues to understand a literary work.	4.3.1.1 Use prior and background knowledge to interpret textual and visual clues to understand a literary work (e.g., inferring, predicting).	5.3.1.1 Use prior and background knowledge to interpret textual and visual clues to understand a literary work (e.g., inferring, predicting).	6.3.1.1 Connect prior and background knowledge to textual or visual clues to understand a literary work (e.g., inferring, predicting).	7.3.1.1 Connect prior and background knowledge to textual or visual clues to understand a literary work (e.g., inferring, predicting).	8.3.1.1 Connect prior and background knowledge to textual or visual clues to understand a literary work (e.g., inferring, predicting).	910.3.1.1 Connect prior and background knowledge to textual or visual clues to understand a literary work (e.g., inferring, predicting).	1112.3.1.1 Connect prior and background knowledge to textual or visual clues to understand a literary work (e.g., inferring, predicting).
K.3.1.2 Identify central ideas and supporting details of a work.	1.3.1.2 Identify central ideas and supporting details of a work.	2.3.1.2 Identify central ideas and supporting details of a work.	3.3.1.2 Identify central ideas and supporting details of a work (e.g., paraphrasing, summarizing).	4.3.1.2 Identify central ideas and supporting details of a work (e.g., paraphrasing, summarizing).	5.3.1.2 Identify central ideas and supporting details of a work (e.g., paraphrasing, summarizing).	6.3.1.2 Determine central ideas and supporting details of a work (e.g., paraphrasing, summarizing).	7.3.1.2 Determine central ideas and supporting details of a work (e.g., paraphrasing, summarizing).	8.3.1.2 Determine central ideas and supporting details of a work (e.g., paraphrasing, summarizing).	910.3.1.2 Determine central ideas and supporting details of a work (e.g., paraphrasing, summarizing).	1112.3.1.2 Determine central ideas and supporting details of a work (e.g., paraphrasing, summarizing).

3.2 Understand the literary techniques and complexities of a work.

K	1	2	3	4	5	6	7	8	9–10	11–12
K.3.2.1 Identify an author's or illustrator's style (e.g., word choice, use of rhymes) word choice, use of rhymes	1.3.2.1 Identify an author's or illustrator's style (e.g., word choice, use of rhymes).	2.3.2.1 Identify an author's or illustrator's style (e.g., word choice, use of rhymes, medium).	3.3.2.1 Identify an author's or illustrator's style (e.g., word choice, figurative language, medium).	4.3.2.1 Identify an author's or illustrator's style (e.g., word choice, use of figurative language, medium).	5.3.2.1 Identify an author's or illustrator's style (e.g., word choice, use of figurative language, medium).	6.3.2.1 Identify an author's or illustrator's style (e.g., word choice, use of figurative language, medium).	7.3.2.1 Identify an author's or illustrator's style (e.g., word choice, use of figurative language, medium).	8.3.2.1 Identify an author's or illustrator's style (e.g., word choice, use of figurative language, medium).	910.3.2.1 Identify an author's or illustrator's style (e.g., word choice, use of figurative language, medium).	1112.3.2.1 Identify an author's or illustrator's style (e.g., word choice, use of figurative language, medium).
K.3.2.2 Describe the characters, setting, and plot of a work (e.g., who, what, where, when, how) and arrange events in sequence.	1.3.2.2 Describe the characters, setting, and plot of a work (e.g., who, what, where, when, how) and arrange events in sequence.	2.3.2.2 Describe the characters, setting, and plot of a work (e.g., who, what, where, when, how) and arrange events in sequence.	3.3.2.2 Compare story elements (e.g., characters, setting, or plot) in two works.	4.3.2.2 Compare story elements (e.g., characters, setting, or plot) in multiple works.	5.3.2.2 Compare and contrast story elements (e.g., characters, setting, or plot) in multiple works.	6.3.2.2 Compare and contrast story elements (e.g., characters, setting, or plot) in multiple works.	7.3.2.2 Compare and contrast story elements (e.g., characters, setting, or plot) in multiple works.	8.3.2.2 Compare and contrast story elements (e.g., characters, setting, or plot) in multiple works.	910.3.2.2 Compare and contrast story elements (e.g., characters, setting, or plot) in multiple works.	1112.3.2.2 Compare and contrast literary elements (e.g., characters, setting, or plot) in multiple works.

Appendix C.4

READS K-12 Chart—Develop a Literary-Based Product

Develop	Kindergarten	First	Second	Third	Fourth	Fifth	Sixth	Seventh	Eighth	Ninth/Tenth	Eleventh/Twelfth
4.1 Develop an original work or a response to a creative work, working in groups or individually.											
				The student will:							
K.4.1.1 Use a teacher or librarian selected method to present an original work or a response to a creative work.	1.4.1.1 Use a teacher or librarian selected method to present an original work or a response to a creative work.	2.4.1.1 Use a teacher or librarian selected method to present an original work or a response to a creative work.	3.4.1.1 Choose a method to present an original work or a response to a creative work from teacher or librarian choices.	4.4.1.1 Choose a method to present an original work or a response to a creative work from teacher or librarian choices.	5.4.1.1 Choose a method to present an original work or a response to a creative work based on appropriateness and personal preference.	6.4.1.1 Choose a method to present an original work or a response to a creative work based on appropriateness and personal preference.	7.4.1.1 Choose a method to present an original work or a response to a creative work based on appropriateness and personal preference.	8.4.1.1 Choose a method to present an original work or a response to a creative work based on appropriateness and personal preference.	910.4.1.1 Choose a method to present an original work or a response to a creative work based on appropriateness and personal preference.	1112.4.1.1 Choose a method to present an original work or a response to a creative work based on appropriateness and personal preference.
K.4.1.2 Connect thoughts and oral language to generate a response to a work read aloud or viewed with teacher or librarian guidance.	1.4.1.2 Generate and organize ideas for an original story or response to a work read aloud or viewed (e.g., webbing or brainstorming) with teacher or librarian guidance.	2.4.1.2 Generate and organize ideas for an original story or response to a work read aloud or viewed (e.g., webbing or brainstorming) with teacher or librarian guidance.	3.4.1.2 Generate and organize ideas for an original story or response to a work read, heard, or viewed (e.g., webbing or brainstorming).	4.4.1.2 Generate and organize ideas for an original work or a response to a creative work read, heard, or viewed (e.g., graphic organizer, group discussion, or brainstorming).	5.4.1.2 Generate and organize ideas for an original work or a response to a creative work read, heard, or viewed (e.g., graphic organizer, group discussion, or brainstorming).	6.4.1.2 Generate and organize ideas for an original work or a response to a creative work read, heard, or viewed (e.g., graphic organizer, group discussion, or brainstorming).	7.4.1.2 Generate and organize ideas for an original work or a response to a creative work read, heard, or viewed (e.g., graphic organizer, group discussion, or brainstorming).	8.4.1.2 Generate and organize ideas for an original work or a response to a creative work read, heard, or viewed (e.g., graphic organizer, group discussion, or brainstorming).	910.4.1.2 Generate and organize ideas for an original work or a response to a creative work read, heard, or viewed (e.g., graphic organizer, group discussion, or brainstorming).	1112.4.1.2 Generate and organize ideas for an original work or a response to a creative work read, heard, or viewed (e.g., graphic organizer, group discussion, or brainstorming).

(Continued)

K.4.1.3	1.4.1.3	2.4.1.3	3.4.1.3	4.4.1.3	5.4.1.3	6.4.1.3	7.4.1.3	8.4.1.3	910.4.1.3	1112.4.1.3
Create an original work or a response to a creative work, adding details and checking for correct sequence with teacher or librarian guidance.	Create an original work or a response to a creative work, adding details and checking for correct sequence with teacher or librarian guidance.	Create an original work or a response to a creative work, checking work against a teacher or librarian produced rubric.	Create an original work or a response to a creative work, checking work against a teacher or librarian produced rubric.	Create an original work or a response to a creative work, checking work against a teacher or librarian produced rubric or peer review.	Create an original work or a response to a creative work, reflecting on progress and editing as needed (e.g., rubric, peer review, checklist).	Create an original work or a response to a creative work, reflecting on progress and editing as needed (e.g., rubric, peer review, checklist).	Create an original work or a response to a creative work, reflecting on progress and editing as needed (e.g., rubric, peer review, checklist).	Create an original work or a response to a creative work, reflecting on progress and editing as needed (e.g., rubric, peer review, checklist).	Create an original work or a response to a creative work, reflecting on progress and editing as needed (e.g., rubric, peer review, checklist).	Create an original work or a response to a creative work, reflecting on progress and editing as needed (e.g., rubric, peer review, checklist).
		2.4.1.4 Identify legal and ethical usage guidelines for copyrighted resources.	3.4.1.4 Practice respect for copyright laws and intellectual property rights (e.g., use standard bibliographic format to credit sources).	4.4.1.4 Practice respect for copyright laws and intellectual property rights (e.g., use standard bibliographic format to credit sources).	5.4.1.4 Practice respect for copyright laws and intellectual property rights (e.g., use standard bibliographic format to credit sources).	6.4.1.4 Practice respect for copyright laws and intellectual property rights (e.g., use standard bibliographic format to credit sources).	7.4.1.4 Demonstrate understanding of and respect for copyright laws and intellectual property rights (e.g., use standard bibliographic format to credit sources).	8.4.1.4 Demonstrate understanding of and respect for copyright laws and intellectual property rights (e.g., use standard bibliographic format to credit sources).	910.4.1.4 Demonstrate understanding of and respect for copyright laws and intellectual property rights (e.g., use standard bibliographic format to credit sources).	1112.4.1.4 Demonstrate understanding of and respect for copyright laws and intellectual property rights (e.g., use standard bibliographic format to credit sources).

4.2 Communicate and evaluate an original work or a response to creative work, working in a group or individually.

K	1	2	3	4	5	6	7	8	9-10	11-12
K.4.2.1 Convey ideas and experiences based on creative works (e.g., re-tell main events in a story, recite nursery rhymes, draw picture).	1.4.2.1 Communicate orally, visually or in writing ideas and experiences based on creative works with teacher and/or librarian assistance.	2.4.2.1 Communicate orally, visually or in writing ideas and experiences based on creative works with teacher and/or librarian assistance.	3.4.2.1 Use appropriate presentation tools and techniques to share product.	4.4.2.1 Use appropriate presentation tools and techniques to share product.	5.4.2.1 Use appropriate presentation tools and techniques to share product.	6.4.2.1 Use appropriate presentation tools and techniques to share product.	7.4.2.1 Use appropriate presentation tools and techniques to share product.	8.4.2.1 Use appropriate presentation tools and techniques to share product.	910.4.2.1 Use appropriate presentation tools and techniques to share product.	1112.4.2.1 Use appropriate presentation tools and techniques to share product.
K.4.2.2 Evaluate product and production process with guidance from teacher or librarian.	1.4.2.2 Evaluate product and production process with guidance from teacher or librarian.	2.4.2.2 Evaluate product and production process with guidance from teacher or librarian.	3.4.2.2 Evaluate product and production process.	4.4.2.2 Evaluate product and production process.	5.4.2.2 Evaluate product and production process.	6.4.2.2 Evaluate product and production process.	7.4.2.2 Evaluate product and production process.	8.4.2.2 Evaluate product and production process.	910.4.2.2 Evaluate product and production process.	1112.4.2.2 Evaluate product and production process.

Appendix C.5

READS K-12 Chart—Score Reading Progress

5.1 Engage in literacy-based motivational program and activities.

The student will:

Score		
Kindergarten	First	Second
K.5.1.1 Participate in school library activities and reading celebrations (e.g., storytimes, puppet plays).	1.5.1.1 Participate in school library activities and reading celebrations (e.g., character parades, puppet plays).	2.5.1.1 Participate in school library activities and reading celebrations (e.g., character parades, author visits).
K.5.1.2 Participate in structured independent reading programs (e.g., Florida Reading Association Children's Book Award).	1.5.1.2 Participate in structured independent reading programs (e.g., Florida Reading Association Children's Book Award).	2.5.1.2 Participate in structured independent reading programs (e.g., Florida Reading Association Children's Book Award).

Third	Fourth	Fifth	Sixth	Seventh	Eighth	Ninth/Tenth	Eleventh/Twelfth
3.5.1.1 Participate in school library activities and reading celebrations (e.g., character parades, author visits).	4.5.1.1 Participate in school library activities and reading celebrations (e.g, family literacy night, author visits).	5.5.1.1 Participate in school library activities and reading celebrations (e.g., family literacy night, author visits).	6.5.1.1 Participate in school library activities and reading celebrations (e.g, School Library Media Month celebrations).	7.5.1.1 Participate in school library activities and reading celebrations (e.g., School Library Media Month celebrations).	8.5.1.1 Participate in school library activities and reading celebrations (e.g., televised book talks or reviews).	910.5.1.1 Participate in school library activities and reading celebrations (e.g., Banned Book Week activities).	1112.5.1.1 Participate in school library activities and reading celebrations (e.g., Banned Book Week activities).
3.5.1.2 Participate in structured independent reading programs (e.g., Sunshine State Young Reader's Award).	4.5.1.2 Participate in structured independent reading programs (e.g., Sunshine State Young Reader's Award).	5.5.1.2 Participate in structured independent reading programs (e.g., Sunshine State Young Reader's Award).	6.5.1.2 Participate in structured independent reading programs (e.g., Sunshine State Young Reader's Award).	7.5.1.2 Participate in structured independent reading programs (e.g., Sunshine State Young Reader's Award).	8.5.1.2 Participate in structured independent reading programs (e.g., Sunshine State Young Reader's Award).	910.5.1.2 Participate in structured independent reading programs (e.g., Florida Teens Read).	1112.5.1.2 Participate in structured independent reading programs (e.g., Florida Teens Read).

(Continued)

	K	1	2	3	4	5	6	7	8	9-10	11-12
	K.5.1.3 Monitor own reading progress using a variety of methods.	1.5.1.3 Monitor own reading progress using a variety of methods.	2.5.1.3 Participate in reading motivation programs with management components (e.g., *Accelerated Reader* or *Reading Counts*). (optional)	3.5.1.3 Participate in reading motivation programs with management components (e.g., *Accelerated Reader* or *Reading Counts*). (optional)	4.5.1.3 Participate in reading motivation programs with management components (e.g., *Accelerated Reader* or *Reading Counts*). (optional)	5.5.1.3 Participate in reading motivation programs with management components (e.g., *Accelerated Reader* or *Reading Counts*). (optional)	6.5.1.3 Participate in reading motivation programs with management components (e.g., *Accelerated Reader* or *Reading Counts*). (optional)	7.5.1.3 Participate in reading motivation programs with management components (e.g., *Accelerated Reader* or *Reading Counts*). (optional)	8.5.1.3 Participate in reading motivation programs with management components (e.g., *Accelerated Reader* or *Reading Counts*). (optional)	910.5.1.3 Participate in reading motivation programs with management components (e.g., *Accelerated Reader* or *Reading Counts*). (optional)	1112.5.1.3 Participate in reading motivation programs with management components (e.g., *Accelerated Reader* or *Reading Counts*). (optional)

5.2 Develop habits for lifelong learning.

	1	2	3	4	5	6	7	8	9-10	11-12
	1.5.2.1 Identify lifelong literacy skills by relating reading, listening, and viewing to real world situations (e.g., online magazines and books) and choosing a literate lifestyle (e.g., reading for pleasure and personal fulfillment).	2.5.2.1 Identify lifelong literacy skills by relating reading, listening, and viewing to real world situations (e.g., online magazines and books) and choosing a literate lifestyle (e.g., reading for pleasure and personal fulfillment).	3.5.2.1 Identify lifelong literacy skills by relating reading, listening, and viewing to real world situations (e.g., hobby magazines, online newscasts) and choosing a literate lifestyle (e.g., reading for pleasure and personal fulfillment).	4.5.2.1 Identify lifelong literacy skills by relating reading, listening, and viewing to real world situations (e.g., hobby magazines, online newscasts) and choosing a literate lifestyle (e.g., reading for pleasure and personal fulfillment).	5.5.2.1 Identify lifelong literacy skills by relating reading, listening, and viewing to real world situations (e.g., hobby magazines, online newscasts) and choosing a literate lifestyle (e.g., reading for pleasure and personal fulfillment).	6.5.2.1 Practice lifelong literacy skills by relating reading, listening, and viewing to real world situations (e.g., hobby magazines, online newscasts) and choosing a literate lifestyle (e.g., reading for pleasure and personal fulfillment).	7.5.2.1 Practice lifelong literacy skills by relating reading, listening, and viewing to real world situations (e.g., career magazines, online newscasts) and choosing a literate lifestyle (e.g., reading for pleasure and personal fulfillment).	8.5.2.1 Practice lifelong literacy skills by relating reading, listening, and viewing to real world situations (e.g., career magazines, online newscasts) and choosing a literate lifestyle (e.g., reading for pleasure and personal fulfillment).	910.5.2.1 Maintain lifelong literacy skills by relating reading, listening, and viewing to real world situations (e.g., career and technical journals, online newscasts) and choosing a literate lifestyle (e.g., reading for pleasure and personal fulfillment).	1112.5.2.1 Maintain lifelong literacy skills by relating reading, listening, and viewing to real world situations (e.g., career and technical journals, online newscasts) and choosing a literate lifestyle (e.g., reading for pleasure and personal fulfillment).

Appendix D

READS Overview

Read as a personal activity	Explore characteristics, history, and awards of creative works	Analyze structure and aesthetic features of creative works	Develop a literary-based product	Score reading progress

READS Component	READS Indicator	Common Core State Standards—English Language Arts*
Read as a personal activity		
	The student will:	
1.1 Select and read literary and informational resources at an appropriate reading level.	1.1.1 Choose age and ability appropriate literature to read based on interest or curriculum need.	• Reading: Informational Text—10 Read and comprehend literary nonfiction in the grade text complexity band . . . • Reading: Literature—10 Read and comprehend literature in the grade text complexity band . . .
	1.1.2 Choose age and ability appropriate informational texts to read based on interest or curriculum need.	• Reading: Informational Text—10 Read and comprehend literary nonfiction in the grade text complexity band . . . • Reading: Literature – 10 Read and comprehend literature in the grade text complexity band . . .
1.2 Select listening and viewing resources for enjoyment and information.	1.2.1 Choose age and ability appropriate resources for listening and viewing activities (e.g., audiobooks, podcasts).	• Reading: Informational Text—10 Read and comprehend literary nonfiction in the grade text complexity band . . . • Reading: Literature—10 Read and comprehend literature in the grade text complexity band . . . • Speaking and Listening—2 Integrate multiple sources of information presented in diverse formats and media (e.g., visually . . .orally) . . .
1.3 Use community resources for recreational and informational needs.	1.3.1 Visit the school or other libraries virtually or in person to access resources.	• Reading: Informational Text—10 Read and comprehend literary nonfiction in the grade text complexity band . . . • Reading: Literature—10 Read and comprehend literature in the grade text complexity band . . .
	1.3.2 Visit museums, galleries, science centers, and parks virtually or in person (e.g., Smithsonian museums, Museum of Science and Industry).	• Reading: Informational Text—10 Read and comprehend literary nonfiction in the grade text complexity band . . . • Reading: Literature—10 Read and comprehend literature in the grade text complexity band . . .

		Explore characteristics, history, and awards of creative works
2.1 Identify and critically analyze literary and media genres and themes.	2.1.1 Demonstrate knowledge of the distinguishing characteristics of literary and media genres (e.g., historical fiction, biography, documentary).	• Reading: Literature—5 Analyze how an author's choices . . . contribute to its overall structure and meaning as well as its aesthetic impact. • Reading: Literature—7 Analyze multiple interpretations of a story, drama, or poem . . . • Reading: Literature—9 Demonstrate knowledge of foundational works of American literature . . .
	2.1.2 Analyze universal themes in text, visual, and digital resources (e.g., alienation from society).	• Reading: Literature—10 Read and comprehend literature in the grade text complexity band . . . • Writing—9 Draw evidence from literary or informational texts to support analysis . . .
2.2 Recognize that social, cultural, political and historical events influence ideas and information.	2.2.1 Analyze and compare a variety of historically and culturally significant works in various formats (e.g., film noir, Greek plays).	• Reading: Literature—6 Analyze a case in which grasping point of view requires distinguishing what is directly stated in a text from what is really meant . . . • Reading: Literature—7 Analyze multiple interpretations of a story, drama, or poem . . . • Reading: Literature—9 Demonstrate knowledge of foundational works of American literature . . .
	2.2.2 Demonstrate an appreciation for cultural and ethnic diversity by selecting appropriate creative and literary works.	• Speaking and Listening—1c Initiate and participate effectively in a range of collaborative discussions: Propel conversations by posing and responding to questions . . . • Writing—9 Draw evidence from literary or informational texts to support analysis . . .
2.3 Appreciate literary and artistic excellence.	2.3.1 Identify award-winning authors, illustrators, and producers of literary and creative works (e.g., Pulitzer Prize winners).	• Reading: Informational Text—7 Integrate and evaluate multiple sources of information presented in different media or formats . . . • Reading: Informational Text—8 Delineate and evaluate the reasoning in texts . . . • Reading: Literature—6 Analyze a case in which grasping point of view requires distinguishing what is directly stated in a text from what is really meant . . . • Reading: Literature—7 Analyze multiple interpretations of a story, drama, or poem . . .
	2.3.2 Demonstrate a knowledge of and respect for the concept of intellectual freedom.	• Writing—9 Draw evidence from literary or informational texts to support analysis . . .

(Continued)

Analyze structure and aesthetic features of creative works

3.1 Identify and analyze key ideas and details of a work.	3.1.1 Connect prior and background knowledge to textual or visual clues to understand a literary work (e.g., inferring, predicting).	• Language—3 Apply knowledge of language to understand how language functions in different contexts . . . • Language—6 Acquire and use accurately general academic and domain-specific words and phrases . . . • Reading: Informational Text—1 Cite strong and thorough textual evidence to support analysis . . .
	3.1.2 Determine central ideas and supporting details of a work (e.g., paraphrasing, summarizing).	• Reading: Informational Text—4 Determine the meaning of words and phrases . . . • Reading: Literature – 1 Cite strong and thorough textual evidence to support analysis of text . . . • Reading: Literature—4 Determine the meaning of words and phrases . . .
	3.2.1 Identify an author's or illustrator's style (e.g., word choice, use of figurative language, medium).	• Writing – 8 Gather relevant information from multiple authoritative print and digital sources . . . • Reading: Informational Text—3 Analyze a complex set of ideas or sequence of events and explain how specific individuals, ideas, or events interact and develop over the course of the text. • Reading: Literature—1 Cite strong and thorough textual evidence to support analysis of text . . . • Reading: Literature—3 Analyze the impact of the author's choices . . .
3.2 Understand the literary techniques and complexities of a work.	3.2.2 Compare and contrast literary elements (e.g., characters, setting, or plot) in multiple works.	• Reading: Literature—6 Analyze a case in which grasping point of view requires distinguishing what is directly stated in a text from what is really meant . . . • Reading: Literature—9 Demonstrate knowledge of foundational works of American literature . . . • Language—4a Determine or clarify the meaning of unknown and multiple-meaning words and phrases: Use context . . . • Language—5 Demonstrate understanding of figurative language, word relationships, and nuances in word meanings. • Reading: Literature—4 Determine the meaning of words and phrases . . . • Reading: Literature—5 Analyze how an author's choices . . . contribute to its overall structure and meaning as well as its aesthetic impact. • Reading: Literature—9 Demonstrate knowledge of foundational works of American literature . . .

READS Component	READS Indicator	Common Core State Standards—English Language Arts*
		Develop a literary-based product
	4.1.1 Choose a method to present an original work or a response to a creative work based on appropriateness and personal preference.	• Speaking and Listening—5 Make strategic use of digital media in presentations . . . • Speaking and Listening—1a Initiate and participate effectively in a range of collaborative discussions: Come to discussions prepared, having read and researched material . . .
4.1 Develop an original work or a response to creative works, working in groups or individually.	4.1.2 Generate and organize ideas for an original work or a response to a creative work read, heard or viewed (e.g., graphic organizer, group discussion, or brainstorming).	• Speaking and Listening—1b Initiate and participate effectively in a range of collaborative discussions: Work with peers to promote civil, democratic discussions . . . • Speaking and Listening—1c Initiate and participate effectively in a range of collaborative discussions: Propel conversations by posing and responding to questions . . . • Speaking and Listening—1d Initiate and participate effectively in a range of collaborative discussions: Respond thoughtfully to diverse perspectives . . .
	4.1.3 Create an original work or a response to creative work, reflecting on progress and editing as needed.	• Writing—1b Write arguments to support claims: Introduce precise, knowledgeable claim(s) . . . • Writing—2a Write informative/explanatory texts: Introduce a topic; organize complex ideas, concepts, and information . . . • Writing—3c Write narratives to develop real or imagined experiences or events: Use a variety of techniques to sequence events . . . • Writing—3d Write narratives to develop real or imagined experiences or events: Use precise words and phrases, telling details . . . • Writing—4 Produce clear and coherent writing . . . • Writing—5 Develop and strengthen writing as needed . . .
	4.1.4 Demonstrate understanding of and respect for copyright laws and intellectual property rights (e.g., use standard bibliographic format to credit sources).	• Writing—8 Gather relevant information from multiple authoritative print and digital sources . . . avoiding plagiarism and overreliance on any one source and following a standard format for citation.
4.2 Communicate and evaluate an original work or response to creative works, working in a group or individually.	4.2.1 Use appropriate methods to share and evaluate product.	• Speaking and Listening—6 Adapt speech to a variety of contexts and tasks . . . • Writing—6 Use technology, including the Internet, to produce, publish, and update individual or shared writing products . . .

(Continued)

		Score reading progress
5.1 Engage in literacy-based motivational programs and activities.	5.1.1 Participate in school library activities and reading celebrations (e.g., Banned Book Week activities).	• Speaking and Listening – 1a Initiate and participate effectively in a range of collaborative discussions: Come to discussions prepared, having read and researched material . . . • Speaking and Listening – 1b Initiate and participate effectively in a range of collaborative discussions: Work with peers to promote civil, democratic discussions . . .
	5.1.2 Participate in structured independent reading programs (e.g., Florida Teens Read).	• Speaking and Listening – 1c Initiate and participate effectively in a range of collaborative discussions: Propel conversations by posing and responding to questions . . .
	5.1.3 Participate in reading motivation programs with management components (e.g., *Accelerated Reader* or *Reading Counts*) (optional).	• Speaking and Listening – 5 Make strategic use of digital media in presentations . . . • Writing – 6 Use technology, including the Internet, to produce, publish, and update individual or shared writing products . . . • Reading: Informational Text– 10 Read and comprehend literary nonfiction in the grade text complexity band . . .
5.2 Develop habits for lifelong learning	5.2.1 Maintain lifelong literacy skills by relating reading, listening, and viewing to real world situations (e.g., career and technical journals, online newscasts) and choosing a literate lifestyle (e.g., reading for pleasure and personal fulfillment).	• Reading: Literature – 10 Read and comprehend literature in the grade text complexity band . . . • Speaking and Listening – 1a Initiate and participate effectively in a range of collaborative discussions: Come to discussions prepared, having read and researched material . . . • Speaking and Listening – 1b Initiate and participate effectively in a range of collaborative discussions: Work with peers to promote civil, democratic discussions . . . • Writing – 6 Use technology, including the Internet, to produce, publish, and update individual or shared writing products . . .

Index

AASL/ALSC/YALSA Interdivisional Committee on School/Public Library Cooperation, 53, 54, 57
Academic libraries, 58–62; community outreach, 59–62; field trips, 59; reading promotion, 60–62; school visits, 59
Accelerated Reader (AR), 54, 265, 275
Adams, Helen R., 160, 165
Adolescent Literacy: A Policy Research Brief, 5
Adolescents, characteristics and needs, 129, 134
Adventure fiction, 91–92
Advocacy, 50, 54–55, 164–65, 245, 252
Aesthetic readers, 277
African Americans in literature, 129, 131–32
Aliterate students, 22, 32
Allington, Richard, 247–48, 249
American Association of School Librarians (AASL), 4. *See also Empowering Learners; Standards for the 21st-Century Learner;* Position statements
American Library Association (ALA), 153
Anticipation guide, 106, 112
Appleman, Deborah, 258
Arnone, Marilyn P., 14
Aronson, Marc, 298, 299
Art, activities, 65, 87, 95, 106, 178, 180, 184, 194, 195, 199
Assessment data, student, 282, 283–84; formal, 51–52; tools, 228, 230
Assessment. *See also* Self-assessment, students
Assignment alerts. *See* Public libraries, assignment alerts
Association of College & Research Libraries' (ACRL) *Strategic Plan 2020*, 58
Association of Library Services for Children (ALSC), 151
A Test of Leadership: Charting the Future of U.S. Higher Education, 58

Atwell, Nancie, 24
Audiobooks, 39–46, 143, 260; activities, 45–46; awards, 151; educational benefits, 42–46; formats, 45; music, 45–46, 56
Author studies, 183, 189–93
Autobiographies, 102
Awards, popularity, 153, 157
Awards. *See also* Literary awards; Art, activities

Background knowledge, 30, 64, 79, 92, 100, 136, 142, 143, 173–76, 180, 246, 289
Banned Book Week, 161, 163, 241
Becoming a Nation of Readers, 30
Beers, Kylene, 22, 23, 32, 43–44, 102, 113
Bibliographic format, 227
Biography, 102–4; activities, 103–4, 106
Biopunk. *See* Science fiction
Blogs, 191–92, 199
Blogs for professional development, 299
Bloom's Taxonomy, 176
Bodart, Joni, 28
Book clubs, 257–62; parent and student, 61
Bookmarks, 26
Books, circulation, 22–23, 46, 50, 54, 55, 56, 246–47, 250, 251, 275, 283
Books on Tape, 42
Booktalking, 27–29, 55
Book trailers, 29, 176, 192, 198, 199
Brainstorming, 217
Burkey, Mary, 43, 45, 46, 260

Callison, Daniel, 63
Campbell, Kimberly Hill, 96, 97, 99, 102, 103, 106, 112
Careers and workplace, activities, 280, 292–94
Cart, Michael, 92, 151
Caspari, Ann K., 58, 63–64
Censorship, 158, 159, 161–64

Center for Digital Literacy, 14
Challenged books, 158, 159, 161–64
Chance, Rosemary, 42, 89, 161
Characters, 197–200
Chick lit. *See* Realistic fiction
Children's Book Council, 33
Children's Literature Comprehensive Database, 114
Choice of reading materials. *See* Self-selected reading
Citizenship role, 295–97
Civics education, 243
Classroom collection of resources. *See* Text set
Cloud computing, 214, 215–17
Collaboration, 3, 6, 8, 13, 42, 49, 51–52, 95, 98, 113, 134–36, 138–40, 153, 161, 177, 179, 180–81, 194–95, 197, 199, 201, 202, 247, 249, 250, 255, 260, 292
Collection development, 42, 103, 107–9, 133, 135, 138, 160–61, 275, 277; audiobooks, 45; native language resources, 140
College readiness, 58
Common Core Curriculum Mapping: English Language Arts, 281
Common Core Curriculum Mapping Project, 102
Common Core State Standards, 221, 228, 274, 298
Common Core State Standards for English Language Arts, 5, 8, 11
Common Core State Standards for English Language Arts & Literacy in History/Social Studies, Science, and Technical Subjects, 88
Conley, David T., 8
Cooperative groups, 223–24
Copyright, 227–28
Council of Chief State School Officers, 5, 8
Cox, Ruth E., 27
Creative Commons, 228
Critical literacy, 135–36
Critical thinking, 103
Cultural and historical context of literature, 142–43
Cultural artifacts, 63–64, 141
Cultural understanding, 136
Curiosity, 281, 290–92, 297, 298
Cyberpunk. *See* Science fiction

Dale, Edgar, 211
Dale's Cone of Experience, 211
DeVoogd, Glenn, 136
Digital natives, 227
Discussion of literature, value, 132–33, 140
Discussions, literary, 245, 259, 260, 262–64
Displays, 24–26, 46, 87, 178

Dispositions, 4, 101, 179, 279, 281, 282, 287–89, 290–92, 295–97; school librarians, 298–99
Diversity, 132, 136
Drama, 104
DVDs, 143

Elders, 290–92
E-learning, 51, 279, 281, 282, 287–89, 290–92, 295–97
Empowering Learners: Guidelines for School Library Media Programs, 4, 46, 53, 58, 158, 243, 277
English Language Arts Standards: History/Social Studies, 5
English Language Learners (ELL), 31, 43–44, 50, 81, 98, 106, 112, 138, 140, 141, 177, 194, 243, 257, 260
Equipment checklist, 213
Equitable access, 158–60, 161
Essays, 99
Essential questions, 77, 102, 281–82, 295–97
Ethnicity, 132
Exceptional Student Education (ESE), 30, 43, 44, 50, 81, 106, 243
Exit passes, 283–84

Facebook, 199, 214, 223
Family literacy events, 241–42
Fantasy, 93–95
Figurative language, 164, 177, 178, 179, 192–93
Fink, Lisa Storm, 81, 95
Fisher, Douglas, 31, 64, 136, 175, 180, 183, 201, 223, 245
Florida Association for Media in Education (FAME), 164–65, 177, 256
Florida Department of Education, 4
Fluency, 42, 106, 177
Follos, Alison G., 30, 31
Fontichiaro, Kristin, 298
Fountas, Irene C., 81
Frey, Nancy, 64, 136, 180, 183, 201, 245
From the Creative Minds of 21st Century Librarians, 14
Frontloading strategy, 143

Gallagher, Kelly, 22, 244, 249, 297
Gay, lesbian, and bisexual literature (GLBT), 133–34
Gedeon, Julie, 52
Genres, 23–24, 77–105, 115, 116, 284; activities, 81, 86–87, 110, 199; definition, 80; rationale for teaching, 77–80
Geography, 141, 142
Global perspective, 133, 138, 140, 141

Glogster, 191, 195
Google Earth, 65
GoogleLitTrips, 59
Goudvis, Anne, 78
Grants, 41–42, 135, 253, 261
Graphic literature, 109–10
Graphic novels, 109–10, 180–81
Graphic organizers, 95, 177, 182, 191, 217, 219; activities, 197, 199, 201, 202
Grimes, Sharon, 173, 176, 179

Habits of mind. *See* Dispositions
Hamilton, Buffy, 299
Harada, Violet, 228
Hart, Betty, 176–77
Harvey, Stephanie, 78
Higher education, 58
Historical fiction, 92–93, 101, 180, 197, 200, 201
Historical literature, 141–44
Hobbies, 22, 24, 256, 289–90
Holley, Pam Spencer, 43
Hughes-Hassell, Sandra, 107
Humor in fiction, 90

Identity issues, adolescents, 129, 134
Illustrator studies, 193–95
Independent learning, 282
Inferring, 90, 96–97, 111, 112, 179–81
Informational text, online, 102
Informational text, selection, 32–33
Information literacy, 3, 52, 56, 60, 256, 280; assessment, 51–52; instruction, 58–59, 143
Inquiry, 4, 58, 59, 98, 280; activities, 103. *See also* Information literacy
Institute for Library and Information Education (ILILE), 52
Institute of Museum and Library Services (IMLS), 63
Intellectual freedom, 157–65; instruction, 161–63; parental support, 165; timeline of documents, 159
Intellectual property rights, 227–28
International Reading Association (IRA), 5
International Society for Technology in Education (ISTE), 5

Johnson, Doug, 158–60, 299
Johnson, Larry, 50, 64–65, 110
Jones, Jami, 254–56, 281

Keene, Nancy J., 28
Krashen, Stephen, 79, 244, 245, 275
Kuhlthau, Carol C., 58, 63–64

Labeling books, 276–77
Lamb, Annette, 50, 64–65, 110, 281
Lapp, Diane, 31, 180, 223
Lattimer, Heather, 96, 102, 104, 109
Learning centers approach, 25, 41, 110, 178, 292
Learning community, 11–12
Learning formats, 279, 282, 291, 295–97
Learning Network, The: *The New York Times*, 13, 14, 59, 97, 109, 163, 191
Lesesne, Teri, 23, 31, 43, 44, 45, 88, 107, 112, 114, 116, 264, 277
Lesson plan approach, 162
Lesson plan outlines, 100, 282–98
Lesson plans, 6, 13
Lexile reading level, 24, 28, 42, 265, 274, 276, 277
Library aides, 139, 140
Library catalog, instruction, 50, 277, 283, 289
Library of Congress Memory Project, 181
Library orientation, 46–52; assessment, 51–52; challenges, 48–49; gaming strategy, 49–50; iPads, 51; iPods, 51: planning, 49–51; web-based, 50–51
Library staff. *See* School libraries, staff
Lifelong learning, 55, 56–57, 277, 280–82
Lifetime reading, 52–53, 59, 107–8, 258, 275–77, 280
Listening skills, 42–46
Literacy, 11–12, 278, 282–83
Literacy committee, 237, 250, 251
Literacy log, 285
Literacy skills, 279, 286
Literary awards, 152, 153–55
Literary canon, 88
Literary devices, 190
Literary elements, 106, 190, 194, 195–202; activities, 99, 106
Literary Genre Framework, 82–86
Literary selections, 87–89
Literature, cultural values, 132
Literature circles, online, 138–40, 259
LM_Net, 29, 49, 115, 132, 240, 242, 243, 258, 259
Loertscher, David V., 8, 237

Magazines, 100, 101, 107–9, 140, 246, 287–94; activities, 252, 287–89
Main idea, 181–83
Maniotes, Leslie K., 58, 63–64
Marzano, Robert J., 79, 177, 245, 253, 254
McGill-Frazen, Anne, 247–48, 249
McKenzie, Jamie, 281, 293
McLaughlin, Maureen, 136
McTighe, Jay, 281, 282
Memoirs, 102–3, 104

Mentoring, students, 24, 253–56, 257
Metacognition, 280–81, 282, 289
Miller, Donalyn, 86
Moreillon, Judi, 78–79, 80, 112, 114, 138–40, 173,
    262, 281
Morning announcements. *See* Schoolwide
    announcements
Multicultural events and activities, 136, 141
Multicultural resources, 136, 137–41
Multiplatform works, 110
Museums, 63–65; virtual collections, 63–65
Museums, Libraries, and 21st Century Skills, 63
Music, activities, 29, 97, 287–89
Mysteries, 90–91
Mythology, resources, 143

National Assessment of Educational Progress
    (NAEP), 3
National Board for Professional Teaching
    Standards for Library Media, 58
National Council of Teachers of English (NCTE),
    5, 13, 164, 223
National Curriculum Standards for Social Studies,
    129, 141, 142
National Education Technology Standards and
    Performance Indicators for Students, 5
National Governors Association Center for Best
    Practices, 5, 8
National Public Radio (NPR), 40, 41, 99
National Science Teachers' Association, 33
Native Americans in literature, 132, 140
NCTE *Beliefs about the Teaching of Writing*, 223
*NCTE/IRA Standards for the English Language
    Arts*, 5, 77
Newspapers, 100, 101, 107–9, 246, 290–94;
    activities, 202
New York Times, The, 39
Nonfiction, 97–104, 264, 298, 264, 298; activities,
    99–104, 107–9
Notetaking, 184

Odyssey Award, 45
Office of Intellectual Freedom (ALA), 161
One book/one community, 61
One book/one school, 239–40
Online informational text. *See* Informational text,
    online
Online reading selection tools. *See* Selection tools
    online
Opening announcements. *See* Schoolwide
    announcements
Orientation. *See* Library orientation

Paraphrasing, 183–85
Parents, 55, 56, 61, 157, 165, 275, 279
Partnership for 21st Century Skills, 63
Pathfinders, 99
Picture books, 105–7, 113, 140, 194, 197;
    definition, 105
Pinnell, Gay Su, 81
Plagiarism, 60, 227–28
Plot, 180, 195–97
Podcasts, 28, 39, 86, 96, 163; directories, 41
Poetry, 96–97, 139; activities, 46, 106, 181, 183,
    202, 242; values, 96–97
Point of view, 93, 136, 201–2
Political cartoons, 134, 143–44
Popularity awards. *See* Awards, popularity
*Position Statement on the Common Core College-
    and Career-Readiness Standards* (AASL), 8
*Position Statement on the School Librarian's Role in
    Reading*, 4
*Position Statement on the School Library Media
    Specialist's Role in Reading*, 58
Position statements. *See* AASL
Poverty, 244, 247–48, 255; resources, 134–36
Preddy, Leslie B., 12, 237, 243, 247, 262
Predicting, 179–81
Prensky, Marc, 11, 227
Prezi, 196–97
Primary sources, 141, 142; documents, 93, 100
Production checklist, 225
Production methods, 214–15
Project-based learning, 211–30
Project design, 214–17, 219–20
Public librarians, 255, 262, 283–84
Public libraries, 52–58, 250, 255, 265; assignment
    alerts, 54; book clubs, 56, 57; digital collec-
    tions, 56; educator cards, 55; school visits,
    54–55; summer programs, 57
Purdue Online Writing Lab (OWL), 184, 227

Questioning, 136, 175–76, 264, 281. *See also*
    Essential questions
Quilts, 143

Read Across America, 57
Reader response to text, 31, 93, 113, 115, 139–40,
    163, 214–15, 246, 280
Reader's advisory, 19, 21–24, 246, 254, 279.
    See also Selection tools online
Reader's theater, 50, 101, 104, 197
Reading aloud, 30–33, 42, 52, 103, 106, 170,
    200–201, 202, 249, 252, 261
Reading comprehension, 173–85

Reading Counts (RC), 54, 265, 275, 276
Reading format, 260, 282
Reading for pleasure, 19, 21, 23, 42, 62, 275, 277
Reading guidance, group, 24–33
Reading guidance, individual, 19, 21–24, 279, 283
Reading habit, 77, 249, 275, 277–80, 283
Reading interests, 23–24, 107, 224, 245, 256, 259, 280, 284, 287–92
Reading ladders, 107, 116
Reading lists, 26
Reading log, 252, 253
Reading motivation, 265, 274–77; activities, 19, 21–33, 60–62; intrinsic, 275
Reading promotion, 19, 24–33, 110, 134, 237–77
Reading rewards, 275, 276
Reading selection strategies, 283–84
Reading stamina, 43
Reading surveys, 23–24
ReadWriteThink, 13, 14, 24, 81, 85, 95, 163, 199
Realistic fiction, 89–93
Real-world texts, 98, 293–94. *See also* Magazines; Newspapers; Informational text; Nonfiction
Recreational reading. *See* Self-selected reading
Reference resources, 99
Reflection, 280–81
Reflection, student, 181, 225–26, 284–87
Religious values, 133
Reluctant readers, 21–22, 29, 43–44, 256
Resiliency, 254–55
Right to privacy, 160
Risley, Todd, 176–77
Romance, 89–90
Rubrics, 199, 228, 230

Saricks, Joyce, 80, 92
Scales, Pat, 162, 165
SCANS report, 5
Schema, 78–79, 173, 175, 179
Schloman, Barbara, 52
School administrators, 6, 23, 24, 31, 52, 61, 237, 242, 246, 247, 250, 251, 252, 276, 280
School and public library cooperation, 52–58
School librarians, allocation of time, 31, 53, 139–40; leadership role, 299; professional development, 60–61, 298–99
School Librarian's Role in Reading Toolkit, 4
School libraries, balanced approach, 3, 7; best practices, 5–6; environment, 19, 47, 49; foundational principles, 9–11; goals, 3, 6; programming, 9–11; promotion, 50; staff, 33, 160
School library, environment, 140, 141

School Library Media Specialist's Role in Reading Toolkit, 173
Schoolwide announcements, 29, 176, 177, 180, 192, 260
Schoolwide events, 239–42
Schrock, Kathy, 230, 299
Science, activities, 32–33, 95
Science fiction, 94–95
Selection tools online, 27–29
Self-assessment, students, 225–26, 228, 230, 249, 280
Self-selected reading, 23, 244, 245, 246, 275, 279
Setting, 142, 175, 180, 200–201
Short stories, 95–96, 112, 113; activities, 96, 112–13
Skype, 191
Small, Ruth V., 14, 265, 275
Small group activities, 43, 44, 51, 87, 106, 113, 162, 180, 183–84, 197, 199, 200–201, 202, 223–24, 288, 292–94, 297
Social issues, 134–36
Social networks, activities, 223
Social skills, 256, 279
Social studies, activities, 52, 54, 92–93, 98, 101, 103, 134–36, 138, 140, 141, 163, 179, 181, 182–83, 183–84, 200–201, 243
Speaking skills, 42, 57, 97
Sports fiction, 91
Standards for the 21st-Century Learner, 4, 5, 12, 52, 101, 138, 160, 179, 211, 227, 243, 279, 280, 281
Standards for the Assessment of Reading and Writing, 5
State readers' choice programs, 26, 54, 86, 240, 252, 264–73, 276
Steampunk. *See* Science fiction
Story map. *See* Graphic organizers
Storytelling, 42, 56
Stripling, Barbara K., 14, 281
Struggling readers, 43–44, 98, 106, 111, 254
Students with disabilities, 133
Summarizing, 183–84
Summer reading lists, 54, 251
Summer reading loss, 247, 249, 250, 251
Summer reading programs, 249–53
Surveys, 261, 299
Sustained silent reading (SSR), 244–47
Svec, Deb, 256–57
Synthesis, 79

Teachers, 2, 6, 13. *See also* Collaboration
Text format, 39, 81
Text set, 50, 55, 79, 80, 106

Text structure, 101
Text-to-self connections, 191
Theme, 111–16; activities, 106
Think-aloud strategies, 31, 98, 115, 176, 181, 183
To Read or Not to Read: A Question of National Consequence, 280
TRAILS (Tools for Real-Time Assessment of Information Literacy Skills), 52, 58
Transliteracy, 211, 279
Transliteracy Research Project, 279
Trelease, Jim, 30, 245

U.S. National Park Service, 64, 65

Valenza, Joyce, 27, 54, 99, 158–60, 228, 281, 296, 299
Virtual courses. *See* E-learning
Virtual field trips, 65, 178
Visualizing, 175, 179, 181
Visual literacy, 178, 181, 184, 194, 197
Vocabulary development, 22, 30, 31, 42, 50, 64, 79, 98, 106, 140, 141, 162, 176–79, 184, 201

Warlick, David, 39
Wiggins, Grant, 281, 282
Wilhelm, Jeffrey D., 44, 77, 81, 129, 142, 143, 193, 201, 223, 262, 264, 298
Williams, T. Lee, 81
Wilson Core Collections, 114, 144
Word choice, 192–93
Word wall, 31, 50, 162, 179
Wormeli, Rick, 183, 184
Writing, activities, 163, 164–65, 284–89, 290–92, 293–94, 298
Writing activities, 95, 102, 103, 106, 223–24
Writing models, 79–80, 102, 103
Writing skills, 42, 185, 217, 223

Young adult (YA) literature, 88, 165
Young Adult Library Services Association (YALSA), 24, 26, 151
YouTube, 199

Ziemba, Jeanne, 29

About the Authors

SYBIL M. FARWELL worked as a school librarian at the elementary, middle school, and high school levels and is now retired, though she considers herself a "lifetime librarian." She is a National Board Certified Teacher in Library Media and earned a Doctor of Education in Curriculum and Instruction from Florida International University. An article on collaboration in school libraries written by Dr. Farwell first appeared in *Knowledge Quest* and was included in AASL's book, *Collaboration*.

NANCY L. TEGER is a program professor for Nova Southeastern University in Ft. Lauderdale, Florida where she earned a Doctor of Science in Information Sciences degree. Previously, she was the library media services program specialist for the Florida Department of Education and the library media supervisor for Miami-Dade County Public Schools. Dr. Teger's articles on block scheduling were published in *Knowledge Quest*, and, in 2008, she was recognized by *Library Journal* as a "Mover and Shaker."